SO-BSJ-293

Beyond Free Trade

Beyond Free Trade
Firms, Governments, and Global Competition

Edited by

DAVID B. YOFFIE

Harvard Business School Press

Boston, Massachusetts

382
B523

The paper used in this publication meets the requirements of the American National Standard
for Permanence of Paper for Printed Library Materials Z39.48-1984.

Library of Congress Cataloging-in-Publication Data

Beyond free trade : firms, governments, and global competition /
    edited by David B. Yoffie.
        p.   cm.
    Includes bibliographical references and index.
    ISBN 0-87584-344-1 (alk. paper)
    1. International trade.   2. Foreign trade regulation.
3. Investments, Foreign.   4. International business enterprises.
I. Yoffie, David B.
HF71.B49   1993   92-29834
382—dc20   CIP

CONTENTS

Part III
POLITICAL COMPETITION

Part IV
IMPLICATIONS

Preface

WHY IS THE UNITED STATES, a country with one of the most advanced markets and the most advanced technology in telecommunications, the world's largest importer of telecommunication products? Why is bauxite mined in Ghana, the site of a world-class aluminum smelter, shipped to North America for processing? Why is Israel, not Japan, Korea, Singapore, and so forth, a leading exporter of microprocessor chips? Why is Holland the home for significant research and development in antifriction bearings when the country has virtually no market for, and little production of, the product? Why is the largest manufacturer of computers in Europe an American-owned firm, the largest manufacturer of TVs in America a European-owned firm, but the largest manufacturer of all major products in Japan a Japanese firm?

These are a few of the puzzles that intrigued me and my colleagues when we embarked on this ambitious research project in 1988. At the time, many books were being written on competitiveness, the global strategies of firms, and the economic ascendance of Japan in the world. We wanted to do something different. We had a nagging sense that those debates were not capturing the depth and complexity of change taking place in the international economy. We were particularly interested in understanding whether there was significant qualitative or quantitative influence of firms and governments on international trade. To be sure, we recognized that some of the global trends of the 1980s were mere extensions of deep-seated patterns begun in the 1950s and 1960s. Yet other trends, we believed, represented long-term structural shifts that could be comprehended only by an in-depth study of firms and governments across industries, across time, and across geographies. New phenomena, such as the dramatic growth of international trade in services and direct foreign investment in the 1980s, massive deregulation of many industries, and the explosion in new forms of collaboration between firms, could have decisive patterns of global competition.

Since there was both continuity and change in world trade, and neither was well predicted or explained by existing theories, we had many important questions to address. We wanted to know why trade patterns seemed to diverge from our prior expectations. Was there an efficient international market for global commerce that had not yet reached its natural equilibrium or were there significant imperfections in markets that governments and firms created and/or exploited? Three major structural changes in international competition seemed especially important in motivating this study: (1) changes in the direction and origin of goods and services crossing national boundaries; (2) changes in the pattern of capital flows and the role of firms in international trade; and (3) a deepening of government involvement in many international transactions.

THE CHANGING PATTERN OF TRADE

Perhaps the most obvious, well-known trend we confronted was the surge in American imports and explosion in Japanese and German exports, which generated enormous imbalances in world trade. U.S. net exports registered global records, year in and year out, through most of the 1980s, while Japan and Germany's net exports registered equally remarkable surpluses (see Figure P-1).

Of course, balance-of-trade deficits by themselves are not necessarily a sign of economic weakness or even a matter for great concern. Trade balances can be influenced by short-term factors such as exchange-rate fluctuations and fiscal policy. Persistent deficits, however, might imply structural shifts in international trade and global competitiveness that cannot be as easily dismissed. Moreover, the slow responsiveness of the American deficits and Japanese surpluses to slowdowns in the U.S. macro-economy and large exchange-rate swings further suggested that other factors, perhaps at the firm, industry, or government level, might be impeding adjustment.

FIGURE P-1
Trade Balances

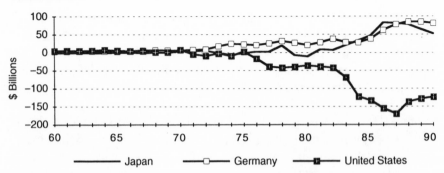

Sources: International Monetary Fund, *Direction of World Trade Statistics,* various years.

A second underlying trend in world trade has been the relatively steady growth in manufacturing exports, which in turn produced high levels of trade between countries with similar factor endowments. These patterns are a striking departure from trade of the nineteenth and early twentieth centuries. Dating back 150 years, trade in the early stages of American expansionism and European colonialism was primarily between rapidly industrializing countries and the producers of food and primary products. Nations such as the United Kingdom, France, and Germany exported manufactured goods to the developing world in exchange for iron ore, bauxite, or whatever raw materials were necessary to fuel the industrial machines of the North. It was a picture of comparative advantage that would have made Adam Smith and David Ricardo proud.

After World War II, trade took a remarkably different turn. Most international transactions over the past several decades have been between countries of similar factor endowments. Three quarters of all exports from the industrial world went to other developed countries. Furthermore, developing countries, typically dependent on markets in industrial nations, also began exporting an increasing percentage of their goods to other developing country markets. By 1989, one third of developing country trade went to nations with similar factor endowments.

The goods traded in this new world were increasingly manufactured products (see Figure P-2). As a consequence, trade was not necessarily a by-product of natural endowments like arable land, climate, and availability of mineral resources. The drivers of trade in manufactured goods

FIGURE P-2
Composition of World Trade (Percentage of manufactures, minerals, and food)

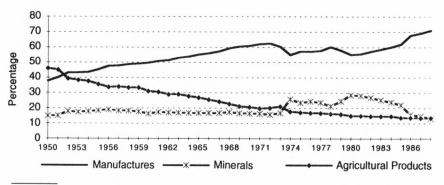

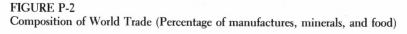

Sources: GATT, *Trade Yearbook,* various years.

could come from the ability of national industries or particular firms to innovate and compete in world markets. This opened the possibility that comparative advantage was not just a function of the God-given attributes, but itself could be manufactured through the accumulation of technologies and skills.

Yet simple notions of comparative-advantage-based factor endowments might still hold true if exports between countries with similar endowments were in different products. For example, if there was inter-industry trade, the United States might export semiconductors, Japan TVs, and Europe machine tools. But theories of international trade confronted yet another challenge if *intra-industry* trade was becoming the norm. Traditional trade theory does not predict intra-industry trade: if countries specialize according to their relative advantage and differences in endowments, two nations would not export the same product to each other. However, what if the United States, Japan, and Europe were all exporting the same products to each other? The notion that country-level factors are driving international trade begins to weaken a little further. In fact, the proportion of intra-industry trade in total trade for a group of eleven industrial countries grew from 46% in 1964 to 60% in 1985.[1] In particular industries, the numbers were even higher: for example, 70% of worldwide exports of antifriction bearings in the mid-1980s went to countries that also exported antifriction bearings.[2]

THE PATTERN OF CAPITAL FLOWS AND THE ROLE OF FIRMS

While the growth in intra-industry trade forced us to search for the most relevant definition of an industry and question whether country factors can best explain patterns of exports, the emergence and maturing of multinational enterprises (MNEs) required us to move beyond countries and industries to look at individual firms. Globalization of firms is clearly not new; MNEs have been around for more than a century. What *is* new is the number of MNEs and their number of home bases. One estimate suggests that, compared to a few hundred large multinationals two decades ago, largely from the United States and the United Kingdom, there are more than 1,000 large MNEs in 1990 from the G-5 (the United States, Germany, France, the United Kingdom, and Japan), plus tens of smaller MNEs from the developing world.[3] Indeed, one of the most striking international phenomena of the 1980s has been the growing role of firms exporting capital across borders in the form of foreign direct

FIGURE P-3
Foreign Direct Investment (total inflows and outflows—United States, Germany, United Kingdom, France, & Japan)

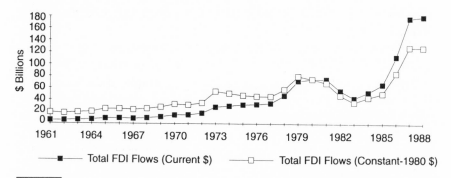

Total FDI Flows (Current $)   Total FDI Flows (Constant-1980 $)

Source: DeAnne Julius, *Global Companies and Public Policies* (New York: Council on Foreign Relations, 1990), 114–122.

investment (FDI). In 1990 alone, the total flows of FDI in and out of the United States totaled more than $100.6 billion. During the latter half of the 1980s, the global flows of new FDI rose by 29% annually— nearly three times the growth of international trade (see Figure P-3). And while the measurement of foreign assets is problematic, one estimate suggests that, during the 1980s, more than $3.5 trillion of business assets worldwide came under "foreign" control.[4]

The sheer magnitude of FDI has to call for a distinction between the competitiveness of multinationals headquartered in one country and the competitiveness of that country as a geographic entity. The line between "who is us" and "who is them," as Robert Reich so boldly put it, begins to become a little blurred. Moreover, most theories of world trade have assumed that international transactions were done at arm's-length. Two independent parties in different countries would buy and sell at market prices. However, by 1989, $102 billion or 28% of all U.S. exports and $93 billion or 19% of all U.S. imports were shipped between affiliates of American firms.[5] If one added intrafirm trade of Japanese and European affiliates, more than one third of all U.S. trade with the rest of the world was internal to corporations (see Figure P-4).

The importance of intrafirm trade is that many simple relationships we had long assumed to be correct might no longer hold true. Arm's-length transactions are generally adjustable in the short run. We usually assume that if prices change because of exchange rates, for instance, firms often cancel or renegotiate arm's-length contracts to reflect current market

FIGURE P-4
Intrafirm Trade (exports from U.S. parents and foreign subsidiaries)

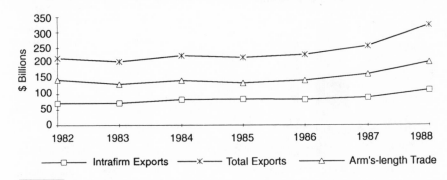

Source: U.S. Department of Commerce, Bureau of Economic Analysis, "Survey of Current Business," October 1991.

prices. When firms are dependent upon their own subsidiaries, some supply contracts may be costly to adjust, constraining the firm's options. On the other hand, transactions within the corporation can also give firms more strategic flexibility to price aggressively (below marginal cost) in foreign markets to hold or gain market share.

Growing FDI and the concomitant growth in intrafirm trade suggested to us a new role for the firm in international trade that had not been fully explored. Moreover, the sheer size, structure, and global concentration of corporations in some industries implied that many international transactions were not taking place in the kind of perfect market that most theories of world trade depended upon. Just looking at global concentration, for instance, we found that many industries we were interested in studying were dominated by a very small number of firms. As Figure P-5 shows, the global sales of the top four firms in telecommunication equipment, construction equipment, mainframe computers, nickel, bearings, and microprocessors all exceeded half the world market.

THE PATTERN OF GOVERNMENT INTERVENTION

The third trend that sparked our interest in this project was the increasingly complex role of government in world trade. Perhaps the greatest achievement of international institutions in the post–World War II era was the consensus on reducing tariffs. Average tariff levels in the industrial countries declined from 10% in the 1950s to less than 5% in 1990. Yet, as any student of international trade knows, tariffs are only one

FIGURE P-5

Global Industry Concentration (market share of top four producers worldwide)

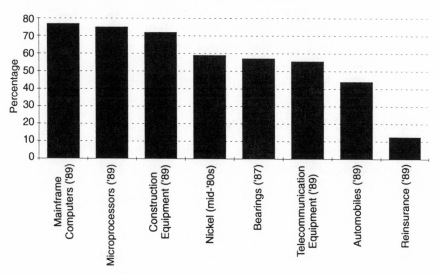

Source: Compiled from statistics in this volume.

manifestation of government intervention in world commerce. Starting as early as the 1950s in textiles, nontariff barriers began to emerge in the industrial countries just as the tariff barriers began to disappear. Nontariff protection has taken on a variety of forms, including voluntary export restraints, licensing procedures, countertrade requirements, restrictive government procurement, technical standards, certification requirements, and so forth.

While measuring government intervention is problematic, there seemed to be a universal consensus that protectionism and sectoral intervention were on the rise. The International Monetary Fund estimated that the proportion of nonfuel imports of industrial countries subject to nontariff barriers rose from approximately 19% in 1981 to 20% in 1984 and to around 23% in 1987.[6] Just looking at selective barriers in the United States, the World Bank estimated that nontariff barriers in textiles, steel, and automobiles were equivalent to a tariff of approximately 25%, a level of protection comparable to that of the late 1940s.[7]

Finally, we were interested in understanding the growing role of government intervention because of its potential effects on regional trading blocs. We started this study about the time the U.S.–Canada Free Trade Agreement was signed and when the Europe 1992 program began to pick up steam. Both agreements were efforts by governments on both sides of the Atlantic to create larger regions in which scale economies could be gained and local inefficiencies eliminated. The dangers, of course, were numerous: trading blocs could divert trade from the optimal partners; they might produce beggar-thy-neighbor policies, as in the 1930s, when free trade zones were sought at the expense of other trade partners; or they might even lead to trade warfare between blocs.[8]

THEMES AND METHODOLOGY

All these macro and micro trends—the structural shifts in international trade in goods, the new role for firms and capital flows, and the growing aggressiveness of government—challenge our understanding of world trade and global competition. The authors of this book have sought to address some or parts of all these issues by exploring international trade at the firm and industry levels. We provide rich qualitative and quantitative data that emerged through primary research on the real actors that engage in international commerce: the firms and, when appropriate, governments that actually move goods, services, and capital around the world. We chose industries that cut across all spectrums of global competition: high technology (e.g., telecommunications and computers) and low technology (e.g., bearings and construction equipment); services (insurance), manufacturing (e.g., semiconductors), and raw materials (copper, bauxite, and nickel); we looked at different geographic regions, especially North-North trade and North-South trade, and industries in which governments were heavily involved (e.g., telecommunications and insurance) and those in which government's role was peripheral (e.g., construction equipment and bearings). Most of our industries were also concentrated at the global level during at least one point in their history. Some industries, like minerals and computers, have become more fragmented over time, while others, like bearings and telecommunications, have become more concentrated over time. Finally, we chose industries that were important because of their sheer size (see Figure P-6): in 1989, these eleven industries represented roughly $1.2 trillion in global production and $370 billion in exports, or roughly 10% of world trade. While our approach clearly lacked some of the precision of the formal models or econometric analyses that dominate international trade research, it did allow us to go deeply into the underlying drivers of global competition.

Beginning in 1988, we ran a monthly seminar at the Harvard Business

FIGURE P-6
Production/Trade ($ billions)

Industry	Global Production	Global Exports
Automobile ('90)	483	161.8[a]
Bearings ('88)	15.5	5.1
Computers ('90)	275	66
Construction Equipment ('90)	35	16.8[b]
Insurance ('88)		
Non-life	551	11
Reinsurance	91.9	36.8
Minerals ('88)		
Aluminum	20.7	20.7[c]
Copper	13	13.0[c]
Nickel	11.2	11.2[c]
Semiconductors ('89)	55.8	19[d]
Color Television ('88)	21.9	8.9[e]
Telecommunications Equip. ('89)	31	7.1[f]

[a]: International Trade Group
[b]: OECD Microtables
[c]: Virtually 100% of these minerals are traded in the ore concentrate, semiprocessed, or metal state.
[d]: Japan and United States only
[e]: UN export data
[f]: OECD Microtables

Source: Compiled from statistics in this volume.

School, where we presented our research to one another. In addition to doing historical research on each industry, the authors interviewed the chairmen, presidents, and various high-level executives of key firms in all parts of the globe. In total, we conducted nearly 500 interviews between 1989 and 1991 in Japan, North America, South America, Southest Asia, and Europe.

The book begins with an overarching framework in Chapter 1, followed by the individual industry studies. While we attempted to make this volume as integrative as possible, each industry study inevitably takes a different perspective. Part I examines regulated competition, in which international trade emerges from the interaction of heavy government intervention and a small number of global firms. In Chapter 2, Laura Tyson and David Yoffie explore the role of government in semiconductors and suggest that government policies in the United States were critical in building national advantage in semiconductors. However, infant-industry protection on trade and investment in Japan undermined those advantages by the late 1970s. The chapter goes on to argue that U.S. government policy subsequently helped stabilize its domestic industry, and as the industry has matured into distinct segments, individual firm strategies are beginning to influence the patterns of trade.

Benjamin Gomes-Casseres, in Chapter 3, examines the evolution of trade and competition in computer hardware. Computers comprise an enormous industry whose various segments have different industry dynamics. Mainframes, for instance, though historically dominated by IBM, were kept in check by government policies around the world. Personal computers, by contrast, comprise a relatively fragmented industry increasingly driven by traditional country advantages. Casseres's thesis is that international alliances heavily influenced the evolution of this industry. These relationships, which encouraged the worldwide diffusion of technology in the industry, now constitute critical elements in most firms' competitive strategies.

Chapter 4 by Richard Vietor and David Yoffie, on the global telecommunication equipment business, argues that global competitiveness in that industry has been a product of dramatic shifts in technology accompanied by asymmetrical deregulation across all major world markets. As the industry consolidates to a half dozen major players, they argue, the legacy of government regulation, combined with the positioning of firms, will determine the patterns of trade and performance in the 1990s and beyond.

Helen Shapiro, in Chapter 5, examines the way state-directed industrialization in Brazil and Mexico substantially influenced international trade and investment flows in the automobile industry. She describes how this politically salient environment first induced multinational auto firms to produce locally, then tried to get those same firms to export significant volumes of vehicles and engines to "Triad" countries.

Part II focuses on industries characterized by less government intervention but intense oligopolistic competition. Chapter 6 picks up this theme with David Collis examining the global bearings industry. Collis finds that the nationality of successful firms becomes increasingly influenced by such firm-specific factors as ownership and organizational capability and less by country endowments as firms mature. He also shows that, in imperfectly competitive markets, the geographic location of activities is biased by the firm's history, risk reduction, personal preferences of managers, and government policy.

Michael Rukstad, in Chapter 7, explores a classic oligopolistic industry in his analysis of construction equipment. Once dominated by Caterpillar, construction equipment turned into a global duopoly in the 1980s with the emergence of Japan's Komatsu. Rukstad illustrates how shifts in demand and global oligopolistic competition in construction equipment affect international trade. Domestic structural changes arising from the oil crisis along with high interest rates and an appreciated dollar fundamentally restructured competition in the 1980s. The location of production and patterns of trade in the 1990s will be driven by the dynamics of the duopoly between Caterpillar and Komatsu, reinforced by the growing consolidation on the fringes.

In Chapter 8, Louis Wells takes a more focused look at oligopolistic competition in minerals. The chapter is concerned specifically with the role of ownership and its implications for the direction of international trade. By exploring international trade in three industries—nickel, bauxite, and copper—with high levels of concentration historically, Wells shows that the structure of the industry, government policies, and ownership of the assets are critical determinants of the direction of trade.

Part III focuses on political competition where industries are relatively fragmented but government has a heavy hand in influencing trade and investment. John Goodman, in Chapter 9 on the global insurance industry, explores two key service businesses: non-life insurance, a trillion-dollar business that has been largely local in character, and reinsurance, a $100 billion industry that has been largely global in nature. The factors driving the limited trade in insurance have been country factors such as capital availability and the international maturity of the manufacturing sector. Historically, trade was also stifled by local regulations that prohibited entry. Paradoxically, Goodman argues, firms in countries with the strictest regulations may be the best positioned for future international expansion.

Part IV provides a summary of the findings, with policy implications for governments and business managers.

The list of people and organizations that should be acknowledged in this book is lengthy. Beyond the contributors to this volume, the first mentions must go to the members of the World Trade and Global Competition seminar, including Mark Wolfson, Ken Froot, Heather Hazard, Herman Daems, and Joe Bower. Some of the preliminary research results from Hazard and Daems's work on television sets have been included in our analysis. Of course, none of the research would have been possible without the contributions of hundreds of senior executives and government officials from more than a dozen countries who gave generously of their time to answer questions, provide data, and point us in the right direction. In addition, the entire venture would have been impossible without the support of the Harvard Business School Division of Research, especially that of Dean John McArthur and research director Michael Yoshino. Not only did the Division of Research provide funding for the interviews and global travel of our faculty, but it also gave us the opportunity to work with research assistants Chris Allen, Jeff Cohn, Maryellen Costello, David Dobrowolski, Nancy Donohue, Julie Herendeen, Conna Hill, Edward Lenk, David Levy, Dianna Magnani, Paul Mang, Krista McQuade, Masao Ogawa, Timothy Sorenson, Toby Stuart, and Masahiro Tanaka. Their long hours and detailed analyses of the industries and data were invaluable. Several individuals should also be mentioned because of their careful readings of the manuscript and their meticulous feedback, especially Tom McCraw, Mark Wolfson, and Ray Vernon.

The entire manuscript was greatly enhanced by the comments of more than eighty participants, from eight countries, in the World Trade and Global Competition Colloquium held at the Harvard Business School from December 1 through December 3, 1991. In connection with the colloquium, we extend a special thank-you to our colloquium speakers, Robert Galvin, chairman of the executive committee of Motorola, and Professor Paul Krugman of MIT, and to the organizers of the colloquium, especially Cathyjean Gustafson and Barbara Bhiladvala.

David B. Yoffie

Boston, Massachusetts
November 1992

NOTES

1. Organization of Economic Cooperation and Development (OECD). *Structural Adjustment and Economic Performance* (Paris: OECD, 1987). The common way to explain intra-industry trade is to claim that the analysis is done at the wrong level of aggregation. If one looks at finer and finer distinctions within industries, what appears to be intra-industry trade really amounts to interindustry trade. For example, Japan and the United States may export semiconductors to each other, but Japan is largely exporting memory products and American firms export logic products. Another answer is to introduce new variables such as economies of scale and product differentiation. The thrust of our

approach is not inconsistent with either of these approaches. We suggest, however, going one step further: in order to understand modern international trade, one must look not only at industry characteristics at low levels of aggregation, but, in some cases, also explore the firms themselves.

2. See David J. Collis, in Chapter 4 of this volume.

3. De Anne Julius, *Global Companies and Public Policies* (New York: Council on Foreign Relations, 1990); Louis Wells, *Third World Multinationals* (Cambridge, Mass.: MIT Press, 1983).

4. This estimate comes from Edward M. Graham, "The Determinants of Foreign Direct Investment: Alternative Theories and International Evidence," unpublished manuscript, Institute for International Economics, October 15, 1991. Exact measurement remains problematic because investments can be leveraged in numerous ways, giving foreign interest greater control than the numbers represent. In addition, there are significant differences between market values and book values of long-term investments. Many European and American investments have been in place for decades, many of those investments fully depreciated. As a consequence, aggregated numbers probably understate the total foreign investment stock. The U.S. Department of Commerce, Bureau of Economic Analysis, has estimated the value of the U.S. direct investment position using current-cost and market-value estimates. The market value of U.S. FDI abroad in 1989 was estimated at $804 billion, compared with the historic cost figure of $373 billion. FDI in the United States, which had a historic cost value of $401 billion in 1989, was estimated to have a market value of only $544 billion. See Julius, *Global Companies and Public Policies*.

5. U.S. Department of Commerce, Bureau of Economic Analysis, September 30, 1991.

6. International Monetary Fund, *Issues and Developments in International Trade Policy* (Washington, D.C.: International Monetary Fund, 1988), 10.

7. J. de Melo and D. Tarr, *Welfare Costs of US Quotas on Textiles, Steel, and Autos*, World Bank Staff Working Paper No. 83 (Washington, D.C.: World Bank Publishing, 1988).

8. Paul Krugman, "The Move to Free Trade Zones," paper prepared for the symposium Policy Implications of Trade and Currency Zones, Jackson Hole, August 22–24, 1991.

1

INTRODUCTION: FROM COMPARATIVE ADVANTAGE TO REGULATED COMPETITION

David B. Yoffie

WHAT DRIVES INTERNATIONAL TRADE? How do we explain who exports what to whom, and who makes what where? Good answers to these questions remain elusive, despite more than two centuries of theorizing. Many continue to argue that national "comparative advantage" drives world trade; factor costs and relative factor endowments determine the pattern of international specialization. Others say that nations have "competitive advantages" in particular industries, that countries with the most intense local competition, the most demanding buyers, and the most advances in infrastructure and skills will dominate trade in those products.

This book takes a different approach. Without denying the obvious relevance of the comparative or competitive advantage of nations, we argue that, under particular conditions, *firms* and *governments* are what really matter in determining international trade. When fragmented global competition is superseded by relatively concentrated global industries, a new logic emerges to explain who exports what to whom, and who makes what where. In global oligopolies, patterns of trade and production become a function of the competitive success and failure of individual firms and governments, not the specific characteristics of the nation-state. It is the visible and guiding hands of multinational corporations and government policy that are the primary drivers of production location decisions and the pattern of exports, not a country's capital endowment, local competition, or domestic demand.

Prior versions of this chapter have benefited greatly from comments of the participants in the World Trade and Global Competition Colloquium, especially the World Trade and Global Competition Interest Group, including David Collis, Ken Froot, Benjamin Gomes-Casseres, John Goodman, Heather Hazard, David Levy, Michael Rukstad, Helen Shapiro, Laura Tyson, Richard Vietor, and Louis Wells.

Of course, most theories of international trade and national comparative advantage never sought to predict particular production locations or the exact direction of exports, just as Newtonian physics never tried to explain the activity of subatomic particles. But in the same way random behavior of subatomic particles forced a reassessment of how much Newtonian physics could explain, we suggest that exceptions to the rules in international trade and the location of production are becoming sufficiently commonplace in globally concentrated businesses to justify a new approach. Only by moving to a new level of analysis can we begin to understand the underlying logic of larger and larger shares of global trade and investments.

This book explores the microfoundations of international trade and global competition. The arguments are based on two premises: first, the typical large multinational firm is no longer overwhelmed by the constraints of its home base's resources or by the invisible hand of the global marketplace. And second, governments are not always inept interveners, unable to turn the tide of a million corporate decisions. One of the paradoxes of modern global competition is that some firms have built the capability to transcend the limitations of their home nation-state, while selected governments have learned how to tip the terms of that competition in favor of domestically headquartered firms. It is this potential for tension between the footloose capabilities of the multinational firm and the growing sophistication of the state which undermines the conventional wisdom about the structure of international trade.

While we do not offer a new, unified theory of international trade, our goal in this study was to understand the role of firms and governments by researching two phenomena: trade patterns (i.e., countries' export shares and the direction of those exports) and the competitive success of firms (i.e., world market share of different national companies). Typically, these are two very different subjects, of interest to two very different audiences. Governments and academic economists are generally concerned with trade patterns, while business executives worry about market share. It is natural for government officials to think about exports. The balance of payments, the autonomy of domestic policy, and the wealth of the nation are often intimately tied to a country's export performance. This concern tends to be especially acute for exports from "strategic" sectors, where loss of competitiveness could mean a threat to national security or a reduction in profits or fewer technological spillovers that would benefit other parts of the economy. In the meantime, corporate managers often anguish over relative market share. For the firm, changes in market share usually signal shifts in competitive advantage and profits. In some industries, firms also required significant shares of a given marketplace to remain viable and achieve adequate economies of scale.

Despite the historical separateness of these two problems, it is our view that the phenomena are intricately linked in global competition of the 1980s and 1990s. One cannot understand either the success of individual firms or the pattern of international trade without observing both. Moreover, we believe that some government policymakers need to be more concerned with the global success of domestically headquartered firms, and executives should be more attuned to their nation's trade performance.

The central theme of this volume is that when industries become globally concentrated, visible hands rather than anonymous market forces emerge to guide trade. While exports and corporate success in relatively fragmented markets can be largely explained by country characteristics, globally concentrated industries need a richer model of global commerce. We suggest that patterns of international trade and production are the complex outcome of five factors: traditional country advantages; the international structure of the industry; specific characteristics of multinational firms; the style and intrusiveness of government policy; and the inertia of history. Our analysis builds on strategic trade theory and administrative theories of the firm, as well as conventional explanations that focus on the characteristics of nations. To understand why we need a broader, more comprehensive framework, this chapter briefly reviews the relevant literature on each factor. It then lays out a series of propositions that emerged from our three-year study. These propositions help us understand the complicated interactions among countries, industries, firms, governments, and history in global competition.

THE CLASSICAL VIEWS

Traditional trade theories have long focused on country-specific variables to explain which countries exported what products to other countries. If we can assume that firms have perfect foresight and costless information, we need only look at the availability of land, labor, and capital to tell us why some countries specialize in the production and export of certain types of products. Furthermore, most theories of international trade have been normative rather than positive. Most economic models tell us what *should* happen to maximize efficiency or welfare, rather than describe reality. Although more recent contributions consider a broader range of factors and have moved closer to the real world, most writings on international trade continue to build normative models that usually regard the national environment as key in determining patterns of world exports.

Comparative Advantage

David Ricardo was the first economist to develop a general theory of trade.[1] Ricardo demonstrated that countries would export and specialize in the production of goods for which they enjoyed "comparative advantage": a nation was said to possess comparative advantage in those products for which its labor was *relatively* productive. He considered labor to be the sole "factor of production," or input into the production process. Trade would take place, even if one country held absolute productivity advantages in all goods, because comparative advantage would cause relative prices to differ between countries. The national environment was thought to influence the types of industries in which domestic labor was more productive. A key insight of this model, which has become a sacrosanct precept of neoclassical economic thought, is that all countries benefit from free trade by exchanging existing output and by each country specializing in the products in which it holds comparative advantage.

While trade theory continued to evolve over the next two centuries, it remained remarkably consistent with Ricardo's original insight. The most significant addendum to Ricardian comparative advantage was known as the factor proportions model, developed by Eli Heckscher and Bertil Ohlin in 1933.[2] The Heckscher-Ohlin theory continued to argue that country factors were the key determinants of trade, but predicted that comparative advantage originated in differences in relative endowments of factors of production rather than in different tastes or technologies. Using restrictive assumptions, Heckscher-Ohlin proposed a two-country, two-factor (capital and labor), two-commodity model, which predicted that a country would export the product for which the abundant factor was used more intensively. As in most neoclassical theory, it assumed that markets were perfectly competitive and that economies of scale were unimportant.

Empirical research by Nobel Prize–winner Wassily Leontief attacked the heart of Heckscher-Ohlin.[3] He uncovered that exports from the capital-rich United States were actually more labor intensive than American products that competed with imports. Despite years of scholarship seeking to save the theory, Leontief dealt a devastating blow to the simple factor model. Moreover, theory and reality seemed to diverge even more in the time since Leontief's famous article. As noted in the Preface, two new trends emerged during the 1960s and 1970s: high and growing levels of intra-industry trade, where large industrial nations were exporting similar goods to each other; and the growth of trade between countries with similar factor endowments. Both trends were inconsistent with a Ricardi-an-Heckscher-Ohlin world. Yet more than a few trade theorists have been hard pressed to give up their elegant models. To this day, the debate on the efficacy of Heckscher-Ohlin rages on. Richard Caves and Ronald Jones suggested that despite the theory's problems, "the spirit of Heckscher-Ohlin theory still remains to suggest that differences between countries in the endowment of broad classes of productive factors such as capital and labor will be reflected in differences in patterns of produc-tion and trade."[4] In the meantime, Gary Hufbauer has retorted that "various authorities have sought to repair the damage [to Heckscher-Ohlin]; their work in some respects resembles the tortured efforts of pre-Copernican astronomers."[5]

By the end of the 1970s there was a growing consensus that theories of factor endowment were most useful for understanding trade in raw materials and the location of labor-intense activities such as electronics assembly in low-wage countries. For other types of industries and for most trade between industrial nations, such conventional trade theory was difficult to apply. The assumptions underlying the Heckscher-Ohlin framework and its subsequent derivatives did not generalize well to the reality of a multiproduct, multicountry world with multiple factors of production. And contrary to the restrictive assumptions made by the theory, imperfect competition existed in many markets, available tech-nologies differed, economies of scale and scope existed, and some factors of production were at least partially mobile between countries.

Responses to the Leontief Paradox

There were many efforts to address the apparent weaknesses in the theory of factor proportions. In the 1960s, one school of thought sug-gested that "supply" variables such as the relative abundance of *skilled* labor and R&D intensity of a nation's industries could explain trade patterns in manufactured goods.[6] Another school, pioneered by Staffan Burenstam Linder, focused on the demand side. Linder argued that "the range of exportable products is determined by internal demand. It is a necessary, but not sufficient, condition that a product be consumed (or invested) in the home country for this product to be a potential export product."[7] However, it was not until Raymond Vernon sought to integrate both demand and supply variables that trade theory started to approximate a realistic world with manufactured, differentiated products.[8]

Vernon's product-cycle hypothesis was a major departure from the neoclassical tradition. Vernon, along with one of the authors in this project, Louis Wells,[9] argued that the United States was a major exporter of innovative products because of its high and growing personal income. In the early stages of a new technology, before a product or process had stabilized, frequent communication would be needed between engineering and marketing, constraining production to be close to headquarters. Moreover, new products would command a price premium, so that little incentive existed for offshore manufacture in cheaper locations. As the product matured and incomes rose in other countries, growing foreign demand would lead first to exports and then to foreign production, often via foreign direct investment (FDI), in the regions of highest demand. Eventually, foreign production would migrate to lower-wage locations, making the United States a net importer.

Product-cycle theory appeared to explain important features of international trade, particularly in manufactured goods. It demonstrated why the United States, at least in the 1950s, would innovate and export a stream of new products to Europe and Japan as well as to developing countries. Intra-industry trade could be explained in terms of different products in the same industry being at different stages of the product cycle. Yet the robustness of the product cycle, like Heckscher-Ohlin, was suspect. Limiting assumptions made the product cycle more of a special case than a general theory of trade. It seemed particularly useful in understanding trade in the first two or three decades after World War II, but its utility diminished thereafter. Vernon himself identified two trends that limited its applicability.[10] First, incomes, tastes, and technological capabilities among the more industrialized countries converged in the 1970s and 1980s, so that entrepreneurs in each country faced similar conditions. No longer could one predict the source of an innovation. Second, with growing international experience and the growth of telecommunications, multinational enterprises (MNEs) were less likely to suffer from a myopic focus on innovation and production for their home market. In an admittedly hypothetical world of costless communication and low transportation costs, Vernon argued that the "global scanner" could serve demand in any market it found from production bases selected for their costs, available resources, and risks.[11]

RECENT THEORIES OF INTERNATIONAL TRADE

Competitive Advantage of Nations

Building on Heckscher-Ohlin and the product cycle, Michael Porter attempted to reinvigorate the role of the country.[12] Arguing that countries have "competitive advantages," Porter synthesized previous approaches into a typology of four country-specific factors that were critical to the competitive success of specific industries in particular countries. According to the model, factors of production, domestic demand, domestic rivalry, and supporting industries, in various combinations, were the key determinants of a country's success in international trade. Porter contended that intense domestic competition was particularly important to international success.

A common feature of all theories of factor endowments and their subsequent derivatives was that national environments play a dominant role in determining which firms succeed. The strategies of individual firms were largely irrelevant in all the models discussed above. While some firms obviously ignore opportunities offered by local demand or factor conditions and others adopt strategies that conflict with the environment, these were destined to be anomalies or the failures of history.

In markets with costless entry and exit, this is exactly what one should expect. If one firm or even a nation does not respond to the natural incentives of its home base, someone else will enter the industry with a lower cost position or better product and steal the business. But what the national environment paradigm does not explain is why proximity to local markets and local factors is critical in an age of multinational corporations and telecommunications.[13] Ascribing a determining role to the environment also creates a methodological risk that national conditions could be used as an ex post rationalization. Country conditions are complex, and some facet can usually be invoked to explain the success of any given industry. Porter, for instance, highlights the role of unfavorable factors in stimulating innovation and exports such as a lack of natural resources or a saturated home market. Competitive success could thus be attributed to either the presence or the absence of favorable environmental conditions. Indeed, Porter found that some factors which determined industry success in one nation or region were also present at the failure of industries in other countries.

Strategic Trade Theory

The apparent weaknesses in country-based explanations of international trade led to the development of various refinements in the 1980s. Borrowing tools from game theory and industrial organization, the focus of these new approaches was to explain patterns of trade and competitive success by examining the strategic interactions of firms and governments rather than national environments. The new models emphasized that international trade and investment could take place under conditions of "imperfect markets" such as oligopoly, barriers to entry, economies of scale, and learning economies. Moreover, in a sharp challenge to many of the neoclassical approaches, formal economic modeling demonstrated that government intervention could be justified in the presence of scale economies and other imperfections.[14]

The theory was called "strategic" for two reasons: first, it made the case that some industries were strategic in that they generated high profits and had positive spillover effects, or externalities, for other sectors of the economy; and second, trade was conceived as the outcome of a strategic rivalry in which there were limited numbers of firms and governments and each party took into account the reactions of competitors. In a world of strategic interactions, firms and nations might be more concerned with relative than absolute gains.

Strategic trade literature added rigor to the analysis of government intervention and trade in imperfect markets. Moreover, one of the great breakthroughs was that its core assumptions more closely reflected the real world: the models demonstrated that small variations in industry structure, like economies of scale, product differentiation, and oligopoly, or minor changes in government policies, like voluntary export restraints versus tariffs, could have a huge impact on the countries involved.[15] Moreover, the models suggested that not only could governments play a meaningful role in altering the outcome of competition between firms, but that a government could improve the welfare of its nation through direct intervention. If one government made credible commitments to trade barriers or subsidizing output, foreign firms might be pre-empted and a country's relative advantage undermined. Rather than trade being a result of large numbers of small firms competing at arm's-length in a global marketplace, the real insight of the new trade theory was to recognize that growing segments of international competition were the product of a few big firms and governments that were strategically self-conscious.

Critics of strategic trade theory pointed out that it was just theory, without hard evidence.[16] Furthermore, the mathematical models had highly restrictive conditions: predicted outcomes and policy recommendations were highly sensitive to assumptions and the availability of sufficient information.[17] Like Ricardian comparative advantage, most of this literature was also normative, unlike the more descriptive product-cycle and Heckscher-Ohlin theses. And most efforts at empirical analysis, which were primarily large statistical studies, also proved difficult and inconclusive.[18]

Despite these weaknesses, the strategic trade policy literature shares with this study an interest in important questions about the changing nature of international trade. In particular, we both want to address the following questions: When industries are comprised of governments and a few large firms, how will trade and location of production differ from predictions of previous theories? And what difference does it make that markets are indeed imperfect, and that firms and governments can strategically intervene?

MULTINATIONAL ENTERPRISES AND INTERNATIONAL TRADE

While strategic trade theory confronts critical issues such as market imperfections, oligopolistic interactions, and the potential role of a strategically conscious government, our study sought to go further by addressing the internal workings of the multinational firm. Despite strategic trade theory's efforts to describe the nature of competition in a reasonably realistic way, firms are usually portrayed as organizations with one production location that act to optimize profits. The existence of MNEs with production, sales, and even R&D in multiple locations creates a gaping hole in most explanations of trade patterns. If the MNE is free to serve markets anywhere in the world from any production location it chooses, then the link between the home base and trade patterns can become rather tenuous.[19] Moreover, the MNE is not a simple, profit-maximizing production function: it is a complex organization run by professional managers. How such complex firms make decisions on production locations and exporting can be critical to understanding international trade.

Unfortunately, there is little in the theory of the multinational enterprise that helps explain international trade; moreover, our understanding of the MNE has many of the same gaps we observed in the theory of international trade. In the neoclassical paradigm of perfect markets, foreign direct investment was traditionally seen as a capital flow serving an arbitrage function between countries with differential returns on capital. Thus capital would flow from capital-rich, low-return countries to capital-poor, high-return ones. During the nineteenth century this may have been consistent with the empirically observed outflow of investment from the United Kingdom to English-speaking colonies and newly independent countries. More recent experience shows that the bulk of foreign investment is among industrial "capital-rich" countries; moreover, there is a degree of cross investment between these countries in the same industries.[20] In other words, capital flows have become remarkably similar to trade flows.

The development of the capital asset pricing model led to an appreciation that financial factors could create an incentive for firms to invest overseas. If international diversification offered opportunities to reduce business, political, and exchange risk, and if individual investors were not free to diversify their portfolios internationally, then a firm could increase its share price by international investment.[21] The concept that firms would invest overseas for portfolio diversification immediately challenged the notion that location of production was purely or even largely a function of country variables. Firms could choose to spread activities across countries, not just to take advantage of country-specific conditions, but to reduce a variety of risks and to maintain a flexible posture in the face of shifting opportunities.[22] A global portfolio could reduce risk from currency fluctuations; it might help smooth balance-of-trade and financial flows, which reduce currency risk and political pressures; it could reduce the risk and potential damage from labor or political disruption in any one place; and finally, it might reduce the effect of fluctuating input prices. The global configuration would also give the multinational opportunities to benefit from changing country conditions, for example, by shifting production to take advantage of currency changes, raising capital where it is cheapest, or accessing new market opportunities and technologies as they arise.

Yet portfolio diversification is only one reason for the multinational firm. In fact, many multinationals do not even ship capital overseas; they prefer to raise money in local capital markets. In addition, it has long been recognized that managers see foreign investment as a means to exploit firm-specific advantages such as technological or marketing capability.[23] Firms might also invest overseas to solve contracting problems with suppliers or distributors.[24] In other words, firms invest overseas for a multitude of reasons, only some of which relate to traditional country-based factors. Many students of foreign investment generally agree with John Dunning's "eclectic theory" of foreign investment,[25] which argues that three forces come together to cause FDI: firms with competitive advantages, such as technology and brand name, have an incentive to exploit them in a foreign country; locational advantages of particular countries, such as factor costs and domestic demand, provide the incentive for production abroad; and ownership of the foreign enterprise can reduce the transaction cost of overseas ventures.

If the multinational enterprise uses foreign investment as a strategic weapon against other firms or to reduce contracting costs, strategic and organizational considerations of the multinational corporation could have significant effects on trade.[26] FDI to serve a local market may replace exports that previously came from the home country. Alternatively, FDI that weakens a local competitor based in the host country could eventually lead to more exports.[27] Furthermore, if contracting problems are indeed important, the direction of shipments—i.e., where do the exports go—may also be a function of who owns the upstream or downstream activities rather than simply going to the lowest cost, most economically efficient location.

The ability of MNEs to coordinate a global network of design, production, and distribution has led some observers to conclude that the link between national competitiveness and the competitiveness of domestically based firms has been entirely broken. Robert Reich forcefully argues that the significance of the location of world headquarters is fading. He cites an example of a new Japanese car that was "designed in California, financed from Tokyo and New York, its prototype was created in Worthing, England, and it was assembled in Michigan and Mexico using advanced electronic components invented in New Jersey and fabricated in Japan."[28] What our research will demonstrate is that this perspective vastly oversimplifies the reality of global competition today. But the growing administrative capabilities of the firm in conjunction with the capabilities of governments to intervene in selected markets are revolutionizing international trade.

FIVE PROPOSITIONS

The literatures of international trade and investments provide an excellent starting point for creating a more robust framework of global competition. To extend the theory, we offer five empirical propositions and several hypotheses that build on the observations of our eight industry studies (see the Preface). The overarching theme is that the complexities of international trade and investment can be understood only by looking at the interplay of five factors: country advantages, industry structure, organizational and strategic attributes of firms, government policies, and corporate inertia. Our propositions describe how these factors interact and the conditions under which each factor plays a role. After presenting the propositions, we offer a new framework for analyzing the dynamics of global trade and competition in oligopolistic and politically salient industries. In Chapter 10, we explore in greater depth the empirical validity of these propositions and their implications for the future.

Country Advantages

The place to begin is by acknowledging that conventional wisdom is appropriate when markets are highly competitive and when an industry's development is in its nascent stage. Thus our *first proposition* is: *when industries are relatively fragmented and competitive, national environments (factors of production, domestic market and domestic demand, and so forth) will largely shape the international competitive advantage of domestically headquartered firms and the pattern of trade.* A correlate to this proposition is that: *in the emerging stage of an industry, country characteristics also play the dominant role in determining international competitive advantage.* Who will make and export particular products in relatively perfect markets or in the very early stages of a new product's life cycle will reflect the comparative or "competitive" advantage of the nation.

The logic here is fairly straightforward: in fragmented businesses, winners and losers are primarily determined by relative cost positions, and some nations are inherently lower-cost production sites than others. Ceteris paribus, as long as the barriers to entry into an industry remain low, production and the platform for exports will gravitate toward the lowest-cost, highest-efficiency manufacturing location. Moreover, in the early stages of an industry, as the early product-cycle theory and later Michael Porter pointed out, country factors can also be crucial, especially if domestic markets have unusual or distinctive local demand characteristics, or if advanced infrastructure and specialized expertise emerges within a country to support particular businesses. With many players competing globally, the competitive advantage of firms is often built on factor abundance at home; firms also are most likely to respond aggressively to local incentives. Managers inevitably look to serve local demand before international demand; they generally react more swiftly to local competitors before international competitors; they see opportunities created by locally unfilled needs before international opportunities.

A related hypothesis is that *the presence of multinational firms should not, by itself, influence patterns of international trade in internationally competitive, fragmented industries: other things being equal, country factors will continue to drive the location of production and the direction of exports.* Many business scholars have argued that as firms expand globally, they develop capabilities that provide them with competitive advantages independent of their original home base. As firms move from being simple exporters to becoming true multinational enterprises with a variety of activities dispersed across multiple locations, they learn how to distribute and manage research, production, marketing, and other functions across different countries.[29] The implication is that the link between national environment and trade can be broken: an American-based company might export disk drives from Japan, Europe, or Singapore, regardless of the country's relative cost position or the national source of the technology.

Yet by itself, the emergence of MNEs with a capability to locate different activities in different locations and then coordinate those activities effectively should have no long-run impact on world trade. In fact, the presence of MNEs could reinforce the traditional model of international trade. Since MNEs can scan the globe to find the lowest-cost locations, any MNE that seeks to maximize profitability will locate its production in the most cost-effective geography, do research and development in the country best suited to that activity, procure globally from the most desirable suppliers, and so forth. Even if firms do not maximize profitability, in highly competitive industries, MNEs cannot afford to place their production, R&D, or other important activities in poor locations. In other words, when facing competition, MNEs will simply reinforce the influence of national environments on trade.

Industry Structure

Yet the role of MNEs in international trade is not always marginal. The very emergence of multinational enterprises with new capabilities can set the stage for a different logic under different industry circumstances. This leads to our *second proposition: if an industry becomes internationally concentrated with high entry barriers, then MNE location and export decisions become a function of global oligopolistic rivalry.* We suggest that country characteristics continue to be important, but all other things being equal, the dynamics of global oligopoly will play the driving role in molding the patterns of trade and production.

When firms compete in international trade in relatively competitive markets, they violate the dictums of national comparative advantage at their peril: if a firm tries to export a product from a country that is an inappropriate location from which to launch a low-cost strategy, that firm is unlikely to stay in business. New entrants will copy the product, producing and exporting from a more suitable site.

This logic does not apply in global industries with a limited number of large companies dominating world production and trade. The defining features of global oligopolies are (1) the success of any one firm is directly affected by the strategies of other firms, and (2) entry into the industry is restricted in some way—typically economies of scale or scope, high R&D costs, capital intensity, or advertising expenses. If these structural features do not exist, entry can also be limited by government regulation or firm strategies that make entry difficult. Firms have a variety of tools at their disposal, such as product differentiation, standard setting, predatory pricing, or proprietary systems (e.g., closed computer architectures), any or all of which constrain new firms or countries from entering a specific marketplace.

Why does this matter for trade? Why should market imperfections and global oligopolies lead to trade patterns any different from what you might expect from country characteristics alone? Trade should follow a different logic in globally concentrated businesses because the industry's structure alters the incentive and constraints faced by firms: in many globally oligopolistic industries, firms earn above-average profits, which can reduce the relevance of comparative costs in production and export decisions; firms may also be able to cross-subsidize between geographic markets or businesses, further reducing the importance of geography in production or export decisions; or firms may be motivated by strategic interaction, multimarket competition, or simply matching moves, rather than efficiency alone. What often becomes important is the firm's *relative* position, not its absolute profit levels. For example, a firm may decide to "invade" a competitor's home market, not because that market is profitable, but because this weakens the competitor. Unlike the situation in competitive markets, where high-cost locations could easily be defeated by new entrants from lower-cost locations, entry is difficult in global oligopolies. In the real world, with differentiated products, brand loyalties, and switching costs, firms have the capacity to hold on to their customers, even in the face of dramatically shifting country advantages. Under these circumstances, it is the competitive advantage of companies that matters for international trade and production, not the comparative advantage of nations.

The Organizational and Strategic Attributes of Firms

But industry structure, like country characteristics, provide only broad parameters from which to predict firm behavior[30] and patterns of trade and investment. This leads to our *third proposition: in global oligopolies, specific firm characteristics—particularly the structure of ownership, discretionary strategic choices, and organizational priorities—have an identifiable influence on location decisions, the direction of trade, and, under certain conditions, the very success of a country in global competition.*

In global oligopolies, where a few firms can organize production according to top management's priorities, the individual firm, with its idiosyncrasies, is no longer a statistical error in explaining the world trade of that industry. *Who* owns the production (i.e., the social, national, and personal backgrounds of the managers), the strategic choices made by those managers, the organizational structure of the firm, the administrative capabilities of that management, all influence a variety of decisions that can significantly bias segments of international trade.

Especially in businesses not easily entered in the short run, managers often exercise prerogatives in ways that are not predictable from a country or even industry perspective. As long as rivalry remains oligopolistic, and the penalties associated with discretionary moves are within reasonable bounds (i.e., 5–10%, not 50%), one should expect that the predilections of management could have a critical impact on where things are produced and the direction of international trade.

Of particular importance is the role of administrative capacity, hedging strategies, and ownership structures. Strategic choices, like the decision to hedge a competitive position, and the facility to execute such choices are critically important for the simple reason that not all firms are alike: the ability to identify competitive advantages and implement a strategy to achieve those advantages varies by firm, not by country. In an oligopolistic structure, where only one or two firms may represent the entire production and exports from a nation, these capabilities to execute a strategy can be critical.

Within a group of relatively successful firms, one can further expect some common strategies. In a strategic setting, where managers are concerned about the moves of rivals, firms will pursue strategies to reduce risk, or to be more specific, to reduce the dangers of another firm's gaining a competitive advantage. Since managers are often measured on their *relative* performance, not profit maximization, one might expect widespread use of risk reduction strategies, like locating in markets similar to those of one's rivals.

Finally, ownership structure—whether the firm's equity is privately held or publicly owned, and whether the holders of equity are individuals or the state—should have equally significant implications for production and export decisions. The motivations of managers can be quite different depending on their time horizon, accountability, and compensation. One might expect firms with substantial private or family ownership, for instance, to have longer time horizons in most capital markets, with greater accountability and compensation tied largely to longer-term performance. Similarly, public state-owned enterprises are generally more motivated by foreign policy considerations, employment, and other non-profit concerns. These differences have a direct influence on investment and marketing decisions.

Government Policies

For most firms in globally concentrated industries, the primary constraints on their export and location choices come from the structure of their industry and their internal, organizational imperatives. But in some industries, even the most concentrated ones, there is another guiding hand that cannot be ignored: government. Government has the capacity to restructure trade flows and even manipulate a firm or industry's competitive advantage. This leads us to our *fourth proposition: extensive government intervention in oligopolistic industries can alter the relative balance between firms of different nations; even in fragmented industries, it can alter the direction of trade and accelerate/forestall major corporate trade decisions.*[31]

Our research found that the impact of government intervention varied by the type of industry. In relatively mature, fragmented industry segments, for example, most routine forms of government intervention, such as tariffs, voluntary restraints, tax breaks for FDI, and environmental policies, merely accelerated existing trends, affecting trade and investment decisions only on the margin. The underlying economics of an industry continued to drive location and export patterns.

However, we also found that in industries with significant scale economies and other market imperfections, government intervention, especially infant-industry policies, could reshape the structure of world trade. Economists have long recognized that it was possible for governments to encourage infant industry through temporary protection. Especially where scale and learning economies exist, and spillover effects make the success of one firm dependent on the existence of others, private capital may view investment in the early stages of an industry as too risky in the absence of government guarantees or tariff protection. Yet many economists have refused to endorse infant-industry protection because so many governments fail in such efforts. Most economists also note that protection seldom turns out to be temporary.[32] We suggest that it is critical to separate normative statements from description and theory: while many governments fail to succor infant industries, strategic government intervention can build businesses that would otherwise not exist.

Corporate Inertia

So far, we have discussed how firms and governments have become visible hands guiding international trade and production in concentrated industries. However, our research also found that one cannot take a snapshot of international trade patterns at any given point in time and hope to explain its underlying logic without looking at the evolution of the industry. This leads to our *fifth proposition: in industries where firms make long-term commitments, corporate adjustments and patterns of trade tend to be "sticky."* Choices made by firms and governments at one point in time will have a lasting impact on patterns of production and trade, sometimes for as long as twenty years.

Most models assume that the world is a tabula rasa—a blank slate that begins again with each new decision. In reality, of course, any institution, be it government or corporation, should be understood as a unique set of assets—intangible as well as tangible—that are a function of investments over time. Actions taken in the past cumulate to build the position of the present. All institutions have a heritage which influences the way that institution does business. What makes many institutions unique is the path by which that institution arrived at its current state.

This "path dependence" can have a manifest impact on the competitive advantage of firms and the organization of international production and trade.[33] This legacy of past choices, or the firm's "administrative heritage,"[34] is both a source of competitive advantage and a constraint, because the competitive profile, the array of resources, can take years to change. Investments in productive capacity in one country may outlive the conditions that drove the initial decision. Physical relocation can be expensive, and the organizational structure of the firm is geared to the existing configuration of production. Put simply, we will argue that history creates the power of inertia and momentum. Patterns of exports and production become "sticky" when firms make large, not easily tradable investments in human or physical capital. Managers who decided twenty years ago to invest in one location rarely reassess that decision, absent a corporate crisis or fundamental change in industry structure. Even if production locations and export platforms are no longer the most economically efficient, because they are sunk costs, it is economically rational to keep those operations in business for years or decades. Firms frequently become committed to certain existing patterns of trade and investment because managers are often tied to particular organizational structures. While such organizational commitments will quickly fail in competitive markets, the slack associated with global oligopolies allows less-than-optimal firm policies to persist for years.

A NEW FRAMEWORK FOR INTERNATIONAL TRADE

Our last four propositions have sought to deepen our understanding of international trade by introducing industry structure, the multinational firm, government policy, and history into the explanation of global competition. Figure 1-1 provides a graphic depiction of how all these factors interact to influence the direction and structure of international trade and production.

The traditional literature on international trade sought to explain activities in the lower left-hand box: that is, industries that had few market imperfections and little role for government. Whenever entry was relatively easy and government intervention relatively modest, the driving forces behind the winners and losers in international competition were determined by some form of *comparative advantage*—factor costs, relative factor endowments, the intensity of local competition, local demand, and so forth. However, if industries were imperfect, if entry was restricted and the number of competitors small, and/or government intervention became significant, the driving forces in international competition changed. New forms of competition supplemented and supplanted country-based comparative advantages.

In this book we argue that there are three additional patterns of compe-

FIGURE 1-1
Drivers of International Trade

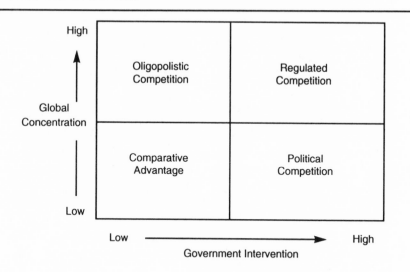

tition, in which outcomes are frequently at odds with models of comparative advantage (see Figures 1-2 and 1-3). In globally concentrated industries where government's role is modest, we suggest that *oligopolistic
competition* propels export and foreign investment decisions. Varying
industry structures have different effects, but one should expect strategic
and organizational choices by managers to be particularly important in
determining the location of production and the direction of exports.

In highly fragmented industries that have significant government intervention (which might be measured as a tariff equivalent or a subsidy
equivalent), *political competition* will supplement competition among
countries. How different governments regulate their industries at home
or use trade barriers at their borders will influence the timing and pace
of shifts in country advantage as well as the level of trade. In these types
of industries, governments will rarely alter the fundamental structure of
national competitive or comparative advantage. Yet if political competition is important, how governments intervene can determine the longevity and exporting success of local industries.

In oligopolistic industries that have extensive government intervention, international trade and competition become a game of strategic
business-government relations. Global competition becomes *regulated*

FIGURE 1-2
Mapping Industries to Drivers of International Trade (circa 1970)

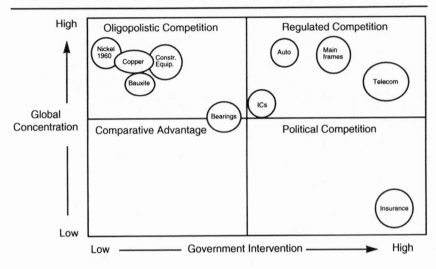

FIGURE 1-3
Mapping Industries to Drivers of International Trade (circa 1990)

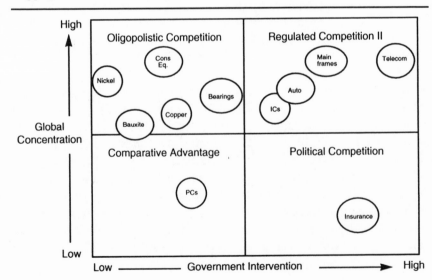

competition, where neither government alone, nor firms and industry alone, can explain the pattern of exports and investments. It is the interaction of business strategy, government policy, and industry structure that is the key driver of global winners and losers.

Finally, patterns of competition are not static. Dynamics are important in two ways. First, industries constantly shift their positions: as the differences between Figures 1-2 and 1-3 indicate, industries evolve, often dramatically. Among our sample, insurance became somewhat less fragmented, especially in Europe in the wake of 1992; copper became significantly less concentrated as barriers to entry declined; bearings were highly concentrated in the 1950s, more fragmented as Japanese firms entered by the 1970s, only to become dominated again by a small number of firms at the end of the 1980s, and so forth. Second, dynamics are also important in a negative sense: long-lived investments in oligopolistic settings are very sticky. Inertia and corporate adjustments tend to be slow in the absence of crises or discontinuous changes in technologies.

In the next eight chapters, all these themes are covered in much greater detail. The roles for countries, industries, firms, and governments are explored with in-depth analysis. In the final chapter, we discuss the implications of these findings for theory, public policy, and managing in a world where there are guiding hands of global trade.

NOTES

1. David Ricardo, *The Principles of Political Economy and Taxation* (New York: Penguin Press, 1971). Originally published in 1817.

2. B. Ohlin, *Interregional and International Trade* (Cambridge, Mass.: Harvard University Press, 1933); Eli Heckscher, "The Effects of Foreign Trade on the Distribution of Income," *Ekonomisk Tidshrift* 21 (1919): 497–512.

3. Wassily Leontief, "Domestic Production and Foreign Trade: The American Capital Position Re-examined," *Economica Internazionale* 7 (February 1954): 3–32.

4. Richard Caves and Ronald Jones, *World Trade and Payments: An Introduction*, 3d ed. (Boston: Little, Brown, 1981), 132.

5. Quoted in Giovanni Dosi, Keith Pavitt, and L. Soete, *The Economics of Technical Change and International Trade* (New York: New York University Press, 1990), 33.

6. This school included work by Donald Keesing, "Labor Skills and Comparative Advantage," in Robert Baldwin and David Richardson, eds., *International Trade and Finance: Readings* (Boston: Little, Brown, 1974), 4–15; R. Bharadwaj and Jagdish Bhagwati, "Human Capital and the Pattern of Foreign Trade: The

Indian Case," *Indian Economic Review*, no. 2 (1967): 117–142; and William Gruber, Dileep Mehta, and Raymond Vernon, "The R&D Factor in International Trade and Investment," in Baldwin and Richardson, *International Trade and Finance*, 16–33.

7. S. B. Linder, "Causes of Trade in Primary Products versus Manufactures," in Baldwin and Richardson, *International Trade and Finance*, 45.

8. Raymond Vernon, "International Investment and International Trade in the Product Cycle," *Quarterly Journal of Economics* 80 (May 1966): 190–207.

9. Louis Wells, ed. *The Product Cycle Theory of International Trade* (Boston: Harvard Business School Division of Research, 1973.

10. Raymond Vernon, "The Product Cycle Hypothesis in a New International Environment," *Oxford Bulletin of Economics and Statistics* 41 (1979): 255–267.

11. Although not specifically mentioned by Vernon, this also raises the possibility of foreign firms innovating for and exporting to the U.S. market. Other criticism of the product cycle included the deterministic nature of the industry cycle. For example, new technologies, product innovations, or the entrance of low-cost competitors can cause an industry to revert to a less mature stage. Similarly, standardized production of mature products might lead to investments in dedicated capital-intense production lines, reducing any incentive to transfer production to a low-wage location.

12. Michael Porter, *The Competitive Advantage of Nations* (New York: Free Press, 1990).

13. Porter, for instance, recognizes that multinationals locate some activities abroad in order to gain advantages offered in foreign environments. He nonetheless emphasizes the importance of understanding the location of the home base because the intensity of incentives, he asserts, is much greater at home.

14. Some aspects of the strategic trade literature built off a very old tradition in the economics literature of infant-industry protection and optimal tariffs.

15. Early work in this area, pioneered by Brander and Krugman, focused largely on the implications of simple market imperfections. For example, J. Brander in his 1981 article, "Intra-industry Trade in Identical Commodities," *Journal of International Economics* 11, 1–14, showed that intra-industry trade could occur in identical goods because of increasing returns to scale and oligopoly; in effect, two firms based in different countries may engage in mutual dumping on the other's territory. Subsequent work developed much more sophisticated, technical models, which explored subtle changes in industry structure and government policy. For instance, J. Brander and B. J. Spencer, "Export Subsidies and International Market Share Rivalry," *Journal of International Economics* 18 (1985): 83–100, demonstrated the possibility that subsidies could raise national welfare by increasing the domestic share of production in an international oligopolistic industry by shifting a proportion of the pool of profits, or rents, to the domestic firms. The basic model assumed two countries that

produced and exported to a third country and were engaged in duopolistic competition. A subsidy worsens domestic terms of trade (i.e., reduces export prices), but more than compensates by increasing the rents accruing to the domestic firm.

16. See, for example, Avinash Dixit, "International Trade Policy for Oligopolistic Industries," *Economic Journal* (Supplement, 1984): 1–16, and Jagdish Bhagwati, *Protectionism* (Cambridge, Mass.: MIT Press, 1988).

17. An example of the difficulty in policy prescriptions was demonstrated by J. Eaton and G. Grossman, "Optimal Trade and Industrial Policy under Oligopoly," Working Paper No. 1236, National Bureau of Economic Research, 1983. Their model showed that when demand and supply are inelastic, the model indicates that an export tax rather than a subsidy is needed. They show that in the duopoly model, a subsidy will raise national welfare when the domestic firm conjectures a more aggressive response by the foreign rival than in fact occurs, and an export tax is optimal in the opposite case. If the home firm has consistent conjectures, meaning it accurately forecasts the rival's response, they show that free trade is the optimal policy. Other theoretical restrictions relate to the number of domestic firms and the amount of domestic consumption as a proportion of the global total. In both cases, a high proportion reduces the possible effectiveness of a subsidy and may require a tax. The most serious policy problem appears to be the identification of appropriate target industries. High profitability by itself can reflect high risk, return on uncapitalized R&D, or short-term market dynamics. The amount of profit-shifting potential depends on demand and supply elasticities, barriers to entry, and the nature of competition, all of which present measurement problems in practice. Even if some likely candidates for support are identified, A. K. Dixit and G. M. Grossman have shown, in "Targeted Export Promotion with Several Oligopolistic Industries," Discussion Papers in Economics No. 71, Princeton University, 1984, that encouraging one industry may bid up the price of common resources and harm other strategic sectors dependent on them.

18. G. M. Grossman and J. D. Richardson, "Strategic Trade Policy: A Survey of Issues and Early Analysis," Special Paper 15, Princeton, International Finance Section, 1985.

19. Some recent empirical research suggests how country base and trade can become disconnected. Robert Lipsey and Irving Kravis, "The Competitiveness and Comparative Advantage of U.S. Multinationals, 1957–1983," National Bureau of Economic Research, Working Paper No. 2051, 1986, show in their study of trade and competitiveness that U.S.-based multinationals had maintained their share of world exports of manufactured goods, while the American exports had dramatically lost ground in international markets. In fact, in several instances, despite being home to a number of successful corporations, the United States has become a net importer. Lipsey and Kravis conclude that the quality of American firms' management and technology were not to blame

for the worsening trade position; rather, U.S.-based MNEs were competing successfully while moving an increasing proportion of their production overseas.

20. The basic problem with applying general equilibrium theory to FDI is that it does not differentiate between manufacturing investment and the capital used to finance it.

21. Stephen Hymer, *The International Operations of National Firms: A Study of Direct Investment*, Ph.D. diss., Massachusetts Institute of Technology (Cambridge, Mass.: MIT Press, 1976). See also M. Adler and B. J. Dumas, "The Microeconomics of the Firm in an Open Economy," *American Economic Review* 67 (February 1977): 180–189. R. Z. Aliber, "A Theory of Direct Foreign Investment," in C. P. Kindleberger, ed., *The International Corporation* (Cambridge, Mass.: MIT Press, 1970, 17–34), offers an interesting variation in proposing that MNEs take advantage of domestic investors' failure to notice the risks to which the foreign assets are exposed.

22. Bruce Kogut, "Designing Global Strategies: Profiting from Operational Flexibility," *Sloan Management Review*, Fall 1985, 27–38.

23. Perhaps the classic statement of the role of firm-specific advantages comes from Richard Caves, "International Corporations: The Industrial Economics of Foreign Investment," *Economica* 38 (February 1971): 1–27.

24. See, for example, O. E. Williamson, *Markets and Hierarchies, Analysis and Anti-Trust Implications* (New York: Free Press, 1975); O. E. Williamson, *The Economic Institutions of Capitalism* (New York: Free Press, 1985); David Teece, "Transaction Cost Economics and the Multinational Enterprise: An Assessment," *Journal of Economic Behavior and Organization* 7 (1986): 21–45; and P. Buckley, "The Limits of Explanation: Testing the Internalization Theory of the Multinational Enterprise," *Journal of International Business Studies*, Summer 1988, 181–194.

25. Dunning has produced a large number of books and articles expounding and refining his eclectic theory. Perhaps the best statement of his position can be found in "Trade Location of Economic Activity and the MNE: A Search for an Eclectic Approach," reprinted in Benjamin Gomes-Casseres and David B. Yoffie, eds., *The International Political Economy of Foreign Direct Investment* (London: Elgar Publishing, 1993).

26. The trade-offs between FDI and trade have been discussed widely. See, for example, Seev Hirsch, "An International Trade and Investment Theory of the Firm," *Oxford Economic Papers* 28 (July 1976): 258–269.

27. K. Kojima, "Japanese-Style Direct Foreign Investment," *Japanese Economic Journal*, Spring 1986, 52–82.

28. Robert Reich, "Who is Them?" *Harvard Business Review*, March–April 1991, 79.

29. Christopher Bartlett and Sumantra Ghoshal, "Managing Across Borders: New Strategic Requirements," *Sloan Management Review*, Summer 1987, 43–53.

30. This argument about the indeterminate nature of industry structure is made by John Sutton, *Sunk Costs and Market Structure* (Cambridge, Mass.: MIT Press, 1991).

31. Governments have recognized trade as a source of national wealth, as well as taxation, for many centuries. Our concern here is not whether government interference with free trade can raise or lower overall national welfare, but whether governments can successfully alter the industrial landscape to promote competitive domestic industries.

32. Robert Baldwin, in "The Case against Infant Industry Protection," *Journal of Political Economy*, May/June 1969, 295–305, discusses, from a skeptical viewpoint, the circumstances under which the infant-industry argument can be sustained. While we argue that infant industry "works," it still may not be pareto optimal. We did not measure whether the short-run costs to the economy were outweighed by the long-run benefits of increased exports, share of market, and profits.

33. This point has been made by such economists as Gene Grossman and Paul Krugman. They typically use the term "hysteresis" to describe what we are calling path dependence.

34. Bartlett and Ghoshal, "Managing Across Borders."

PART I
Regulated Competition

2

SEMICONDUCTORS: FROM MANIPULATED TO MANAGED TRADE

Laura D'Andrea Tyson and David B. Yoffie

THE SEMICONDUCTOR INDUSTRY has never been free of the visible hand of government intervention. Policy choices have heavily influenced competitive advantage in production and trade, particularly in the United States and Japan. Some of them, like public support of basic science, R&D, and education in the United States, have had general objectives. Others, like the provision of secured demand for industry output through military procurement in the United States and preferential procurement of computers and telecommunication equipment in Japan, have been industry-specific. The semiconductor industry has been an explicit target of industrial policy, whether in the guise of military policy in the United States or of commercial policy elsewhere in the world.

Conditions creating advantage in this industry have been manipulated by policy, not inherited like features of the national landscape. Nor has trade in this industry ever been free in the classic sense. Rather, it has been manipulated by a myriad of formal and informal policies that have powerfully affected the levels and directions of trade flow among nations.

INDUSTRY ECONOMICS AND THE EVOLUTION OF COMPARATIVE ADVANTAGE

The Ascent of the U.S. Firms

The semiconductor industry originated with the invention of the transistor by Bell Laboratories in 1947.[1] That the industry was born in the

We benefited greatly from the comments of many reviewers, including the Institute for International Economics, BRIE, Michael Borrus, Ken Flamm, Clyde Prestowitz, Charles Ferguson, Garth Saloner, Richard Heimlich, Gordon Moore, and many senior industry executives. We are especially grateful to Masao Ogawa, Julie Herendeen, Eric Vayle, and P. Konstantina Koiusis for their research assistance. This chapter has appeared in revised form as a chapter in Laura Tyson, *Who's Bashing Whom?: Trade Conflicts in High Technology Industries* (Washington D.C.: Institute for International Economics, 1993).

United States is not surprising; indeed, it is consistent with theories of trade that emphasize two kinds of country-based variables—the availability of factors of production and the level of domestic demand. At the time, the United States was the unparalleled leader in technological, scientific, and engineering capabilities—the most important factors behind the development of the semiconductor industry and the driving force behind competition in the industry until the 1980s.

American leadership partly reflected America's policy commitment to scientific training and to funding basic research. A number of technological indicators show the U.S. superiority, including high R&D spending as a percentage of gross national product, large cadres of engineers and scientists as a percentage of the labor force, and U.S. dominance in world patents through the early 1960s.[2]

The United States also possessed demand conditions that supported the industry's development in the form of a secure defense market. In the early years of the industry, the military purchased up to 100% of its output, and even as late as 1968 claimed nearly 40%.[3] In addition, the military's heavy procurement of computer output throughout the 1960s produced a derived defense demand for semiconductor output.[4] The steady direct and indirect defense purchases reduced the risk of investment in R&D and equipment. The government's willingness and ability to buy chips in quantity and premium prices allowed a growing number of companies to refine their production skills and develop elaborate manufacturing facilities.

These improvements brought increases in the number of elements contained on a single integrated circuit (IC), coupled with steep declines in price. More than any other product in industrial history, ICs benefited from an amazingly steep learning curve. In 1964 a chip containing about sixty-four components was priced at around $32. By 1971 the price of a chip containing more than a thousand components was about $1.[5] The rule of thumb in the industry was that costs fell 30% to 40% with every doubling in volume. Semiconductor manufacturing gained such steep learning economies because it routinely yielded more defective than sound chips. For complex new products, yields as low as 25% were quite common, while mature products might yield 90%. The need to raise yields led firms to manufacture "technology drivers"—high-volume products with simple designs. When a firm mass-produced a technology driver, it would hone its manufacturing skills, then transfer its learning to more complicated, lower-volume, higher-value-added devices. Dynamic random-access memories (DRAMs) were particularly well suited for this purpose because they had less complex structures than other ICs, allowing their producers to distinguish quickly between a flaw in the design and a flaw in the manufacturing process. For particular products, other high-volume ICs, such as electrically programmable read-only memories (EPROMs) and static random-access memories (SRAMs), could also serve as technology drivers.

Having invented DRAMs, EPROMs, and SRAMs, American firms enjoyed obvious first-mover advantages. Product cycles were quite long, so the returns from a first-mover position in a particular product could be generous. These profits helped finance R&D and capital spending for the next product generation. The government also paid for a large share of R&D through the early 1970s, providing roughly one-half the total from 1958 through 1970.[6]

From its inception, the semiconductor industry has been one of the most R&D-intensive industries; R&D expenditures average more than 10% of revenues. It has also been a highly capital-intensive industry; as much as 30% of sales is spent on capital equipment. At the same time, variable costs have always been small and have gradually declined. The basic inputs into semiconductor production are sand (silicon) and electricity. Distribution and transportation costs have been tiny (1–2%). The only significant variable costs have been labor outlays for final chip assembly. And by the 1980s, variable labor costs could be largely automated away.

Investment patterns in semiconductors have been lumpy, producing chronic booms and busts. Excess capacity emerges approximately every five years. The cyclical nature of the industry, together with steep learning curves, has promoted a practice of forward pricing. The industry leader of the late 1960s and early 1970s, Texas Instruments, was well known for pricing well below costs in the early stages of a product to build volume, gain market share, and move down the learning curve.[7] By the early 1980s American producers were voicing sharp criticism of their Japanese competitors for similar pricing tactics.

The history of the American industry through the mid-1970s is one of product innovation driven by the entry of new firms. Between 1966 and 1972, thirty merchant firms entered the market. Managers and technicians who had left established companies were the principal entrepreneurs. The U.S. environment nurtured this pattern of competition in several ways. First, there were no policies or norms favoring permanent relationships between firms and their most valued employees. Indeed, salaried employees in the United States have always enjoyed great mobility. Second, the venture market supplied the financial capital necessary for entry on attractive terms. Third, the military was not only the largest consumer of leading-edge components in the 1960s but also bought very expensive products from brand-new firms that offered the ultimate in performance in lieu of reassuring track records.[8] Fourth, some technological information needed for successful operation was freely available through university and academic channels, in which research continued to be funded by huge federal investments.[9] Indeed, the conditions of federal funding often required cooperation between industry and the supported university infrastructure. Fifth, the U.S. antitrust environment worked to the advantage of the merchant firms and to the disadvantage of formidable vertically integrated competitors like IBM and AT&T.

As a result of a 1956 consent decree, AT&T could not participate in the emerging U.S. semiconductor market. It was required to give any company access to its technologies—at a royalty to be set by a court if the parties could not agree. The low-cost availability of AT&T's technological information greatly facilitated the entry of Texas Instruments, Fairchild, and others. In the case of IBM, no court order precluded it from competing in the semiconductor market, but the credible threat of antitrust action deterred it from entering the merchant market.[10] The U.S. antitrust and patent environment also encouraged the flow of technological information through cross-licensing. Cross-licensing, which became a popular mechanism for avoiding lengthy and risky patent disputes, promoted technological exchange and access among companies.

These factors shaped an industry with a distinctive character whose biggest players were not part of vertically integrated systems producers, but were so-called merchant firms specializing in semiconductor products. This structure gave rise to strategies and forms of competition that infused the industry with great vitality through the mid-1970s.

The underlying economics reinforced the potential sustainability of America's advantages in semiconductors. Learning-curve effects were so powerful that they kept the U.S. merchant industry quite concentrated despite the proliferation of new vendors. In 1965, for example, the four largest merchants accounted for 69% of total shipments, and the eight largest accounted for 91%. In 1972, even with many new entrants, the comparable figures remained high at 53% and 67%.[11] Furthermore, U.S. industry leaders did not rest on their laurels; right from the beginning, they sought to exploit their first-mover and country-based advantages by developing global strategies. Even the smallest semiconductor companies maintained international sales offices with exports that averaged about 20% of sales.[12] Transportation costs were insignificant and there were no credible foreign competitors, leaving the way open for American companies to move abroad aggressively.

Initially, global strategies focused on exporting, but direct investment eventually became more important. Foreign investment emerged for two reasons: first, U.S. manufacturers wanted to take advantage of low labor costs in Southeast Asia for the assembly of their products; second, government protection limited market access in Japan and Europe. The shift to offshore assembly operations became important between 1964 and 1972, as firms in the increasingly competitive industry tried to compete on cost. The natural division of production into wafer fabrication, assembly, and testing allowed the assembly stage to be located apart from fabrication and testing with little impact on learning economies. The assembly stage required low-skilled labor that was available abroad at a steep wage discount—yielding up to a 50% reduction in manufacturing costs. Not for another decade could a high percentage of labor costs be automated out of assembly.

The policies of the United States and several newly industrializing countries supported the offshore assembly strategy. Under American tariff schedules 806 and 807, imported articles assembled in whole or in part from U.S.-fabricated components were dutiable only to the extent that value was added abroad. This meant a big tariff break on the offshore assembly of chips. Moreover, beginning in 1967, the governments of Mexico, Taiwan, Singapore, Malaysia, and Korea established "export platforms" to encourage foreign investment. The inducements offered by these platforms included tax-free exports, import tax reductions, and tax holidays. By 1978 the top nine U.S. producers had thirty-five offshore assembly operations in ten developing countries in Latin America and Southeast Asia. By that time more than 80% of the semiconductors shipped in the United States were assembled and tested overseas, mainly in these countries (see Figure 2-1).[13]

The second type of foreign investment, integrated fabrication of chips, came mainly in Europe, where high tariff rates (17% of value), preferential procurement procedures, and pressure by governments (especially the British and the French) encouraged foreign investment to serve their growing markets. Investment in Europe was heavy from 1969 to 1974, by which time forty-six affiliates, eighteen of which were engaged in complete manufacturing operations including fabrication, had been established.[14]

Tariffs, quotas, and other forms of border protection encouraged U.S.

FIGURE 2-1
Proportion of U.S. Semiconductors Produced Within the United States and Abroad

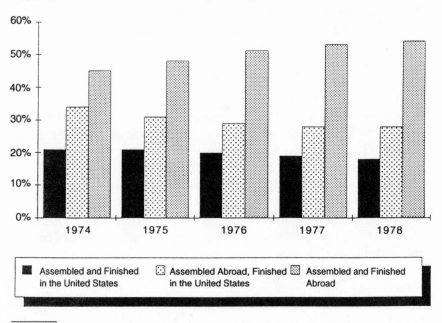

Source: Joseph Grunwald and Kenneth S. Flamm, *The Global Factory: Foreign Assembly in International Trade* (Washington, D.C.: Brookings Institution, 1985), 84.

companies to consider direct investment to serve the Japanese market, but the Japanese blocked it. They avowedly pursued a strategy of import substitution through creating and promoting indigenous suppliers. The Europeans, on the other hand, used import substitution, at least in part, to replace U.S. imports with local production by American companies. The difference in these strategies is apparent in the numbers: Japanese companies have always supplied the lion's share (90%) of the Japanese marketplace, while American companies, either through export or local production, have supplied 50–70% of the European market, with the remainder supplied primarily by domestic enterprises.[15]

Texas Instruments refused to license its key integrated circuit patents to Japanese firms and petitioned Washington for trade protection based on patent infringement by the Japanese. It alone was able to extract permission from the Japanese government to establish a wholly owned manufacturing subsidiary in Japan in 1968. The requirements posed by the Japanese government for investment by other U.S. companies were so unattractive that few chose to exercise this option until after direct controls were abolished in 1978. By that time, for the reasons we note below, the growing strength of Japanese firms had reduced the incentives to invest in the Japanese market.

Implications for Trade

Initially, the United States enjoyed a trade surplus in integrated circuits; but even while American firms remained dominant in the world semiconductor market, direct investment reduced net export earnings. The United States began to run a trade deficit in integrated circuits as early as 1971, although overall semiconductor trade showed a surplus through 1977 (Table 2-1). In the early years, most U.S. imports consisted of assembled products from U.S. affiliates located in newly industrializing countries (NICs); toward the end of the 1970s, however, the Japanese share of imports rose dramatically. Most U.S. exports of finished integrated circuits served four markets—Britain, France, West Germany, and Japan. Exports of unfinished circuits went mainly to five Southeast Asian assembly locations for final assembly and packaging. The manufacturers then re-exported these products either to the United States or to the other four markets.

Consistent with these trade trends, by the late 1970s an estimated 80% of the fabrication by U.S. firms was still done at home and 20% abroad, mainly in Europe. The reverse numbers applied in assembly—about 80% of assembly by U.S. firms was performed abroad and only 20% at home.[16]

THE CREATION AND RISE OF THE JAPANESE INDUSTRY

In Japan the semiconductor industry is a successful and dramatic story of infant-industry promotion and protection. As part of its aim to establish a competitive indigenous computer industry, the government wanted to create a competitive indigenous semiconductor industry. While military objectives predominated in the United States, the objective was purely commercial in Japan. Moreover, while U.S. support was designed to expand the technological frontier, Japanese support was an acknowledged catch-up effort.

The Japanese government protected the domestic market from the inception of the industry in the 1960s through the mid-1970s. Tokyo rejected all applications for wholly owned subsidiaries and for joint ven-

TABLE 2-1
U.S. Semiconductor Trade ($ millions)

	Exports					Imports			
	Total	Integrated Circuits	Transistors, Diodes & Rectifiers	Other[a]		Total	Integrated Circuits	Transistors, Diodes & Rectifiers	Other[a]
1966	130.4	8.9	91.0	30.5	1966	44.6		28.7	15.9
1967	152.4	26.5	81.4	44.1	1967	46.5		26.7	19.8
1968	204.5	36.2	89.5	78.8	1968	76.6		44.7	31.9
1969	345.7	72.4	138.6	134.7	1969	111.2		59.0	52.2
1970	416.9	99.8	146.2	170.9	1970	167.7	69.4	59.8	38.5
1971	370.5	91.2	99.9	179.4	1971	187.0	94.2	60.4	32.4
1972	469.6	103.5	126.0	240.1	1972	328.8	180.5	100.1	48.2
1973	848.6	217.7	195.8	435.1	1973	610.5	365.3	160.6	84.6
1974	1,247.5	313.5	215.6	718.4	1974	953.5	606.3	235.9	111.3
1975	1,037.0	262.1	111.6	663.3	1975	802.0	581.5	138.5	82.0
1976	1,385.9	320.4	120.3	945.2	1976	1,098.0	813.7	153.1	131.2
1977	1,490.5	348.1	70.6	1,071.8	1977	1,403.2	1,025.0	173.5	204.7
1978	1,521.4	471.9	85.4	964.1	1978	1,827.4	1,405.2	179.1	243.1
1979	2,075.1	650.1	90.9	1,334.1	1979	2,587.7	2,035.4	195.0	357.3
1980	2,782.3	833.5	95.2	1,853.6	1980	3,395.6	2,780.4	212.2	403.0
1981	2,832.7	768.4	87.3	1,977.0	1981	3,645.5	2,982.1	264.0	399.4
1982	3,058.9	836.3	81.8	2,140.8	1982	4,397.0	3,501.0	263.9	632.1
1983	3,673.5	1,025.7	97.9	2,549.9	1983	5,330.1	4,150.2	257.4	922.5
1984	4,651.5	1,391.3	118.8	3,141.4	1984	8,284.2	6,135.8	345.9	1,802.5
1985	3,693.1	1,140.6	123.1	2,429.4	1985	6,369.7	4,423.9	259.4	1,686.4
1986	4,185.4	1,148.1	138.8	2,898.5	1986	6,685.7	4,539.0	303.7	1,843.0
1987	6,229.0	1,622.8	131.4	4,474.9	1987	8,561.9	6,038.1	336.8	2,187.0
1988	8,035.4	2,588.5	168.4	5,278.5	1988	12,089.8	8,767.6	425.2	2,896.9
1989	9,530.6				1989	12,301.6			
1990	10,709.6				1990	12,143.5			

Sources: 1966–1972: U.S. Department of Commerce Publications #ES-2:15; 1973–1976: U.S. Department of Commerce Publications #ES-2:17; 1977–1982: U.S. Department of Commerce Publications #ES-2:19; 1983–1986: U.S. Department of Commerce Publications #ES-2:20; 1987–1988: Compiled from U.S. Department of Commerce Publications #FT-246; 1989–1990: Compiled from Official U.S. Department of Commerce Statistics.

(Breakdowns for 1989–1990 were not available because of a change in classification from SIC to a Harmonized System).

[a]Other semiconductor devices.

tures in which foreign firms would hold majority ownership.[17] It restricted foreign purchases of equity in Japanese firms. It used high tariffs, restrictive quotas, and approval registration requirements to control imports. It required approval for all patent and technical assistance licensing agreements. Through controls over the acquisition of foreign technology, the Ministry of International Trade and Industry (MITI) acted as a monopsonist buyer of such technology and doled it out among Japanese firms. These tight border controls held the U.S. share of the Japanese semiconductor market far below its market shares in the rest of the world. In 1975, U.S. firms had 98% of the U.S. market, 78% of the European market, and only 20% of the Japanese market.[18]

In response to foreign pressure, the Japanese government phased out its formal trade barriers by 1976 and its formal foreign investment restrictions by 1978. Beginning in 1971, the government targeted a series of advanced technologies, including semiconductors, and provided financing to stimulate their cooperative development. Between 1971 and 1977, more than sixty projects received total financial support in the multihundred-million-dollar range in such areas as electron-beam exposure and large-scale integration (LSI) production equipment, discrete devices, basic materials research, and low-power, high-performance semiconductors[19] (see Table 2-2). All these projects called for cooperation and cofinancing by competitors in the precommercial stages of developing a new technology—stages at which it is difficult to exclude others from the use of results and hence the returns to knowledge creation are not easily appropriable.

These programs, along with related efforts to support Japan's developing computer industry, raised the value of more sophisticated integrated circuits as a share of total Japanese semiconductor output from 27% in 1971 to about 42% by the end of 1975. By 1976 the Japanese had developed a significant LSI capability, and they dominated their domestic market in all but the most sophisticated IC devices. They had also lifted their share of the domestic installed base of general-purpose digital computers to more than 60%.[20]

The Japanese achieved this performance despite the availability of U.S. semiconductor and computer products at lower prices, and at higher quality, capability, and reliability levels than theirs. The "counter-liberalization measures" taken by the Japanese government to guarantee "that liberalization [would] not adversely affect domestic producers nor produce confusion" seemed to work.[21] Despite the abolition of formal barriers, the government held foreign penetration in check by a variety of

TABLE 2-2
MITI-Sponsored Joint Research and Development Projects in Microelectronics

Project	MITI VLSI	Opto Electronics	Super Computer	New Function Elements	SORTEC[b]	Optoelectronic Devices	Fifth-Generation Computer
Time Frame	1975–1979	1979–1986	1981–1989	1981–1990	1986–1996	1986–1996	1981–1991
Technological Focus	VLSI Manufacturing	Optical Semiconductors	High-Speed Devices	VLSI Device & Process	Synchotron Lithography	Optical Semiconductors	VLSI Logic
Government Funding[a] ($ millions)	112	80	135	140	62	42	N/A
Participants	NEC Hitachi Fujitsu Toshiba Mitsubishi	NEC Hitachi Fujitsu Toshiba Mitsubishi Oki Sumitomo	NEC Hitachi Fujitsu Toshiba Mitsubishi Oki Sharp	NEC Hitachi Fujitsu Toshiba Mitsubishi Oki Sharp Sanyo Sumitomo Matsushita	NEC Hitachi Fujitsu Toshiba Mitsubishi Oki Sharp Sanyo Sumitomo Nippon Sheet Glass Matsushita Nippon Kogaku	NEC Hitachi Fujitsu Toshiba Mitsubishi Oki Sharp Sanyo Sumitomo Nippon Sheet Glass Fujikura	NEC Hitachi Fujitsu Toshiba Mitsubishi Oki Sharp

[a]Yen: dollar conversion average for the period.
[b]Funded through Japan Key Technology Center. SORTEC was a consortium of 13 companies—Hitachi, NEC, Fujitsu, Mitsubishi, Matsushita, Oki, Canon, Sanyo, Toshiba, Sharp, Sumitomo, Sony, and Nippon Kogaku.

Source: Reprinted by permission from Thomas Howell et al., The Microelectronics Race: The Impact of Government Policy on International Competition (Boulder, Colo.: Westview Press, 1988), 47.

offsetting policies, including R&D support, government-sponsored joint R&D and production ventures among the Japanese companies, preferential procurement policies—Nippon Telephone and Telegraph (NTT) would not buy any foreign systems products, nor would it buy domestic systems products containing foreign semiconductors—and other administrative means, and by the purchase decisions of the Japanese companies themselves.

Of all the support programs of the 1970s, the most successful was the very large-scale integration (VLSI) cooperative R&D program designed to help Japanese firms reach state-of-the-art capability in the production of memory devices and logic circuits. The Japanese strategy to move into the most sophisticated memory products reflected aims and needs in telecommunications and computers. By the late 1970s these needs could be met only by purchasing more sophisticated memory devices from American firms, which had a commanding lead, or by developing Japanese production capabilities for such devices. Consistent with their infant-industry approach, the Japanese chose the latter option.

By 1980 this option had paid off. The VLSI program helped the participating firms develop one-micron-device technology, submicron process technology, and 64K DRAMs. The dramatic success of VLSI was partly a function of a temporary shortfall in American production capacity in 1976–1977. This in turn was the result of the 1975 recession, during which American business cut back on its capacity expansion plans. When the semiconductor market recovered in 1976–1977, U.S. companies were caught short, forcing their customers to search for other sources of supply and opening the door to new competitors. By that time, the Japanese were ready to step in.

Japanese firms also capitalized on another American mistake at this time: through the 1970s, most U.S. firms were fabricating chips with bipolar and NMOS technology, low-cost techniques used since the 1960s. During the mid-1970s, however, Japanese firms were more aggressive than their American rivals in adopting a new process technology called CMOS, which produced chips with superior features. By 1983–1984, as a result of an innovation in lithography equipment, the cost of CMOS fell. According to some analysts, "U.S. memory producers had looked down on CMOS technology as . . . insufficient for the stringent requirements of computer memories. . . . All of a sudden, the long acquaintance of the Japanese with CMOS technology turned out to be an important competitive advantage."[22]

The choices of process and product technology by the Japanese, i.e.,

CMOS and DRAMs, proved critical to the success of their infant-industry strategy. DRAMs are the largest volume commodity product of the semiconductor industry. They are a standardized good with almost perfect substitution capability among the various manufacturers producing at the industry norm. Because they are standardized and require the least investment in support and distribution services, DRAMs are also one of the easiest product lines for newcomers to adopt. The only significant entry barriers into DRAMs are scale economies and the learning curve. Scale, in particular, became increasingly important after the mid-1970s. While it cost only $3 million to build a fabrication facility in 1970, its price approached $75 million by 1980. In addition, intellectual property protection poses barriers to entry, but relatively weak ones, because there are multiple ways to design a standard part. In the 1970s, moreover, intellectual property protection for semiconductors was fairly weak.

A policy of promotion and protection helped Japanese companies gain the scale and technical experience they needed to become formidable competitors in the DRAM market. Protection allowed Japanese producers to reach minimum scale; promotion reduced the risk of making the big capital investments necessary to enter. Such policies would not have succeeded had the Japanese tried to target other semiconductor products, like logic, where competition often depends on proprietary design innovations, and where U.S. companies had significant first-mover advantages. On the other hand, the targeting of DRAMs helped create knowledge in large-scale production process technology that had spillover benefits for Japanese companies in their efforts to break into other less commodity-like product lines in the 1980s.

The effects of promotion and protection must also be understood in the context of a particular industrial structure. The Japanese semiconductor industry is dominated by six multidivisional, vertically integrated firms that make electronics systems products serving end markets in consumer electronics, computers, and telecommunications equipment: NEC, Hitachi, Toshiba, Fujitsu, Mitsubishi, and Matsushita. Together these firms form an even more concentrated oligopoly structure than in the American merchant market; in the mid-1970s, for example, they controlled 79% of domestic sales.[23]

Some 20% of these firms' production is consumed internally; in memory devices, the figure is even lower. The main Japanese semiconductor firms are neither captive producers, like IBM and AT&T, nor merchant producers, like Intel and National Semiconductor. Yet, together, they account for approximately 60% of total Japanese semiconductor consumption.

The structure of Japanese companies and their close relationships with one another and with various parts of the Japanese government, especially MITI, the Ministry of Posts and Telecommunications (MPT), and NTT, have been important factors behind the continued difficulties of American producers to gain access to the Japanese market. During the 1970s American companies penetrated the Japanese market primarily with advanced product innovations not yet produced by the Japanese. As Japanese suppliers became competent in the production of these devices, American suppliers saw their shares of the Japanese market level off or decline, even as Japanese demand grew. This pattern, of course, is also characteristic of many other industries in which foreign companies have tried to gain access to Japanese markets.

The Japanese often attribute the failure of U.S. companies to gain market share in Japan after trade liberalization to an alleged mismatch between Japanese demand and American supply. According to this explanation, U.S. producers—whose lines were heavily tailored to computer, industrial, and defense applications—did not offer the products required for Japan's consumer electronics applications.

But this explanation cannot be the whole story. The structure of Japan's market was roughly 50% data processing and communications, 40% consumer electronics, and 10% industrial and defense. While it is true that American firms did not offer specialized products for many consumer electronics applications, such products accounted for only 20–25% of total Japanese demand. Commodity products like DRAMs, EPROMs, and microcontrollers, supplied by most U.S. producers, could be used in many Japanese consumer applications. In addition, U.S. producers were competitive suppliers of data-processing and communication chips; if they had obtained 60% of the Japanese demand for these applications, as they had done in Europe, they would have captured roughly 30% of the total Japanese market. Preferential procurement of Japanese chips for these applications was consistent with NTT's "Japan-only" procurement strategies, which persisted through the 1980s, and with Japan's infant-industry strategy in computers.[24]

There is a strong prima facie case that the incentives and business practices of the Japanese firms themselves played a role in restricting the access of American producers once the Japanese government stopped acting as a gatekeeper. Each of the six firms is part of a keiretsu—with implications for preferential sales arrangements among member firms and for restrictive distributional arrangements that block access to distributional channels by nonmember companies. All participated in cooperative research and production activities sponsored by MITI, which encouraged specialization and communication and discouraged competition among the companies. All participants were active in the Electronics Industries Association of Japan, a legal trade association that has a long history of exchanges of company production and sales information. Four of the six firms—Matsushita, Hitachi, Toshiba, and Mitsubishi—had a history of overt and clandestine methods of cartelizing the consumer electronics market in Japan and coordinating export efforts abroad.[25] The two others—NEC and Fujitsu—were the beneficiaries of continued preferential NTT policies in the procurement of computers and telecommunication equipment.[26] Finally, all functioned in a lax antitrust environment in which there was no particular sanction against cooperative or collusive behavior.

The continued difficulties of American companies to access the Japanese market can be explored in one of two ways. One possibility is that the Japanese companies worked in undocumented and undetected ways to cartelize the Japanese marketplace at the expense of foreign companies. Similar efforts involving some or all of the same companies have been documented in the television and office computer industries.[27] The structure of the Japanese industry was obviously more conducive to cartel-like behavior than that of the American industry. Such behavior was also made more likely by the exemption of the computer and semiconductor industries from Japan's antimonopoly law.

The alternative explanation is that the patterns of specialization, distribution, cooperation, and trust fostered by decades of protection and promotion and by the keiretsu system led Japanese companies to prefer buying from one another rather than from an outsider, even when that outsider was a new Japanese entrant and especially when that outsider was a foreign company supplying competitor firms, like IBM, in lucrative downstream markets. In a recent study, Robert Lawrence concluded, "Producer keiretsu relationships are a significant barrier to the entry of foreign products into Japan."[28]

As far as the effects on international trade and American producers are concerned, it is not germane whether the cartel explanation or what Ronald Dore calls the "relational handshake" is the correct one. Access to the Japanese market by American companies continued to be limited to products not offered by their Japanese competitors. And the Japanese authorities sanctioned, if not encouraged, this behavior.

The structure of the Japanese industry presented another serious roadblock to Americans. Because of their vertical integration and keiretsu linkages, the Japanese companies had very deep pockets—they had access to cheap and patient capital to finance massive investment spending even during periods of market slowdown and to withstand sustained losses when pricing aggressively to build market shares. Only the two U.S. merchants that were partly diversified, Texas Instruments (TI) and Motorola, could afford to invest countercyclically or absorb losses for long periods. The consequences of these differences in industrial structure were first felt in the aftermath of the 1975 recession. Strapped for cash, American firms cut capacity expansion during the downturn, but Japanese firms cross-subsidized their investment, giving them their first opportunity to gain market share in the United States. By 1983 the Japanese companies were outinvesting the American companies, a trend that persisted through 1990.

The deep pockets of the Japanese also allowed them to wage an aggressive pricing war in the depressed market conditions of 1985–1986. This helped push seven American companies, including Intel, Motorola, AMD, and National Semiconductor, out of production of DRAMs by 1986, leaving only two, and ensured the virtual domination of the latest generation of DRAM chips by the Japanese.

Finally, Japan's successful thrust down the learning curve in DRAMs gave its companies another competitive advantage in the marketplace: by 1980 they were delivering to their U.S. and Japanese customers fewer defects per shipment, by an order of magnitude, than their American counterparts. Yet this advantage should not be interpreted to suggest that Japanese firms had simply become better. By the middle of the 1980s American firms had responded to the competitive challenge, and there was no appreciable difference in defect rates delivered to customers between U.S. and Japanese suppliers.

THE STAGNATION OF THE EUROPEAN INDUSTRY

The European approach to the semiconductor industry was similar to that of the Japanese in one respect—the use of protection to promote national producers.[29] European semiconductor producers were buffered by a steep 17% tariff that survived both the Kennedy and Tokyo rounds of the General Agreement on Tariffs and Trade (GATT) tariff reductions, by rules of origin that blocked the use of imported semiconductors in European electronics manufactures crossing the European Community–

European Free Trade Association (EC-EFTA) boundary, and by informal nontariff barriers, including preferential procurement practices,
which encouraged European production by foreign producers to serve
the European market. As a result, American producers invested heavily
in European production facilities.

The objective of the Japanese was to promote Japanese industry, while
the Europeans increasingly sought to promote a European production
base, regardless of ownership. The Japanese forced U.S. firms to transfer
technology to their Japanese competitors if they wanted to profit from
growth in the Japanese market, while the Europeans allowed American
companies to earn a return through their facilities in Europe without
transferring their technological know-how to budding European competitors. The Americans could thereby pre-empt the developing European
market for advanced products, which some observers believe underlay
the European producers' failure to gain a growing share of the world
markets.[30]

Another factor behind their weakness was the fragmentation of the
large European market into much smaller national markets, which eliminated the potential for pan-European product specialization. Ironically,
such fragmentation discouraged cooperation among European companies from different European nations while encouraging cooperation between them and American firms. As a result, U.S. companies were able
to operate in most of the major European countries, thereby capturing
the benefits of scale denied to their European competitors.

Failure of promotional policies in the computer industry also aggravated Europe's difficulties in semiconductors. European governments
protected national computer markets with high tariffs and promoted national champions via direct subsidies and preferential procurement. The
failure of this strategy kept the European computer industry lagging well
behind its U.S. competitors.[31] In this respect, the European situation
was similar to that in Japan. Like the Europeans, the Japanese had
targeted the computer industry and pushed their producers into head-on
competition with IBM. Both strategies failed. But whereas the Europeans
continued to target the computer industry directly, with relatively modest
support for the semiconductor industry, the Japanese shifted attention to
their semiconductor industry as a means to build strength in computers.
Finally, in the second half of the 1980s, in response to the precipitous
decline in the fortunes of their semiconductor industry between 1975
and 1985 and the mounting challenge of the Japanese, the Europeans

belatedly began to develop significant programs to support their semiconductor producers.

The weakness of the European computer industry resulted in limited demand for the high-performance chips that drove technology development in the United States. Instead, European semiconductor producers focused on products for the telecommunication and industrial markets, where European producers remained strong. As a consequence, the European semiconductor companies produced mainly for European users, doing little business in the rest of the world. Indeed, the largest integrated national champions promoted through national policies, like Thomson and Siemens, were primarily interested in developing semiconductor capacities that served their internal needs and only secondarily interested in serving as commodity component producers for other users.

Intent on producing specialized proprietary chips in a sheltered environment, European companies failed to build state-of-the-art manufacturing skills that were crucial to competitive success in commodity memory products. When these products became the fastest-growing segments of the global semiconductor market, the share of the European companies in this market fell sharply, even in Europe. Flamm estimates that between 1975 and 1985, Europe's share of the global merchant semiconductor market dropped about 50%.[32] During this period, the share of European companies in their own market declined from 50% to 35%.[33]

EFFECTS OF DEVELOPMENT STRATEGIES ON TRADE FLOWS AND MARKET SHARES

The spectacular rise in the world market share of the Japanese semiconductor industry at the expense of its American counterpart, beginning in 1978 and continuing through 1985, is a well-known story. Companies headquartered in the United States produced 55% of global semiconductor revenues in 1978, while Japanese companies produced 28%. By 1986 U.S. firms captured only about 40% as Japanese companies claimed around 46%.[34] In 1985 the famous crossover occurred—the Japanese companies' global share jumped ahead of the U.S. companies' share (see Table 2-3). The rankings of individual U.S. companies dropped accordingly.[35]

Japan's growing strength in IC production was reflected in its trade and in the share of its firms in world markets. In the U.S. case, domestic firms retained leadership in ICs through the early 1980s, but suffered a

TABLE 2-3
Worldwide Semiconductor Market Share, 1981–1990

	1981	1982	1983	1984	1985	1986	1987	1988	1989	1990
United States	51.40%	51.40%	49.00%	48.40%	45.40%	41.50%	39.00%	36.50%	35.40%	39.70%
Japan	35.50%	35.30%	38.80%	39.70%	41.70%	45.90%	48.20%	51.00%	51.30%	48.00%
Europe	12.90%	12.70%	11.30%	11.00%	11.70%	11.20%	11.00%	9.70%	9.70%	12.30%

Sources: Dataquest, Semiconductor User Information Service News Letter, various issues.

TABLE 2-4
Japanese Semiconductor Trade, 1967–1990

Year	Exports Integrated Circuits ($ millions)	Total	Year	Imports Integrated Circuits ($ millions)	Total
1967	NA[a]	16.6	1967	5.0	17.0
1968	NA[a]	18.7	1968	12.0	27.5
1969	NA[a]	27.1	1969	21.8	47.7
1970	NA[a]	27.2	1970	57.4	92.5
1971	NA[a]	27.9	1971	69.6	89.8
1972	6.8	42.0	1972	54.2	81.3
1973	9.5	84.3	1973	122.5	181.8
1974	22.9	130.8	1974	154.7	206.3
1975	45.5	140.8	1975	134.9	182.9
1976	76.7	236.0	1976	199.4	280.7
1977	177.9	309.4	1977	207.6	291.7
1978	248.2	480.4	1978	291.4	378.0
1979	494.5	753.8	1979	449.6	556.2
1980	808.8	1,087.6	1980	480.3	609.3
1981	904.9	1,326.5	1981	517.8	686.7
1982	1,144.8	1,425.9	1982	511.4	641.2
1983	1,784.2	2,150.0	1983	642.4	785.9
1984	3,271.2	3,778.3	1984	935.6	1,137.4
1985	2,439.7	2,920.9	1985	693.8	836.3
1986	3,107.4	3,797.3	1986	867.7	1,026.2
1987	4,096.6	5,005.4	1987	1,125.4	1,306.6
1988	6,598.3	7,915.4	1988	1,761.0	2,003.1
1989	8,313.0	9,681.1	1989	2,246.9	2,547.0
1990	7,595.1	9,005.4	1990	2,589.1	2,921.3

Note: During 1965–1966, the Japanese exported only discrete semiconductor devices (DSDs); these included germanium transistors, silicon transistors, germanium diodes, silicon diodes, and silicon diodes for silicon rectifiers. Thus, the data do not include integrated circuits (ICs) for this period.
[a]In 1967–1972, the Japanese did not distinguish between ICs and DSDs.
Source: Japan Electronics Bureau, JETRO.

growing trade deficit. This situation contrasted sharply with the Japanese experience: government policies and firm export strategies combined to produce higher shares for firms and significant trade surpluses in ICs for Japan. Through 1978 Japan ran a net trade deficit in ICs (see Table 2-4). Thereafter, as Japanese 64K DRAMs began to hit the market, IC exports expanded rapidly. Japan's trade surplus in ICs grew from $43 million in 1978 to $2.3 billion by 1984. Imports from the United States more than doubled during this time, while exports to the United States grew tenfold. Japanese firms focused their trade activity increasingly on the U.S. market: chips destined for the United States rose from 24% to 45% of Japanese exports.

U.S. companies lost market share to Japan in almost all product lines, but the Japanese gain in share was most extreme in the DRAM market.

FIGURE 2-2
Worldwide DRAM Market Share, 1978–1989

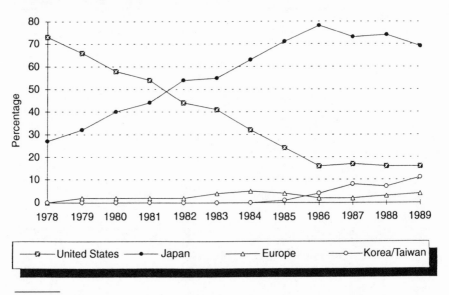

Sources: Compiled from *Dataquest* and Semiconductor User Information Service *News Letter*, various issues.

In less than a decade American companies went from market dominance to a minor role as the Japanese gained ascendance and then dominance in this critical product (see Figure 2-2). The crossover in DRAM market shares occurred in 1981.

Slightly more than half the decline in the U.S. global market share in semiconductors between 1978 and 1985 was the result of faster growth in the Japanese market, which was served mainly by Japanese suppliers. The remainder of the decline resulted largely from the growing penetration of the U.S. market by Japanese producers.[36] From 1978 to 1985, semiconductor imports from Japan increased from under 5% of total U.S. semiconductor consumption to 17%. In contrast, U.S. companies' share of total Japanese semiconductor consumption was stagnant—10% in 1978 and 9% in 1985.

FROM MANIPULATED TO MANAGED TRADE: THE 1986 SEMICONDUCTOR TRADE AGREEMENT

Had governments withdrawn from involvement in semiconductor markets after 1985, Japanese firms would probably have moved from a position of rough parity to virtual dominance. The changing economic structure of the industry made it even more likely that Japan's huge, vertically integrated firms would capture greater shares of the world market in the late 1980s and the 1990s. Rising economies of scale in production were making it almost impossible for small merchant firms to invest in new fabrication facilities.[37] But governments continued to shape the domestic environments and the structure of international trade. In an unprecedented move, the United States negotiated a path-breaking agreement with Japan in the mid-1980s.

The Semiconductor Trade Agreement (SCTA) addressed two issues: access to the Japanese market and alleged dumping by Japanese firms. It suspended the dumping suits and the Section 301 case in return for stipulated actions by the Japanese government to improve market access for American companies and to terminate dumping by Japanese firms.

On market access, the Japanese government agreed to provide sales assistance to U.S. and other foreign companies in Japan and to encourage long-term relationships between domestic users and foreign suppliers. In a confidential side letter to the official agreement, Tokyo went further and stated that it "understood, welcomed, and would make efforts to assist foreign companies in reaching their goal of a 20% market share within five years." That would double the foreign share.

On the dumping issue, the SCTA suspended the EPROM and DRAM investigations without the imposition of duties (despite an assessment of dumping margins of up to 188% for individual Japanese suppliers). The Japanese producers agreed not to sell their products in the United States at prices below their (average) cost of production, plus an 8% profit margin.[38] The Japanese agreed to have MITI monitor export prices on a wide range of semiconductor products, including EPROMs, 256K DRAMs, 1M DRAMs, Application Specific Integrated Circuits (ASICs), and 8-bit and 16-bit microprocessors, to prevent Japanese producers from selling at less than fair market values in the United States or in third countries. The Department of Commerce was given the responsibility to calculate foreign market values (FMVs) for each Japanese manufacturer for each product based on that producer's costs and to monitor the production costs and prices of all Japanese products covered by the agreement. The United States reserved the right to add or drop products from the monitoring arrangement.

The antidumping provisions of the SCTA had several distinctive features. First, the agreement permitted monitoring of costs and prices on a wide range of products, including several that had not been the subject

of the pending dumping investigations. The U.S. government anticipated that this arrangement would deter or prevent dumping of such
products in the future. It had long been a complaint of the semiconductor
industry and other industries that by the time a finding of dumping is
actually made, substantial and irreparable harm has been done to American producers. The SCTA tried to address this complaint by heading off
dumping before it occurred. Second, the agreement was structured to fit
the global nature of competition in the semiconductor industry. Because
American and Japanese producers competed around the world, an agreement that simply halted dumping by Japanese producers in the U.S.
market would leave American producers exposed to unfair Japanese competition in third-country markets. If Japanese producers offered more
attractive prices in such markets, U.S. and other consumers would switch
their purchases there, and the United States would become what the
industry called a "high-price" island.

A third distinctive feature of the dumping provisions of the agreement
was their focus on the cost and pricing behavior of individual firms. The
Semiconductor Industry Association (SIA), cognizant of the concerns of
its U.S. customers about higher prices, opposed both an import quota
and a price floor as mechanisms for responding to Japanese dumping.
The evidence indicated that individual Japanese companies differ greatly
on costs. So the agreement was structured to allow low-cost Japanese
producers to continue to compete on price with high-cost Japanese producers, and as their costs fell, so would the FMVs. From the U.S.
perspective, this competition would have two beneficial effects: it would
limit any price increases growing out of enforcement of the agreement,
and it would discourage further expansion of capacity by Japan's high-cost
producers, thereby making it easier for lower-cost American producers
to win shares of the Japanese market.

Effects of the Agreement on Trade and Pricing

Effects on market access.   After 1986 Japanese firms had the benefit
of the world's fastest-growing domestic chip market. By 1988 Japan's
share of world consumption had exceeded that of the United States and
approached 40% (see Figure 2-3). In the absence of a trade agreement
in such a scale-sensitive business, limited access to the world's largest
market (Japan) could work greatly to the disadvantage of U.S. and European firms.

Did the market access agreement have any impact on U.S. and other

FIGURE 2-3
Worldwide Semiconductor Consumption

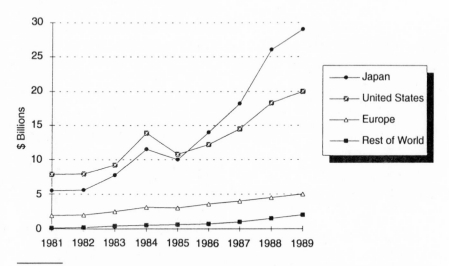

Sources: Compiled from *Dataquest,* Semiconductor User Information Service, *News Letter,* various issues.

foreign-affiliated firms' exports to Japan? The quantitative evidence suggests that after the U.S. government retaliated against Japan in March 1987, market share started to rise (see Figure 2-4); furthermore, interviews with industry officials suggest that government pressure on Japanese firms improved the prospects for U.S. sales in Japan. As of the end of 1990, the foreign share of the Japanese market was approximately 13.35%, up from 8.5% when the agreement was signed and its highest level ever.

The increase in share has been largely the result of concerted action by the Japanese producers to realize a 20% foreign market share in their purchases. Hitachi, NEC, Mitsubishi Electric, Oki Electric, and Toshiba achieved this objective in 1991, and Sony, Fujitsu, and Matsushita promised to do the same. The real effort by the Japanese companies to increase foreign access began only in late 1987, however, with the formation of the Electronic Industries Association–Japan (EIAJ) Users Committee, a group consisting of sixty major Japanese companies, including the semiconductor companies, each of which adopted a market access plan of its own. In addition, in 1988 the Japan Automotive Parts Industry Association began to explore its role in stepping up purchases of foreign semiconductors. These actions mirrored a larger effort by the Japanese to

FIGURE 2-4
Foreign Semiconductor Market Share in Japan

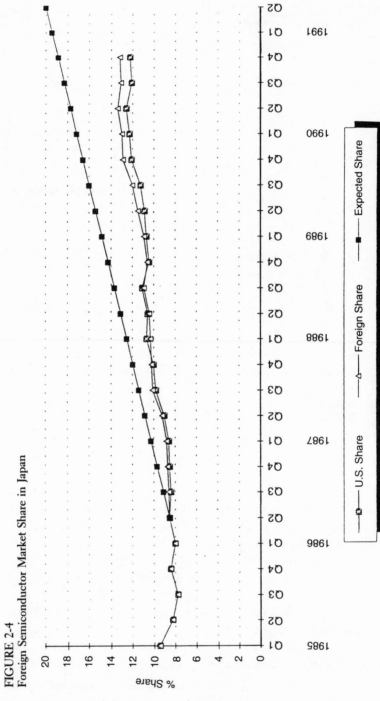

52

Source: SIA, A Deal Is a Deal: Four Years of Experience Under the U.S.–Japan Semiconductor Agreement, The Fourth Annual Report to the President, November 1990.

increase imports of manufactured goods. Japanese authorities encouraged greater imports through beneficial tax treatment and jawboning. Japan's action came in response to steady pressure from U.S. trade negotiators for reduction of the U.S. trade imbalance.

Meanwhile, the share of European, Korean, and Taiwanese industries in Japan increased from 0.3% to 0.7% between the end of 1986 and the second quarter of 1990. This is a large proportional increase on a very small base.

After the signing of the SCTA, American firms increased their efforts to boost sales in the Japanese market. In its 1990 report, the SIA noted that between 1986 and 1989, U.S. suppliers added thirty sales offices to the forty-two in place. They also opened more than sixteen new design centers—a fourfold increase—six new test and quality centers for a total of eighteen, and four new failure analysis centers for a total of fifteen. Overall, U.S. corporate personnel expenditures in Japan have increased by 32%, capital expenditures by 162%, and sales expenses by 86%.[39]

Evidently, few American companies believe that direct investment in Japan will solve the market access problem. While many U.S. producers have chosen to invest or increase production in Europe in anticipation of increased protectionism, only a handful have put money into Japanese production facilities—TI, Motorola, Analog Devices, and LSI Logic. Most American suppliers have preferred to make less expensive investments in design, testing, and sales.

Some American companies have formed alliances with Japanese firms to improve their access to the Japanese market, the most notable example being Motorola's with Toshiba. Motorola packages and markets DRAM dice manufactured by Toshiba and has acquired memory technology to produce 256K, 1M, and 4M DRAMs and 256K and 1M SRAMs. In return, Toshiba has received 8-, 16-, and 32-bit microprocessor technology from Motorola. Using the technology acquired from Toshiba, Motorola is making its own 1M DRAMs in Japan and Scotland and has transferred the process to its Arizona facilities. For Motorola, which actually withdrew from the DRAM market in 1985, DRAMs are now the company's largest revenue-producing memory product. Even so, its share of the global DRAM market remains small.

The 20% target for foreign market share established by the SCTA was unattainable solely through the sale of memory devices. In addition, Japanese companies would have to design proprietary foreign devices into their electronics systems products. The market trend toward ASICs, a segment containing many leading-edge American companies and products, gave American firms an opportunity to have their designs locked into Japanese systems and not easily replaced. Moreover, design-in procedures require close relationships between Japanese systems engineers and foreign semiconductor engineers. So the design-in of ASICs is an important route for the entry of American products into Japan's huge consumer electronics market.

Sustained U.S. pressure, backed by the threat of further trade action, seems to have helped boost the U.S. market share after mid-1989. Tough talk by the Bush administration in 1989 and SIA lobbying efforts evidently spurred Japanese manufacturers to action. Fears that the SIA might get the White House to make semiconductors a U.S. trade priority under the Section 301 provision of the 1988 Trade Act led to a series of initiatives to facilitate the development of long-term relationships between U.S. suppliers and Japanese users. These initiatives, complemented by the efforts of American suppliers to expand their Japanese sales, paid off in a dramatic increase in U.S. share between mid-1989 and the end of 1990.

Effects on pricing.   In the first few months after the conclusion of the agreement, prices of semiconductor memory devices exported from Japan jumped sharply. U.S. customers reported that prices of 256K DRAMs had risen anywhere from two to eight times the pre-agreement price. Shortly thereafter, the Commerce Department adjusted its foreign-market-value calculations on the basis of more recent cost data, and by early 1987 U.S. customers were reporting that the revised FMVs were not far from what the market itself would have produced.

Sustained price increases came only after the imposition of sanctions on Japanese companies for failure to comply with provisions of the agreement. By March 1987, SIA members were convinced that the Japanese were violating the agreement by selling below FMVs in third markets and by failing to increase their purchases from U.S. producers. Evidence of the former came from documentation of sales at less than FMVs by Japanese companies in the Far East.[40] Evidence of the latter came from the fact that the U.S. share of the Japanese market had not risen since the signing of the agreement.

In an unprecedented move, the Bush administration responded with a decision to impose sanctions on the Japanese producers. It did so in a highly charged atmosphere in which both houses of Congress voted to encourage the administration to apply sanctions, and in which a DoD

FIGURE 2-5
DRAM Pricing, 1987–1989

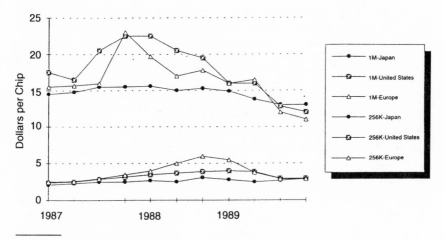

Source: Dataquest, biweekly data.

study pointed with alarm to declining U.S. competitiveness in semiconductors and the semiconductor equipment industry.

Shortly after the imposition of sanctions, the prices of DRAMs began a precipitous increase lasting through the end of 1988. All the available data series show an unprecedented and sustained increase in 256K DRAM and 1M DRAM prices beginning shortly after the sanctions were imposed (see Figure 2-5). The average price per bit of DRAM memory increased in 1987 for the first time. DRAM prices jumped again in 1988 and remained far in excess of reasonable estimates of FMVs for the leading Japanese producers throughout 1988 and 1989. DRAM prices in Japan, although also slightly higher than before the agreement, were noticeably lower than prices in the United States, Europe, and East Asia through the middle of 1989.

The most dramatic price increases occurred in 1988, when spot prices for 256K DRAMs tripled over a four-month period,[41] and American consumers reported great difficulty in obtaining adequate supplies at any price. The price hikes and supply interruptions caused several U.S. systems vendors to ration memory shipments, delay new product introductions, and hike prices. The increase in spot prices for DRAMs was especially severe—they rose three to six times higher than long-term contract prices, with the result that the effective price paid by consumers depended heavily on the percentage of demand they had to purchase on the spot market.

By early 1989 most major U.S. consumers reported that they could obtain adequate supplies, and the gap between spot and large contract prices had disappeared. By mid-1989 the regional price differentials had also disappeared—prices in Japan roughly equaled prices in other major markets. In addition, 256K and 1M DRAM prices were trending down, partly in response to the introduction of the next-generation 4M DRAM device, whose price had fallen continuously since its appearance in the second half of 1988 (see Figure 2-6).

But the prices of all DRAM products remained high enough to yield hefty profits for their Japanese producers. Flamm estimates that higher prices in 1988 meant about $4 billion of extra net income on global DRAM sales on the order of $10 billion. Since the Japanese had the lion's share of the DRAM market, they earned the lion's share of these so-called bubble profits. The two remaining American DRAM producers, TI and Micron Technology, also profited handsomely from the surge in DRAM prices. According to one Wall Street semiconductor analyst, between 30% and 40% of TI's semiconductor operating profit in 1987, and as much as 60% in 1988, was attributable to DRAM sales. Micron, which specialized in DRAM production, enjoyed a sixfold rise in revenues between 1986 and 1988 and became profitable for the first time in three years. The Japanese, in turn, plowed their bubble profits back into R&D and investment. As a consequence, the gap between capital and R&D spending by Japanese companies and American companies expanded still further. By 1988 Japanese capital spending was nearly $2 billion higher than that of the United States, and the R&D spending of the top five Japanese companies exceeded the R&D spending of the top five American merchant firms by about $1.5 billion. Thus, the agreement had the perverse result, from the American perspective, of disproportionately strengthening the Japanese companies for future rounds of competition in new products.

Did the SCTA cause the dramatic price increases in DRAMs and the huge additional profits for the Japanese producers that occurred after the middle of 1987? Most critics of the agreement think so. But the chain of causality between the agreement and the price hikes is not as simple or as direct as many observers believe. For one reason, higher DRAM prices after 1987 were partly the result of a cyclical upsurge in demand stemming from growth in the computer industry. And to some extent

IM DRAM Average Cost[a] and Average Selling Price

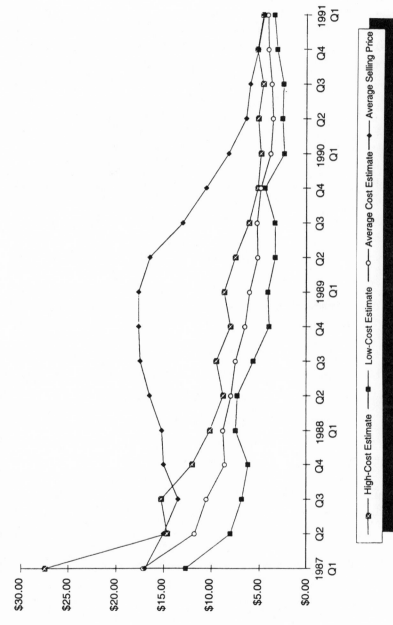

High-Cost Estimate   Low-Cost Estimate   Average Cost Estimate   Average Selling Price

[a]Average cost estimates for Japanese producers are based on actual cost data submitted to the Department of Commerce. The high-cost estimate is 20% above and the low-cost estimate is 20% below the data submitted to the Commerce Department. According to the Commerce Department, the cost estimates are more useful for ascertaining a trend than they are for estimating actual costs at a given point in time.

they were also the result of unanticipated technical difficulties associated with bringing new 1M supply capacities into production.

Second, contrary to what many have asserted, the SCTA did not establish an overall price floor. Indeed, U.S. negotiators were careful not to do so. The purpose of calculating FMVs for individual Japanese companies was to allow the more efficient ones to sell at lower prices than the less efficient ones, thereby encouraging competition among the Japanese suppliers and preventing an overall price floor.

Third, throughout 1989 DRAM prices remained far above the individual FMVs for most, if not all, of the Japanese producers, even the high-cost producers like Oki. And, finally, as is demonstrated below, similar antidumping provisions on EPROMs in the SCTA did not have similar effects on world prices. Overall, the evidence indicates that the SCTA helped push DRAM prices higher by promoting cartel-like behavior on the part of the Japanese firms, which MITI encouraged and facilitated.

There is little doubt that shortly after the negotiation of the agreement and with renewed vigor after the declaration of sanctions in the spring of 1987, MITI imposed production and investment cutbacks and export controls on all Japanese producers. Indeed, Flamm describes a four-part program of export controls that included export allocations and an effective minimum price floor on DRAM exports for different regional markets.[42]

If MITI had acted simply to enforce the provisions of the trade agreement, it hardly needed to restrict production and exports so much that it would force prices to soar above the FMVs of the highest-cost Japanese producers. Perhaps MITI forecast mistakenly, but since the agency habitually made accurate forecasts of semiconductor production, investment, and domestic demand every three months, that explanation is hard to swallow. A more compelling explanation, which is consistent with MITI's history of continuous involvement in the industry since its inception, is that it worked closely with the firms and encouraged cartel-like behavior that benefited all of them.

According to this explanation, MITI acted as an agent to facilitate cooperation among the Japanese firms to reduce U.S.–Japan trade friction, but it did so in ways that would best serve Japanese interests and in ways that were characteristic of its approach to industries suffering losses—it stipulated production and investment cutbacks to remove "excessive competition" while allowing the weakest domestic firms to survive.

Although MITI's actions pressured Japanese companies to cooperate, their behavior suggests that they themselves came to see the attractions of cooperation. Certainly the dominance of these companies in global DRAM supply made a cooperative outcome feasible. Several clues indicate collusive behavior on the part of the Japanese producers in 1988 and 1989. In 1988 Japanese producers began to assert that a new pricing rule prevailed in the semiconductor industry. According to industry spokesmen, DRAM prices for each previous generation of memory device had tended to decline asymptotically toward the $3 level as mass production of that generation peaked—the so-called pi-rule of pricing. In future generations of products, however, the Japanese contended that the so-called bai-rule would apply, meaning that every new generation of product would approximately double in price as mass production peaked.[43]

Other clues include continued restraint on investment in 1988 despite huge inventory rundowns, higher prices, higher profits, and surging demand, and repeated comments by Japanese industry spokesmen about the value of cooperation and the desirability of avoiding the kind of "excessive competition" that had caused huge losses in 1985 and 1986. In product lines they dominated, Japanese producers seemed to behave as if profitability mattered more than market share. And higher DRAM prices certainly meant higher profits. In 1989, for example, an estimated one half of Toshiba's total earnings came from its semiconductor division.[44]

Probably the most telling evidence of cartel-like behavior came at the end of 1989 when, in response to weakening demand and prices, Toshiba, the acknowledged production, cost, and price leader in 1M DRAMs, announced its decision to cut production. The other Japanese producers made similar announcements the same day. At this juncture, DRAM prices were still much higher than the average costs of production (and far higher than the marginal costs of production) of the leading Japanese producers. Yet rather than cut prices to sell more and gain market share at the expense of higher-cost producers, the low-cost producers chose to cut production—hardly the action one would expect in a competitive market.

What, then, was the role of the SCTA in getting the Japanese companies to behave more cooperatively? There can be no conclusive answer. Perhaps even in the absence of the trade agreement these companies would have realized the extent of their market power and started to behave more cooperatively, since they had succeeded in driving out

American competition. Their keiretsu structure, the absence of credible antitrust enforcement, a long history of cross-share holding, shared R&D efforts, and other links among these particular Japanese firms, plus their competition with one another in a variety of other downstream systems markets, made a cooperative outcome more likely.

On the other hand, the timing of the appearance of cooperative behavior on the part of the Japanese companies, following so closely on the sanctions, suggests an alternative explanation. This explanation, consistent with the theoretical literature on the effects of trade restrictions on company strategies in imperfectly competitive industries, sees the trade agreement as an external threat or prod that precipitated a change in industry behavior.[45] It is difficult to realize a collusive arrangement in a heavily concentrated industry even when it works to the benefit of all the players. But external pressure may encourage or even necessitate such an arrangement temporarily, and if the firms see the benefits to be had, they may continue to behave cohesively even after this pressure has been removed.

Market power played a big role in the choice of the cooperative outcome in DRAMs. In EPROMs, where several American companies retained large shares of the world market at the time of the trade agreement, the outcome was quite different. According to some industry observers, after the agreement Japanese firms became noticeably less aggressive in seeking market share in EPROMs. Following a brief increase in prices in the second half of 1987, the prices of 256K EPROMs remained stable during most of 1988, then began to fall sharply by year's end. Meanwhile, prices of 1M EPROMs fell throughout 1988 and 1989. During much of the period, EPROM prices in the United States and Europe actually remained lower than in Japan. American and other buyers reported no shortages in EPROM supplies, and American EPROM suppliers like Intel asserted that, because of competitive market conditions, EPROM prices never rose much above marginal costs. Finally, MITI acknowledged that it could not control EPROM supply because it had no influence over the production and investment decisions of global players who were not Japanese.

The divergence of results in DRAMs and EPROMs helps to illustrate how government policy can affect trade in high-technology industries. It is especially important for understanding differences between national oligopolies and cross-national oligopolies. Because of significant internal economies and dynamic feedback effects in production, the semiconductor industry is inherently oligopolistic. Moreover, because technological and capital costs of entry have risen sharply, the market power of incumbents has been growing.

Whether potential market power is exercised, however, depends on the ability of individual firms to commit to a cooperative strategy. For a variety of reasons, such a strategy seems more likely to emerge when an industry or segment is dominated by a small number of Japanese firms, as the semiconductor industry was in the mid-1980s. First, there is no credible threat of antitrust prosecution. Second, information is regularly exchanged among firms through a number of publicly sanctioned channels, including industry associations, MITI panels, and government-organized and -sponsored R&D projects. Because most large Japanese firms are members of large business groups, they compete with one another in many product markets. And the greater the extent of multiproduct competition, the greater the long-run costs of deviating from a cooperative strategy in a particular product line. Furthermore, because of their financial structure, Japanese firms can credibly threaten to lose money for a long time to deter the entry of new competitors in an industry they dominate. Thus, ceteris paribus, a Japanese oligopoly is more likely to be cooperative than an oligopoly composed of American or other companies with different financial structures.

On the other hand, a collusive or cooperative arrangement in an oligopoly is inherently unstable and can quickly dissolve under changing market conditions. This appears to be the case in the Japanese memory oligopoly. Slack demand, the growing threat of Korean suppliers in 256K and 1M chips, and jockeying for position in new 4M and 16M generations have undermined Japan's ability to maintain collusion. Prices of all memory devices have fallen precipitously since September 1990. As of mid-1991 the price of 4M DRAMs was too low to recoup the cost of new production lines needed to make them.

Effects on market shares. Though still one of the highest technology industries (as measured by R&D as a percentage of sales), by 1991 the semiconductor industry was maturing: growth had slowed and radically new product introductions were few and far between. As a consequence, it was less appropriate to describe semiconductors as a homogeneous industry and more important to define trade and market leadership according to segments.

Perhaps the most positive effect of the SCTA was in EPROMs: the U.S. share in the global marketplace grew from 42% in 1985, prior to the signing of the agreement, to 53% in 1989 (see Figure 2-7). Data

FIGURE 2-7
Worldwide EPROM Market Share, 1978–1989

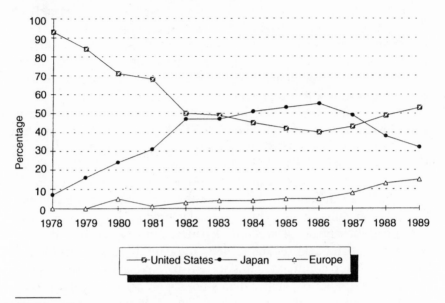

Source: SIA, *A Deal Is a Deal,* 35.

from 1990 show a continued increase in the U.S. share. The Japanese share dropped by 15 percentage points. By 1988 the U.S. world market share exceeded the Japanese share in EPROMs. Japanese firms have also increased purchases of U.S. EPROMs as part of their market access efforts.

In the meantime, the EPROM market has become less concentrated since the agreement, with the top four firms declining from 59% in 1985 to 53% in 1990. American firms, especially AMD, National, and TI, as well as the European firm SGS-Thomson, view EPROMs as an important technology driver that they should not cede to their Japanese competitors. Ironically, the SCTA, a managed trade agreement, stimulated more competition in EPROMs and made the market less profitable over the long run for all participants.[46] The agreement may have had yet another perverse effect on the EPROM segment: although the SCTA seems to have made the Japanese less aggressive in their push toward broad market domination, it may have stimulated Japanese firms to focus their investment at the high end of EPROM performance. While Japanese firms have largely withdrawn from lower density (256K and under) EPROMs, they have been active in 1M EPROMs and new products

FIGURE 2-8
1M EPROM Market Share Leaders, 1990

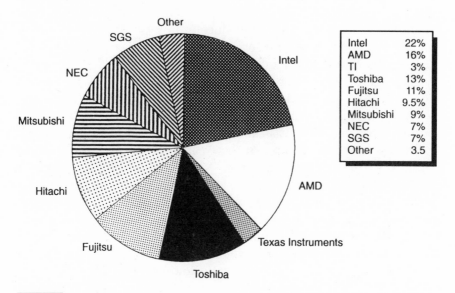

Intel	22%
AMD	16%
TI	3%
Toshiba	13%
Fujitsu	11%
Hitachi	9.5%
Mitsubishi	9%
NEC	7%
SGS	7%
Other	3.5

Source: Created from *Dataquest*, Semiconductor User Information Service, *News Letter*, February 1991.

called flash memory. Although two American firms continue to lead in that category, as Figure 2-8 shows, the Japanese in 1990 had gained some 45% of the market compared with America's 41%.

The EPROM experience stands in sharp contrast to DRAMs, for which the U.S. share stabilized at 16% after 1986 (see Figure 2-2), partly because of investments by Micron and TI and the re-entry of Motorola. Except for Micron, which invested solely in the United States, more than 80% of DRAM capacity expansion projects by American producers have occurred abroad, mostly in Japan and Europe. Even though prices bulged in 1988 and 1989, the barriers to entry remained enormous. The minimum scale for a state-of-the-art facility approached half a billion dollars; product life cycles became shorter, leaving less time for late entrants to recoup investments; and new entrants have to fear retaliation from the Japanese with their considerable experience advantage. Nonetheless, the Japanese share of the DRAM market declined from about 80% to about 70% from 1986 to 1989, the victim mainly of a surge in share by the Koreans. Aided by government subsidies and a government commitment to support a Korean semiconductor industry, the Korean companies were undeterred by high barriers to entry in memories or by the Japanese threat of a pre-emptive price war.[47] The contrast between them and many American companies is revealing. The American merchant firms that exited DRAM production in 1985–1986 believed that the Japanese companies, with government help and their own deep pockets, could outlast them in a disastrous price war (see Table 2-5).

Although the Japanese continue to dominate the markets for 4M and 16M DRAMs, the frontier-technology products, Samsung, the largest Korean producer, moved into the 1M market in 1990. Largely as a result of this move, the East Asian producers maintained their share of the global semiconductor market in that year, even as the Japanese share declined for the first time since 1982—from 52% in 1989 to just under 50% in 1990.[48] This decline can be attributed largely to the rapid growth in the microprocessor segment, where American firms still dominate, and to a sharp drop in prices and revenues in the memory segment, where Japanese firms still dominate. The collapse of prices in the DRAM market, in turn, was partly the result of efforts by the Japanese companies to respond to the Korean challenge at the low end of the DRAM market.

Effects on trade patterns.   So far the SCTA has not fundamentally altered trends in the directions and shares of U.S. and Japanese international trade. Imports as a percentage of U.S. consumption have continued their erratic upward trend, increasing from about 50% of U.S. consumption before the agreement to more than 60% in 1990 (see Table 2-6). The bulk of imports into the United States—on the order of 65% to 70%—still originates, however, from the foreign subsidiaries of U.S. companies. Thanks in part to higher DRAM prices, the share of Japanese imports in total U.S. consumption has more than doubled, rising from about 10% before the agreement to more than 21% in 1989. In value terms, after increasing steadily between 1986 and 1989, imports from Japan declined by nearly 15% in 1990, but according to Department of Commerce estimates, this represents only a 0.7% decline in the volume of imports from Japan.[49] Semiconductor imports in value terms declined by 1.3% from 1989 to 1990 but were still nearly 82% higher than in 1986, and imports of integrated circuits in 1990 were 130% above their 1986 levels (see Table 2-1). In 1990 the U.S. trade deficit in semiconductors was about $1.4 billion, compared with a 1986 shortfall of about $2.5 billion. This drop reflects the higher growth of exports over imports. Japan, however, has remained a minor export market for U.S. semiconductors, accounting for about 10% in 1989 and 1990.

TABLE 2-5
DRAM Pricing, 1987–1989 (dollars per chip)

	1987	Q2	Q3	1988	Q2	Q3	Q4	1989	Q2	Q3	Q4
1M-Japan	14.5	14.8	15.5	15.5	15.6	15.0	15.3	14.9	13.8	13.0	13.0
1M-United States	17.5	16.5	20.5	22.5	22.5	20.5	19.5	16.0	16.0	12.8	12.0
1M-Europe	15.5	15.7	16.0	23.0	19.7	17.0	17.8	16.0	16.5	12.0	11.0
256K-Japan	2.1	2.3	2.5	2.5	2.7	2.5	3.1	2.8	2.5	2.7	2.9
256K-United States	2.4	2.5	2.9	3.2	3.5	3.7	3.9	4.0	3.9	3.0	3.0
256K-Europe	2.5	2.6	3.0	3.5	4.0	5.0	6.0	5.5	3.8	2.9	2.9

Source: Dataquest, biweekly data.

TABLE 2-6
Imports as a Share of U.S. Consumption of Semiconductors

	Total Imports	Imports from Japan
1982	57%	8%
1983	49	8
1984	50	12
1985	53	11
1986	47	10
1987	53	12
1988	61	16
1989	63	21

Source: Dataquest.

Imports continued to make up a small share of Japanese consumption of semiconductors during the course of the agreement. After shrinking to about 6% in 1986, imports as a percentage of Japanese consumption rose to about 10% in 1989 (see Table 2-7). But in 1982 imports amounted to 14% of consumption. The bulk of American sales to the Japanese market—approximately 75% in 1989—did not originate from U.S. locations (see Table 2-8). Motorola and Intel gained disproportionately during the first two years of the agreement, enjoying a 260% increase in their sales in Japan. Undoubtedly, a large portion of the increment came from their offshore locations—Intel's and Motorola's assembly operations in Southeast Asia and the Philippines and Motorola's Japanese subsidiary.

EVOLUTION OF INTERNATIONAL TRADE IN SEMICONDUCTORS

The future of international trade in semiconductors will depend on three variables: oligopolistic competition in particular market segments, direct investment decisions by businesses, and the degree of intervention by governments. These, more than such other important elements as

TABLE 2-7
Imports as a Share of Japanese Consumption of Semiconductors (percentage)

	1982	1983	1984	1985	1986	1987	1988	1989
Imports from the United States	10	10	9	6	5	5	6	7
Imports from Non-United States	4	3	2	1.5	1	1.5	2	3

Sources: Ministry of Finance, Dataquest.

TABLE 2-8
U.S. Exports and Sales of U.S. Companies in Japan, 1984–1989
($ millions)

	1984	1985	1986	1987	1988	1989
Imports from the United States	278	149	169	256	371	543
Sales of U.S. Companies	965	695	948	1,255	1,956	2,147

Sources: Compiled by authors from Japan Ministry of Finance and *Dataquest* data.

factor costs, domestic competition, and the size of local markets, will be the drivers of trade.

Oligopolistic competition has become especially important because the industry has fragmented into segments and become highly concentrated in some of them. Of the three segments we have discussed— EPROMs, DRAMs, and microprocessors—firms have realized significant market power in microprocessors and somewhat less in DRAMs. As a consequence of market power in microprocessors, individual firms' decisions virtually determine patterns of trade. During the 1970s, when microprocessors were in their infancy and made largely by U.S. firms, the market was highly competitive: many firms competed energetically to win designs. Even through the early 1980s, competition was intense for the microprocessor market because customers required manufacturers to license multiple sources. In the latter half of the 1980s, however, leading microprocessors became sole-sourced products that involved significant switching costs for users. As long as a manufacturer had a proprietary design, customers became locked in because software vendors wrote most of their programs for particular chips. By 1990 two firms dominated this field: Intel with a 53% share of the world market and Motorola with a 13% share.[50] Since by 1990 more than $30 billion worth of software had been written exclusively for Intel's chip, it had a very strong position. The consequence for international trade in microprocessors is that Intel can build its chips at geographically dispersed plants that fit its organizational priorities and strategy with little regard for country-based advantages.

The competitive dynamics in DRAMs also reflect the oligopolistic features of the DRAM market. In the 1990s, however, it is becoming harder to treat this market as unified, for three reasons:

• The high and low ends of this market are likely to become more distinct, especially with the expansion of Korean and Taiwanese manufacturers.

- Since DRAMs have lower switching costs than microprocessors, the market tends to be competitive in older-technology, lower-density chips. When 4M DRAMs are on the frontier, 1M and 256K become increasingly like commodities; when 16M DRAMs are the frontier, 4M and 1M become commodities with less concentration. In competitive DRAM segments, costs and prices will still help determine these trade flows. Even in these segments, however, it is hard to imagine that the Japanese will cede their domestic market to lower-cost foreign producers. The structure and behavior of the Japanese producers make their domestic market less competitive than the American or European market, even in low-end products. Therefore, foreign penetration in Japan even in these products is likely to remain limited, although import penetration may climb sharply as the Japanese move some of their labor-intensive processes to lower-cost locations in East Asia.

- Competition in DRAMs will continue to be affected by government intervention. Korea and Taiwan have adopted strategies similar to Japan's. They hope to offset the first-mover advantages of Japanese DRAM producers through infant-industry policies of promotion and protection. They have also been helped by the yen exchange rate and encouraged by the rents earned by Japanese producers in 1988 and 1989. As most cartels do, the Japanese DRAM cartel created an attractive market to enter. The capital barriers to entry in DRAMs are high, but their deterrent effects depend in part on government policy. The strategies of the East Asian NICs have put pressure on the Japanese to move faster to the next generation of memory products or to move into the logic segments where American producers are strong.

By far the biggest influence on future trade in DRAMs is likely to be the explosion in Japanese foreign investment, encouraged in part by ongoing trade friction. Japanese producers fear that Europe and the United States will close markets for their products. The SCTA, as well as changes in the EC's dumping and domestic content laws, have stimulated enormous growth in Japanese foreign investment, especially in the United States and Europe. Before 1990 Japanese firms had limited foreign investment: many firms had assembly plants in Southeast Asia for very low-end products, but only four had fabrication plants outside Japan, with five factories in the United States and none in Europe. By 1990, however, virtually every Japanese firm had announced plans for new facilities: eleven, ten of which were memory, were slated for the United

States, and ten, eight of which were memory, were proposed for Europe.

In interviews at Japanese firms, their managers argued that "in terms of costs, management of engineers, and the control of production, it was better to produce in Japan." Nonetheless, these firms have decided to invest abroad. The rationale most often used is trade friction, but we also heard other familiar reasons like being close to the customer, access to new engineering talent and technology, and access to foreign capital. The pattern of investment confirms Frederick Knickerbocker's hypothesis that in oligopolistic industries, smaller companies often follow the industry leader overseas.[51] In semiconductors, the largest Japanese producer, NEC, pioneered investment in the United States and was the first to invest in Europe. The other large semiconductor firms—Hitachi, Mitsubishi, Toshiba, and Fujitsu—lagged two or three years behind NEC, while smaller firms either eschewed foreign fabrication (e.g., Sony) or have postponed making investments as long as possible (e.g., NMB).

If a few Japanese firms continue to dominate the high end of the DRAM market, as seems likely, the pattern of DRAM trade should look very different at the end of the 1990s from what it is today. Export growth from Japan will decline, replaced by local Japanese production in the United States and Europe. On the other hand, if the market becomes more competitive—if Korea and Taiwan successfully challenge NEC, Toshiba, and the other Japanese giants—then trade in DRAMs will follow a more conventional path as new low-cost producers gain share.[52] For the reasons listed earlier, foreign penetration of the Japanese market is likely to remain limited, although import penetration from Japanese production facilities abroad is likely to grow, especially if the Koreans and Taiwanese become a more significant threat.

While the EPROM market is the least concentrated and most competitive, production in the 1990s will not necessarily migrate to the lowest-cost locations. The strategic considerations of selected U.S. and European firms will continue to influence EPROM trade. Most semiconductor firms operate on the philosophy that they must have a large-volume technology driver to improve their manufacturing yields. Since most American and European firms exited from DRAMs (the technology driver of the Japanese firms), EPROMs remain one of their best hopes. For these firms, the barriers to exit are enormous: they fear that if they leave the EPROM business, they may ultimately lose competitiveness in their higher-margin products. Therefore, many firms are willing to treat EPROMs as a loss leader, producing a trade pattern that largely reflects the staying power of individual firms. In sum, American and European firms may remain significant players in EPROMs, even though they enjoy limited locational advantages.

Moreover, the location of production and/or assembly for EPROMs will not necessarily be a company's home base. Firm-specific logic continues to guide locational choices such as fabricating in Silicon Valley, Israel, or Scotland, assembling in Southeast Asia, and shipping to final markets around the world. Although American firms closed some inefficient overseas plants in the 1980s, National Semiconductor, Texas Instruments, Intel, AMD, and others continue to operate from developing countries and European locations that they set up in the early 1970s. National Semiconductor's experience is typical: it established plants initially to economize on labor costs and take advantage of government incentives. As the industry changed, National sold or closed some inefficient facilities but expanded only in old locations. Even though Japan might have been "the best" new location, for instance, National preferred to maintain its existing network. It followed an internal organizational logic in making location decisions rather than treating previous foreign investments as truly sunk costs. From the firm's perspective, it may be cheaper in terms of human and other resources to continue from an existing site than to start, de novo, at a new location.

CONCLUSIONS

Trade patterns in the semiconductor industry have never been explainable solely on the basis of traditional country variables. From the industry's inception, government policies, first in the United States, then in Japan and Europe, and now in the newly industrializing countries, have manipulated factor costs, demand, and competitive rivalry. By the mid-1980s government policies went even further to manage trade flows and pricing directly.

The effects of heavy government intervention varied by the type of policy employed and by how well it matched the industry's condition at the time it was employed. During the nascent phases of semiconductor development, U.S. military procurement guaranteed secure demand at a time when the technological risks might have been prohibitive for most firms. Japanese government policies were very different, but also appropriate for their time. When the industry was a little more mature, Japanese protection and promotion policies also sought to reduce the risk in semiconductor production, but they did so through less competition, both at home and from abroad. In almost classic John Stuart Mill fashion, Japan demonstrated that, under the right conditions, infant-industry protection works.

Government intervention in any large domestic market would inevitably affect international trade in semiconductors because of the industry's unusual economics. With large-scale economies and steep learning curves at the plant level, and extraordinarily high R&D requirements at the corporate level, few firms in any country could survive and prosper without selling overseas. Moreover, these industry features gave first movers strong competitive advantages—leaders could often set standards, forcing followers to play catch-up, and leaders could move down the learning curve, raising barriers for late arrivals. Since such early moves often lasted through the current generation of products, it behooved firms to enter international markets as aggressively as they entered domestic markets.

In a free market, the first-mover advantages initially accumulated by U.S. firms should have pre-empted Japanese competition, but the Japanese government prevented this outcome. Similarly, if the market had been free of government intervention in the 1980s, Japanese first-mover advantages should have blocked Korea and Taiwan as entrants. Repeatedly, government intervention foiled competitive advantages won by other nations. The scale and learning economies of semiconductors created a potentially significant role for government intervention. The government of the United States in the 1960s, Japan and Europe in the 1970s and 1980s, and Korea in the 1980s and 1990s capitalized on that opportunity.

The semiconductor experience also teaches us about the powerful influence of history on firm production and export decisions. As long as key segments of the semiconductor market remain free of challenge by new low-cost producers, incumbents have the latitude to manufacture and assemble products in locations that do not identically match country advantages. If the semiconductor industry had started in this decade, with Japanese and American firms holding the same positions they held in 1990, the structure of world exports would be very different. The volume of products shipped from Southeast Asia would be much reduced; U.S. exports would be much greater; and facilities in Ireland, Scotland, Israel, and various locations on the European continent might not even exist.

Corporate experience can have an abnormally large impact on semiconductor trade for at least two reasons: first, the increasing segmentation of the market and the growing concentration in individual segments; and second, the "strategic" nature of certain high-volume, technology-driver products like EPROMs and DRAMs. In the first case, when segments are concentrated and not easily entered, small (and, under some conditions, even large) differentials in costs do not matter. Firms will produce in older facilities as long as they can price to recover their costs and they have mechanisms other than price (like proprietary technology) to deter entry. In the second case, firms are willing to sacrifice profits on strategic product lines to retain their market positions in other product lines. Moreover, the economies of scope between a commodity product and a high-margin product can be so great that profits earned on the high-value IC more than compensate for losses in the commodity business. Even when new lower-cost locations emerge, incumbents may continue to produce their strategic lines in existing locations because the total cost of relocation exceeds the marginal cost of staying put.

Finally, the semiconductor experience demonstrates the difficulties of predicting the effects of trade policy on trade flows when the industry is oligopolistic and many of the big players have extensive global operations. The effects of the SCTA on trade patterns depended on the production, investment, and trade decisions of a small number of Japanese and American companies. Because of differences in their structure and strategies, these companies reacted differently. In DRAMs, for example, the Japanese companies, with the help of MITI, formed a temporary collusive arrangement that worked to their benefit. As a result, the SCTA initially *reduced* DRAM competition. In contrast, the SCTA increased competition in the EPROM market as American and European companies vied for the share made available by the retreating Japanese.

The choices of individual firms about production locations also influenced how the SCTA affected trade. Had TI and Motorola responded to improved incentives for DRAM production by further expansion of their U.S. facilities and reduced expansion of their facilities in Japan, more of the increase in the share of American companies in the Japanese market would have come from an increase in U.S. exports. Instead, most of the increase in American sales to the Japanese market came from the production of American companies in Japan and third-country locations (see Table 2-8). Although the SCTA seems to have been a qualified success in improving access for American companies to the Japanese market, it was less successful at boosting direct exports of semiconductors to Japan from U.S. locations. Since American firms produced some of their products in Japan and assembled other products in Southeast Asia, the U.S.-Japanese trade balance in semiconductors was not materially changed.

In fact, the SCTA had remarkably little effect on trade patterns in the United States and Japan. Imports into the United States continued to grow, both in value terms and as a share of U.S. consumption, through 1989. The drop in U.S. imports in 1990 was the consequence of lower DRAM prices—in real terms, imports from Japan were virtually unchanged. They continued to rise as a share of U.S. consumption through the period, although sales from the foreign subsidiaries of American companies still accounted for the bulk of U.S. imports. The Japanese increased imports for consumption, especially in 1988–1990, reversing a decline between 1982 and 1986, but the overall share remained below levels realized in the early 1980s. Japan's trade surplus in semiconductors continued to grow through 1989, but fell in 1990, mainly as a result of lower DRAM prices.

Judged by trade results alone, the SCTA appears to have had little effect. Judged by its impact on prices, market shares, and competitive dynamics in key industry segments, however, the SCTA appears to have had some important consequences. The evidence indicates that the agreement was a qualified success with some of its objectives—the U.S. share of the global DRAM market stabilized; the steep decline in the U.S. share of the global EPROM market was reversed; and the share of U.S. companies in the Japanese market rose.

Nor did the trade agreement reduce competition across all market segments, as most critics of managed trade arrangements had predicted. Competition in the EPROM market actually heated up. Competition in the DRAM market decreased initially, as the agreement allowed the Japanese producers to consolidate their market power. But eventually the DRAM market too became more competitive as a result of several factors, including an increase in production by American companies like TI and Motorola; the growing strength of South Korean suppliers, promoted by their government and attracted by the hefty profits earned by the Japanese; and the expansion of production capacity in Europe, encouraged in part by European policies to develop a regional supply base in semiconductors in the wake of supply shortages and higher prices in 1986–1988.[53] Moreover, if the improved access of foreign producers to the Japanese marketplace ultimately weakens the market power of the keiretsu firms, as the trade agreement intends, then users of semiconductors may benefit further from heightened competition.

Even if we limit our assessment of the agreement's benefits to the producer side of the equation, an important question remains: Did the United States gain as a result of the benefits realized by U.S. companies, even though at least some had production operations abroad? On the one hand, the SCTA allowed American companies to enhance many of their high-value-added activities, especially in R&D and fabrication, and the lion's share of these activities is still located in the United States.[54] On the other hand, much of the gain in the market share of U.S. companies reflected augmented sales from their subsidiary operations. And ironically, in the long run America as a production site for semiconductors may benefit most from the FDI of Japanese firms trying to protect their share of the American market from future trade barriers.

Looking to the future, the massive flow of Japanese foreign direct investment motivated by the threat of trade protection in the United States and Europe is likely to be the single most important factor determining shifting trade patterns in the semiconductor industry in the remainder of this decade. Nations will continue to promote domestic semiconductor producers and manipulate or manage trade flows, but patterns of global competition and trade will increasingly be affected by the globalization strategies of all the major producers, regardless of their nationality or country base.

NOTES

1. For more comprehensive, in-depth studies of the evolution of the American and Japanese semiconductor industries, see Michael Borrus, James Millstein, and John Zysman, "U.S.-Japanese Competition in the Semiconductor Industry," *Policy Papers in International Affairs* 17 (Berkeley: Institute for International Studies, University of California, 1983); Michael Borrus, *Competing for Control: America's Stake in Microelectronics* (Cambridge, Mass.: Ballinger, 1988); and Clyde Prestowitz, *Trading Places: How We Allowed Japan to Take the Lead* (New York: Basic Books, 1988).

2. For comparative numbers on these and other indicators of U.S. technological structure, see Richard R. Nelson, "U.S. Technological Leadership: Where Did It Come From and Where Did It Go?" *Research Policy* 19 (1990): 117–132.

3. Borrus, Millstein, and Zysman, "U.S.-Japanese Competition in the Semiconductor Industry."

4. For an in-depth study of DoD's involvement in the creation of the nation's semiconductor and computer industries, see Kenneth Flamm, *Creating the Computer: Government Industry and High Technology* (Washington, D.C.: Brookings Institution, 1988).

5. David B. Yoffie, "Global Semiconductor Industry 1987," Case No. 388-052 (Boston: Harvard Business School, 1988); Borrus, *Competing for Control.*

6. Kenneth Flamm, "Policy and Politics in the International Semiconductor Industry," paper presented at the SMEI ISS Seminar, Newport Beach, California, January 1989.

7. See Dieter Ernst and David O'Conner, *Competing in the Electronics Industry—The Experience of Newly Industrializing Countries,* unpublished draft (Paris: OECD Development Center, 1991), 79.

8. Ibid. Ernst and O'Conner argue that the Defense Department's support of small merchant firms was critical to semiconductor development in the United States, since the predominant firms in the 1950s, committed to the discrete technology based on germanium, were extremely slow to adopt new circuit technologies based on silicon.

9. For a complete discussion of the role of American universities in the creation and diffusion of technological knowledge, see David C. Mowery and Nathan Rosenberg, "The U.S. National Innovation System," Consortium on Competitiveness and Cooperation, Center for Research in Management, Working Paper No. 90-3, University of California, Berkeley, September 1990.

10. W. Edward Steinmueller, "Industry Structure and Government Policies in the U.S. and Japanese Integrated Circuit Industries," Publication No. 105, Center for Economic Policy Research, Stanford University, December 1986.

11. Ibid.

12. Borrus, Millstein, and Zysman, "U.S.-Japanese Competition in the Semiconductor Industry."

13. Ibid., 37.

14. Kenneth Flamm, "Semiconductors," in *Europe 1992: An American Perspective,* ed. Gary Clyde Hufbauer (Washington, D.C.: Brookings Institution, 1990).

15. On the American share of the European market, see ibid. On the American share of the Japanese market, see Borrus, Millstein, and Zysman, "U.S.-Japanese Competition in the Semiconductor Industry," and Prestowitz, *Trading Places.*

16. Borrus, Millstein, and Zysman, "U.S.-Japanese Competition in the Semiconductor Industry," 35–42.

17. Dennis Encarnation, *Rivals Beyond Trade* (Ithaca, N.Y.: Cornell University Press, 1992).

18. Borrus, Millstein, and Zysman, "U.S.-Japanese Competition in the Semiconductor Industry," 38.

19. Ibid.

20. Borrus, *Competing for Control.*

21. Prestowitz, *Trading Places,* 47.

22. Ernst and O'Conner, *Competing in the Electronics Industry,* 37.

23. Steinmueller, "Industry Structure and Government Policies in the U.S. and Japanese Integrated Circuit Industries."

24. For an examination of this strategy, see Marie Anchordoguy, *Computers, Inc.: Japan's Challenge to IBM* (Cambridge, Mass.: Harvard University Press, 1989).

25. See Kozo Yamamura, "Caveat Emptor: The Industrial Policy of Japan," in *Strategic Policy and the New International Economics*, ed. Paul Krugman (Cambridge, Mass.: MIT Press, 1986), and Pat Choate, *Agents of Influence* (New York: Alfred A. Knopf, 1990), Chapter 6.

26. For the role of preferential procurement in the development of the Japanese computer industry, see Marie Anchordoguy, "Mastering the Market: Japanese Government Targeting of the Computer Industry," *International Organization* 42 (Summer 1988): 509–543.

27. Kozo Yamamura and Jan Vandenburg, "Japan's Rapid Growth Policy on Trial: The Television Case," in *Law and Trade Issues of the Japanese Economy*, edited by Gary Saxonhouse and Kozo Yamamura (Seattle: University of Washington Press, 1986).

28. Robert Lawrence, "Efficient or Exclusionist? The Import Behavior of Japanese Corporate Groups," *Brookings Papers on Economic Activity* 1 (1991): 311–330.

29. For complete discussions of the history of the European semiconductor industry, see Borrus, *Competing for Control*, Chapter 8, and Flamm, "Semiconductors," in *Europe 1992*. A similar position on the detrimental effects of American direct investment on the European semiconductor industry is taken by Ernst and O'Conner, *Competing in the Electronics Industry*, 78.

30. See for example Giovanni Dosi's arguments in "Technical Change and Survival: Europe's Semiconductor Industry," Sussex European Paper No. 9, Sussex European Research Center, 1981. See also Ernst and O'Conner, *Competing in the Electronics Industry*, 78.

31. For a comprehensive discussion, see Flamm, *Targeting the Computer*.

32. Flamm, "Semiconductors," 236.

33. Borrus, *Competing for Control*, 196.

34. Following standard practice, all the market-share figures cited in the following discussion are based on dollar-denominated revenues of companies headquartered in the particular country divided by total dollar-denominated industry revenues. The result is that market-share calculations for individual countries are sensitive to changes in exchange rates. For example, the increase in the dollar's value against the yen between 1981 and 1985 inflated the U.S. market share and reduced Japan's market share. The opposite is true for the 1985–1989 period, when the fall in the dollar's value reduced the U.S. share and increased Japan's share.

35. These data include merchant producers. Since no reliable production or revenue estimates exist, wholly captive manufacturers, the most significant

being IBM and AT&T, are excluded. Including IBM and AT&T would change the absolute rankings, but it would not alter the trends.

36. *The Semiconductor Industry*, report of a Federal Interagency Staff Working Group, Washington, D.C., November 16, 1987.

37. Charles Ferguson made this argument in "From the People Who Brought You Voodoo Economics," *Harvard Business Review*, May–June 1988, 55–62. By 1985 a plant with minimum efficient scale was approaching $150 million in cost; by 1991, the comparable figure was $500 million. Any firm without stable cash flows from nonsemiconductor businesses or a large volume commodity IC business, such as DRAMs, would have difficulty in keeping up with its larger, better-financed Japanese competitors.

38. These restrictions on the Japanese did not apply to their U.S. production facilities. The Europeans adopted a similar exclusion in their pricing agreements with the Japanese in 1989 and 1990. The U.S. exclusion encouraged a surge in Japanese investment in such facilities by the end of the decade.

39. SIA, *A Deal Is a Deal: Four Years of Experience Under the US–Japan Semiconductor Agreement, The Fourth Annual Report to the President*, November 1990, 4–15.

40. Ibid., 60.

41. For detailed price information, see Kenneth Flamm, "Measurement of DRAM Prices: Technology and Market Share," working paper (Washington, D.C.: Brookings Institution, November 1990).

42. See ibid. and Flamm, "Policy and Politics in the International Semiconductor Industry." A 1988 GATT panel ruling in response to a complaint by the European Community found MITI's system of production and export restrictions to be impermissible under GATT law, and MITI formally terminated it.

43. For a discussion of these pricing rules of thumb, see *Japan Electronics Almanac* (Tokyo: DEMPA Publications, 1989).

44. Report by Hajume Karatsu to the National Research Council, June 1991.

45. See, for example, Kala Krishna, "Trade Restrictions as Facilitating Practices," *Journal of International Economics* 26 (1989): 251–270, and Avinash Dixit, "Optimal Trade and Industrial Policy for the U.S. Automobile Industry," in *Empirical Methods for International Trade*, ed. Robert Feenstra (Cambridge, Mass.: MIT Press, 1988), 141–165.

46. According to the manager of one of the leading EPROM manufacturers, firms were unlikely to break even in EPROMs in 1991 with less than 10% of the market. If this is so, only the top four firms were breaking even.

47. For a complete discussion of South Korean promotional and protectionist policies in the semiconductor industry, see Thomas Howell et al., *The Microelectronics Race: The Impact of Government Policy on International Competition* (Boulder, Colo.: Westview Press, 1988), 148–164.

48. "Preliminary 1990 Worldwide Semiconductor Market Share Estimates: The Microprocessor," *Dataquest* report, 1991.

49. U.S. Department of Commerce, International Trade Commission, *U.S. Industrial Outlook, 1991* (Washington, D.C.: U.S. Government Printing Office, 1991), 4.

50. If one measures 32-bit microprocessors, the industry was even more concentrated, with Intel commanding approximately 75% of the market, AMD roughly 13%, and Motorola roughly 12%.

51. Frederick Knickerbocker, *Oligopolistic Reaction and Multinational Enterprise* (Boston: Division of Research, Harvard Business School, 1973).

52. According to one American manager in 1991, some Japanese firms were trying hard to create a new cartel to undermine Korea's and Taiwan's ability to use their factor-cost advantage to change the pattern of trade. Some Japanese firms were allegedly using their positions in critical segments of the semiconductor equipment business as a source of leverage to get the Koreans to ease up in their DRAM pricing.

53. For an insightful analysis of the European strategy, see Flamm, "Semiconductors."

54. Laura D'Andrea Tyson, "They Are Not Us: Why American Ownership Still Matters," *American Prospect*, Winter 1991, 37–49.

3

COMPUTERS: ALLIANCES AND INDUSTRY EVOLUTION

Benjamin Gomes-Casseres

IN THE SPAN OF A FEW DECADES, the computer industry became one of the most important high-technology segments of the global economy. By 1990 computers were critical to firm and national competitiveness in numerous other sectors, and the industry represented more than $300 billion in sales and $70 billion in international trade annually—the largest in the information technology sector.[1] While it was intimately linked to related segments, I define it here as the manufacture and sale of data-processing (DP) systems, including peripherals but excluding software, services, telecommunication equipment, and semiconductors.[2]

As computers revolutionized the business world, the industry itself experienced radical changes. Foremost among these were the appearance of new firms and massive shifts in patterns of international trade and competition. An industry dominated by the United States and by a handful of U.S. firms evolved into a truly international industry with intensive competition among diverse firms. Technological change, firm strategies, and government policies all played a part in this evolution.

The causes and consequences of these changes in the global computer industry are the broad subjects of this chapter. In addition, I focus on one aspect of firm behavior that is closely related to these structural changes: the role of interfirm alliances. The rapidly rising use of alliances by leading firms was nowhere as dramatic as in computers. This phenom-

I received valuable comments on earlier versions of this chapter from participants in the Harvard Business School World Trade and Global Competition seminar and colloquium (especially from Richard Vietor and David Yoffie), in the Competition and Strategy seminar (especially from Michael Porter), in the Science and Technology seminar, and from Tom McCraw, Robert Hayes, Bruce Kogut, Warren McFarlan, Ray Corey, and Roger Kay. Paul Mang, Donna Hill, Chris Allen, and Maryellen Costello assisted in the research on alliances. The Harvard Business School Division of Research funded the project. Executives at twenty computer firms in the United States, Japan, and Europe shared their time, thoughts, and information with me, and the Gartner Group and International Data Corporation provided useful data. The views expressed here—and any errors—are mine.

enon deserves attention in its own right, as well as for the light that it sheds on the industry's evolution.

INDUSTRY EVOLUTION: NARROWING GAPS

The first computers were developed more or less independently in Britain, the United States, and Japan, but the commercial computer industry had its start in the United States.[3] From the 1950s to the end of the 1970s, the United States developed into the dominant producer and exporter of computers, and U.S. firms held dominant market shares everywhere except in Japan.

IBM stood out early among the U.S. first movers and by the mid-1960s had become by far the largest producer of computers worldwide. Its production activities were spread worldwide and IBM was often the leading exporter from its host nations. When Europeans in the 1960s talked about *Le Défi Américain*, and when the Japanese began to target U.S. dominance, they invariably had IBM in mind.[4] The company's deep penetration of foreign markets and the dominance of its proprietary technology represented tremendous hurdles for the challengers.

Few in the mid-1970s predicted the structural shifts that followed, although IBM World Trade's Management Committee warned in 1972:

> The Japanese manufacturers have demonstrated commitment to an over-seas marketing strategy. . . . In light of the Japanese Government's demonstrated support of this exporting strategy for computers, the effect of our action programs in Japan will be at best to delay the inevitable schedule by perhaps one year.[5]

Within a decade and a half after this warning, the pattern of international competition in computers had changed dramatically. The position of the United States as a production site for computer products declined in favor of Japan and a select group of newly industrializing countries (NICs) in Asia.[6] Moreover, the position of U.S. firms, including IBM, declined while that of a handful of Japanese firms rose. Finally, the European trade balance became deeply negative, and the shares of European firms even in their own markets stagnated or declined.

In short, the early gaps between the capabilities and market position of U.S. and non-U.S. firms had narrowed substantially by the late 1980s, as had the gap between IBM and second-tier computer vendors. As a result, rivalry between firms from different nations increased, as did the interdependence among their individual strategies and performance. For example, while U.S. firms, especially IBM, previously could often dictate market and technological trends, by the 1990s they had to respond daily to serious pressures and initiatives from non-U.S. firms. Patterns of trade and global competition reflected the changing structure of the industry.

What led to these shifts? The answer is complex and multifaceted—technological change, government policies, firm strategies, and industrial development all played parts.

Basic technologies were diffused worldwide, often through alliances between the U.S. and non-U.S. firms. Furthermore, wholly new technologies helped modify the key success factors in the industry. The new Japanese entrants took advantage of these trends to expand in personal computers, laptop computers, and peripherals. In the mainframe segment, technical standards remained dominated by IBM's proprietary systems, but Fujitsu and Hitachi developed the capabilities to make products that were fully compatible with IBM's. Technological change thus created opportunities for the second-mover firms.

In addition, the development of Asian and European economies and accompanying government policies helped the second movers catch up with the U.S. first movers. Initially, the United States offered conditions in which computer firms flourished while firms elsewhere labored under serious disadvantages. Over time, other countries, Japan in particular, developed conditions favoring the industry. Often governments helped in this process. Public policies everywhere regulated trade, foreign investment, and domestic spending in the industry; in a few celebrated cases, governments all but created domestic computer firms. The rise of Japanese and the Asian NICs was intimately tied to the economic and policy environment at home.

The narrowing gaps between U.S. and non-U.S. firms and the relative decline of IBM signaled growing rivalry in the industry. Compounding this trend was the rise in the United States of new computer firms focused on microcomputers and other new segments. Together, the appearance of new technologies, the rise of new competitors, the interpenetration of markets by firms from different nations, and the growing technical capabilities of non-U.S. firms led to a dramatic increase in interdependence among firms. In this context, interfirm collaboration took on increasingly important role.

INTERNATIONAL ALLIANCES AS CAUSE AND EFFECT

These shifts in competitive advantage of firms and nations relate closely to the role of international alliances.[7] There were striking patterns in the way firms from different nations used alliances, and these patterns correspond closely to the shifting competitive structure of the industry. The data I collected show that:

- America was the technology generator—its firms formed alliances that diffused technology and sold product based on this technology;
- Europe was the large, fragmented market with weak domestic firms— its firms used alliances to source product, offering market access in return; and
- Japan was the rising manufacturing base—its firms used alliances to enter new markets with local product and to acquire technology.

Interfirm alliances, in fact, were both cause and effect of the competitive shifts. Historically they helped close the gap between the second-mover European and Japanese firms and the American first movers. But as this gap narrowed, international alliances took on additional roles.

International collaboration played key roles in helping Japanese firms catch up with the Americans and in getting some European firms off the ground. Each of the three Japanese leaders used ties with American and European firms in the 1970s and 1980s to learn new technologies and to overcome marketing barriers to entry. While few counterexamples exist with which to judge their impact, the firms that used international alliances most intensively seemed to prosper more than others in this catch-up phase.

By the 1990s the role of international alliances was changing. First, their popularity continued to increase, as new industry conditions created incentives for cooperation between firms. Second, they were being used for novel purposes—incumbents began to use them to defend market share, and new entrants used them to gain support in emerging segments. More than ever before, competition began to revolve around groups of allied firms rather than around individual players. As such, interfirm collaboration had become a critical element of firm strategy, not only for second movers catching up, but even for industry leaders like IBM.

The close relation between alliances and other drivers of industry evolution suggest that neither can be understood in isolation. In the rest of this chapter I will analyze each in great detail, beginning with the roles of countries, firm strategy, and government policy in industry evolution. After that, I will examine explicitly the role of alliances in this process.

SHIFTING TRADE PATTERNS: COMPARATIVE ADVANTAGE AND FIRM STRATEGY

The United States was still the largest market for computers in 1990, but the Asian and European markets had been growing faster. As Figure 3-1 shows, Asian consumption of data-processing equipment rose between 1984 and 1989 from $19 to $71 billion (24% p.a.), European consumption from $31 to $90 billion (19% p.a.), and U.S. consumption from $66 to $98 billion (7% p.a.). The share of the United States in world demand fell from 57% to 38%, while those of Asia and Europe rose to 28% and 35%. Still, in 1990 the United States accounted for the bulk of the 2 million people employed in the industry worldwide; the top 100 DP firms had 1.2 million employees in the United States, compared with more than 270,000 in Asia and less than that in Europe.[8]

The industry could be segmented in a number of ways, and the economics of production varied between segments. One way was to separate peripherals from central processing units (CPUs), which in turn could be classified by size and cost. Sales of mainframe systems and personal computers (PCs) each accounted for 22% of the total in 1988, but the latter was growing four times as fast as the former. Sales of peripherals, such as disk drives and printers, were also growing fast, partly because they were used with PCs. Peripherals represented about one third of the total. During the 1980s the minicomputer segment (14% of total) was squeezed between booming PC sales and continued strong mainframe sales.[9]

The cost of goods sold was proportionately higher in PCs and peripherals than in mainframes. But selling expenses were lower for PCs and peripherals, because they were usually sold through indirect channels. Mainframes required direct sales and service. About one third of the employees in leading computer firms worked in manufacturing, one-quarter in sales, one-tenth in research, and almost one-fifth in maintenance and repair. Labor costs were not critical in competitiveness, though they could be important in the production of components. Even in PCs, direct labor accounted for less than 5% of total variable cost, and overhead for another 10%. More important were costs of components such as semiconductors, printed circuit boards, and disk drives, which accounted for about three quarters of variable costs.

FIGURE 3-1
Consumption of Data-Processing Equipment, 1975–1990

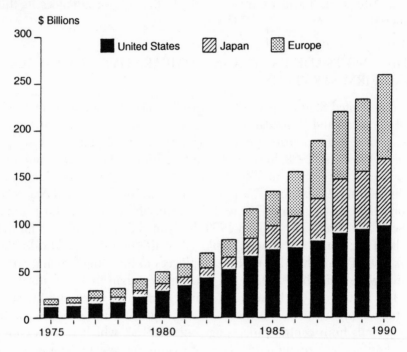

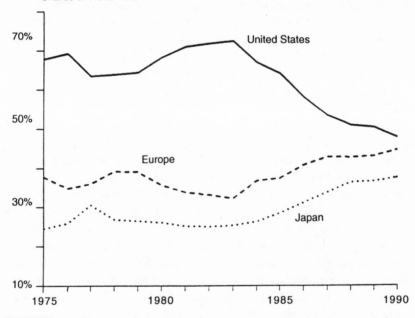

Sources: *Electronics*; Gartner Group, *Yardstick Worldwide*.

Demand and costs of production influenced the location of plants and sales worldwide, and thus the pattern of trade. These factors changed over time, accounting for some of the competitive shifts in the industry. But there were also other factors—related to firm strategies and government policies—that influenced the global structure and evolution of the industry.

Early Trade Patterns: IBM's Global Strategy

From the early 1960s, the United States, the birthplace of the modern industry, was the largest exporter of computer products. Still, non-U.S. production grew quickly, and major markets in Europe and Japan soon came to be served primarily by local production. Much of this local production, however, as well as what little exports these countries had, bore the logo of IBM. In 1960, IBM was already operating in 87 countries; it had 19 manufacturing plants abroad, and employed 30,000 people outside the United States.[10] By 1972 IBM World Trade was active in 126 countries with 22 manufacturing plants and 115,000 employees. Between 1967 and 1972, IBM World Trade's revenues grew at 22% per year and represented 44% of IBM's total volume.[11]

The pattern of trade in the 1960s and early 1970s, therefore, reflected IBM's international production strategy. Starting in the mid-1960s, the company pursued a goal of balanced trade in North America, Western Europe, and Japan.[12] IBM's booming foreign sales grew largely through local (or regional) production rather than by exports from the United States. IBM reportedly accounted for all of Japan's exports in 1972,[13] and cross shipments among IBM plants in Europe were thought to account for the bulk of exports registered by European countries in the mid-1960s.[14] At this time, IBM accounted for three quarters of the markets in West Germany, Italy, and France, half the market in the United Kingdom, and about two-fifths in Japan.[15]

Evolution of Trade in the 1980s: The Role of Country Environments

By 1990 international trade in computer products was substantial. Imports and exports of data-processing equipment and parts[16] amounted to about one quarter of world consumption. This share varied historically and across regions, as indicated in Table 3-1, Top. The importance of imports in consumption rose sharply in the United States from 5% in

TABLE 3-1
Trade and Consumption of Computers and Parts, 1978–1990
(SITC 752 plus 7599 in $ billions)

	1978	1981	1984	1987	1990	Annual Growth 1978–1990	Trade as Share of Consumption				
							1978	1981	1984	1987	1990
Imports											
By United States	0.9	1.8	8.1	15.3	23.4	31%	5%	5%	12%	19%	24%
By Asia	0.8	1.7	3.2	5.2	12.2	25%	15%	19%	17%	12%	17%
By Europe	3.1	6.0	10.2	18.8	27.8	20%	33%	44%	33%	30%	31%
Total	4.8	9.5	21.4	39.3	63.4	24%	15%	17%	18%	21%	24%
Exports											
By United States	4.4	9.0	14.0	18.8	25.9	16%	26%	26%	21%	23%	26%
By Asia	0.8	2.0	8.5	18.9	33.3	36%	16%	22%	44%	42%	47%
By Europe	1.8	2.9	4.9	9.3	11.8	17%	20%	21%	16%	15%	13%
Total	7.1	13.9	27.5	47.0	71.0	21%	22%	24%	24%	25%	27%
Consumption											
By United States	17.1	35.0	65.8	82.1	97.8	16%					
By Asia	5.4	8.7	19.2	44.7	71.4	24%					
By Europe	9.3	13.7	31.2	61.7	89.7	21%					
Total	31.8	57.4	116.2	188.5	258.9	19%					

Parts as Share of Total DP Trade
(SITC 7599 divided by 752 + 7599)

	1978	1981	1984	1987	1990
Imports					
By United States	57%	61%	55%	52%	33%
By Japan	26%	29%	30%	34%	41%
By Europe	27%	29%	31%	28%	29%
By NICs	77%	58%	50%	57%	51%
Total	35%	37%	42%	40%	34%
Exports					
By United States	40%	44%	48%	51%	39%
By Japan	46%	35%	20%	26%	36%
By Europe	34%	36%	41%	41%	33%
By NICs	98%	89%	56%	35%	30%
Total	41%	43%	42%	40%	36%

Sources: Trade data from the United Nations; consumption from *Electronics* and Gartner Group, *Yardstick Worldwide.*

1978 to 24% in 1990; elsewhere, the role of imports varied less. Asian exports as a share of Asian consumption more than doubled, from 16% to 47%.

These and other data illustrate the rapid development of Japan, and to a lesser extent the Asian NICs, into successful computer exporters. At the same time, the position of the United States declined. A world industry that was dominated by U.S.-based production in the early 1970s became one in which the United States and Japan held more or less similar positions. The slow decline of Europe as a production site was less remarkable than that of the United States, since Europe had never held a dominant position in the industry.

While U.S. imports and Asian exports grew robustly during the late 1970s and 1980s, Europe remained the most dependent on imports and the least successful in exports. [17] Over time, the difference in trade pattern between Japan and Europe became more pronounced, as the trade balances in Figure 3-2 show. This trend helped spur European efforts in the early 1980s to revitalize the region's information technology industry through such collaborative programs as ESPRIT, Jessi, and Eureka. While the United States continued to run a surplus in this industry, in absolute terms its surplus fell from $3.5 billion in 1978 to $2.5 billion in 1990, and relative to total computer exports it declined from 80% to 10%.

The structure of trade.   Changes in the balance between parts and finished goods traded internationally accompanied the changes in the importance of trade. Worldwide, parts for data-processing equipment accounted for about 40% of total exports of equipment and parts during this period, as shown in Table 3-1, Bottom. The most striking changes in this indicator are the "graduation" of Japan and the NICs, which developed from exporters of parts to exporters of finished goods. The share of parts in Japanese exports fell from 46% in 1978 to 36% in 1990, and that of the NICs in this study from 98% to 30%. At the same time, Japan stepped up imports of parts.

The shifting competitive positions of these regions is clearly shown by the data in Figure 3-3. Between 1978 and 1990, the share of the United States in world exports of DP equipment fell from over 60% to under 40%; at the same time, the share of Japan rose from 10% to 40%, and the share of the Asian NICs rose from nothing to over 20% (Figure 3-3, Top). If parts were included, the same trends would be apparent, but the share of U.S. exports would remain some 10 percentage points higher than Japan's in 1990.

FIGURE 3-2
Imports and Exports of Computers and Parts, 1978–1990

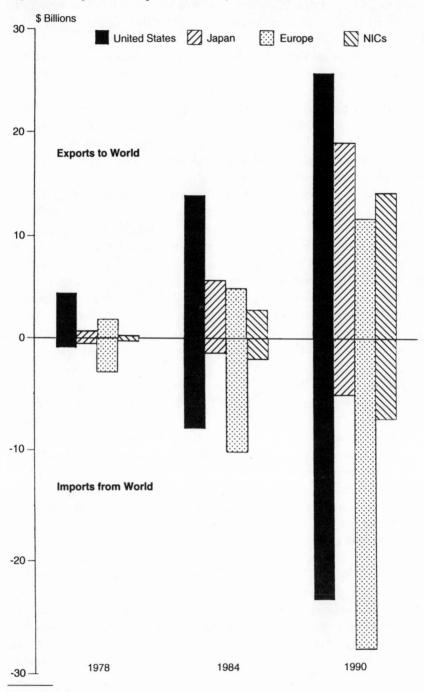

Source: United Nations.

FIGURE 3-3
Export Shares and Comparative Advantage by Region, 1978–1990 (DP equipment only; SITC 752)

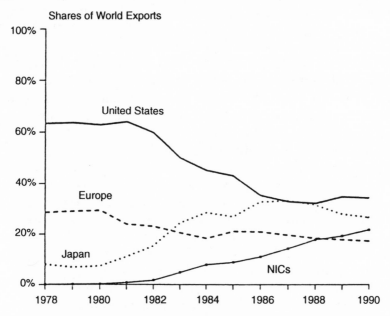

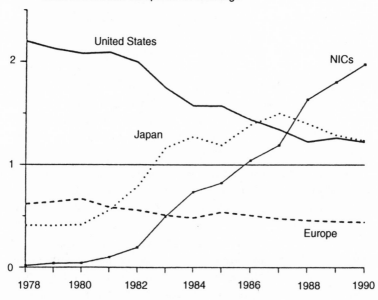

Notes: RCA calculated using Balassa method: share of computers in total exports for each region divided by share of computers in total world exports. An index greater than one indicates comparative advantage, and less than one indicates disadvantage.
Source: United Nations.

Given the macro-economic factors behind the overall U.S. trade deficit and Japanese surplus, it is more instructive to examine the indexes of revealed comparative advantage (RCA)[18] in Figure 3-3, Bottom. The development of the Asian exporters shows up even more dramatically using this measure. Japan's RCA index rose from 0.4 in 1978 to 1.2 in 1990, and that of the Asian NICs rose from practically zero to 2.0 in 1990. At the same time, the United States went from a strong comparative advantage in computers in 1978 (an index of 2.2) to virtual parity with Japan in 1990. Europe maintained a strong comparative disadvantage in computer exports during this period.

Labor costs, a critically important country factor in neoclassical trade theory, are only partly responsible for these shifts. First, wages were a small component of production cost, as I noted above. Second, electronics wage differentials between Japan, the United States, and Europe were narrowing during this period. From the mid-1970s to the mid-1980s, Japanese wages were half those in the United States, but this gap had closed by 1990. European wages fluctuated around the U.S. level over most of this period. Labor costs remained low only in the Asian NICs, even though these too rose from about one-sixth to one-half those in the United States.[19]

Only the Asian NICs were successful in labor-intensive segments. Most of the major computer firms had manufacturing plants in the NICs for components like keyboards, printers, disk drives, and tape drives.[20] In 1990 Taiwan exported $5.2 billion in computer products, making it the second-largest Asian exporter behind Japan. Its exports represented 66% of world exports of PC system boards and 20% to 40% of monitors, power supplies, keyboards, graphics cards, and scanners. Thirty percent of these exports were made by subsidiaries of foreign firms, and 47% were sold by Taiwanese firms on an OEM basis to foreign firms.[21]

The rise of Asia fits Michael Porter's model of competitive advantage of nations better than it does the neoclassical trade model. Porter argued that the competitiveness of a nation's firms depended on the availability of advanced factors of production domestically, the nature of home demand, the presence of related industries locally, and the degree of rivalry in the industry.[22] The volume and sophistication of demand for computers grew fast in Japan, and many of the leading-edge technologies (e.g., laptop computers) become popular there first. The computer industry in Japan benefited directly from the blossoming of such related industries as semiconductors, consumer electronics, and office printing and copying. Japanese universities turned out large numbers of electronic engineers, and government as well as firms invested heavily in R&D. Occupying the top tier of Japan's computer market were four highly competitive firms of roughly equal market size—Fujitsu, NEC, Hitachi, and IBM. This degree of rivalry was unparalleled in Europe or the United States, where IBM still occupied positions far above the next firm.

The country conditions behind the rising competitive advantage of the Asian NICs were somewhat different, as low labor costs were more important. Also, domestic demand was less important, and technology was usually acquired from the outside through licensing or foreign direct investment. But related industries also played important roles, as skills first applied in simple consumer electronics were transferred into assembly of computer products. While they remained dependent on Japan and the United States for their supply of key components like microprocessors and liquid-crystal display screens, the Asian NICs invested heavily in production of commodity semiconductors.

The direction of trade. The destination of regional exports and the origins of imports also changed in distinct ways during the 1980s, as shown in Figure 3-4. In short, the United States became the premier importer of Japanese and NIC goods and the dominant exporter to Europe and the rest of the world. By 1990 the United States ran $4 billion trade deficits with both Japan and the NICs in this study, and an equally large surplus with the rest of the world. Japan, in turn, ran trade surpluses with all the regions, with Europe and the United States each taking $4 billion in net exports. The Asian NICs, which depended even more on the United States as a destination for their exports, ran deficits only with Japan.[23]

This pattern was difficult to explain solely with country-based theories of comparative advantage. If Japan had a comparative advantage vis-à-vis the United States—as suggested by the direction of Japanese exports—and the United States had a comparative advantage vis-à-vis Europe and the rest of the world—as suggested by the U.S. export pattern—then wouldn't Japan have an even stronger incentive to export directly to these areas?

The explanation for this pattern probably lies in the role of firm-level strategy and government policies in determining trade flows. From the Japanese firms' point of view, the United States was a larger, more accessible market than Europe, partly because these firms had exported large quantities of consumer electronics to the United States. Europe had traditionally been more closed to Japanese imports and fragmented, partly

FIGURE 3-4
Computer Trade Balances by Region, 1978–1990 (bilateral balances in $ billions)

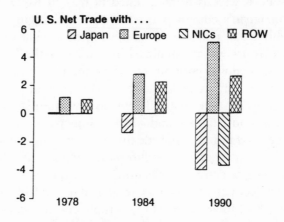

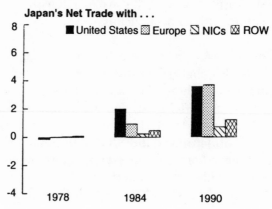

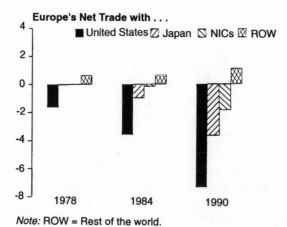

Note: ROW = Rest of the world.

Source: United Nations.

because local governments favored national firms for their substantial computer purchases. Several other factors made a presence in the U.S. market more important to these firms than a presence in Europe: the United States had more sophisticated demand and more advanced technology and was home to the leading firms in the industry. Firm-level barriers to entry and implicit and explicit European protection of locally based firms thus led to a stronger drive by Japanese firms to export to the United States than to Europe.

This pattern changed slowly during the 1980s as Europe became a more important destination for Japanese exports. Country competitiveness may thus well have been driving trade patterns, but the latter seemed to respond with a lag of several years. In other words, the first-mover, firm-specific advantages created by U.S. firms in Europe were not insurmountable by the Japanese, but they led to inertia in market shares.

For the U.S. firms, Europe and Latin America were the traditional destinations of exports and foreign investment. Studies of U.S. foreign investment usually found that U.S. multinational corporations went to "familiar" countries—the United Kingdom and those on the European continent—before Asia. The Japanese market was relatively closed to U.S. firms;[24] only IBM was strong in Japan, and then only by virtue of its local production. At the same time, foreign investment in Europe helped U.S. firms establish important first-mover advantages there. As a result, more than 32% of the total sales of U.S. data-processing firms were in Europe in 1990, compared with 11% in Asia (see Table 3-2).

Foreign Direct Investment and Intrafirm Trade

Overall, U.S. computer firms, led by IBM, have been disproportionately active abroad. The assets of their foreign affiliates amounted to $58 billion in 1986, or fully 20% of the total foreign assets of U.S. manufacturing firms.[25] These assets represented 58% of the total assets of the parent firms, a higher share than for any of the other major industrial categories tracked by the U.S. Department of Commerce. Furthermore, just over half the foreign assets of U.S. computer firms were in Europe in 1986, down from 66% in 1982.

What explained this heavy reliance on foreign direct investment? First, U.S. firms had dominant capabilities in the industry; such strong firm-specific advantages normally helped foreign firms overcome the inherent advantages enjoyed by local host-country firms.[26] Second, local favoritism usually obliged American firms to use foreign subsidiaries to supply

TABLE 3-2
Geographic Position of Computer Firms, 1984–1990

	Market Shares of Firms in Each Market (by nationality of firm)			Relative Weight of Geographic Markets in Each Firm's Sales (by nationality of firm)		
	1984	1990	Annual Growth		1984	1990	Annual Growth
Total Market Sizes ($ billions)				Total Sales ($ billions)			
United States	66	98	6.8%	IBM	43	65	7.2%
Europe	31	90	19.2%	All U.S.	95	175	10.7%
Asia	19	71	24.5%	Japanese	14	64	28.1%
Other	8	16	12.6%	Europeans	15	34	14.9%
World Total	124	275	14.2%	Total	124	275	14.2%
Share of U.S. Market accounted for by:				Weight of U.S. Market in Total for:			
IBM	39%	26%		IBM	60%	39%	
All U.S.	94%	88%		All U.S.	65%	49%	
Japanese	2%	6%		Japanese	10%	10%	
Europeans	4%	4%		Europeans	17%	13%	
				All	53%	36%	
Share of European Market by:				Weight of Europe in Total for:			
IBM	34%	27%		IBM	25%	38%	
All U.S.	63%	62%		All U.S.	21%	32%	
Japanese	3%	7%		Japanese	6%	10%	
Europeans	34%	30%		Europeans	72%	79%	
				All	25%	33%	
Share of Asian Market by:				Weight of Asia in Total for:			
IBM	18%	13%		IBM	8%	14%	
All U.S.	35%	28%		All U.S.	7%	11%	
Japanese	61%	69%		Japanese	81%	77%	
Europeans	4%	3%		Europeans	5%	5%	
				All	15%	26%	
Share of Other Markets by:				Weight of Other Markets in Totals:			
IBM	41%	38%		IBM	8%	9%	
All U.S.	83%	79%		All U.S.	7%	7%	
Japanese	6%	11%		Japanese	3%	3%	
Europeans	11%	6%		Europeans	6%	3%	
				All	6%	6%	
Share of World Market by:							
IBM	34%	24%					
All U.S.	76%	64%					
Japanese	12%	23%					
Europeans	12%	12%					

Source: Gartner Group, *Yardstick Worldwide.*

growing foreign demands. From the beginning, IBM allowed its country managers considerable autonomy, as long as they followed financial and product policies approved by headquarters. IBM's foreign plants specialized by product or component, while the two major regions—Europe and Japan—were nearly self-sufficient. IBM claimed it produced in Europe 90% of what it sold there. In Japan, IBM said, it ran a surplus in trade, with 30% of production being exported.

Not all U.S. computer firms followed such strategies, and those that did not often failed in foreign markets.[27] Some entrants, like RCA and GE, never made a substantial commitment to foreign markets, preferring instead to export or license technology. Neither established a presence abroad, and both exited the business in the 1970s. Sperry invested more in foreign markets, including an early marketing joint venture in Japan that led to Nihon Unisys's strong position there. Digital Equipment Corporation's (DEC's) European production strategy was similar to IBM's— DEC produced most of what it sold in the region and became a strong contender in Europe.

Did intrafirm trade account for the regional trade patterns? In 1982 the United States ran an intrafirm trade surplus of $1 billion with Europe—about 25% of total net trade between the regions.[28] With Japan, the intrafirm trade balance was probably also positive for the United States, at about $200 million, compared with a net deficit for total DP trade between the regions.[29] A great deal of trade between the regions thus took place through the mediation of U.S. multinationals.

This was not the full extent of the role of U.S. firms in Europe and Japan. A rough estimate of the importance of local production by foreign firms—as distinct from trade by foreign firms—appears in Table 3-3. Taking total consumption, and subtracting (1) sales in the local market by domestic firms and (2) imports from foreign firms abroad, leaves a residual that could be ascribed to local production by foreign firms. By this method, local production by foreign firms in 1990 accounted for only 6% of U.S. consumption, but 21% of Asian consumption and 48% of European consumption. In both Japan and Europe, local production by foreign firms was twice as large as imports.

These are admittedly rough estimates. But they support the view that world competition in computers could not be understood by looking only at trade flows among countries. Corporate strategies were critical—they mediated trade flows and accounted for a large part of "domestic" production. The trade data in this section showed that the gap between the United States and Asia as production sites for computer products narrowed substantially during the 1980s. While firm strategies reinforced this trend, the country-level data did not address the relative position of firms from different nationalities. Did a comparable trend also appear in the competitive positions of U.S. and Asian firms? The next section explores this question.

TABLE 3-3
How Regional Computer Markets Were Served in 1990

Item and Assumption	$ Billions	%	Source
U.S. Market			
Total Market Size	98	100%	Gartner Group
Sales by U.S. Firms	86	88%	Gartner Group
Imports from Foreign Firms	6	6%	UN Data and Gartner Group
Remainder assumed to be accounted for by local production by foreign firms	6	6%	
Asian Market			
Total Market Size	71	100%	Gartner Group
Sales by Japanese Firms	49	69%	Gartner Group
Imports from World	7	10%	UN Data
Remainder assumed to be accounted for by local production by foreign firms	15	21%	
IBM Sales		13%	Gartner Group
Other FDI		8%	
European Market			
Total Market Size	90	100%	Gartner Group
Sales by European Firms	27	30%	Gartner Group
Imports from World	20	22%	UN Data
Remainder assumed to be accounted for by local production by foreign firms	43	48%	
IBM Sales		27%	Gartner Group
Other FDI		21%	

Assumptions
1. National firms supply domestic market from local production;
2. Imports are from foreign firms producing abroad;
3. IBM supplies regional markets from local production;
4. For the United States, imports shown are total estimated to be from foreign firms; and
5. Imports into Asia include Japan, Taiwan, Hong Kong, South Korea, and Singapore.

THE ROLES OF FIRMS AND GOVERNMENTS: REGULATED COMPETITION

During the 1980s the global competitive structure of the computer industry changed in tandem with the changes in trade structure I described above. But these changes did not take place in a vacuum. By the second half of the 1970s there were strong established interests and patterns of competition in the industry, which would not change easily. I will therefore examine first the structure of the industry from the 1960s through most of the 1970s, and then the processes that led to change, starting in the late 1970s and accelerating during the 1980s. These two periods correspond roughly to a technological shift—the first was the heyday of large systems and the second the rise of microcomputer technologies.

Throughout the two periods under consideration, some aspects of global competition remained fairly constant. The economics of the industry, for example, led to a classic oligopolistic structure. The mainframe segment was much more concentrated than others, with a C4 ratio in 1990 of 0.77 compared with 0.51 for microcomputers and 0.30 for peripherals.[30] IBM alone accounted for 0.51, 0.24, and 0.10 of the sales in these segments. These ratios were somewhat lower than those for the 1970s, but not by much. They indicate the great extent of the barriers to entry facing new firms.

U.S. firms dominated the world computer industry almost since its inception. In 1984 U.S. firms accounted for 76% of world computer sales and 94% of U.S. sales. But their position in Europe (63% of market) and in Asia (35%) was stronger than that of U.S. firms in most other comparable industries. (See Table 3-2.) These foreign markets were, in turn, critical to the U.S. firms. The share of foreign sales in IBM's total, for example, grew steadily from 20% in 1960 to a peak of 54% in 1979; after that it declined, but rose again to 59% in 1989.[31]

The way computer firms chose to deploy their resources internationally could be crucial to their performance. In this sense, the success of individual firms depended on firm-specific factors, such as how they were organized, their internal capabilities, and their strategies. The dominant U.S. firms in the 1970s came from the same home-country base, but not all built on the same set of firm-specific advantages. While the European, and especially the Japanese, firms were still in their infancy, it did not take exceptional management of these advantages to enable the U.S. firms to penetrate foreign markets. But by the mid-1970s this began to change, as the foreign firms gained capabilities and market position, first in their home country, and later abroad. The narrowing gaps between firms led to increased rivalry, which in turn called for new strategies, including the use of alliances.

Traditional Global Competition: U.S. Dominance

Five competitive themes characterized the nature of global competition during the large systems era of the 1960s and 1970s. Several of these themes continued to apply to the 1980s, but by then other trends seemed to overtake them in importance.

The first theme was the role of the United States as the lead market for computer development.[32] While the British developed early computing machines to decode enemy messages, and the Japanese also had early rudimentary computers, the industry first flourished commercially in the United States. As with the later rise of Japan, the birth of the industry in the United States also agrees with Porter's model of competitive advantages of nations.[33] There were advanced factors of production available as the United States came out of the war with a strong university system deep in science and technology skills. Demand was strong from booming high-technology industries, including the National Aeronautics and Space Administration and defense. The office-equipment and semiconductor industries, which developed rapidly for these same reasons, supported the rise of the computer industry. Finally, there was more rivalry among computer firms in the United States than anywhere else.

The second central theme of traditional competition in computers was the dominance of IBM, which I have noted. It was by far the largest computer company worldwide, accounting for 39% of the market in the United States in 1984, 34% in Europe, and 18% in Asia (see Table 3-2). The strength of this firm grew out of the country environment I described above, but it was bolstered by firm-based advantages specific to IBM. Foremost among these advantages were the company's marketing and service capabilities. With the appearance of IBM's 360 family of computers in 1964, IBM's dominance grew, and the cohesion of the company's global strategy increased. This family of computers was the first to share a common architecture, allowing users to upgrade without losing their investments in software and training. During this time, IBM insisted on full control of its subsidiaries abroad, because it wanted the freedom to ship products from one unit to another, to rationalize production across countries, and to pursue similar pricing and marketing strategies in neighboring countries.[34] The interests of local partners might have interfered with such an integrated global strategy. The company even left the lucrative Indian market in 1978 rather than accede to government demands for a jointly owned local subsidiary.[35]

Over time, the factors leading to IBM's dominance snowballed, as they could be expected to do in a business where technical standards and service were important. Product and geographical integration strategies begot growth, which begot further scale and reputation, which begot further software support, which begot market share, and so on.

Scale, scope, and standards.   The experience of IBM suggests that Alfred Chandler's model of firm-specific advantages rooted in scale and scope also applied well to this industry.[36] This was the third competitive theme, but the role of scale and scope was different from the capital-intensive industries Chandler studied. While production scale was important in some parts of the industry, such as fabrication of semiconductors and printed-circuit boards, competitive advantage depended much less on capacity utilization than in, say, chemicals. But scope was critical when several products used the same manufacturing process, drew on the same research base, or were sold through the same channels.

In particular, scale and scope were critical in R&D, which of course was the key to winning the technological races among firms. Leading firms invested almost 10% of revenue in R&D and another 10% in capital expenditures. Again, there were substantial differences by market segment. Developing a new mainframe computer requires about $500 million and five years, much more than a new minicomputer or PC. Consequently, IBM's scale and scope advantages proved much less important in the new microcomputer segments than in larger systems.

Still, the competitive battle between computer companies was by no means only a technological race. In the PC market, for example, prices for nearly identical systems in 1990 varied by a factor of 2 or 3 times, depending on a vendor's reputation and service. In larger systems, reputation premiums of about 15% were more common. In mainframes, scale in terms of a firm's installed base was also important for another reason. IBM had initiated the practice of leasing computers early on; this meant that annual income was a function of this base rather than of annual output. The capital requirements of market entry using leasing represented important barriers for new firms. Because of this, only large, well-funded firms could hope to challenge IBM—or firms that could depend on their governments for help.

In addition, scale and scope were essential in the battle of technical standards. As in the telecommunication and television industries, technical standards played a key role in the computer industry, where they referred to hardware and software architectures. But technical standards in computers were not usually set by governments, as they were in the other industries. Standards for connecting systems and components were often set by industrywide consortia, but those of operating systems were usually set by individual firms, using their own market power. IBM's proprietary architecture had long been dominant in mainframes, even though Fujitsu and Hitachi became successful with their own architectures in Japan. In minicomputers, DEC and other firms operated with their own proprietary architectures. There were two main standards in PCs—the MS-DOS system based on Microsoft software, Intel microprocessors, and IBM system architecture, and the Macintosh system based on Apple software and architecture and Motorola microprocessors. Here again, the Japanese market allowed an alternative to flourish—NEC's proprietary architecture dominated half of that market.

There were thus two forms of competition between computer firms: between and within standards. Factors crucial in the former, such as network effects, software availability, and component compatibility, were much less important in the latter. Competition within one standard revolved more around price/performance ratios and service. To scale and scope, therefore, we must add another crucial "s"—standards.

Global competition.   The fourth theme characterizing traditional competition in computers was that it took place at two levels, global and local, simultaneously. The global aspect had to do with the universality of computing functions—scientific applications and many business functions were similar from one country to another; customization of the product could usually be achieved through minor software changes. Furthermore, the importance of scale in R&D and the snowball effects of scale, scope, and standards favored firms that could exploit large and multiple geographic markets. In short, the core computer technologies were highly transferable from country to country, and there were great incentives for maximizing world sales and market share. These features were typical of a global industry.[37]

At the same time, however, strong forces were encouraging the local presence of firms. Note first that, to the extent that final manufacturing offered limited economies of scale, the production cost disadvantages of running several local assembly plants were low. In addition, there were great advantages to being close to the customer—to provide maintenance and service and to tailor computer systems to customer needs.[38] The complexity of these systems and the extent to which buyers depended on them made such services essential. These factors led to the growth of locally oriented computer firms in every major market—Bull in France, Siemens-Nixdorf in Germany, ICL in the United Kingdom, Olivetti in Italy, and Fujitsu, NEC, and Hitachi in Japan.

In Japan, language differences created extra advantage for locally oriented firms. The large Kana-Kanji alphabet required different computer designs and components; Japanese computer firms were the first to develop such "Japanized" computer systems, even though each was much smaller than IBM Japan. Conversely, language and cultural differences reportedly represented barriers to entry for Japanese computer systems makers in Europe and the United States.[39]

The strategy and structure of the successful U.S. firms suggested that different parts of the value chain exhibited different incentives for local or global strategies, as follows:

Value-Added Component	*Optimum Geographic Scope of Strategy*
Basic research	Global
Systems development	Global
Applications development	Mixed, depending on universality
Component production	Mixed, depending on scale effects
System production	Regional
Sales and marketing	Local
Service and maintenance	Local

Impact of government policy.   More or less explicit government pressures provided further incentives for localization strategies. This was the fifth competitive theme in the traditional structure of the industry.

In Japan, government policy clearly favored local firms and regulated IBM's expansion, as I will explain further. In Europe, governments and state-owned enterprises were important buyers of the equipment produced by the local "national champions," which also received some direct public funding and research support. By the 1990s in Europe, pressures for local production had not waned but had become subtler. Government buyers continued to apply what one executive called "goodness" equations to evaluate how much a sale would contribute to domestic value-added, skills development, and the balance of payments.

These and similar policies affected the international strategy of IBM and other U.S. firms. Jacques Maisonrouge, CEO of IBM World Trade, said in 1973: "Political power is stronger than economic power when the two collide."[40] In accordance with this motto, IBM regularly traded off global efficiency for responsiveness to local political constituencies. For example, it continued to expand local production and R&D in Japan and the major European countries, even when exports from the United States or from a smaller number of plants might have been more efficient. In theory, competitive bidding among IBM plants determined the allocation of production, but a 1987 study by a former IBM manager noted: "The balancing act involved in assigning new production requirements often revolves around political factors that are little related to economics."[41]

Government policy in the United States had a less direct effect on competition. The key instrument of policy there was antitrust regulations, and during the late 1960s and the 1970s IBM's policies were under constant review by the U.S. Justice Department. The effects of this antitrust scrutiny constrained IBM's moves and helped open up opportunities for competitors. For example, IBM decided in 1968, partly because of the antitrust pressure, to stop selling its hardware and software "bundled" together. This meant that customers could buy IBM-type hardware from other vendors and use it with software purchased from IBM. The door was opened to the sale of plug-compatible machines (PCMs), which became a big business for Fujitsu and Hitachi in the 1980s.

Creative Destruction: The Rise of Japanese Firms

The evolution of computer competition after the 1970s was characterized by the declining role of the traditional American suppliers. While new U.S. firms appeared in emerging segments, the most dramatic trend was the rise of non-U.S. firms, particularly Japanese firms. What led to this result? Comparing the firm strategies and government policies in Japan and in Europe helped explain it.

The weakness of European firms stemmed from country conditions, firm strategy, and government policy. American firms, as previously noted, had established first-mover advantages in these markets that smaller European firms could not easily overcome. Furthermore, the fragmented nature of these markets made it difficult for them to develop regional scale to challenge the world scale of American competitors. Early European efforts to collaborate regionally to counter the "American challenge" (like the Unidata project involving Siemens, CII, and Philips) floundered on national jealousies, and later efforts (ESPRIT and Eureka) were too little too late. This experience highlighted the unassailable position that U.S. firms had achieved in Europe.

The development of the Japanese market followed a much different pattern. Although IBM had been a presence in Japan since before World War II, and enjoyed the largest sales until 1979, it was surpassed in the 1980s by Fujitsu and NEC and equaled in sales by Hitachi. As a result, while the U.S. and European markets showed IBM leading with about 25% of each market, and a slew of second-tier firms following with between 3% and 5% market shares, the top tier of the Japanese market was split four ways: Fujitsu, NEC, IBM, and Hitachi each held between 12% and 15% of the market in 1989.

Japanese government policies. This outcome followed from two related factors. First, American firms never established as strong a first-mover advantage in Japan as they did in Europe. While the Ministry of International Trade and Industry (MITI) allowed IBM to operate a wholly owned subsidiary in Japan, it did so only after IBM agreed to license key patents to Japanese firms and submit every product introduction for MITI approval. Imports of IBM computers were not only strictly controlled by quotas, but also had import duties imposed on them. These policies gave the Japanese firms breathing room in which to develop.

Second, the Japanese government encouraged, supported, and cajoled the leading Japanese firms into developing computer capabilities. MITI subsidized joint research by three groups of Japanese companies: Fujitsu and Hitachi, NEC and Toshiba, and Matsushita, Mitsubishi, and Oki. By the early 1980s these domestic alliances had been dissolved, but the head start that the companies got had been crucial.[42] In addition, to overcome the IBM advantage from its large installed base of leased computers, the government funded the Japan Electronic Computer Company to provide lease financing for firms buying Japanese computers.[43]

The Japanese firms flourished in this environment. In 1975 NEC was the only Japanese firm among the fifteen largest data-processing firms worldwide, ranking eleventh. In 1990 there were five Japanese firms in this elite group—with Fujitsu ranking second, NEC fourth, and Hitachi fifth.[44] Among the seven firms that were new to the top fifteen since 1975, four were Japanese, two American, and one European. Between 1984 and 1990 alone, the share of Japanese firms in the world market almost doubled, from 12% to 23%, as IBM's share fell from 34% to 24%. Annual sales of Japanese firms grew at 28% in this period, compared with the 14% growth of the world market. The Japanese position in Asia was strengthened by 8 percentage points during these years, again mostly at the expense of U.S. firms. The Japanese share of U.S. and European markets remained small, but rose, respectively, from 2% to 6% and from 3% to 7% (see Table 3-2).

Japanese firm strategies. The growth of the Japanese firms was strongest in mainframes (their world market share increased from 11% to 28% in 1984–1990), in microcomputers (9% to 24%), and in peripherals (20% to 38%).[45] The explanation for this pattern lay partly in the division of labor pursued by Japanese firms after the collaborative programs of the early 1970s. Fujitsu and Hitachi concentrated on challenging IBM's position in mainframes, partly through development of PCMs. NEC and Toshiba, with their greater capabilities in consumer electronics, focused on small machines and peripherals. Production costs were more important in these segments than in others, so that these companies could enter and compete on low-cost strategies.

The financial profile of the Japanese computer firms during the second half of the 1980s differed in some ways from those of their American and European competitors. They typically ran thinner operating margins—much thinner than IBM, whose dominance enabled it to earn monopolistic rents. Even so, under the intensifying competition of the 1980s, IBM's operating income fell from 26% of revenue in 1984 to 16% in 1990, still higher than the 7% of Japanese firms and the 2% *loss* for the struggling European firms. R&D spending as a share of revenues was similar across the company groups, with IBM outspending the others, but both IBM and the Japanese gradually increasing their R&D spending.[46]

On one dimension the Japanese firms differed radically from IBM, as did European firms like Siemens and Bull. Their DP businesses were parts of larger corporations whose net income on average was two or three times as large as operating income from data processing. The DP units' sister operations in semiconductors, consumer electronics, and telecommunications probably helped these firms reach the scale and scope required in components and provided them with some captive demand. Siemens, for example, had large internally generated demand for computing systems based on its industrial contracting business, and all the large Japanese firms had large internal markets for business computing equipment.

Because of these conditions and strategies, the firm-specific capabilities of Japanese firms grew fast. This trend was closely related to, but different from, the growing advantages of Japan as a production site. Firm capabilities were typically embodied in the scale, organization, personnel, and intellectual property of the firms, not in their country environments. One way to measure R&D-based capabilities in a high-technology industry is by the number of patents granted to the firm. By this measure, Japanese firms were nearing parity with American firms in computers: in 1988, 40% of U.S. computer patents were granted to Japanese firms, compared with 45% to American firms. The share of Japanese patents had taken a spectacular jump from 15% in 1978, as the share of European firms declined from 13% to 9%.[47]

If these patent statistics are an indication, the competitive environment in computers in the 1990s promises to be much different from that of the 1970s, when American firms were unchallenged technologically and comfortable in their market positions. The new environment featured greater technological parity between American and non-American firms, and greater strategic interdependence among them. This in turn was likely to call for new firm strategies, including more sophisticated use of alliances.

THE ROLE OF INTERNATIONAL ALLIANCES

The evolving role of international alliances in computers was intimately linked to competitive and technological trends. Aside from the narrowing of competitive gaps between nations described above, at least three technological trends were important. Each modified the incentives for vertical integration across businesses and the potential benefits of collaboration between firms.

First, equipment and components became more standardized. Memory chips, disk drives, displays, keyboards, and printers almost became commodities. This meant that assemblers and system integrators could build systems from readily available parts. In contrast, 1970s components usually had to be designed specifically for each system, leading to strong incentives for vertical integration. By the 1990s suppliers of different components tended to specialize, leaving to system assemblers the task of combining parts from independent sources. The value chain for computer hardware was thus broken up, and links between its various parts were often established through alliances.

Second, "open" systems gained ground against proprietary systems. The MS-DOS system in PCs, for example, was open because software and hardware designers could use it for nominal fees. In workstations, the UNIX operating system—widely licensed by AT&T—gained popularity at the expense of proprietary systems. Open systems spread rapidly in Europe and Japan, where firms and governments sought ways to reduce the control of dominant American firms. Like the decline in economies of scale and scope in systems production, this trend reduced the incentives for vertical integration, as hardware components and software could be combined more freely by users and resellers, and through collaboration between separate firms.

The third trend in the industry was downsizing. The rising power of smaller machines led to the substitution of mainframes by minis, and minis by workstations and PCs. Downsizing generally hurt firms making large computers and those making smaller systems, but minicomputer vendors suffered the most. As demand for mainframes used in storage and processing of massive sets of data remained strong, the functions of minicomputers were gradually taken over by PCs, workstations, and smaller network servers. This trend, too, reduced the benefits of vertical integration, as scale and scope were less important in making the smaller systems. The center of gravity of the industry shifted to fields where interfirm alliances offered the greatest benefits.

The Rise of Interfirm Collaboration

These were among the reasons for the rising importance of international alliances in computers. To explore this phenomenon, I conducted a search of industry and business periodicals between 1975 and 1989 and coded details of 226 alliances (see Table 3-4).[48] The broad definition of alliance used here covers a range of structures and activities, which falls structurally in the gray area between open-market purchases and internal company transactions.[49] Still, 39% of the deals were structured as supply agreements, some of which arguably might be classified as market purchases. In addition, 16% were structured as technology licenses, which some would consider purchases on the "market" for technology. Still, for reasons that I will discuss later, these supply agreements and technology licenses were unlikely to be pure market transactions. The rest—mostly joint R&D projects (17%), equity joint ventures (13%), and equity investments (5%)—fell more clearly in the above definition of alliances. The remaining 10% constituted various hybrid forms. Finally, unless otherwise noted, I have focused on relationships that were international, that is, involving firms of different national origins.[50]

Trends over time.   In the early 1980s, alliances were already common in the computer industry, but there was no evidence at the time that their popularity was growing.[51] But the 1980s saw an increase in the formation of alliances in computers, from under four a year in 1975–1980 to twenty-six per year in 1985–1989; the data by nationality of firm are shown in Figure 3-5, Top.[52] This rise was one and a half times that in world consumption of DP equipment, which rose from an average of $32 billion in 1975–1980 to an average of $150 billion in 1985–1989. This suggests that the new wave of alliances was a response to changing structural conditions rather than to the gradual rise in business volume.

TABLE 3-4
Methods Used in Survey of Alliances

The data reported in Figure 3-5 and Figure 3-6 were collected in a search of press reports I made with the help of Paul Mang, Donna Hill, and Chris Allen. Using the Predicasts PTS PROMT on-line database, we searched for articles within the computers and auxiliary equipment (3573) industry classification in the period 1973 to November 1989, using the key words:

Alliance	Collaboration
Joint Venture	Cooperative
Joint Development	Licensing
Joint Production	Consortium
Joint R&D	Sourcing
Equity Investment	Acquisition

Based on a prior analysis of the coverage that various news sources gave to alliance activity in the United States, Europe, and Asia, we searched only among the following:

Computer Weekly	*Information Week*
Computer World	*The Financial Times*
Electronic Engineering Times	*The Japan Economic Journal*
Electronic News	*MIS Week*
Electronics	*The Wall Street Journal*

Because we were interested in data on how the world's leading data-processing firms used alliances, we searched for articles that reported on one or more of the following twenty-four firms. (To take account of mergers and name changes, we conducted a search on the old names too.) Note that we did not only look for alliances among these twenty-four firms, but for all those involving at least one firm as a partner. In fact, the bulk of the alliances included partners outside this group.

American Firms		*Japanese Firms*	*European Firms*	
IBM	AT&T	Fujitsu	Siemens	Philips
DEC	Compaq	NEC	Olivetti	ICL
Unisys	Amdahl	Hitachi	Bull	Ericsson
HP	Tandy	Toshiba	Nixdorf	
NCR	Sun	Matsushita		
Apple		Mitsubishi		

This search yielded more than two thousand titles with abstracts. We reviewed manually and coded the abstracts and, when necessary, the original articles, using a classification system that recorded such items as partner names, date, structure, activities, motivations, and contributions. Since the search was not limited to "international" alliances, the coding system also distinguished these from purely domestic alliances. In total, there were 226 international and 303 domestic alliances; only the former are used in this chapter. The coding process also separated the formation of alliances from changes in existing alliances; only the former are used in this chapter. Finally, we discarded complete mergers and other nonalliance activities captured by the key words. Further details are available from me.

Furthermore, new formations rose abruptly during the first half of the 1980s, a period of dramatic changes in the pattern of global competition in computers.

Computer firms used alliances in all parts of the value chain. About one third were devoted to trading goods and components, another third

FIGURE 3-5
International Alliances of Leading Computer Firms, 1975–1989

Alliances Formed Annually by
Twenty-four Top Computer Companies

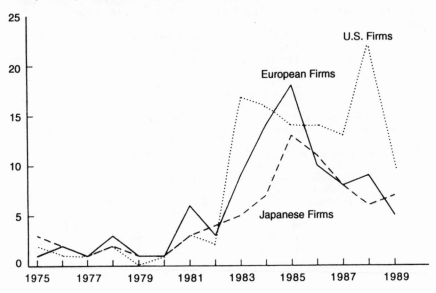

Types of International Alliances

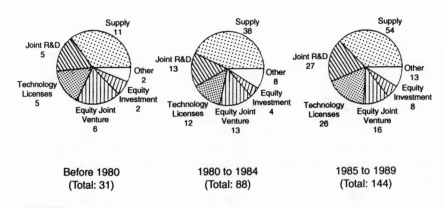

Source: Survey of press reports; see *Table* 3-4.

to technology development and transfer, and about one fifth to manufacturing. Over time, however, the role of technology development and transfer in alliances tended to increase; before 1984, 29% were structured as joint R&D and technology licenses, compared with 37% in 1985–1989 (see Figure 3-5, Bottom).[53] This growth in technology-oriented alliances was motivated by the narrowing technological gaps between firms from different national origins, particularly between Japanese and American firms.

Another reason for the increasing popularity of alliances was defensive. IBM, for example, saw its market position erode in Japan and Europe in the early 1980s, partly because local firms were aggressive in the new microcomputer segments (e.g., Olivetti in Europe) or had simply reached a stage where their products were good enough to challenge IBM's (Japanese firms). So IBM abandoned its earlier stance against sharing control of subsidiaries and entered into many alliances with local firms. In 1982–1984 IBM Japan formed only four alliances with local firms involving some equity investment; in 1987–1989 it formed twenty-five such alliances. Following the example set by IBM Japan, IBM Europe expanded its stock of equity-based alliances from six in 1987 to 150 in 1990.[54] DEC and other incumbents pursued similar defensive alliance strategies in the second half of the 1980s.

Goals of alliances. To explore the role of alliances in transferring capabilities between firms, I classified the alliances in the sample by the "contributions" of each partner.[55] Figure 3-6 shows how the contributions of the firms in an alliance were matched—that is, what one firm contributed in return for the other's contribution. Alliances in which technology was "traded" for technology were common in all groups, but Japanese firms engaged in fewer technology-for-technology deals. Europeans typically contributed market access in exchange for products from the partner, and Japanese firms did the reverse. In fact, Europeans used their offer of market access to get all the items listed—product, market, and technology—and Japanese firms did the same with their offer of supplying product. American firms typically used technology as "payment" for all three items (although mostly for technology), and Japanese and European firms offered all three items in return for *acquiring* technology.

The results of another variable—motivations of the partners—confirmed this picture. The extent to which firms sought technology varied little across nationalities, with only a slightly higher tendency for

FIGURE 3-6
Contributions of Partners in International Alliances (total number of alliances for
1975–1989, paired as shown)

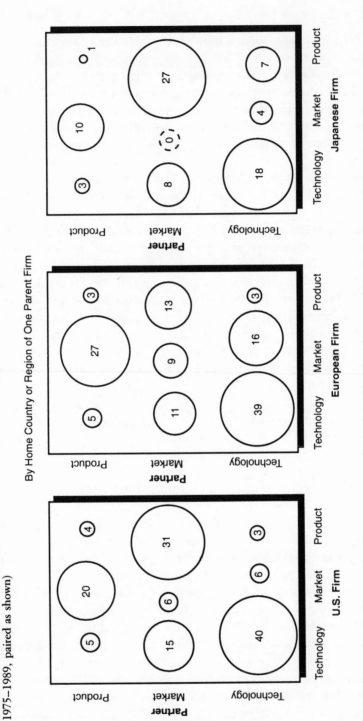

By Home Country or Region of One Parent Firm

Note: Read this figure by matching the partner based in the designated region with the foreign partner. For example, in the box at left, fifteen alliances involved U.S. firms contributing technology for market access and twenty involved offering market access for products.

Source: Survey of press reports; see Table 3-4.

110

non-American firms to enter into alliances for this purpose than American firms. There were greater differences in the use of sourcing and market-access alliances. In general, American and Japanese parents sought market access more often than did European firms, which in turn sought to source products from partners more often than did the Americans and Japanese. European and Japanese alliances were driven by the need to acquire technology more often than were American alliances.

Alliances and competitive strategies.   To explore why alliances were used and what effects they had on global competition, I found it useful to define three ideal types of alliance strategies. Because partner strategies often differed, an alliance strategy was specific to one firm's motivations and competitive goals, not to the structure or content of the alliance itself. I derived this typology inductively—it seemed to sum up the data well. But my scheme also corresponds well to the three theoretical schools of thought on joint ventures described by Bruce Kogut—transaction costs, organizational knowledge, and strategic behavior.[56]

I call the first type of strategy *supply alliances*. Their main purpose is to minimize the transaction costs of trade and product exchanges. The typical basis for such an exchange is a complementary capability of one firm that the other lacks. In a supply alliance, the firms exchange goods and services produced by these different capabilities, enabling each firm to exploit its assets better.

The motivation for doing this through a supply alliance would be reduction of the transaction costs of negotiating, monitoring, and enforcing the agreement. Transaction costs can be high when one partner has to make investments specific to the needs of the other, or when the market and technology are changing in uncertain ways.[57] The contracting costs can usually be reduced through a long-term relationship between the firms; sometimes an agreement with broad commitments is enough, but at other times equity investments may be needed.

The second strategic type is *learning alliances*. The object here is to develop new skills, not merely to trade at low cost the output of existing capabilities. Generally, transaction costs in technology transfer also play a role in these alliances. But the objectives, activities, and ultimate effects differ from those of supply alliances. Firms attempting to learn new skills through these relationships structure their agreements to permit the fastest and most effective transfer of technology and to afford room for growth and development of firm capabilities.[58]

Learning alliances may involve two firms trying to learn together, as in a joint R&D project, or one firm transferring skills to the other, as in a licensing relationship. Because the firm's capabilities and know-how in question are often tacit, embodied in people and organizational routines, or for other reasons "sticky" or "embedded,"[59] cooperation between firms is required for their transfer. Moreover, as in the supply alliances, learning alliances are predicated on an initial need to combine contributions from two firms, either to develop new capabilities or to transfer capabilities from one to the other.

The third ideal type is *positioning alliances.* Their purpose is to help a firm overcome or create marketing barriers to entry.[60] Because of the important role of local service in the computer industry, aggressive firms might form alliances with intermediary organizations that are already strongly positioned to serve particular customer groups. Firms on the defensive in this market positioning game might try to tie the intermediaries more closely to them by deepening their relationships or making additional equity investments.

Positioning strategies are all the more important because of the high costs to buyers in switching from one system or vendor to another. As a result, it takes special effort to convince old buyers to switch, and there are great incentives to capture new buyers. The mutual dependence created when a major buyer or intermediary selects a computer firm's system encourages the formation of long-term relationships, often backed by equity. Furthermore, in wholly new segments of the industry, where several competing technical standards exist, firms can use positioning alliances to gather "sponsors" for their systems and so expand the market for their technology.

These three alliance strategies are not mutually exclusive. In fact, major alliances between computer firms often exhibited elements of two or all of these ideal types, as I will discuss below. Still, the effects of each type of alliance strategy differ from those of the others, and the typology helps in understanding the role of interfirm collaboration.

Alliances and industry evolution.   To see how my typology applies, it is useful to examine what role alliances played in two distinct market segments—mainframes and workstations. In 1990, the first was a mature segment with modest but steady growth worldwide in which IBM dominated in market share and technology standards. The second was an emerging market experiencing burgeoning growth in which no dominant players or standards had emerged. Furthermore, marketing and technological barriers to entry were much higher in mainframes than in workstations, whereas in workstations it was still unclear which barriers to entry would become most important. In both segments, however, alliance activity was intensive—more so, in fact, than in the middle segment of minicomputers or in the more commodity-oriented segments of PCs and peripherals.

My focus on mainframes and workstations will illustrate the different roles that alliances played in the competitive shifts the industry experienced in the 1970s and 1980s. In mainframes, alliances helped encourage the narrowing of gaps between nations. In workstations, alliances were more consequence than cause of these narrowing gaps. In other words, as the industry evolved from its traditional pattern of competition to the new environment of the 1990s, the role of alliances shifted from what was typical in the mainframe segment to what was characteristic of the workstation segment. The two segments thus provide two snapshots of an evolving story.

Alliances in Mature Markets: Mainframes

All major mainframe producers, with the exception until the early 1990s of IBM, used alliances at one time or another. For many of the non-American producers, such arrangements had been important in overcoming the substantial barriers to entry in the business.

Bull, for example, acquired mainframe technology from GE in the 1970s and later maintained a close technological and equity relationship with Honeywell Information Systems. NEC, which also had a licensing relationship with Honeywell, joined with Bull in a three-way joint venture in 1987, when Honeywell began to divest from the computer business. Siemens and ICL, both of which had originally acquired mainframe technology from RCA, later developed supply and technology agreements with Fujitsu. By 1990 Fujitsu was an important supplier to Siemens, and it came to own 80% of ICL. Fujitsu's most important cross-border alliance, however, was its part ownership and close relationship with Amdahl in the United States.

Aside from these interregional alliances, both the Europeans and the Japanese formed alliances with other firms from their home regions to pool their capabilities. In the 1970s Siemens, Philips, and CII (a predecessor of Bull) formed the short-lived Unidata alliance, which foundered on conflicting partner goals and strategies. The Japanese firms joined in the three domestic alliances encouraged by MITI in the 1970s and in other joint development arrangements.

Alliances as causes of narrowing gaps.   The evidence suggests that
European and Japanese second-mover firms used alliances as vehicles for
learning. In that sense, NEC's and Bull's relationships with Honeywell,
Siemens's and ICL's relationships with RCA, and Fujitsu's relationship
with Amdahl helped the Europeans and Japanese overcome technological barriers to entry. (The same was true for Fujitsu's relationship with
ICL, even though ICL itself was not one of the first in the industry.)
The American firms, in each case, developed basic technical capabilities
early on, but were overtaken by IBM, Sperry, and Burroughs. These
second- and third-tier American firms were the only ones willing to
share technology with the foreigners—IBM, Sperry, and Burroughs
rarely entered into such arrangements.

Each of these learning alliances ended in the absorption of, or at least
eclipsing of, the first mover by the foreign second mover: Bull and NEC
together acquired Honeywell's computer business in 1987, Siemens
bought RCA's technology (but not its U.S. business) and built on it when
RCA exited computers. ICL was acquired by Fujitsu. The only American
firms willing to transfer technology to the second movers were those
already in retreat, or at least in trouble; they expected to get financial or
product help from their foreign partners. The foreign firms, in turn, built
strong local businesses, often with support from their national governments. The basic technology, therefore, was transferred across borders
and strengthened the foreign firms. But the latter also used service, standards, and local scope to build sustainable positions domestically.

Amdahl was an exception to this pattern—it remained a strong U.S.
firm even though it was partly owned by Fujitsu and was dependent on
it for key technology. In fact, Amdahl maintained important design skills
in the United States and pushed Fujitsu's technological capabilities as
the partners pursued IBM in the U.S. market. Fujitsu thus continued
to learn from this relationship.

Several of these mainframe deals also exhibited elements of supply
strategies. ICL and Amdahl, for example, purchased many key components from Fujitsu. In both cases, Fujitsu supplied them with highly
complex printed-circuit boards (with 60+ layers), specially designed
semiconductor chips, and sometimes with complete CPU "cubes." At
the same time, both ICL and Amdahl sold Fujitsu's high-end disk drives.
Both parties gained from these transactions, quite apart from any long-
term learning gained from the relationship.

Fujitsu's business with these two firms clearly helped it acquire manufacturing scale, which was important at the component level; Fujitsu's

sales to Amdahl, ICL, and Siemens accounted for about half its total output of CPU components. At the same time, Amdahl and ICL came to depend on a single source for these components; Fujitsu's manufacturing capabilities in this field are reportedly surpassed only by IBM's. Furthermore, both companies usually gain quick access to Fujitsu's new technologies and collaborate with Fujitsu in joint design work.[61]

Because of the importance of these transactions to both sides and the highly specific nature of the technology, this approximates a bilateral monopoly situation, creating a strong incentive for vertical integration. Fujitsu's acquisition of ICL achieved just that, but full acquisition is not always necessary to reduce the hold-up risks inherent in bilateral monopolies. A strong equity position, as Fujitsu has in Amdahl, appears to suffice. In both cases, a long-term arrangement between the partners accommodated product exchange by reducing transaction costs.

Hitachi's relationships with foreign partners suggest that, in the absence of high transaction costs, supply alliances can be much looser and need not involve equity investments. Hitachi supplied IBM-compatible machines to Olivetti and to Comparex (a joint venture between Siemens and BASF), but owned equity in neither European firm. The European partners normally provided only service and sales capabilities, but since the Hitachi machines were fully plug-compatible with IBM models, the partners' investments were not specific to Hitachi machines. In fact, Siemens had a similar arrangement with Fujitsu in the early 1980s, but sold the business to Comparex during Fujitsu's intellectual property dispute with IBM. Comparex merged this Fujitsu-based business with the Hitachi-based business originally managed by BASF.

These mainframe alliances also exhibited some elements of positioning strategies. As I have noted, Fujitsu, NEC, and Hitachi benefited from the sales and service organizations of Amdahl, ICL, Bull, and Comparex. Amdahl's sales and maintenance organization, for example, numbered more than 4,000 people and ICL's almost 11,000. Furthermore, Amdahl's salespeople aggressively pursued potential and traditional IBM customers. Amdahl claimed a 20% market share in those segments in which it competed head to head with IBM. One anecdote has it that a potential buyer sporting merely a coffee mug that read "Amdahl" when an IBM salesperson visited quickly got a $1 million discount on IBM equipment.

Because PCMs had to have a lower price/performance ratio than the IBM original, Amdahl had to keep up continuously with IBM technology and service. Whether Fujitsu by itself could have pursued such an aggressive marketing strategy vis-à-vis IBM is doubtful. In Japan, Fujitsu's market was much more insulated from IBM competition—although its M-series machines operated IBM application programs, IBM machines could not run Fujitsu software. Fujitsu systems were thus proprietary, and incompatible with Hitachi's and NEC's as well. In addition, Fujitsu had a strong Japanese sales and service organization. Amdahl helped Fujitsu position its products effectively in competition with IBM outside of Japan.

Fujitsu's relationship with ICL may have fulfilled a similar function. Fujitsu became involved with ICL in the early 1980s, when ICL was nearly bankrupt. Had that happened, IBM would likely have captured much of ICL's share in the U.K. market—Siemens and Bull were simply not strong enough in the United Kingdom, and the Japanese firms were practically absent, so Fujitsu's support for ICL helped position it in Europe.

Measuring effects of mainframe alliances.   The most significant alliances in mainframes showed elements of each ideal type—supply, learning, and positioning. How important were these arrangements in the overall volume of business in this segment?

One way to judge the impact of alliances on learning is to compare the progress of firms that used them differently. Fujitsu and Hitachi were partners in the MITI project to develop IBM-compatible mainframes and drives, and both remained active in this business, aside from making proprietary equipment. But Fujitsu developed its computer business through its strong alliances with Amdahl and ICL, while Hitachi had only OEM marketing agreements in Europe and an investment in a marketing unit in the United States. Fujitsu developed into the second-largest computer firm worldwide (including its recent 80% acquisition of ICL), with $15 billion in sales, compared with Hitachi's $9 billion.

The differences between NEC and Toshiba—partners in the second MITI group—also underscored the importance of international alliances for learning. NEC gained from its long, multifaceted relationship with Honeywell and Bull. Toshiba never developed a strong alliance for computers, although it had early contacts with GE. Toshiba's rise in computers was mostly based on its strength in technologies important for laptops.[62] While NEC had other factors working in its favor, these differences in alliance strategy helped make it an $11 billion computer vendor, compared with Toshiba's $4 billion.

Examples in Europe tended to support the pattern observed in Japan.

Siemens, Philips, and CII (later Bull) participated in the failed Unidata regional alliance in the 1970s. After that, Siemens worked closely with RCA, and Bull with Honeywell, but Philips formed no substantial international alliances. In 1991 Philips withdrew from computers, and Siemens and Bull were among the few European firms likely to survive in the long run. Olivetti, a late entrant in computers, grew on the strength of its sales network and volume manufacturing skills, focusing mostly on PCs; it made alliances a key part of its competitive strategy in the 1980s.

The volume of product exchange through these arrangements was another measure of their impact, particularly in supply alliances. My best estimate—based on sketchy and sensitive interview data and some assumptions—is that Hitachi, Fujitsu, and NEC together sold almost $800 million worth of product annually through their U.S. mainframe alliances and $1.1 billion through their European mainframe alliances. Together, this amounted to about 14% of total Japanese exports of data-processing equipment and parts (SITC 752 and 7599).[63]

Market shares provide another measure of the importance of alliances in the mainframe business. Direct sales by Japanese firms accounted for 3% of mainframe sales in the U.S. market in 1989; when these firms' alliances were included, their share was 15%.[64] In absolute terms, the Japanese firms sold somewhat more than $500 million worth of mainframes in the United States in 1989; their allies sold more than $3 billion. Of course, much of the value-added in these sales was generated in the United States, often by the partners, not the Japanese component suppliers.

Yet another way to quantify the effects of mainframe alliances was by the Japanese firms' equity ownership of the U.S. and European firms. Fujitsu could be assigned 43% of Amdahl's overall revenue (or $870 million) plus 80% of ICL's overall revenue (or $3.6 billion)—a total of $4.5 billion, which was fully one third of Fujitsu's own (unconsolidated) DP revenues.[65]

Alliances in Emerging Markets: Workstations

The industry environment in the workstation segment differed in many ways from that in mainframes. The lack of a dominant standard or player in workstations, the rapid growth of demand and change in technology, the radically different economics of production compared with mainframes, and the general uncertainty surrounding workstation competition affected how alliances were used. My three-part classification of alliance strategies also applied in this environment, but the relative importance of the strategies differed from that in mainframes.

Whereas alliances in mainframes were primarily intended to help second-mover firms overcome technological barriers to entry and reduce transaction costs, those in workstations were intended to help contending firms overcome or create new marketing barriers to entry. Positioning alliances took on more importance in workstations than in mainframes, and supply and learning alliances, less importance.

The main ties in the workstation segment revolved around American firms, which had a clear lead in developing technology and standards in the segment. But these firms were all using alliances as part of their strategy to establish sustainable competitive positions. Many of these alliances pertained to new reduced instruction set computing (RISC) chip designs.[66]

There were two groups of American firms in the RISC segment. Those which were well established in the computer industry—HP, DEC, and IBM—did not use alliances extensively. When they did, it was on limited projects for certain purposes. But two new firms in the field—Sun Microsystems and MIPS Computer Systems—used alliances extensively in a battle over channels and standards. MIPS's and Sun's strategies fed on each other, as each raced to find as many partners as possible to push its systems.

MIPS's strategy included licenses to six firms to produce the chip itself; it selected strong partners in both Japan (NEC) and Europe (Siemens). The chip designs of each licensee were identical, ensuring complete "pin compatibility" among MIPS chips worldwide. MIPS licenses guaranteed not only that there would be no more licensees but also that current licensees would maintain rights to new generations of RISC chips for ten years. MIPS made this promise to reassure adopters of the chip that MIPS would not monopolize production after the firm had penetrated the market. At the same time, MIPS also provided OEM buyers full systems or boards at any level of integration. The idea was to help firms enter the market quickly and cheaply and allow them the option of integrating backward later. MIPS sold no systems under its own name—an assurance that it would not compete directly with its OEM buyers.[67] This strategy came to be questioned in 1992, when MIPS was acquired by Silicon Graphics, which sold workstations under its own name. Furthermore, MIPS's original alliance network began to come apart when DEC—an original supporter of MIPS technology—introduced and began to push its own RISC design, called Alpha.

Sun's strategy was a bit different. Sun licensed its "SPARC" instruction set for others to incorporate in their chip designs. This was another way of spreading the use of this RISC architecture, although the chips made by different semiconductor manufacturers were then not pin compatible. Furthermore, Sun produced systems and sold them under its own name—actually, it was known in the industry for its aggressive sales force. At the same time, Sun sold through so many OEM vendors in Japan that none was reportedly making money on the business. Sun was also inviting clones of its systems in another attempt to maximize the number of machines on the market using its RISC architecture.

These firms appeared to be using positioning alliances almost exclusively. They did not aim primarily to learn from the alliances or to minimize transaction costs but, initially at least, to overcome marketing barriers to entry. These barriers were maintained by the established firms that sold workstations and related machines through their existing channels and tried to dominate the emerging industry by virtue of the distribution scale and scope they had built in other computer markets.[68]

Aside from overcoming existing entry barriers, Sun's and MIPS's alliances aimed to establish a dominant architecture or at least, in MIPS's words, make its architecture "pervasive worldwide." In this sense, each was also seeking to raise new standards-based barriers to entry through these same alliances. The goal was to use alliances to get products out quickly (overcoming barriers), which would encourage software houses to write applications for these systems, which in turn would lead to a critical mass of demand and applications. That mass allowed the firm a certain amount of protection from vendors outside its standard.

Alliances as consequences of narrowing gaps. This pattern suggests that, in emerging industries without dominant players, especially when standards and network effects are important, firms use alliances to jockey for position. This helps them create the scale and scope that in turn help determine which standard will dominate. American firms' extensive use of international alliances in this battle was again a function of the narrowing gaps between the capabilities of U.S. and foreign firms and a recognition of the importance of local presence in foreign markets. In contrast, when mainframe computers spread commercially in the early 1960s, IBM and its rivals competed for dominance without such alliances. By the 1990s a competitor could not win a similar battle without getting the big Japanese, and to a lesser extent European, producers on its side.

It was unclear how far this strategy could go. Previously, computer makers' proprietary standards had been controlled by the originators, creating an umbrella that allowed a degree of monopoly pricing. But what would happen if the strategy to create the standard itself brought many firms under this umbrella? These firms in the end would be competing with one another inside the standards umbrella. Their only ties to one another were their agreements with the originator of the standard (e.g., Sun and MIPS). Could this originator "regulate" competition under the umbrella? Or would such competition be based purely on price/performance ratios, as in the IBM-compatible PC segment? If price/performance became the key to success, Asian manufacturers would probably be better placed than the American first movers.

Measuring effects of workstation alliances.   Few data were available on the product flows through workstation alliances. The direction of the flow, however, was clear—from the United States to Europe and Japan. Sun sold $400 million in Asia in 1989, all through OEM channels; this was roughly 10% of exports of U.S. data-processing parts and equipment to Japan and the Asian NICs. The effects of MIPS's alliances on trade were minimal. The company's total sales just exceeded $150 million, about one third of which was abroad; in addition, MIPS imported heavily from Kubota in Japan.

The most important effects of the workstation alliances could not be measured quantitatively. Like those in mainframes, they tended to heighten competition by allowing second-mover firms to overcome the entry barriers set up by the first movers. The RISC workstation alliances, however, also aimed to contribute to the establishment of one or more dominant standards, and as such they may ultimately reduce competition in the industry. In the end, they may reduce competition *between* standards and increase competition *within* standards. Through that route, what started out as a U.S.-dominated industry was likely to open up to participants from different countries, with strong advantages likely for those able to achieve scale and low manufacturing costs.

Another effect of workstation alliances was the way they were changing the nature of competition. A pattern was emerging where *groups* of firms, tied together in a network of alliances, competed with one another instead of with individual firms.[69] The formation of broad industry consortia in the RISC field was only the most concrete example of this trend. Compaq and Microsoft joined MIPS and its allies in the Advanced Computing Environment (ACE) consortium, which competed head to head with Sun's, HP's, and Motorola's consortia in a battle to bring RISC computing to commercial users.[70] IBM's reaction was an indication of the significance of these new consortia: it formed an unprecedented alliance with Apple and Motorola to develop the Power PC, a RISC-based system.

The implications of such network competition for international trade are still unclear. The RISC consortia are for the most part blind to national boundaries—they generally include American, European, and Japanese firms. Competition between RISC standards, therefore, was not likely to depend on differences among countries or among the nationalities of firms. Within each standard, however, international differences in cost of production would be key. The multinational membership of the consortia also suggests that, in the future, there will be less room for proprietary national standards, such as NEC's PC architecture in Japan.

CONCLUSION: INDUSTRY EVOLUTION AND ALLIANCE DYNAMICS

The findings in this chapter suggest that for firms in certain positions, and in certain industry environments, international alliances can be critical elements in competitive strategy. Yet because their role changes with industry and firm evolution, alliances cannot be a permanent feature of a company's strategy. Individual interfirm relationships must either be transitional or be adjusted substantially as time passes. This combination creates the tension that leads to the multitude of alliance structures that we normally observe and to their inherent instability.[71]

This dynamic view of alliances has implications for technology management. The study suggests that alliances assist in the international diffusion of technological capabilities in three ways: directly when they enable the transfer of know-how between firms; indirectly when, by helping a firm overcome nontechnological barriers to entry, they enable it to develop skills and capabilities through growth; and finally, they give firms access to complementary technologies without much reallocation of resources.

My research also has addressed issues of more theoretical interest. Existing economic theories of alliance formation usually revolve around transaction-cost minimization. For example, equity joint ventures help align the incentives of two partners in a joint enterprise and so reduce contracting costs involved in securing the commitments that each will make to the enterprise.[72] In a static world, that might indeed be their main motive. Even in dynamic worlds, transaction-cost minimization probably plays a role in the precise design of alliance structures. But my study suggests that the transaction-cost model underemphasizes the function of alliances as facilitators of change.

My approach suggests that alliances be distinguished according to their broad goals, only one of which is transaction-cost minimization. The three ideal types—supply, learning, and positioning alliances—are likely to obey different economic rules and have different economic effects.

Finally, my evidence addresses government policy issues. The computer industry in Japan is a classic example of an infant industry that benefited from government protection.[73] At the start, U.S. firms were far ahead of the Japanese. Moreover, there were important externalities as well as scale and scope economies in the industry, which provided added incentives for infant-industry protection. The Japanese government's policies were typical—restrictions on imports and on foreign investment and subsidies to domestic firms. Yet similar policies implemented in the 1980s in Europe were much less effective. This result illustrates the importance of the timing of government policy as well as the role of the general country environment.

These patterns of trade, competition, and alliance formation are not unique, of course. In many other high-technology industries, international alliances have played roles similar to those they played in computers—diffusing technological capabilities and facilitating market entry by second movers. Dramatic shifts in competitive advantage have occurred in such other industries as semiconductors, consumer electronics, and automobiles. In these industries, too, the initially dominant position of U.S. firms has been eroded and, in a few cases, replaced by the Japanese. By any measure, the United States and U.S. firms still dominate the computer industry. Only time will tell whether this truly sets the industry apart or whether we are simply looking at the early chapters of a familiar story.

NOTES

1. According to the Computer and Business Equipment Manufacturers Association (CBEMA), electronic data-processing equipment accounted for $330 billion (or 50%) of the $660 billion consumed worldwide in the information technology industry. The next largest segments were software and services ($140 billion, or 21%), and telecommunication equipment ($120, or 18%). CBEMA,

Information Technology Industry Global Market Analysis: 1989 (Washington, D.C.: CBEMA, 1989).

2. This definition is admittedly a bit fuzzy around the edges. Large-scale integration of semiconductors is creating "computers on a chip," and telecommunication equipment is being integrated with DP equipment.

3. See Kenneth Flamm, *Creating the Computer: Goverment, Industry, and High Technology* (Washington, D.C.: Brookings Institution, 1988).

4. See Jean-Jacques Servan-Schreiber, *The American Challenge* (New York: Avon Books, 1968), and Marie Anchordoguy, *Computers Inc.: Japan's Challenge to IBM* (Cambridge, Mass.: Council on East Asian Studies and Harvard University Press, 1989).

5. Minutes of February 28, 1972, quoted in Leo A. Morehouse and John W. Rosenblum, "IBM World Trade Corporation," Case No. 9-374-303 (Boston: Harvard Business School, 1974).

6. The strongest Asian NICs in computers were Taiwan, South Korea, and Singapore. Unless otherwise stated, however, the trade data on NICs offered here refer only to South Korea, Singapore, and Hong Kong, the countries on which comparable data are available.

7. In this study, "alliances" are defined broadly as a class of interfirm relations that are short of merger but of longer duration and more substance than arm's-length market exchanges.

8. Gartner Group, *Yardstick: Top 100 Worldwide, 1991 Edition* (Stamford, Conn.: Gartner Group, 1990).

9. In 1988 *Electronics* defined PCs as systems costing under $5,000 and mainframes as systems costing between $400,000 and $5 million. Minicomputers cost between $20,000 and $1 million. The growth rates and market shares are from this source.

10. "Q: What Grows Faster than IBM? A: IBM Abroad," *Fortune*, November 1960, 166.

11. Morehouse and Rosenblum, "IBM World Trade Corporation."

12. No region was meant to be self-sufficient. Rather, the aim was to balance any imports against exports. In fact, when IBM Japan received approval from MITI in the mid-1960s to increase its production in Japan substantially, it reportedly agreed to export one third of its production. From 1965 to 1969, IBM Japan actually exported about 25% of its production. See Anchordoguy, *Computers Inc.* The share today is still about 30%. In Europe, IBM claims to produce 90% of its sales in the region, which implies imports of 10% of sales.

13. Ibid., 11.

14. Alvin J. Harman, *The International Computer Industry: Innovation and Comparative Advantage* (Cambridge, Mass.: Harvard University Press, 1971), 61–62.

15. Ibid., 20.

16. All the trade data in this study are based on the standard international

trade classification (SITC), Revision 2, where SITC 752 covers calculating and automatic data-processing equipment, and SITC 7599 covers parts and accessories suitable for use solely or principally with calculating and automatic data-processing machines. SITC 7599 does *not* include semiconductor and other generic electric components, which are listed under SITC 776. The parts included in SITC 7599 are semifinished equipment, printed-circuit boards, mechanical components specifically for computers, and so on.

17. Unless otherwise noted, the trade data and analysis for Europe exclude trade among Belgium, France, the Netherlands, the United Kingdom, West Germany, Italy, and Sweden. The data shown for Europe thus represent estimates of European trade with non-European countries.

18. Using the now standard Balassa method, this index is defined as the share of computers in a country's exports divided by the share of computers in world exports. An index over one means that the country's export pattern reveals a bias toward computers—i.e., a comparative advantage in computers.

19. CBEMA, *Global Market Analysis;* and Robert Hayes, personal communication.

20. See United Nations Centre on Transnational Corporations, *Transnational Corporations and the Transfer of New and Emerging Technologies to Developing Countries* (New York: UN, 1990), 44–45.

21. I could not include these data on Taiwan in the totals for NICs in this chapter because they were not comparable to the other data available. The Taiwanese numbers appear in an informative Special Advertising Section in *Byte,* October 1991.

22. Michael E. Porter, *The Competitive Advantage of Nations* (New York: Free Press, 1990).

23. Based on UN data for SITC 752. Regional groupings as defined elsewhere in this chapter.

24. During the 1960s, Japanese import duties for computers ranged between 15% and 25%, and the goverment also imposed import quotas. After the government removed most of this protection in the early 1970s, there remained strong incentives for domestic production, such as government procurement that represented a quarter of the market. See Anchordoguy, *Computers Inc.,* 168–171.

25. National Science Board, *Science and Technology Indicators: 1989* (Washington, D.C.: U.S. Goverment Printing Office, 1989), Tables 7-17 and 7-18, 381.

26. This is a well-known theme in the international business literature, first discussed in depth in Richard E. Caves, "International Corporations: The Industrial Economics of Foreign Investment," *Economica,* February 1971, 1–27.

27. For a comparative analysis of U.S. computer firms abroad in the early 1970s, see Harman, *The International Computer Industry.*

28. More recent data on interfirm trade are not yet available. In 1981 the

overall trade balance for data-processing equipment *and parts* between the United States and Europe was $3.7 billion.

29. No direct information is available on the intrafirm trade balance with Japan; my estimate is based on world total minus Europe and major less-developed countries. Note that this measure of intrafirm trade is based on sales to and from "affiliates" and so does not include foreign sourcing from independent parties or allies.

30. The C4 ratio is equal to the market share of the top four firms. Here it is calculated as the share of the sales of the top 100 firms worldwide, using data from Gartner Group, *Yardstick Worldwide*. The C8 ratios for these segments were 0.91, 0.62, and 0.46.

31. Flamm, *Creating the Computer; Electronics*, various issues; and Gartner Group, *Yardstick Worldwide*.

32. See Kenneth Flamm, *Targeting the Computer: Government Support and International Competition* (Washington, D.C.: Brookings Institution, 1987).

33. Porter, *The Competitive Advantage of Nations*.

34. See Morehouse and Rosenblum, "IBM World Trade Corporation."

35. For a discussion of IBM's 1978 dispute with India over ownership issues, see Joseph M. Grieco, "Between Dependency and Autonomy: India's Experience with the International Computer Industry," *International Organization*, Summer 1982, 609–632.

36. Alfred D. Chandler, Jr., *Scale and Scope: The Dynamics of Industrial Capitalism* (Cambridge, Mass.: Harvard University Press, 1990). For analysis of the role of scale and scope in computers, see Nancy S. Dorfman, *Innovation and Market Structure: Lessons from the Computer and Semiconductor Industries* (Cambridge, Mass.: Ballinger, 1987), 63–74.

37. See Michael E. Porter, "Competition in Global Industries," in Michael E. Porter, ed., *Competition in Global Industries* (Boston: Harvard Business School Press, 1986), 15–60.

38. These patterns are comparable to what David Yoffie and Richard Vietor found in telecommunication switching equipment. See their comparison of the incentives for local production in central office switches and PBXs in Chapter 4, this volume.

39. These cultural barriers tended to be highest in large systems, for which service is most important, and lower in PCs and peripherals, for which users require less direct vendor support. The barriers are usually lower where supercomputers and workstations are used, like scientific and technical fields, but Japanese executives expect them to rise as these systems spread in commercial applications. Similarly, they are expected to rise in PCs and peripherals as the systems become more closely tied to desktop publishing and graphic arts applications.

40. Nancy Foy, *The Sun Never Sets on IBM* (New York: Morrow, 1974), 158.

41. David Mercer, *The Global IBM: Leadership in Multinational Management* (New York: Dodd, Mead, 1987), 168.

42. See Martin Fransman, *The Market and Beyond: Cooperation and Competition in Information Technology Development in the Japanese System* (Cambridge, England: Cambridge University Press, 1990).

43. See Anchordoguy, *Computers Inc.*

44. McKinsey & Co., *The 1990 Report on the Computer Industry*, 1–13; Gartner Group, *Yardstick Worldwide.*

45. Gartner Group, *Yardstick Worldwide.*

46. Data in this paragraph and the next are based on ibid.

47. National Science Board, *Science and Technology Indicators: 1989.*

48. Many of these alliances have more than one activity or purpose, and each partner may make several different types of contributions. Consequently, when the activities, motivations, and contributions in the alliances are tabulated graphically, the totals usually add up to more than the total number of deals; in all cases, only shares of this total are shown.

49. An early description of different forms of alliances using transaction cost concepts appears in Peter J. Buckley, "New Forms of International Industrial Cooperation," in Buckley and Mark Casson, *The Economic Theory of the Multinational Enterprise* (London: Macmillan, 1985), 39–59.

50. This includes, of course, alliances between IBM Japan and local Japanese firms.

51. Pankaj Ghemawat, Michael E. Porter, and Richard A. Rawlinson, "Patterns of International Coalition Activity," in Porter, *Competition in Global Industries*, 345–365.

52. In adding the data in Figure 3-5, Top, I eliminated double counting. An alliance between an American firm and a Japanese firm would appear twice in Figure 3-5, but only once in the totals mentioned in the text.

53. The totals in Figure 3-5, Bottom, differ from the number of alliances in my sample (226), because many alliances featured more than one structure and so were counted more than once in these pie charts.

54. Many of these were small local alliances that were not reported in the international press, so they are not included in the data in Table 3-4, Figure 3-5, and Figure 3-6. Still, in these data, too, the increase in IBM's alliances was dramatic.

55. I coded both "motivations" and "contributions" for each partner. As could be expected, one firm's motivations usually corresponded to its partner's contributions.

56. Bruce Kogut, "Joint Ventures: Theoretical and Empirical Perspectives," *Strategic Management Journal* 9 (1988): 319–332.

57. A broader interpretation of the rationale for international collaboration—but one closely related to the transaction-cost perspective—is in Peter J. Buckley and Mark Casson, "A Theory of Cooperation in International Busi-

ness," in Farok J. Contractor and Peter Lorange, eds., *Cooperative Strategies in International Business* (Lexington, Mass.: Lexington Books, 1988), 31–54.

58. Recent work on the role of alliances in transferring skills is reported in Gary Hamel, "Competition for Competence and Inter-Partner Learning Within International Strategic Alliances," *Strategic Management Review* 12 (1991): 83–104.

59. Eric von Hippel, "The Impact of 'Sticky' Data on Innovation and Problem Solving," MIT Working Paper 3147-90-BPS, April 1990, and Joseph L. Badaracco, Jr., *The Knowledge Link: How Firms Compete through Strategic Alliances* (Boston: Harvard Business School Press, 1991).

60. Note that the preceding two forms of alliances might also be interpreted in a barrier-to-entry framework. The learning alliances, in this view, would help firms overcome technological barriers to entry, and the supply alliances help in overcoming transaction-cost barriers.

61. The Fujitsu-Amdahl collaboration is described in Jack Baranson, *Technology and the Multinationals: Corporate Strategies in a Changing World Economy* (Lexington, Mass.: Lexington Books, 1978), 75–84. See also Taiyu Kobayashi, Richard Cleary, trans., *Fortune Favors the Brave: Fujitsu, Thirty Years in Computers* (Tokyo: Toyo Keiza Shinposha, 1983), 77–110.

62. Even IBM formed an alliance with Toshiba to develop liquid-crystal display technology, underscoring the latter's strength in laptop technologies.

63. If mainframes represent a similar proportion of Japanese exports as they do of the U.S. market (about one-third), then the share of Japanese exports through alliances may represent more than 40% of total exports in that segment alone. Adding one more major product exchange done through a U.S.-Japanese alliance gives a more complete measure. Canon reportedly sells about $1 billion worth of laser-printer engines to Hewlett-Packard for the HP Laserjet series. Adding this to the amount I have adduced above suggests that these alliances account for at least 20% of Japanese exports of computers and parts.

64. Based on data from the International Data Corporation.

65. Furthermore, including 80% of ICL in Fujitsu's worldwide revenues makes it the second-largest computer firm, replacing DEC, which long held that position.

66. Reduced instruction set computing (RISC) systems used semiconductor and operating system architectures that reduced the number of lines of code the processor had to execute for any given operation, thus dramatically improving performance (speed).

67. Further details on MIPS's alliance strategy is in Benjamin Gomes-Casseres and Krista McQuade, "MIPS Computer Systems," Case No. 9-792-055 (Boston: Harvard Business School, 1992).

68. Another example of how an existing firm network served a new market was Olivetti's PC business. It had an excellent sales force, reputation, and distribution network for typewriters, even in Japan, which it used to become the

largest European PC maker in Japan. Toshiba formed a joint venture with Olivetti because it wanted access to Olivetti's distribution network in Japan!

69. This pattern is not unique to computers. See an analysis of and application to the automobile industry in Nitin Nohria and Carlos Garcia-Pont, "Global Strategic Linkages and Industry Structure," *Strategic Management Journal* 12 (1991): 105–124. The argument that U.S. firms ought to form networks of alliances to compete more effectively against Japanese keiretsu is made in Charles H. Ferguson, "Computers and the Coming of the U.S. Keiretsu," *Harvard Business Review*, July–August 1990, 55–70.

70. MIPS's strategy and the competition among industry consortia are described in Gomes-Casseres and McQuade, "MIPS Computer Systems."

71. See the related arguments in Bruce Kogut, "Joint Ventures and the Option to Expand and Acquire," *Management Science*, January 1991, 19–33.

72. For an overview of the role of transaction costs in international strategy, see Jean-François Hennart, "The Transaction Cost Theory of the Multinational Enterprise," in Christos N. Pitelis and Roger Sugden, eds., *The Nature of the Transnational Firm* (London: Routledge, 1991), 81–116.

73. The infant-industry argument for government support is described within the context of the strategic trade theory in Paul Krugman, ed., *Strategic Trade Policy in the New International Economics* (Cambridge, Mass.: MIT Press, 1986).

4

TELECOMMUNICATIONS: DEREGULATION AND GLOBALIZATION

Richard H. Vietor and David B. Yoffie

THE 1980s WERE AN extraordinary time in the world telecommunication-equipment industry; more than half a century of regulation crumbled as new technologies revolutionized the business. For the first time, global competition became a possibility. Governments proclaimed their borders open, unleashing companies like AT&T, Siemens, and NEC to attack one another's markets.

If national comparative advantage drove this industry, there should have been a fairly predictable division of labor. Firms in Japan, America, Europe, and the newly industrializing countries (NICs) each brought a distinctive set of national advantages and corporate attributes to the competitive landscape. Low-wage countries should have become the major exporters in the labor-intensive segments of the industry, such as telephone sets. In the more advanced customer-premise equipment, like private branch exchanges (PBXs),[1] Japan (by virtue of its strength in low-cost manufacturing and digital technologies) should have been the winner. And in the high end, especially central-office switches, the United States should have dominated. It had the largest and most sophisticated market for advanced features, and AT&T's Bell Laboratories led in several key technologies.

These conventional predictions proved wrong: country characteristics were not decisive. Factor costs could explain trade and competitive success in the low end of global telecommunications, but in the higher-value-added portions of the industry, especially PBXs and central-office switches, a much more complex pattern of international competition

We have benefited greatly from the comments of a large number of reviewers, including the Harvard Business School World Trade and Global Competition Interest Group, Dick Rosenbloom, John Meyer, and senior executives at AT&T, Bosch, Ericsson, NEC, and Siemens. We are especially grateful to Masao Ogawa for research assistance in Japan, Julie Herendeen for preparing trade data, and Toby Lenk for preparing performance and market-share data.

emerged. In the late 1980s government policy largely determined trade and investment flows; in the 1990s, the success of different national firms began to play an increasingly important role.

The driving forces behind trade and competition in telecommunication equipment, we suggest, come from: (1) a disjuncture in technology, (2) global but asymmetric deregulation, and (3) a positioning struggle among a handful of large telecommunication firms from Europe, Japan, and North America. We begin with technological change because it altered the economics of telecommunications. The emergence of integrated-circuit technology, followed by the digitization of switching, made much of the installed base of equipment obsolete. This technological revolution also altered the economies of production. To be a competitive equipment supplier, a firm required much greater scale economies in R&D and manufacturing, which undermined small niche players and firms in single geographies. Furthermore, the new digital technology created the potential for significant scope economies: while independent switching companies once could thrive in small protected markets, digital technologies conferred cost and technical advantages to those in multiple product lines. These new economies forced companies like Rolm, Mitel, and Intecom to disappear or to merge, while large firms like AT&T, Alcatel, and Siemens strengthened their dominant positions. The underlying economics are likely to leave this industry with only six global players by the turn of the century.

The changing economics of telecommunications also left government regulatory policies outmoded. All industrial countries began their telecommunication industries in the 1980s. The United States deregulated first, followed much later and to a lesser degree by Japan and then Europe. The timing and structure of this action proved to be decisive for trade and investment. When the United States opened its markets, competitors around the world flooded the country. Most of the global flows of products and capital can be attributed to the United States' unilateral opening. Yet open borders did not produce much trade in switching equipment or lead to a fundamental restructuring of competitive positions. Six years after the reduction in formal trade barriers, trade barely existed. And while competitors invaded new markets through direct investment, joint ventures, and strategic alliances, Japanese firms continued to dominate Japan, European firms Europe, and North American firms the United States. The enduring legacy of regulation continued to stifle competition.

But the intersection of partial deregulation and the exploding demand for new digital technology created a window of contestability in the mid-to-late 1980s. A few small contracts opened during this period, which gave foreign firms their first opportunity to penetrate competitors' market-places. The widest openings appeared in the U.S. market, while limited bids emerged in Europe and Asia. Winning these bids was critical: once a competitor's product was installed, the customer became locked into the switch and its add-on products for years to come. Hence, the success of firms' positioning during this transition period of contestable markets should have an enduring impact on trade and global market structure in telecommunication equipment.

The future of international trade in telecommunications will be determined by government regulation and the success of firms in executing their strategies. Global telecommunications has moved from a business defined by politics to a business of globally regulated competition. Government remains critical because deregulation has proceeded in fits and starts. Moreover, the key players have bet on different approaches to equipment. At one extreme, AT&T has tried to wed integrated-circuit and computer technology with telecommunication services; at the other extreme, companies like Northern Telecom, Ericsson, and Alcatel have focused narrowly on telecommunication equipment. NEC, with its communication and computer strategy, Fujitsu, Hitachi, and Siemens fall along the middle of the spectrum. To date, the focused, full-line producers have been the superior performers. But ultimately, the countries and companies that win in telecommunication equipment will be those which successfully implement their visions while mastering the confusion among multiple regulatory systems.[2]

THE GLOBAL TELECOMMUNICATION MARKET

In trying to grasp the global telecommunication markets, most analyses stumble over the mere definition of its boundaries. Just a decade or so ago, telecommunications meant the telephone business—point-to-point transmission of voice (analog) communications, with a small overlay of data (digital) transportation. Since 1980, however, the technological and functional boundaries between telecommunications and computing have become blurred. Modern digital switches *are* computers. If a piece of such equipment or its database is used to move information (digital or analog, voice, video, or fax) or to manage its movement, it is generally deemed part of telecommunications. If it's used to manipulate or manage the information itself, it is generally considered to be computing.

Given these boundaries, the best estimates of the global market—equipment and services together—put its size at $425 billion in 1987 and forecast 1993 at $700 billion.[3] Demand for equipment constitutes one fifth of the total. Most of the services and equipment sales are concentrated in Japan, North America, and Western Europe. North America accounts for a larger portion of both the equipment and service markets (38% and 44%, respectively) than its share of installed main telephone lines (37%). Europe has 38% of installed main lines and only 28% of world service revenue.

Only certain segments of this business have become international, much less global. Prior to 1980, the only cross-national commerce was in low-value-added, customer-premise equipment—telephones, keysets, and small PBXs. Even international long-distance telephone service was essentially a domestic business: AT&T Long Lines contracted with the state-owned telephone monopolies of other countries to provide international circuits jointly. The originating carrier collected the toll, paying the terminating company a fee, typically a dollar. Since only the fee shows up on the balance of payments, the United States, which originates more calls, records a deficit.

Technological Developments

During the 1980s technological innovation dramatically changed the entire telecommunication sector. The most important, as in electronics more generally, was the advent of integrated circuits. This technology, together with advances in time-division multiplexing and pulse-code modulation,[4] made possible the evolution of telecommunication networks from electromechanical (pre-1960s), to analog electronic (1960s–1970s), to digital (1980s–1990s). The shift to digital meant that electronic communication was transported and switched in the form of digital pulses rather than analog waves. This step permitted vast improvements in quality, speed, and capacity, with collateral reductions in unit costs.[5] It also created the possibility of advanced services like integrated services digital networks (ISDNs).[6]

Central-office equipment. The world market for telecommunication equipment totaled approximately $90 billion in 1987; just under half that amount belonged to the central-office segment. Central-office equipment embraces a range of high-technology digital switches, transmission equipment, transmission media, and software, for which the buyers are generally public telecommunication companies. Although end-users with very large private networks occasionally buy this equipment, the central-office market is overwhelmingly an "industrial market," in which the equipment is used to provide services for resale.

A modern telecommunication network consists of a hierarchy of central-office switches connected by varying combinations of fiber optic cables, copper cables, microwaves, and satellites; the interface between transmission lines and switches is made possible by other, highly sophisticated electronic equipment. Each central-office switch interconnects hundreds or thousands of local lines that extend ten or twenty miles to customer premises, where they connect telephones, PBXs, and other terminal equipment. The switch, in other words, is the hub of the system; the transmission lines the spokes; and the terminal equipment the nodes. Of the estimated $42 billion to $44 billion world central-office-equipment market, transmission equipment constituted more than half, with switching equipment (and software) just less than half ($20 billion in 1989).[7] For the United States in the mid-1980s, when digital switch conversion with advanced software proceeded at a rapid clip, central-office equipment constituted a higher proportion, about 58%, of telecom equipment sales.[8]

Digital switches. Central-office switches form the heart of the public telecommunication network. In the late 1970s new digital switching technology began to be deployed, first in France, then in the United States (after 1981), to replace the installed base of analog electronic and even older electromechanical switches. For most of the principal equipment manufacturers, large digital switches became the flagship products of their lines. A digital central-office switch (COS) consists of arrays of several hundred circuit boards, containing thousands of integrated circuits, wired together in metal cabinets of 400 to 1,000 cubic feet in size. Digital COSs range in size from 5,000 line units to more than 100,000 lines (connecting remote modules up to forty or fifty miles away). Switches are also highly differentiated products, which could be segmented by differences in size and degree of functionality. Ericsson switches, for instance, originally designed for international markets, were traditionally vanilla-like—i.e., adaptable but simple and deployable in relatively small increments. At the other extreme, AT&T switches, like the 5ESS, were designed for a more advanced network, with larger concentrated volumes of usage, greater functionality (especially centrex—the generic name for feature-rich services performed directly in the central office by digital switches), and extraordinary levels of reliability.

Software represents a significant portion of the value (and development

FIGURE 4-1
Central-Office-Switch Revenues
World Market by Type of Sales

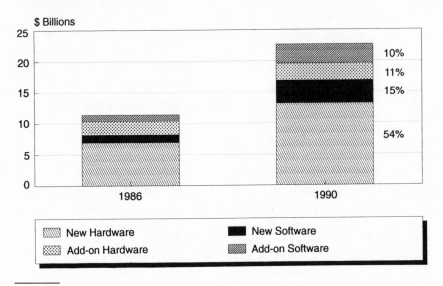

Source: Northern Business Information, *World Public Switching Market: 1991 Database*, 199.

costs) of a digital switch. Most of the switches currently available on the world market were developed in the early 1980s, but the software has evolved considerably since then. AT&T, for example, produced seven editions of the generic codes for its 5ESS model between 1981 and 1990; beyond this are annual feature additions and substantial customizations for different customers in various countries. A 1986 estimate put the value of feature additions at $1.6 billion out of total shipments of $5.1 billion for the United States (see Figure 4-1).[9] Estimates of software's share of the overall value ranged from 30% to 50%. Countries and firms packaged hardware and software differently, however: European and Japanese firms usually sold hardware and software together in multiyear contracts; AT&T and Northern Telecom in the United States often sold hardware aggressively up front, adding software enhancements in later years.

Research and development. The development costs for central-office switches are heavy, and for generic software continuing. Only companies with considerable financial resources and technical personnel, or substantial government support, have entered this business. Fewer still survived the 1980s. In addition to development costs ranging from $800

FIGURE 4-2
Central-Office-Switch Suppliers
COS R&D Spending, 1987

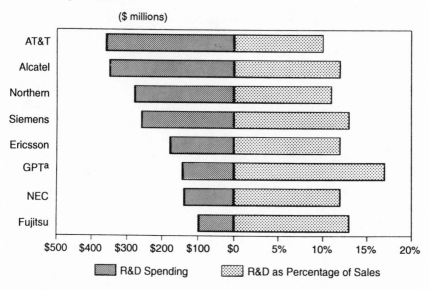

($ millions)

AT&T	
Alcatel	
Northern	
Siemens	
Ericsson	
GPT^a	
NEC	
Fujitsu	

$500 $400 $300 $200 $100 $0   5%   10%   15%   20%

▨ R&D Spending   ▨ R&D as Percentage of Sales

^aPrior to Siemens/GEC joint venture

Source: Arthur D. Little Decision Resources—Spectrum (December 1988).

million to more than $1 billion for each manufacturer's switch, there are annual expenses for software modifications of as much as $200 million per firm (see Figure 4-2). The top eight firms spent, for example, just under $2 billion on COS R&D in 1987. To recover costs of this magnitude, most firms had to get government subsidies (directly through transfers or indirectly through high domestic switch prices) or win a significant share of their domestic markets as well as some share of the world market beyond their borders. If a firm in a small country, like GPT in the United Kingdom, could not sell overseas, its ratio of R&D to sales would inevitably become unsustainable without government subsidies, even with a monopoly at home (see Figure 4-2).[10] In the 1990s international market share will increase in importance as government-owned telephone authorities (PTTs) face increasing competitive pressures that will limit their ability to subsidize national champions. In addition, growth in the leading suppliers' home markets may stagnate as the conversion from analog to digital switches nears completion.

Manufacturing. Central-office equipment—switches, transmission equipment, and media—has long been manufactured in very large-scale plants. Although the development of electronic switches has greatly reduced economies of scale in manufacturing from the levels obtained with electromechanical equipment, they are still significant. Even in the largest national market—the United States—the dominant supplier (AT&T) produces all its 5ESS switches at a single plant, its 4ESS (interexchange) switches at a single plant, its transmission equipment at a single plant, and its fiber cable at a single plant. Similarly, Northern Telecom produces its DMS switch and its transmission equipment at single plants in the United States. Since all other markets are smaller, the efficient manufacturing scale for digital central-office switches is presumably a single plant with capacity of as much as 6.5 million lines.[11] Under this assumption, the 1989 world market of 40 million lines could support at most six players of equal size at an efficient production scale.[12]

Economies of scope. The need for economies of scale in R&D is the dominant feature driving globalization in COSs. Economies of vertical integration, however, also appear important. Certainly, managers we interviewed from the less-integrated firms believe that vertical integration imparts a huge advantage. Japanese and German executives unanimously expressed trepidation over AT&T's reputed competitive advantage from the integration of Bell Labs, Network Systems's switch manufacturing, terminal equipment and computer manufacturing, long-distance services, and private-network design and management capabilities. While the economic significance of these scope economies remains unclear, a firm can evidently realize advantages by spreading its R&D costs for related software and hardware products over a very large revenue base by making its own customized components, thereby maintaining an extensive distribution organization that can offer after-market service in telecommunication services as well as equipment. The components and integrated circuits used in switching and transmission equipment are so specialized that some degree of vertical integration is desirable, either in equipment or with the design and production capabilities common to computer manufacturing.

All the world-scale manufacturers of central-office switches are multiproduct firms, integrated at least into premise equipment (e.g., PBXs)—Northern Telecom, Ericsson, and Alcatel—and even further into computers—NEC, Fujitsu, AT&T, and Siemens (see Figures 4-3, 4-4, and 4-5). All appear to gain some cost savings from shared product lines.[13] Moreover, they gain related scope economies in the

FIGURE 4-3
PBX and COS Activity

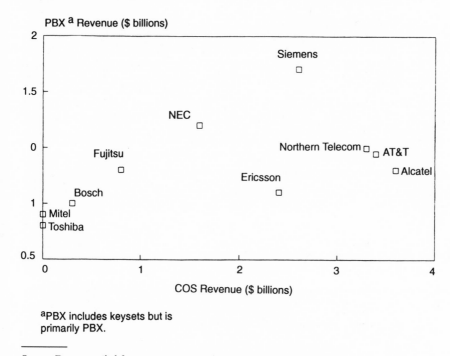

^aPBX includes keysets but is
primarily PBX.

Source: Data compiled from company annual reports and authors' estimates.

process of product design, integration, and upgrading. Given the integrated character of telecommunication networks and the shortening product life cycle inherent in digital technology, multiproduct vendors obtain (or at least plan to obtain) a significant advantage from product integration in a customer's network. For instance, when a glitch in a network appears, a niche vendor has difficulty fixing it; the glitch could come from a variety of hardware or software components. But a full-line vendor, with hundreds of design-and-manufacturing engineers on-line (literally) to deal with a problem, can service any or all of its network products at once.

Entry (and exit) barriers. Historically, the largest barrier to entry into any of the national COS markets was regulation (discussed below). But even in the absence of political obstacles, most COS equipment markets of the world were tough to enter. Any new entrant would have to contend not only with scale and scope considerations, but also with users' high

FIGURE 4-4
Switching and Adjacent[a] Revenue

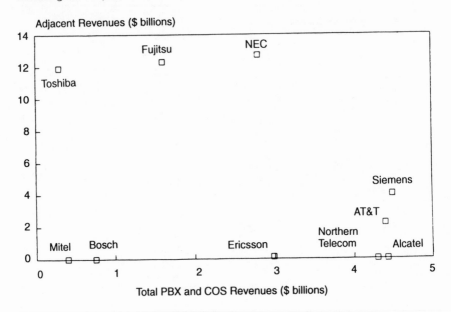

Adjacent Revenues ($ billions)

aComputers and semiconductors; excludes
AT&T services.

Source: Data compiled from company annual reports and authors' estimates.

switching costs and long replacement cycles. To minimize the cost of
maintaining such a highly complex product, most telephone operating
companies preferred to buy two, and at most three types of COSs. Furthermore, the mean time between failures of a switch, like the AT&T
5ESS, was approximately forty years; once a 5ESS was installed, AT&T
had a virtual lock on that account and add-on business for four decades.

Even for incumbent firms in the COS business, there remained the
vast differences from one national network to another. Economic resi-
dues from past political regimes, these differences were costly to overcome: firms had to customize their software and establish large aftermarket service organizations before they could become credible suppliers
in a new country. Just the cost to adapt a COS to a second market ranged
from $30 million to $500 million.[14] Indeed, some switches simply won't
work at all in a foreign market. After spending hundreds of millions
trying to adapt its switch for the United States, Alcatel gave up. Similarly,

FIGURE 4-5
Sales by Major Equipment Category, 1989

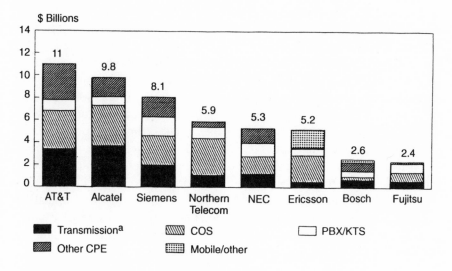

aIncludes Northern Telecom cables.
Note: These data pertain only to telecommunication equipment sales.

Source: Data compiled from company annual reports and authors' estimates.

the Nippon Telephone and Telegraph (NTT)–sponsored switch, made by all four NTT suppliers (NEC, Fujitsu, Hitachi, and Oki), was unworkable outside Japan. NEC and Fujitsu developed entirely separate products for export markets.

In addition to these local customization costs, potential vendors must go through elaborate testing and certification procedures that are both time-consuming and expensive. Then, once a contract is signed, many national governments insist on production in local manufacturing plants, often with ancillary laboratories. Even were this not a political prerequisite, local presence may be crucial because of a related barrier to entry: the need for responsive service and engineering support. For PTTs, the costs of equipment failure are so high that few will buy a nonlocal vendor's switch unless they are confident about the vendor's ability to provide fast service.[15]

Exit is also difficult for many of the same reasons. Public networks entail a huge and complex base of installed equipment for which the national vendors retain responsibility. Products must be supported and upgraded for decades. Exit, under these circumstances, is politically infeasible. Similarly, once a company has introduced products and sold equipment into a public network, withdrawal from the market can blot its reputation in markets.

Distribution and customer base. Distribution channels were generally not important in the central-office market, since the customer base was very limited, centralized, and well defined: the customers were government-owned (or recently privatized) telephone companies, together with the government ministries. In the United States, the customer base was more fragmented: there were 1,500 small, local telephone companies (comprising 5% of the market), five large independent operators (10% of the market), seven regional Bell holding companies, and GTE (together totally 85% of the U.S. demand for COSs). An average Bell operating company covered a territory and population equal in size to Germany. In all these markets, long-term engineering relationships, overlaid by political deals, tied vendor and buyer together.

Terminal (or "customer-premise") equipment. If COSs were the hub of the network, customer-premise or terminal equipment was the "nodes" incorporating a vast, fragmented market. Terminal equipment varies over a wide range of price and functionality, from $19 vanilla phones manufactured in Taiwan, to multimillion-dollar PBX switching systems. In between, the range covers a spectrum of telephones, modems, recorders, facsimile machines, keysets, video and data terminals, and PBXs in every conceivable size. The customer base includes residential buyers, businesses, resellers (retailers and wholesalers), and telephone companies themselves (as distributors). The total market for customer-premise equipment (excluding computer terminals) was approximately $30–$35 billion in 1989. PBXs accounted for the largest (just under one-third), although it was declining.

Private branch exchanges. PBXs are multiline, business telephone systems that provide a group of users with internal switching functions and pooled access to external telephone lines connected to the public network. For an isolated group of users, a PBX provides the same functions as the public network's central switches. PBXs have been used since the late nineteenth century, evolving through a series of technologies: human switchboard operators, electromechanical devices, electronic, and most recently, digital.

Modern PBXs automatically establish and route calls within a single location or between an extension and an external line. Since most users do not regularly call outside their location, the PBX provides a time-sharing function for external lines, which lowers total costs. This has been especially true in regulatory regimes in which rates for usage (e.g., long-distance) have been employed to subsidize rates for access (e.g., flat-rate, local service). To avoid or minimize these cross subsidies, large-business customers have historically combined on-premise PBXs with external private lines, which are generally priced at a fixed monthly rate.[16]

Digital PBXs have also provided business customers with features not previously available from the public network, e.g., more precise billing and usage data, conference calling, call identification, and voice messaging. As ISDN capabilities become more widely available in the early 1990s, analysts predict a new round of purchasing or upgrading. PBXs, like the range of COSs, require software of varying complexity and ancillary hardware.

Only in the United States have PBX-like features been available directly from the central-office public network. Since the early 1980s, the regional Bell companies, and some of the independents, have offered versions of centrex. Indeed, by 1990 most of the Bell companies deployed centrex services as the heart of their business-customer strategies. This accounts, in part, for the decline in PBX sales in the United States during the late 1980s. And it has probably aggravated the intense price competition in which PBX manufacturers worldwide have engaged for several years.[17] Not surprisingly, AT&T and Northern Telecom, which together dominate the U.S. market, are world leaders in centrex-like software features.[18] In Europe and Japan, PBX penetration among business customers (proportionately) has been much deeper, and the public telephone companies have shown no particular interest in centrex. Most of the PTTs in Europe have distributed PBXs to business customers, often in competition with the same manufacturers.

PBX product differentiation is considerably more diverse than COSs. As of 1987, for example, Dataquest reported 130 PBX models in the United States alone (from 35 manufacturers).[19] PBX systems varied widely in size and feature richness. At the low end, systems with 100 lines or fewer accounted for less than one third of the market, at prices of $500 to $600 per line. Larger systems, with 100–1,000 lines, held more than one third of the market, at prices of $700 to $800 per line. At the high end, systems with more than 1,000 lines accounted for just less than a third of the market at prices of $900 to $1,000 per line.[20]

Some PBXs are sold as stand-alone products. Some companies, like NEC and Fujitsu, market PBXs as part of an integrated hardware package that might include telephones, computers, and other private-network equipment. Depending on a customer's needs and size, both these approaches appear sensible, although the piece-part approach seems to be losing ground to the fully integrated system vendors. In both cases, PBX sales generate considerable after-service business through expansion, software upgrading, and addition of ancillary units.

R&D and manufacturing. The research and manufacturing requirements of the PBX business are similar, but smaller than those of the central-office switch business. Development of a competitive PBX requires substantial up-front research and efficient manufacturing operations. The same sorts of microelectronic components, circuit boards, wiring, and frames go into both PBXs and COSs; at the higher ends, only the software is different. Small PBXs can be and have been manufactured in relatively unsophisticated plants, at a much smaller scale.

Like COSs, the PBX business exhibits both scale and scope economies. Although scale has clearly been less significant than in network equipment, one estimate has suggested that a midsize digital PBX requires an investment of more than a half billion dollars, over three to five years, for a product life cycle of seven years.[21] Scope economies were rather unimportant in the 1970s. At the time, the fastest-growing, most successful digital PBX suppliers were niche players like Rolm, Intecom, and Mitel. By the 1980s, however, single-business PBX firms were hard pressed to survive. While measuring scope economies remains elusive, it was no accident that PBXs were no longer the primary business of any major competitor (see Figure 4-3). In interviews, managers reported varying benefits from scope, including design skills and knowledge of telecommunication networks gained in COSs, design skills that leveraged integrated circuit technology, and common distribution, which gained leverage from a firm's office-automation products.[22]

Entry (and exit) barriers. Entry barriers are much lower in customer-premise equipment generally, and for PBXs as well. There are many more potential customers, and purchasing is not only less monopsonistic but less nationalistic. Entry via export, without the political imposition of local manufacturing, makes start-up less costly and less risky. Elaborate certification requirements and competition from the PTTs are the most serious political obstacles. Unit volumes, to justify entry costs, are much lower than for network switches. For smaller, less complicated products, the equipment to software ratio is higher, and local customization requirements are therefore lower.

Nonetheless, entry is far from frictionless. Differences in electrical systems, interconnection standards, and network protocols impose customization costs that can be onerous. Rolm indicated that it spent "millions" to modify its product for introduction into Japan. AT&T, meanwhile, had through 1990 declined to enter Europe, except the United Kingdom, presumably because of high entry costs, intense local competition, and political hurdles. The greatest barrier in PBXs was distribution. There are thousands of large customers and hundreds of thousands of smaller customers in any market. Although indirect distribution through local telephone companies or PTTs is feasible, that approach severely dilutes margins. Direct distribution requires an immense organization, which can scarcely stand alone in competition with multiproduct distributors of computers, PBXs, and diverse terminal equipment. For many foreign firms, the cheapest way to gain distribution was through acquisition.

GOVERNMENT REGULATORY POLICY REGIMES

The 1980s technology revolution was matched by an equally dramatic revolution in government policy. With few exceptions, national telecommunication markets were closed, mostly state-owned monopolies until the late 1970s. There was no competition, either domestic or international, in services or equipment, and there was no global market. Telecommunications was universally deemed a public utility, vital to defense and commerce, and thus a closely controlled enterprise. Rates were elaborately structured to generate cross subsidies, from long-distance to local services, and from business users to residential users. Supply relationships were either vertically integrated (as in Bell Canada and AT&T), or virtually integrated through oligopolistic procurement arrangements. Competition was generally incompatible with regimes of this sort. By force of government policy, international trade was simply stifled.

Technological change undermined these regimes. The advent of microelectronics, then digital switches, computers, microwave, satellite, and optical transmission eroded historical scale economies on which tariff barriers were based and created too many entrepreneurial opportunities for policymakers and incumbent suppliers to withstand. Large users, often multinational firms, demanded advanced services and more efficient rates, bypassing the public network if they could not get them. Regulation was *forced* to accommodate. Moreover, the United States used trade pressure to facilitate the process in Japan, and was helped by multinational corporations in both Japan and Europe, which pressured their respective governments to offer services and rates competitive with their U.S. counterparts. Once global deregulation was under way, the possibilities for international trade and global competition emerged. Still, the differences among regulatory regimes would significantly determine the terms of that competition.

United States

The opening up and eventual disintegration of national telecommunication monopolies occurred first in the United States. By 1990 this process had progressed much further in the United States than elsewhere, much to the competitive disadvantage of its principal national supplier, AT&T. Historically, AT&T was the only privately owned national telephone system among the major industrial countries.[23] It was also the only exchange-service provider that was vertically integrated into equipment manufacturing. The Bell System, which served 82% of the local-service market and 100% of long distance, did not allow non-Bell equipment to be connected to its network. The Federal Communications Commission (FCC) regulated AT&T's interstate service as to price, profitability, and interconnection. State public utility commissions regulated local rates.

Prior to 1968, AT&T had a virtual monopoly on telecommunication equipment sold in the United States. GTE and Stromberg-Carlson supplied COSs to non-Bell companies, but AT&T had effectively controlled approximately 90% of the central-office and terminal-equipment markets. Then, in a landmark decision involving the Carterfone Company, the FCC ruled that AT&T could not arbitrarily prohibit interconnection of non-Bell terminal equipment. In one giant step, the FCC opened the huge U.S. market to competition, domestic and foreign. Over the next twelve years, the remaining restrictions were removed. By 1980 terminal equipment was deregulated altogether, and AT&T's installed base of telephones, keysets, and telex machines was detariffed.[24]

Similarly, in private-line services and then long distance, the FCC and and the courts gradually allowed competitive entry and, eventually, subsidized competition.[25] By the late 1970s several vendors were selling private-line services, and MCI offered a switched, long-distance service in direct competition with AT&T.[26] Partly because of AT&T's responses to these competitive and regulatory changes, the U.S. Justice Department brought an antitrust suit against it in 1974. In January 1982, having exhausted efforts to gain legislative relief, AT&T agreed to divest its local operating companies. AT&T was allowed to retain Bell Labs, AT&T Long Lines, and Western Electric (renamed Network Systems), creating a new company with $34 billion in assets. The Justice Department dropped its suit and withdrew a previous consent decree that had prevented AT&T from entering the computer business.[27]

The twenty-two operating companies were reorganized into seven regional holding companies, each with some $11 billion to $14 billion in assets. Under the terms of the decree, the Bell companies were awarded the lucrative *Yellow Pages*, the Bell name, and a jointly owned piece of Bell Labs (renamed Bell Communications Corporation). But they were restricted indefinitely from providing long-distance services across court-ordered market boundaries (called LATAs), from manufacturing equipment, and from offering information services.[28] In the years since the divestiture, the U.S. government has implemented two additional regulatory reforms. In 1986 the FCC ruled that local telephone companies must unbundle their tariffs and introduce "open network architecture" to make access to the network fully competitive for all service vendors. The same decision freed AT&T from a previous requirement to keep services and equipment sales organizationally separate.[29] In 1988 the FCC changed the method by which it regulated AT&T's rates from a rate-of-return basis to a capped-price basis. This decision was designed to give AT&T greater competitive flexibility and an incentive to operate efficiently.[30]

These domestic regulatory reforms affected the U.S. market structure and in some areas had perverse effects on AT&T. In customer-premise equipment, when the Carterfone decision had opened the market, it fostered new entry and sharp price competition. Although AT&T still dominated PBX sales, new entrants such as Rolm and Mitel, as well as foreign suppliers like NEC and Fujitsu, suddenly were free to challenge AT&T's position. Until the late 1980s, however, AT&T had few opportunities to respond to foreign competitors in their closed home markets, and it remained constrained at home by antitrust laws from using its corporate scope to respond to competitive assaults. While AT&T was allowed to combine its service and equipment sales organizations, it still could not offer its customers bundled contracts in which equipment networks and services were jointly priced.

Even more significant, the artificial restrictions on regional operating companies gave them an incentive to encourage foreign suppliers. Anticipating eventual competition with AT&T, they suspected that AT&T Network Systems was withholding technological capabilities from its switches to gain a competitive advantage with its PBXs and its own long-distance networks. Therefore the Bell operating companies sought foreign suppliers to supplement their AT&T offerings and promote more price competition. This move opened the way for Northern Telecom, a subsidiary of Bell Canada, to enter the U.S. market, and it opened the door for NEC, Fujitsu, Siemens, and others to bid on Bell operating company tenders.

Japan

Like the United States, Japan went through a regulatory convulsion. "The telecommunications market in Japan," proclaimed the Ministry of Posts and Telecommunications (MPT) in 1989, "has become one of the most open markets in the world."[31] Hyperbole aside, this was a far cry from 1979, when the president of NTT allegedly suggested that "the only thing NTT would buy from the United States was mops and buckets."[32]

Before 1985 Japan's telecommunication system was a national monopoly, closed to any sort of competition, much less foreign entry. Under a series of laws enacted in the early 1950s, the Ministry of Posts and Telecommunications took control of Nippon Telephone and Telegraph, the state-owned utility that provided all local and domestic long-distance service in Japan.[33] The ministry designed rates, as in the United States, to foster universal service: thus, long-distance usage and business customers generally subsidized the flat-rate residential service. NTT also maintained the Electronic Communications Laboratories, which conducted and financed joint research in conjunction with its four DenDen or "family" suppliers, NEC, Fujitsu, Hitachi, and Oki. In effect, regulation created a market structure in which these four firms were virtually the only vendors to NTT, which allocated market shares for COSs and other terminal equipment in roughly equal proportions.[34] These arrangements, cross-subsidized by local rates, enabled Japan's equipment manufacturers to develop the technical capabilities and scale necessary to catch up with American and European suppliers.[35]

In the early 1980s trade frictions with the United States, complaints from large Japanese customers about high rates and inadequate service, and efforts by MITI to assert its computer-based authority over telecommunications, precipitated a policy debate that culminated in the enactment of two laws in 1985, the Telecommunications Business Law and the NTT Private Corporation Law.[36] The former drastically reorganized entry and licensing conditions for domestic and international telecommunication services. It divided service vendors into two groups. Type I carriers were facility-based companies, like NTT and KDD, with their own regional, long-distance, cellular, paging, or satellite networks. Type I carriers needed MPT permission to offer a service; rates were regulated, and foreign capital was limited to one third. Type II carriers were non-facility-based service vendors. These companies provided all sorts of value-added services over circuits leased from Type I carriers. For "special" Type II carriers, such as providers of value-added, data, and packet-switching networks, registration with the ministry and notification of services was required; the services themselves, however, were unregulated. "General" Type II carriers, which included mostly resellers of voice and data services, were not regulated.[37] This law also set the stage for the liberalization of technical standards and licensing procedures for terminal equipment, subsequently negotiated in talks with the United States.

The new NTT law mandated its privatization through a series of public offerings. Two thirds of the stock has since been sold to the public at prices indicating a total market value of $250 billion, making NTT the world's most valuable company. NTT has since organized more than 170 affiliates, operating in many less-regulated or unregulated lines of business. The ministry, unlike its counterparts in the United States and the United Kingdom, imposed no restrictions on relations between NTT's regulated and unregulated units.[38]

Five years after the enactment of these laws, the structure of Japan's domestic telecommunication industry had just begun to change. By maintaining NTT's and KDD's rates at noncompetitive levels, the government encouraged competitive entry. While NTT maintained a virtual monopoly on local residential service, and provided itself with superior access in bundled tariffs in dense commercial regions, it nonetheless faced three new common carriers in long-distance, four in cellular, twenty-four in paging, two in satellites, and four new regional companies (organized by electric utilities) that could provide local service selectively—bypassing NTT, in dense commercial regions. In the Type II sector, twenty-three special and more than six hundred general companies had been organized.[39] Most of these firms were Japanese, although a few of the value-added networks (VANs) included foreign-capital participants, including IBM and AT&T.

Driven by competitive pressures, the prospect of further deregulation, and even the threat of divestiture, NTT made some strides to cut costs and reduce rates. Still, competitors and customers alike continued to complain of NTT's bureaucratic operations, excessive costs, discriminatory access, and high rates. A committee of the Diet, which had played a key role in the earlier legislative reforms, proposed the divestiture of NTT; MITI and the Keidanren (Federation of Economic Organizations) seemed to concur. But the Ministry of Posts and Telecommunications objected, and after a year of further study and debate, the divestiture initiative appeared dead and nearly forgotten.[40]

Unlike the situation in the United States, where regulatory change created strong incentives for much greater foreign competition, all regulatory changes in Japan, even taken together, had a minimal impact on international competition. Despite MPT's assertion that Japan was "the most open market in the world," foreign firms' inroads into customer-premise and central-office equipment remained limited. The most notable foreign success was the $250 million contract NTT awarded Northern Telecom to replace switches over five years. It was the first non-DenDen company to do so. While Northern Telecom's revenues have grown to more than $600 million in Japan, its share amounted to only 2–3% of the Japanese market by 1990. Siecor, a partner of Siemens, sold some fiber; Rolm sold a few PBXs, but not enough for a profit; and Motorola, by dint of its continuing political harassment, succeeded in entering Japan's cellular market. And in services, the aforementioned joint-venture VANs were established, but without significant sales or profitability records by the end of 1990.

The pattern seemed obvious. In each strategic sector of the telecommunication market, political and regulatory authorities decided that one foreign supplier was enough.

Europe

Changes in public telecommunication policies were nearly as momentous in Europe as they were in Japan and the United States, albeit a bit more gradual. Prior to 1987, however, it would have been a misnomer to refer to "European" telecommunications. Each European Community (EC) country had its own regulatory system, with national service monopolies and several large producers holding leading positions in different countries. For instance, as of the mid-1980s in COSs, CGE and Thomson dominated France; Plessey and GEC the United Kingdom;

Italtel Italy; Philips the Netherlands; Ericsson Sweden and most of Scandinavia along with small shares in France, the United Kingdom, and Italy; ITT Belgium, Switzerland, and a strong position in Germany with its SEL subsidiary. Germany had three additional suppliers, but Telenorma (later purchased by Bosch) and TeDeWe licensed their technology from the dominant firm, Siemens. The same players dominated PBXs in their countries.

As the economies of scale exploded in telecommunication equipment, this extreme fragmentation became highly problematic. While the United States held 35% of world demand and Japan 12%, no one European state represented more than 8%.[41] To address this problem, the European Community began moving toward integration of telecommunications and, by necessity, regulatory liberalization. The first steps toward integration entailed an elaborate and politically complicated process, which we can only summarize here. Prior to 1987, little real progress had been made.[42] But in June of that year, the European Commission, the EC's governing body, published a "green paper" on telecommunications, inviting comments on a series of broad principles. The most salient of these were:

- acceptance of exclusive provision of network infrastructure and basic services by public telecommunication administrations;
- free (unregulated) provision of all other services and Community-wide interoperability of network standards;
- free (unrestricted) provision of terminal equipment and Community-wide compatibility of type approval (with a possible exception for subscriber's first [conventional] telephone set);
- separation of regulatory and operational activities of telecommunication administrations; and
- obligatory interconnection, equal-access provision, and open procurement, and eventual reduction of cross subsidies by public telecommunication administrations.[43]

The Commission recognized that such measures were necessary to achieve economic competitiveness through scale and that market integration in Europe would be impossible without an integrated communication network.

Although the Commission's schedule for implementing these recommendations had slipped some, remarkable progress had nonetheless been made by the end of 1990. The Commission's competition tsar, Sir Leon Brittan, twice resorted to Article 90 directives (orders that circumvent discussion by the Council of Ministers) to force PTTs to liberalize.[44] In 1988, when the Commission applied this directive to terminal equipment, France objected loudly and challenged in court. In 1989, Sir Leon did it a second time, with regard to services, causing a major flap among the weaker EC members.[45] Two other important directives awaited Commission approval: rules for unbundled, nondiscriminatory access to networks and competitive procurement of central-office equipment. Since this reform provided for 50% local EC content and allowed preferential treatment of European companies, American trade officials still deemed it unacceptable.[46]

Of course, country-by-country implementation of these rules and guidelines was another matter, one that varied widely among member states. The United Kingdom, after the liberalization of entry and pricing in 1981 and the privatization of British Telecom in 1984, had the most open telecommunication market in Europe. The Netherlands and Belgium remained quite closed and monopolistic; France, among the most important markets, liberalized competition, especially in information services, with its successful Minitel network, but remained virtually closed to imports or non-French procurement.[47]

Because it is the home base for Siemens (and Bosch), Germany is an especially interesting case. Before mid-1989, the German telephone operating entity and regulatory authority were one and the same—Deutsche Bundespost, which supplied all telecommunication services. It had a monopoly on first telephones and distributed other terminal and PBX equipment, often in competition with the vendors. Its dominant suppliers (excluding ITT's SEL subsidiary) were German firms, particularly Siemens. Unlike the PTTs in most other European countries, the Bundespost's responsibility for postal and telecommunication services was established in the Basic Law, Germany's constitution.

Legislation to separate the Bundespost operational and regulatory functions was introduced unsuccessfully in the early 1980s. Later a government commission recommended against privatization and supported the government's retention of basic monopoly service, but urged rapid decontrol of equipment and value-added services.[48] By the time its report was submitted to the German government in 1988, European liberalization was well under way. Finally, the German political establishment recognized the risk of being left behind.

In the summer of 1988 the government reversed course. The Bundespost was reorganized into three operating units, one being Deutsche Bundespost Telekom. A separate entity would have the authority for approving equipment, and interconnect standards would be established as a separate entity. Services were divided into two categories: "duty" and "competitive." Telekom was obliged to provide the former and could choose to provide any of the latter. To the extent that it continued to be an equipment owner and distributor, it could manage those businesses as a separate division, with separate (e.g., unsubsidized) accounts. Foreign entry and investment in the competitive services were unrestricted. Subsidies between Telekom and Posts were to be phased out quickly, while subsidies among telecommunication services would be phased out more gradually.[49] With these changes, Germany would join the United Kingdom out in front of EC liberalization and integration.

This scarcely meant, however, that foreign firms could easily establish themselves in the German market or win procurement contracts from Deutsche Telekom. Substantial economic and technical barriers remained, and the very close ties between Telekom and the half dozen German equipment suppliers were likely to persist.[50] But for non-German firms, with competitive terminal equipment (especially such as cordless phones, cellular phones, and PBXs) and central-office products, this sudden opening represented a possible window of opportunity for the early 1990s, open as long as it would take German firms to make structural adjustments to real competition.

"GLOBALIZATION" AND INTERNATIONAL TRADE

As deregulation spread beyond the United States during the 1980s, first to the United Kingdom, then to Japan, and eventually to Europe, conventional wisdom might have anticipated a quickening of trade, shifting market shares, and industry consolidations. With economies of scale greater than any one local market could support, firms would inevitably globalize, seeking out new, large markets that would allow them to amortize their fixed R&D and manufacturing expenses. But which countries and firms should win? In a truly free market, theory would suggest the emergence of comparative specialization. The firms most competitive in price or performance would dominate. While firms did aggressively seek markets outside their home bases and the industry did consolidate, trade in COSs and PBXs grew slowly, and no firm has grabbed significant market shares from a direct competitor since the mid-1980s. The long legacy of regulation and close ties between operating companies and their suppliers stifled true global rationalization.

Nonetheless, the rising economies of scale and the opportunity to buy

FIGURE 4-6
Consolidation in the World PBX Market, 1983–1990 (percentages are world market shares in 1989)

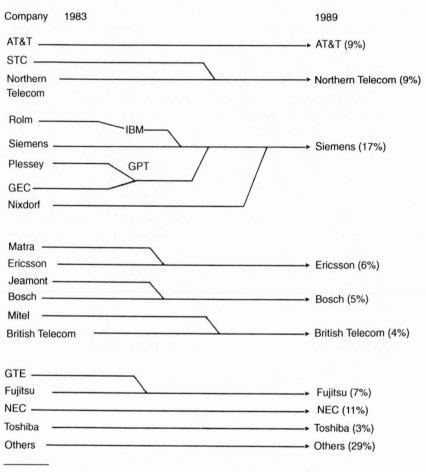

Sources: Northern Business Information data and authors' estimates.

foreign firms in the new regulatory era spurred a boom in acquisitions. In 1989, the once fragmented equipment industry had only seven firms with approximately 87% of the world COS market and a four-firm concentration of 63%; the same seven had 66% of the world PBX market (C4 of 46%) (see Figures 4-6 and 4-7). In PBXs, for instance, several of the world's largest vendors in 1983 were no longer independent by 1990.[51] At the end of the 1980s, ten firms held significant shares that together accounted for 78% of the global market (Siemens's acquisition

FIGURE 4-7
Consolidation in the World COS Market, 1983–1989 (percentages are world market shares in 1989)

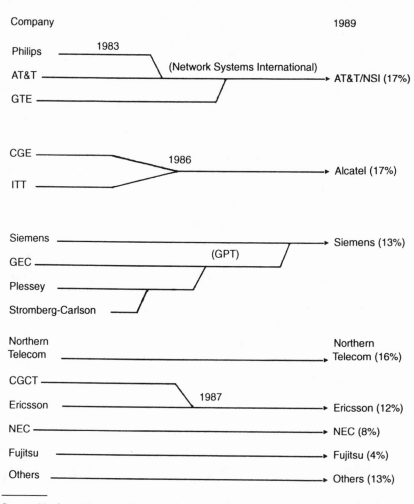

Sources: Northern Business Information data and authors' estimates.

of GPT and Rolm boosted its world share nearly 10 points, from 8% to just over 17%). Seven of those firms (together with their acquisitions), with 66% share, were also the dominant firms in COSs. The eighth, Bosch, manufactured switches in Germany. Mitel—ninth—and Toshiba—tenth—were the only leading PBX players with no position in central-office switches (see Figure 4-3).

Despite all this consolidation, however, true globalization had not materialized. Outside the United States, firms attacked foreign markets, but deregulation had not translated into greater sales opportunities in the 1980s. American and Japanese firms made little headway in Europe, and American and European firms had even less success in Japan.

The same phenomenon occurred in COSs: firms merged, were acquired, but outside the United States, no one made much headway in a foreign competitor's home market. A field of fourteen major COS firms in 1982 had narrowed to seven by 1990 (see Figure 4-7). While firms merged, however, they had not rationalized their product lines. Acquiring companies spoke of product "migration" strategies, but none had been implemented by 1990. Technological incompatibilities, national political considerations, and the need to serve existing customers with established networks prevented abrupt changes. The result was persistent excess capacity; a customer could still buy a GTE switch, a Thomson switch, an ITT switch, or a Rolm PBX, but only under a different corporate label.

The minor switch manufacturers—Hitachi and Oki in Japan, Bosch and TeDeWe in Germany—were limited to a protected share of their home markets. Italtel, the largest COS firm in Italy, entered into an agreement with AT&T. All the remaining seven major firms were vertically integrated within telecommunication equipment, and four— AT&T, NEC, Siemens, and Fujitsu—more broadly in computing and electronics. Yet despite the high worldwide concentration ratio, no one firm had achieved truly global status, that is, a significant presence in all three major markets. In Japan, the domestic oligopoly persisted (though Fujitsu surpassed NEC as market leader), with virtually no foreign entrants. In Europe, Alcatel remained in the lead by dint of offering two incompatible switches. And while it has a strong position in dozens of developing-country markets, Alcatel has opted out of both the American and Japanese markets for COSs. Siemens, too, was strong in Europe, but only through its recent acquisition. No non-European firms had any significant market share in Europe: AT&T had merely established a presence, and Northern Telecom had none. In 1990 it bought STC, a British cable and transmission company, for almost $3 billion in the hope of creating a strong European beachhead (see Figure 4-8).

The pattern in the United States, where deregulation occurred much earlier, differed slightly: significant foreign inroads did occur. Northern Telecom, for example, grabbed share from AT&T in the early 1980s before any other markets in the world were open to bid. Northern Tele-

FIGURE 4-8
Regional COS Market Shares, 1989

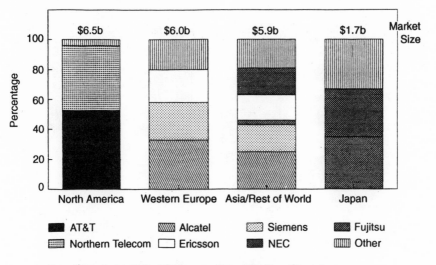

Note: Other in the United States consists of Siemens/Stromberg, Ericsson, and NEC. Fujitsu is also trying to enter. In Western Europe, Other consists primarily of Italtel/AT&T, Bosch, and TeDeWe. In Japan, Other consists of Hitachi, Oki, and Northern Telecom.

Sources: Northern Business Information data and authors' estimates.

com had an early lead in digital switches, and its first-mover advantages allowed it to maintain almost half the U.S. market, even after AT&T introduced its 5ESS digital switch. In the meantime, four other foreign firms (Siemens, NEC, Ericsson, and Fujitsu) have invested heavily in the United States, and each has been awarded small contracts from Bell operating companies. Foreign incursions into PBXs were equally dramatic. Even if one excludes Siemens's acquisition of Rolm's 20% market share, foreign competitors such as NEC and Fujitsu were able to grab another 40% of the U.S. PBX market in the 1980s (see Figure 4-9). The openness of the U.S. market welcomed foreign competition.

International Trade

The economics of the industry, especially the rising scale economies in R&D, clearly drove firms to consolidate and attack foreign markets.

FIGURE 4-9
Regional PBX Market Shares, 1989

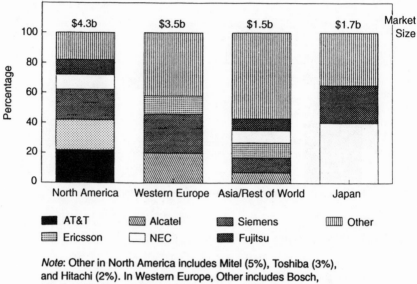

Note: Other in North America includes Mitel (5%), Toshiba (3%), and Hitachi (2%). In Western Europe, Other includes Bosch, Mitel, and Philips. In Japan, Other includes Hitachi (16%), Oki (8%), and Toshiba (6%).

Sources: Northern Business Information data and authors' estimates.

But what effect did this have on international trade? How did this deregu-lated, oligopolistic structure organize production and shipments around the world? To answer these questions, we analyzed trade in telecommu-nication equipment and parts between the United States, Japan, and Germany, and between each of those countries and the EC, the newly industrialized economies (NIEs) of Hong Kong, Singapore, Taiwan, and Korea, and the rest of the world, from 1978 to 1988. We have also compiled export and import data for the United States from 1982 to 1988 that disaggregate "switches," although the data unfortunately do not distinguish between COSs and PBXs.[52]

The U.S. telecommunication trade profile exhibits several clear trends. Over the six years through 1988, U.S. exports grew 10% annu-ally, while imports grew 23%. The balance turned negative, from a surplus of $275 million to a deficit of $2.6 billion (see Figure 4-10). By 1988, imports from Japan exceeded exports to Japan by a factor of ten, resulting in a bilateral deficit of $2.2 billion. Similarly, in its balance

FIGURE 4-10
Telecommunication-Equipment Trade: Japanese Exports and Imports, 1978–1988

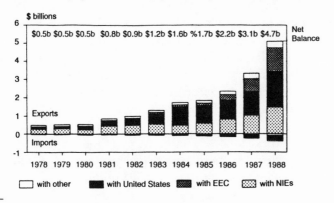

Sources: OECD Microtables, 81TC 76-41 and 76-491.

Telecommunication-Equipment Trade: U.S. Exports and Imports, 1982–1988

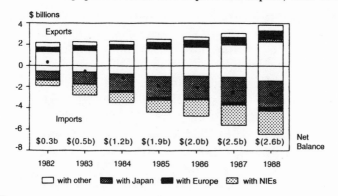

Sources: OECD Microtables, 81TC 76-41 and U.S. Department of Commerce, 900.

Telecommunication-Equipment Trade: EEC Exports and Imports, 1978–1988

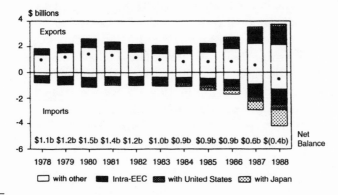

Sources: OECD Microtables, 81TC 76-41 and 764-91.

with the four Asian NIEs, the United States moved from a small deficit of $100 million to a deficit of $1.7 billion. Together, Japan and the NIEs accounted for 72% of U.S. imports, but only 20% of U.S. exports. The United States has run a persistent trade surplus with Europe, reaching $417 million in 1988.

For Japan, the growth rates in trade are deceptive but the results unsurprising. Between 1978 and 1988, exports grew at 26%, while imports grew at 33%. But in 1978, Japan's telecommunication imports from the rest of the world totaled a mere $23 million; exports were twenty times as much. By 1988 these exports had grown to $5.1 billion, while imports remained only one-thirteenth ($391 million) as much. The destination of Japan's exports, meanwhile, had shifted. In 1978, about one-fifth went to the NIEs, and the same to the United States. But by 1988, the NIEs' share had dropped to 7% and Europe took 26%, while the United States' had risen to 39%.

In the EC, exports by member countries expanded 7% annually in 1978–1988, while imports grew at 18%, resulting in a 1988 trade deficit of $446 million, down from the $1,066 million surplus in 1978. As with the United States, Japan was the country that contributed the most to this decline; the EC's bilateral balance with that country went from −$27 million in 1978 to −$1,233 million in 1988. Japanese imports displaced intra-EC trade, rising from 4% of total EC imports to 30% over the ten-year period to 1988, while intra-EC imports fell from 58% of the total to 30%. We presume that most of the Japanese exports to Europe consisted of facsimile machines. While the NIEs had made significant inroads into the low-end terminal-equipment market in the United States, countries like Taiwan, Hong Kong, and Korea were largely kept out of that segment in Europe. As a result, the EC bilateral trade deficit with the NIEs was a relatively small $100 million in 1988.

Turning to the limited data on switches and parts, we can sharpen the focus on global competitiveness. First, it becomes apparent that most trade in telecommunications consists of smaller terminal equipment (not switches) and parts. In the United States, telephones, fax machines, cellular and cordless sets, and other terminal equipment accounted for most of the import growth up to 1988. Since the United States is less competitive in small terminal equipment (like telephones, keysets, facsimiles), two thirds of its exports are parts. Yet, while it is certainly competitive in switches, only one sixth of the total is switches. For Japan, facsimile constituted more than half of exports in 1987, and if we could isolate telephones, modems, and keysets, we would probably be left with a number about equal to the total of switches ($419 million) and parts ($675 million). Parts constituted about one third of exports and imports alike for Germany. As for switches, Germany exported mainly within Europe (and some PBXs to the United States), but imports scarcely at all (even digital switches from Alcatel's SEL subsidiary were made in Germany).

Although it is difficult to further disaggregate these trade figures for switches, we have concluded that *central-office switches do not trade*. At best, there is trade in electronic components. The numbers for Japan and Germany mostly reflect PBXs, and for the United States either PBXs or COSs shipped by Northern Telecom (a Canadian company that manufactures in the United States) possibly to Canada, and AT&T products to less-developed countries.[53] Even international trade in *PBXs* among the advanced competitor countries *remains extremely limited*, excluding intra-European trade. Billions of dollars of trade in the low end of customer-premise equipment—telephones, keysets, and facsimiles—went from the NIEs and Japan to the United States. But imports served only 5% of the switching market (PBX and COS) in the United States. Since major foreign competitors control half of this total market, imports represent only 10% of foreign firms' market share. All the companies we have examined made alliances or foreign direct investments to assemble, make, and distribute PBXs and COSs in their target countries. In other words, despite the large scale in manufacturing, local presence measured global competitiveness, not international trade.

Thus, eight years after the introduction of digital switching and six years of true international (e.g., extra-European) competition, a most peculiar oligopoly emerged. The industry was increasingly concentrated, yet home-country dominance and historical positions elsewhere still accounted for most relative market shares in COS equipment; only in the U.S. PBX market did share appear to feel the effects of foreign competition.

FUTURE EVOLUTION: CONTESTABLE MARKETS AND COMPETITIVE MOVES

The new economics of digital switching and the willingness of governments to open their markets to competition clearly drove trade in telecommunication equipment. The most open market—the United States—was the most competitive market and target for the bulk of the world's exports of goods and capital. But as other areas slowly opened, what would determine the future of international competition in this field? Would the huge, sophisticated domestic market make the United States and AT&T the winner? Would Japan dominate this business, as it has so many other electronic-related industries? Or would European firms emerge as key players?

Central-office switches and PBXs have become global oligopolies, still heavily influenced by government policy. In this type of environment, relative costs are not very important, nor is technological prowess or proximity to large sophisticated customers and suppliers. Rather, success is determined by two factors: the degree to which governments continue supporting their local champions and the administrative strength of the various firms in executing their strategies. Governments remain important, even in a period of deregulation, because deregulation has not meant free markets. Governments remained deeply involved. In the future, governments will continue to affect international competition if they allow cross subsidies from domestic to international sales[54] and if they use their monopsonist powers to hinder foreign rivals in the home market. In an industry whose scale economies in R&D are great, a government's strong commitment can discourage foreign competitors' investments; moreover, cash flow generated from domestic subsidies can lead to high investment levels and significant competitive advantages.

Execution of strategies by firms will be equally important. No matter how much a government spends on telecommunication equipment, it cannot assure the success of its firms in such a high-technology business. Moreover, all the large players in COSs and PBXs have different visions of how to compete, visions that vary by firm, not by country.[55] The complexity of designing, manufacturing, and selling telecommunication equipment globally can overwhelm any company's administrative capability. International success, we believe, will be a function of how well firms position their companies during the critical transition through the mid-1990s, while deregulation and the need for new digital switches creates a brief opening in many world markets.

Every contract during this period is significant. PTTs are experimenting with new switches to augment their existing networks. If PTTs could mix and match different switches from a variety of suppliers, markets might become increasingly contestable over time. But the history of regulation produced incompatible switches in virtually every country, and few, if any, telephone operating companies want more than two or three switch vendors. The costs of servicing and maintaining the network grow with the number of incompatible suppliers. Therefore, while large telecommunication markets in Japan, Germany, and elsewhere were opening in the late 1980s and early 1990s, they were not likely to stay open very long. Barring another technical revolution, the market would effectively close once the second or third supplier was chosen. If a vendor could become such a new second or third supplier, it would secure a revenue stream for years to come.

To take advantage of this window, the large vertically integrated companies around the world plunged into acquisitions, alliances, and foreign investments. Siemens achieved the largest level of revenue outside a home area primarily through aggressive acquisition. Alcatel and Ericsson were second and third in revenue outside a home area, but neither had penetrated North America or Japan (see Figures 4-8 and 4-9). Their achievement was the result of relentless pursuit of the rest of the less-developed-country markets. Share gains also varied considerably by segment: AT&T and Fujitsu achieved little in PBXs outside their home bases, but Siemens, through acquisition (Rolm, GPT, and Nixdorf), became the world's largest PBX supplier. Overall, the greatest surprise was the general lack of success outside the home area (see Table 4-1).

Although the effects of strategic behavior were scarcely evident, the real consequences should be clear by the mid-1990s. Firms built different track records in the 1980s and have staked out different positions in the global oligopoly. Of course, it is no simple matter to categorize corporate strategies in this industry: the firms varied widely in their financial positions (see Table 4-2), scale and scope (see Tables 4-3 and 4-4), and geographic focus. One important distinction is geographic positioning in competitors' home markets. As Figure 4-11 indicates, Japanese and some European firms have targeted U.S. markets, but not each other's; U.S.-based firms have targeted markets peripheral to Japan, France, and Germany, but have not attacked each other frontally. And Alcatel alone has yet to attack the switching markets of its non-European competitors. Although it remains to be seen which of these strategies is viable under regulated competition, Robert Galvin, the chairman of Motorola, is convinced that to survive in global competition, a firm "cannot allow sanctuary for competitive enemies."[56]

Another strategic distinction can be made between those firms which have a vision and strategy of integrating equipment and services to provide "information movement and management" (IM&M) (i.e., the networked office of the future), and those which focus primarily on wholesale and retail equipment markets. The IM&M strategy has been adopted by the major Japanese players and AT&T; the less-integrated firms, like

TABLE 4-1
Regional Market Shares in Public and Private Switching, 1989

Area	Public Switching		Private Switching	
United States:		$ 6.0b		$ 4.0b[a]
	1 AT&T	53%	1 AT&T	22%
	2 Northern Telecom	43%	2 Northern Telecom	20%
	3 Siemens/Stromberg }		3 Siemens	20%
	3 Ericsson }	4%	4 NEC	10%
	3 NEC }		5 Fujitsu	10%
			6 Mitel	4%
			7 Toshiba	3%
			Other	11%
Western Europe:		$ 6.0b		$ 3.5b
	1 Alcatel	33%	1 Siemens	26%
	2 Siemens[b]	25%	2 Alcatel	20%
	3 Ericsson	22%	3 Bosch	14%
	4 Italtel/AT&T[c]	11%	4 Ericsson	12%
	5 Philips/AT&T	3%	5 Mitel	5%
	Bosch/TeDeWe/Other	6%	Philips/Northern Telecom/Other	23%
Japan:		$ 1.7b		$ 1.7b
	1 Fujitsu	35%	1 NEC	40%
	2 NEC	32%	2 Fujitsu	25%

162

3	Hitachi	15%		
4	Oki	15%		
5	Northern Telecom	3%		

Rest of World:

		$ 5.9b
1	Alcatel	25%
2	NEC	18%
3	Siemens	18%
4	Ericsson	17%
	Other	22%

World:

		$20.1b
1	Alcatel	17%
2	AT&T[c]	17%
3	Northern Telecom	16%
4	Siemens[b]	13%
5	Ericsson	12%
6	NEC	8%
7	Fujitsu	4%
	Other	13%

3	Hitachi	16%
4	Oki	8%
5	Toshiba	6%
	Other	5%

		$ 1.5b
1	Siemens	10%
2	Ericsson	10%
3	NEC	8%
4	Fujitsu	8%
5	Alcatel	7%
	Other	57%

		$11.0b
1	Siemens	17%
2	NEC	11%
3	Northern Telecom	9%
4	AT&T	9%
5	Alcatel	7%
6	Fujitsu	7%
7	Ericsson	6%
8	Bosch	5%
9	Mitel	4%
10	Toshiba	3%
	Other	22%

[a]Canada and the United States bring the total for North America (except Mexico) to $4.3b.
[b]Siemens figures include all COS sales of GPT.
[c]World share figures for AT&T in 1989 reflect joint venture with Philips but do not reflect any results from the latest deal in Italy.

TABLE 4-2
Financial Position of Leading Telecommunication-Equipment Suppliers, 1989

(All figures in $ billions)	AT&T	Alcatel	Siemens	Northern Telecom	NEC	Ericsson	Bosch	Fujitsu	Toshiba
Revenue	36.1	14.7	34.0	6.1	20.7	6.4	17.0	15.4	25.6
Assets	37.7	13.2	35.8	6.4	22.2	6.7	12.3	17.9	31.2
Operating Income	4.3	1.3	0.6	0.5	1.2	0.7	1.2	1.2	1.3
Net Income	2.7	0.6	0.9	0.4	0.5	0.3	0.3	0.5	0.8
R&D Expenditure	2.7	1.0	3.8	0.7	3.3	0.7	1.0	1.8	1.6
Operating Return on Sales	11.8%	8.6%	1.7%	8.6%	5.9%	11.5%	7.1%	7.8%	4.9%
Net Return on Sales	7.5%	3.7%	2.6%	6.2%	2.5%	4.7%	2.0%	2.9%	3.1%
Operating Return on Assets	11.4%	9.6%	1.6%	8.3%	5.5%	11.2%	9.8%	7.1%	4.0%
Net Return on Assets	7.2%	4.2%	2.4%	5.9%	2.3%	4.5%	2.8%	2.7%	2.5%
R&D as % of Sales	7.3%	7.0%	11.3%	12.0%	16.1%	10.9%	5.9%	10.3%	6.3%
Telecommunications:									
Service Revenue	19.5	—	—	—	—	—	—	—	—
Equipment Revenue	11.0	9.8	8.1	5.9	5.3	5.1	2.6	2.4	1.0
As % of Total Revenue	30%	67%	24%	97%	25%	79%	15%	15%	4%
Equipment Operating Profit	NA	1.0	NA	0.5	NA	0.7	NA	NA	NA
As % of Equipment Revenue	NA	9.8%	NA	8.9%	NA	14.5%	NA	NA	NA
Est. Equipment R&D	1.2	0.9	0.9	0.7	0.8	0.6	0.2	0.2	0.1
As % of Equipment Revenue	12.2%	9.4%	11.3%	12.4%	16.1%	11.8%	9.4%	10.3%	6.3%
Degree of accuracy:	c	a	b	a	b	a	a	b	d

Notes: NA = Not applicable.
a—Able to estimate from annual reports.
b—Estimated multiplying corporate R&D ratio to equipment sales. Many firms actually cross-subsidized telecommunication equipment from other activities; for instance, Fujitsu and AT&T certainly spend more than the corporate rate.
c—AT&T is estimated by adding $0.5 billion to the figure attained by method b above. A leading competitor to AT&T estimated that from $0.5 to $1.0 billion of equipment R&D was cross-subsidized from service revenues.
d—Toshiba reports revenue of over $12 billion in one sector, Information and Communication Systems and Electronic Devices. However, the major communication product is PBX equipment, with $200 to $300 million in sales. The figure of $1.0 above thus represents a rough cap to Toshiba's telecommunication equipment revenue.
Sources: Annual reports, company interviews and documents, Eurostrategies report to the EC, "Report on the European Telecommunications Industry."

TABLE 4-3
Corporate Revenue Breakdown for Leading Telecommunication-Equipment Suppliers, 1989

(All figures in $ billions)	AT&T	Alcatel	Siemens	Northern Telecom	NEC	Ericsson	Bosch	Fujitsu	Toshiba
Telecommunications:	32.7	12.9	8.1	6.1	5.3	6.0	2.7	2.4	1.0
Service	19.5	—	—	—	—	—	—	—	—
Equipment	11.0	9.8	8.1	5.9	5.3	5.1	2.6	2.4	1.0
Other	2.2	3.1	—	0.2	—	0.9	0.1	—	—
Activities adjacent to public and private switching:	2.2	—	4.0	—	12.7	0.1	—	12.3	11.9
Data processing/office	1.5	—	3.1	—	8.4	(c)	—	9.5	8.1
components/semiconductors	0.7 (a)	—	0.9	(b)	4.3	0.1	—	2.8	3.8
Activities adjacent to terminal equipment (faxes, phones, etc.):	—	0.6	—	—	2.7	—	1.1	0.7	7.3
Consumer Electronics	—	—	—	—	1.6	—	1.1	0.7	7.3
Other	—	0.6	—	—	1.1	—	—	—	—
Nonadjacent activities	1.2	1.2	21.9	—	—	0.3	13.3	—	5.4
Total Revenues	36.1	14.7	34.0	6.1	20.7	6.4	17.1	15.4	25.6

Notes:
a—This is an estimate of AT&T's external component sales only, and thus understates the true level of activity.
b—Northern does have some semiconductor manufacturing activity, but sells few components externally and provides no figures to indicate the size of the activity.
c—Ericsson divested its data-processing group, after sustaining several years of heavy losses, in 1987.

TABLE 4-4
Estimated Equipment Sales by Category, 1989

(All figures in $ billions)	AT&T	Alcatel	Siemens (a)	Northern Telecom	NEC	Ericsson	Bosch	Fujitsu	Toshiba (b)
Public Switching (COS)	3.4	3.6	2.6	3.3	1.6	2.4	0.3	0.8	—
Transmission	2.0–2.3	2.1	1.4	0.6	1.2	0.3	0.7	0.6	—
Cables	1.1–1.4	1.6	0.6	0.5	—	0.2	—	d	—
Total Network Equipment	6.8	7.3	4.6	4.4	2.8	2.8	1.0	1.4	—
Private Switching (PBX, KTS)	1.0	0.8	1.7	1.0	1.2	0.6	0.5	0.8	0.3
Total Switching	4.4	4.4	4.5	4.3	2.8	3.0	0.8	1.6	0.3
Terminals/Other CPE	3.2	1.7	1.8	0.5	1.3	0.1	0.8	0.2	0.7
Mobile/Other	c	c	c	c	c	1.6	0.3	c	c
Total Telecommunication Equipment	11.0	9.8	8.1	5.9	5.3	5.1	2.6	2.4	1.0

Notes:

a—Siemens cable revenues are underreported because Siemens does not consolidate revenues from Siecor, Siemens's 50/50 joint venture with Corning Glass Works.

b—This, again, represents a rough total for Toshiba's activities.

c—For these companies it was not possible to split out mobile activities from the above "terminal/other CPE" category.

d—Any transmission and cabling activity resides in the figure for transmission.

FIGURE 4-11
Geographic Thrusts

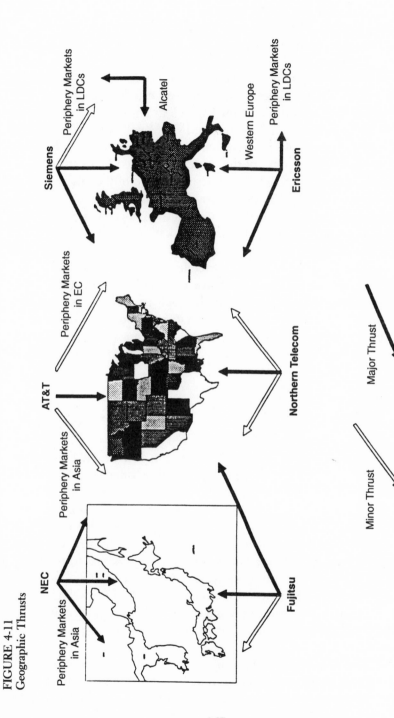

Source: Based on the authors' interpretation of company strategies.

167

Northern Telecom, Ericsson, and Alcatel, largely sell telecommunication equipment, eschewing the broader electronics field. Siemens is somewhere between these two groups. The difference among these strategies could have profound implications for the 1990s. Through 1990, the IM&M strategy was an unhappy marriage—no firm had really integrated computing and telecommunication technology into viable commercial products. While we remain dubious that IM&M will emerge in the next decade, its success would severely reduce Europe's presence in global telecommunications because of the strategies adopted by its firms.

To contrast these approaches, we describe three of the largest players on each continent—AT&T, NEC, and Siemens—and briefly summarize the strategies of the focused firms—Ericsson, Alcatel, and Northern Telecom. Through the early 1990s, the focused firms were generally more profitable and grew faster than the firms investing in multiple technologies and trying to realize synergies across different businesses. Furthermore, companies with extensive international experience, such as Ericsson and Alcatel, have generally had an easier time adjusting their products to foreign markets and operating in foreign environments. While firms such as AT&T and Northern Telecom have been learning quickly, their lack of global experience has had negative consequences on their businesses.

AT&T

Between World War II and the early 1980s, AT&T possessed great operational strength and effectiveness derived from its sweeping horizontal and vertical integration. Before divestiture in 1984, AT&T was capable of making all its own equipment as well as offering many of the most advanced telecommunication services. Even after divestiture, AT&T remained the world's largest telecommunication firm, with $33 billion in revenue in 1984. Although divestiture stripped AT&T of its local operating companies, it left the company with the Bell Laboratories, the entire range of electronics businesses, domestic and international long distance, and value-added services. AT&T's scale and scope made it unique among the world's telecommunication firms. Moreover, AT&T was perhaps the strongest brand name in the global telecommunication business, with a reputation for reliability and technological sophistication.

AT&T's greatest weakness coming into the 1980s was that it had been a regulated monopoly that excelled in technology, but not marketing; in addition, it had always dominated its domestic market, but had little international experience. After being forced by foreign authorities and the U.S. Justice Department to divest many of its early international subsidiaries, including NEC, Bell Canada, and ITT, AT&T shied away from international sales after World War II. These two legacies conditioned AT&T's strategy for the latter half of the 1980s. To become a more aggressive, marketing-oriented competitor at home, AT&T management eventually took some drastic steps to make its organization more cost-effective and responsive to the market. In 1988–1989, CEO Robert Allen decentralized responsibility, requiring each division to have its own bottom line and all staff organizations to contract with operating divisions for services. This policy forced operating managers to cut unnecessary overhead and learn to focus their organizations and strategies. But it denied AT&T a great potential asset: economies of scope, that is, sharing marketing and development costs across related product lines (such as COSs and PBXs, produced by separate divisions) and exploiting the common customer base that was serviced by the long-distance and value-added telecommunication service organization and equipment groups. AT&T not only marketed products in isolation of one another, but also developed competing products (centrex for local operating companies and PBXs for end-users) and competing customer-service organizations. Therefore AT&T did not have an organization designed for its strategy of information movement and management. Nor was it well positioned for international expansion. AT&T's products were developed for the U.S. market exclusively: while the firm's flagship COS, the 5ESS, may have been the world's most sophisticated, reliable product, it was also one of the most expensive to customize for a foreign market. The legacy of regulation, combined with the fragmentation of the domestic businesses, helped undermine AT&T's global performance.

At home, regional Bell companies—eager to diversify suppliers after divestiture—sought equipment from AT&T's competitors. AT&T was obliged to cut prices sharply to maintain domestic share and it bought GTE's central-office switch business to preempt foreign competitors from gaining a sizable foothold in the United States. This stiffer competition, coupled with declining loyalty in the customer base, put pressure on AT&T: price per line in COSs, for instance, dropped to between $80 and $300. According to executives at NEC and Siemens, prices per line in Germany and Japan in 1989 were 100% higher, though the differences narrowed somewhat in the early 1990s.[57] The competitive attack damaged AT&T's margins and research efforts at home. Aggravated by an expensive attempt to build up a computer business, AT&T's nonservice margins declined steeply in the later 1980s. AT&T also redirected its research at Bell Laboratories into more applied short-term projects. If extrapolated into the future, these trends were even more ominous: if foreign competitors continued to gain ground in the U.S. market, AT&T could lose significant scale in the 1990s.

At the same time AT&T was being attacked at home, it pursued a strategy of aggressive expansion into Europe and Japan to further its goal of generating 25% of its revenues from non-U.S. sales. Recognizing its lack of international experience, AT&T launched a patchwork of strategic alliances: Philips would help AT&T break into Europe's COS market; Olivetti would supply AT&T with personal computers; a joint venture with Spain's PTT, Telefonica, would make integrated circuits; Italy's SGS would distribute AT&T chips; Denmark's NKT would manufacture optical fiber under license from AT&T; throughout Asia, AT&T signed distribution and joint-venture manufacturing agreements, including joint operations with Lucky Goldstar in Korea for COSs and fiber cable, a COS alliance in Taiwan, and two agreements in Japan—a joint venture with Ricoh to manufacture keysets and a distribution arrangement with Toshiba to sell PBXs.

AT&T's initial global strategy could best be described as sell-all-product categories in all major regions of the world, relying on a combination of local assembly, direct sales, indirect sales through distributors and local partnerships to market the products. As a retired AT&T executive in Tokyo recalled, "AT&T had been a monopoly, and we believed that everyone in the world must want AT&T's products."[58]

Launched in 1983, the strategy suffered a myriad of setbacks. In Japan, NTT rejected the AT&T switch in favor of Northern Telecom's, and Toshiba decided to develop and market its own PBX in competition with AT&T; in Belgium, AT&T lost a $500 million contract to Siemens and Alcatel; in France, AT&T lost a bid for a small manufacturer of central-office switches when the French government sold it to Ericsson; in England, Siemens won its bid for GPT, locking AT&T out of the British switch market; in Italy, AT&T sold off its stake in Olivetti; and the joint venture with Philips, which failed to produce the expected synergies, was bought out by AT&T in 1990.

In virtually every case, AT&T insiders as well as local Japanese and Europeans traced the failures to AT&T's poor execution and lack of international experience. In the postmortem of the failed NTT bid, for instance, many AT&T executives thought that AT&T had priced its product very competitively, but NTT rejected the 5ESS because AT&T

would not furnish the key software customers would need for servicing the switch, which AT&T provides to Bell operating companies. Similarly, AT&T's failure in France was widely attributed to poor understanding of the foreign politics underlying the decision; and its failure with joint-venture and alliance partners was the product of hasty decisions in the mad rush to expand overseas.

The historic separation of operating units by regulation did not help. Country managers had responsibility but no real power. Thus American production executives made decisions along functional lines, depriving AT&T of the benefits of economies of scope and strong input from country managers.

By the late 1980s, however, AT&T executives were more fully aware of these shortcomings. While the failures of a few years earlier had shut AT&T out of certain major switching markets for years to come, the international strategy became more focused, both geographically and by product. By 1988 AT&T was generating $980 million in revenue from overseas sales, representing 20% annual growth; $811 million came from Network Systems. Product sales in Europe were about half ($530 million) of the total. The joint venture with Philips ultimately became profitable, generating about $300 million in annual sales to Holland alone. Rather than attack the German, French, or Japanese markets head-on in switching, AT&T pushed transmission equipment (which was easier to sell and cost less to customize) in the big markets and switches in the peripheral markets of Europe and Asia. The main product thrust worldwide was central-office equipment, while customer-premise equipment, like PBXs, got little support.

AT&T's most notable success under this revised strategy was a victory over Siemens, Alcatel, and Ericsson in 1989 to win a contract with Italtel, Italy's state-owned telecommunications company. The Italtel deal demonstrated learning and more maturity on the part of AT&T. AT&T also won significant nonswitching contracts in Japan in the late 1980s, including a $154 million optical transmission system. By 1990 AT&T's international equipment sales exceeded $1.5 billion, a sixfold increase in only four years.

AT&T remained the most feared competitor in the business. By virtue of its scale and scope, every leading Japanese and European executive we interviewed believed that AT&T had the financial and technological wherewithal to be *the* global telecommunication leader. These same executives also believed, however, that AT&T's lack of strategic focus across business units and its slow learning about international competition threatened to disable its advantages. Yet ultimately, whether America remains a large net importer of telecommunication equipment or becomes a significant base for exports will increasingly depend on AT&T's ability to hold off foreign incursions into its home market while solving its international corporate problems.

NEC

If AT&T's legacy of regulation at home partially undermined the firm's ability to gain advantage through economies of scope, NEC's strategy was to maximize advantage by leveraging technology across its three businesses—computers, semiconductors, and telecommunications—and within business units—especially between PBXs and COSs. NEC expressed this strategy in a slogan: C&C—computers and communications. In the belief that computers and communications would merge, NEC also wanted to become the leader in semiconductors, a critical upstream business. By the late 1980s it had realized this goal and vied with Fujitsu as the top producer of computers and telecommunication equipment in Japan.

NEC's home base in Japan was both an asset and a liability for competing internationally. Historically, NTT, NEC's largest telecommunication customer, lagged in a variety of basic services that were offered in the United States and some countries of Europe.[59] NEC, however, had a strategy that consciously sought to counteract its country-based disadvantages. NEC management recognized in the late 1970s that the digital switch was a disjuncture in technology that provided a great opportunity to break into international markets. Before NTT started to develop digital switches for the local market, NEC launched an independent R&D effort for a digital switch to sell overseas. The result was the NEAX, a low-cost, low-functionality digital switch, which NEC at first marketed to the developing world.

Although its initial U.S. foray in the late 1970s failed owing to quality problems, NEC staked out a strong position in digital switches outside the industrial world. By 1990 NEC had installed switches in fifty-five countries, with dominant shares in New Zealand (100%), Thailand (80%), Malaysia (60%), Hong Kong (50%), Argentina (50%), China (35%), Brazil (32%), Venezuela (32%), and Chile (30%). These products were exported from Japan except in Brazil and Malaysia, where local assembly was required. To minimize the added costs of building two incompatible switches, the NEAX and the D60\D70 were produced in the same facility along with PBXs, which allowed for shared overhead along with shared component and board manufacturing and shared test equipment. Nonetheless, NEC probably lost money on its overseas switch business.

By the latter half of the 1980s, lured by the size and relative openness of the U.S. market, as well as a sophisticated customer base, NEC again retargeted its strategy. NEC managers believed that only four firms would be able to compete in the switching business in the year 2000. Unless the company was successful in the United States, it would not survive. On the other hand, NEC managers did not believe that Europe would be a market open enough to justify heavy investment at the end of the 1980s.

Like AT&T, however, NEC could not make much headway in a large industrial country outside its home base. After spending some 100 billion yen (roughly $770 million) to enter the American market, including the construction of an assembly facility in Texas, NEC found its share of the COS market mired at less than 1% for several years. With little prospect of ever showing a profit, NEC announced in 1992 that it would ultimately withdraw from the U.S. market.

NEC's performance in PBXs outside Japan was similarly anemic. While holding about one third of the Japanese PBX market, NEC had gained almost 10% of the American market but only 0.3% in Europe by the mid-1980s. Exports to the United States faltered somewhat in the late part of the decade because of poor distribution and increased competition.

NEC's approach, which closely mirrored Fujitsu's, was a three-pronged strategy of aggressive exports to the developing world, local manufacturing in the United States, and retaining a dominant position in Japan with an incompatible product. NEC's strategy was a "typical Japanese" focus on low cost with a willingness to underwrite losses in telecommunication equipment for years in order to build a market position. But NEC has been much less successful in high-value telecommunication equipment outside Japan than in other electronics businesses. This was partly due to its locational disadvantages, like Japan's weak telecommunication market, and partly to NEC's technological shortcomings. NEC could not translate C&C into competitive advantage in telecommunication equipment. Still, its secure position at home (granted by regulatory authorities) has given NEC freedom to invest heavily for long periods (fifteen years) without needing or expecting a financial return. Regulation in Japan had provided NEC with cash flow to support overseas expansion while losing money in its U.S. activities.[60]

If NEC is ultimately successful in building a beachhead in the United States, it will be hard to attribute exclusively to NEC's Japanese origins. NEC's success, if it develops, will come from its unique corporate structure, which maximizes integration across technologies. Oki and Hitachi, confronting similar national constraints and advantages, are even less likely to succeed in international markets. Ultimately, if NEC is one of the survivors, the credit will go to NTT's indirect subsidies and protection combined with the firm's ability to execute C&C.

Siemens

If AT&T followed a differentiation strategy bolstered by international investments and alliances, and NEC followed a low-cost strategy augmented by local manufacturing and assembly in the United States, Siemens's strategy was to alter the structure of the COS and PBX industries in Europe and the United States. To Siemens, even more than to NEC and AT&T, the global telecommunication industry was an oligopolistic chess game; the key was to put the company's pieces in the right position to build a stable oligopoly.

Siemens was not just a diversified telecommunication firm, but a broadly diversified industrial company with revenues of $34 billion in 1989, including, in billions, semiconductors ($0.9), data-processing and office equipment ($3.1), energy and automation ($7.4), electrical and automotive systems ($3.0), power plants ($4.9), lamps ($1.3), and telecommunication equipment ($8.1). Siemens exported from Germany nearly 25% of its total revenue, and nearly 40% of its customer-premise equipment business and 24% of its COS business.

Siemens's competitive advantages in telecommunications abroad came from several sources:

1. Siemens's corporate scope gave it significant monetary resources, including cash and liquid securities of $11 billion and $3.7 billion in corporate R&D in 1989. If it was strategically important, Siemens could cross-subsidize any business.
2. Like NEC, it had a sanctuary at home for telecommunication equipment. Its close working relationship with the Deutsche Bundespost, combined with weak domestic competition for telecommunication

equipment, allowed Siemens to generate the funds it needed for international expansion.[61] The home base was also important because the Deutsche Bundespost was on the leading edge of ISDN installations.

3. Siemens had built a strong international position, especially in Western Europe. After it acquired GPT, the company owned a quarter of the Western European COS market. About 70% of Siemens's COS sales were made outside its home country (27% elsewhere in Europe, 34% in developing countries, and 9% in the United States), compared with less than 10% for either AT&T or Northern Telecom and about 25% for NEC and Fujitsu.

4. Siemens had a potential advantage in the way it configured its international network: unlike NEC and AT&T, which largely centralized their R&D function at home, Siemens had extensive R&D facilities outside Germany, especially in the United States. Distributed R&D gave Siemens the opportunity to tap foreign country-based advantages. In PBXs, for instance, Siemens used its U.S. R&D organization to develop its digital switch at a time when the United States was leading in digital technology.[62]

Siemens's organization, like AT&T's, separated PBXs from COSs. Each division had its own bottom line and strategy; little effort was made to maximize scope economies across these products. Siemens did not have high profit expectations for its international telecommunication business: senior executives did not expect the PBX and COS divisions to generate profits in the United States until the mid-1990s.[63] Although analysts historically considered Siemens a conservative, sleepy company "about as exciting as yesterday's sauerkraut," the company had displayed a surprising aggressiveness in the late 1980s.[64] From 1985 to 1990, Siemens spent $3.5 billion on acquisitions and joint ventures, the most significant being the joint purchase of GPT (with GEC) in the United Kingdom (which also gave Siemens control over Stromberg-Carlson's share in the United States), Rolm in the United States, and Nixdorf in Germany.[65] Siemens was also an aggressive bidder for CGCT in France and the joint venture with Italtel (won by AT&T).[66]

While NEC was largely seeking to build its own international network, and AT&T relied heavily on partners to penetrate foreign markets, Siemens had an explicit strategy to acquire market share in Europe and the United States. Like NEC and AT&T, the Siemens geographic focus was on its home market, defined as Europe, and the American market; Japan was virtually written off. Siemens's acquisition strategy was also the most significant move by any global competitor to force the anticipated consolidation. By acquiring the manufacturing assets of Rolm for approximately $1 billion, for instance, Siemens achieved what no other major foreign producer could in the United States: a large local distribution network, which made it the second-largest player in the domestic PBX market. Just as Siemens's dominant position in the German market had allowed it to provide "price leadership" in Germany, one might conclude that Siemens hoped its acquisition of Rolm would give it leverage to influence the structure of the U.S. PBX industry.

The 40% acquisition of GPT won for Siemens the dominant position in the U.K. COS market (82%), a dominant position in the U.K. PBX market (78%),[67] and a small share of the U.S. market. The combination of Siemens's meager sales of its own COS (only 1.3% of the market in 1989) and Stromberg's switch made Siemens the third-largest supplier in the United States. By 1990, five of the seven regional Bell operating companies in the United States had ordered Siemens switches.

Germany's success in telecommunications was increasingly being determined by the strategy of its dominant firm. Yet Siemens's ability to execute its chosen strategy was far from certain. Acquisitions had bought Siemens market share, but left the company saddled with at least four incompatible PBXs (its own, Rolm's, Plessey's, and Nixdorf's), and three incompatible COSs (its own, Plessey's, and Stromberg's). The potential diseconomies of scale in R&D were enormous: Siemens had to support the installed bases of seven systems spread over North America and Europe as well as much of the developing world. Should these diseconomies undermine Siemens's cost competitiveness, or impede its ability to be a leader in the next generations of COSs and PBXs, the potential for German dominance could evaporate as quickly as it emerged.[68]

AT&T, NEC, and Siemens were all broadly diversified firms spending vast sums of capital to become bona fide global players. Yet none of the three was considered highly profitable outside its home markets. The less diversified, less vertically integrated players, on the other hand, not only held dominant positions in their home markets, but were also making money in NIE and third-world markets outside their national base: Northern Telecom, Alcatel, and Ericsson thrived as focused players. To date, they have not been disadvantaged by their lack of broad scope, but the evidence may suggest that their exploitation of scope *within* telecommunications—their internal coordination of R&D and marketing—may even make them the most formidable competitors of the 1990s.

Northern Telecom

A 53%-owned subsidiary of Bell Canada Enterprises (Canada's national telephone company), Northern Telecom was one of the top three or four manufacturers of COSs and PBXs in the world. The company became a player of global significance by being a first mover in digital switches. After installing its first DMS-10 in Florida in 1977, the Bell System (i.e., at the time, AT&T), ensured Northern Telcom's success with a $100 million order in 1979. Outperforming NEC, Northern Telecom exploded to capture almost the entire digital COS market in the United States in 1984. In fact, according to one analyst, in 1989 Northern Telecom had the largest world market share in COSs (18.8%) and PBXs (10.6%).[69]

What made Northern Telecom distinctive was its dedication to telecommunication equipment (versus computers, semiconductors, and other related electronics produced by AT&T, Siemens, NEC, and others) and the close technical and marketing relationship between its telecommunication technologies: while the architectures were different, collaboration among engineers in both divisions allowed for some sharing of technology as well as the development of common interface standards. Moreover, while AT&T potentially had several salespeople from various divisions calling on customers, Northern Telecom avoided the conflict by using single marketing account managers for all its products.[70] Northern Telecom's weakness, like AT&T's, is its North American orientation; despite proclaiming a goal of 20% for non-American sales, Northern Telecom sales outside the United States and Canada remained less than 10% of revenues in 1989.[71]

Alcatel

Out of the formation of Alcatel NV in December 1986 emerged the second-largest telecommunication equipment company, with annual sales estimated near $11 billion in 1991. It capped a series of consolidations that began in France in 1976 when CIT, owned by Compagnie Générale d'Electricité (CGE), purchased Telic, and continued with the purchase of Thomson in 1984. Then CGE's telecommunication activities merged with those of ITT (approximately $6 billion in sales in 1986). In many ways, Alcatel and ITT were a good fit. CGE, though it dominated France, had minuscule foreign sales and lacked the size to compete in an industry dominated by large corporations like AT&T and NEC.

ITT, though large, had run into financial difficulties with the development of its digital COS, the System 12. Under pressure at home from a hostile takeover attempt and reeling from System 12 problems, ITT needed a partner for its communication business. The merger combined ITT's strong positions in Germany, Italy, Spain, Belgium, and Norway with CGE's position as France's national champion and created the leading European competitor.[72]

Alcatel, like Northern Telecom, concentrated on telecommunication equipment. The company was also geographically focused. Three quarters of its sales are to Europe (18% in France), with the remaining quarter to less-developed nations. Alcatel forswore the North American switch market, preferring not to "lose lots of money there trying to break in."[73] Partly by avoiding the U.S. market, Alcatel was one of the more profitable telecommunication companies (see Table 4-2), and its financial performance had improved considerably over its first three years. The strongest contributor to this improvement was the Public Network Systems group, where COS activities resided. However, like Northern Telecom, Alcatel stressed cooperation among its various telecommunication groups.

Ericsson

Swedish-based Ericsson is the sixth-largest telecommunication equipment supplier. Among the industry leaders, it had the smallest home-market base, with only $500 million in revenue in Sweden. Always an aggressor in foreign markets, in 1991 Ericsson derived 49% of its revenue from other European countries and 37% from areas outside Europe, including 10% from North America. Its AXE switch was designed with export markets in mind; the architecture allowed it to be easily adapted to particular markets. In trying to penetrate the U.S. COS market with AXE, the company set up development facilities in Texas in 1984. By 1989, three Bell companies had approved Ericsson's switch, and two, U.S. West and Southwestern Bell, had placed substantial orders. Ericsson also produced and sold to outside customers just under $100 million of microelectronic components annually and sourced a significant amount of semiconductor components from third parties. Like Alcatel and Northern Telecom, Ericsson concentrated on telecommunication equipment.[74] Ericsson's attempt to penetrate the North American COS market did not have an adverse impact on financial performance; the operating margins of the group responsible for central-office activities grew from 11% in 1986 to 20% in 1989, while revenues doubled.

Niche Players

While the broadly integrated firms expanded aggressively but made little money, and the big focused firms generally prospered, the single-business niche players were swallowed by bigger fish. Mitel Corporation is perhaps the best example of the problems of inadequate scale and scope in the world telecommunication-equipment industry. The company, founded in Canada in 1971, became a successful supplier of PBX equipment in North America (85% of revenues in 1980). Sales reached $111 million in 1981, and operating profits totaled $21 million. The company strategy in the 1980s was to supply a worldwide family of PBX products with integrated voice/data capability. By 1984 sales had more than tripled to $343 million, with one-third derived from overseas markets, primarily Europe. In the same year, however, R&D expenses reached $62 million, or 18% of sales, and operating yield dipped into the red for the first time in the decade.[75] As competition heightened, revenue growth slowed and losses mounted, forcing Mitel to seek a partner with financial clout. British Telecom ultimately purchased 51% of Mitel in 1986 for $322 million. Through 1990 Mitel continued to struggle, finally achieving a roughly break-even performance on the strength of an R&D subsidy from British Telecom.

Rolm, an American PBX manufacturer, encountered many of the same difficulties. It was perhaps the most successful PBX firm in the 1970s, but its management decided in 1982 that the R&D required to compete against AT&T and Northern Telecom exceeded its own resources. IBM, seeking an entrée into telecommunications, eagerly took a 15% stake for $229 million. The logic was simple: PBXs would evolve to handle computer data in addition to phone traffic, and IBM wanted to position itself for the melding of computers and communications. A more down-to-earth synergy existed, in theory, at the distribution level. IBM could sell Rolm's products through its own sales force to its installed customers, many of whom owned AT&T equipment. IBM also hoped that it could sell Rolm equipment to its overseas customers. Two years later, IBM bought the rest of the company for an additional $1.3 billion.

By 1988, however, it was apparent to IBM that the theoretical synergies between PBXs and computing were not on the horizon. Despite a rationalization of the Rolm sales force, the IBM/Rolm combination could not counter the fierce competition, price erosion, poor market growth, and large well-financed competitors that were more closely focused on a broad range of telecommunication equipment. In late 1988 IBM retreated from telecommunications by selling most of Rolm's assets to Siemens.

The only big niche players that survived the 1980s were part of larger enterprises committed to the telecommunication marketplace, like Toshiba and Bosch. Bosch's approach may indicate which niche players can survive in the 1990s. This diversified supplier of automotive and radio equipment had roughly $2.6 billion in telecommunication revenue in 1989: approximately $300 million in COSs, $500 million in PBXs, and $800 million in other customer-premise equipment, as well as $1 billion in transmission equipment, including a rapidly growing mobile communication segment. With 92% of its sales located in Europe, and a very small position in COS equipment, the company was committed to a European focus. While restricting itself to Germany was insufficient (Bosch purchased Jeaumont Schneider, a leading French PBX supplier with $100 million in revenue), management argued that Bosch's combined $1.3 billion in customer-premise-equipment revenue gave the company sufficient size to support ongoing R&D. Management also noted that money spent in the United States would be better invested in Europe to advance its own technology.[76] Finally, the company decided to expand in the telecommunication field by pushing hard in mobile communications. The combination of Bosch's commitment to telecommunications and its geographic focus may enable it to sustain itself in the 1990s.

CONCLUSIONS

What can we learn about world trade from the experience of the global telecommunication-equipment business? Are there also lessons for government policy and managers from this story?

First, the evolution of trade in telecommunications highlights important differences from the standard trade theories that focus on country attributes as the primary driver of international trade patterns. In a Ricardian or Heckscher-Ohlin world—where governments and firms have no material role—one might expect a pattern of trade and competition quite different from the story we have outlined. If country characteristics, like factor endowments, had determined international trade in telecommunications, the United States would probably be the leading COS exporter and Japan perhaps the winner in PBXs. Moreover, as countries deregulated, international trade should have expanded. If one took a broader view of country factors, incorporating product life-cycle characteristics (such as scale economies and the role of domestic demand) or variables of domestic rivalry and related and supplier industries, one would still declare the U.S. champion.

Yet in our study country factors were not decisive in determining trade patterns in the high end of telecommunication equipment. Trade among developed and developing countries emerged as one might expect, and industrial nations exported high-value-added goods, like COSs, to the developing nations where technological and comparative price advantage mattered. However, which firms (or countries) exported to the developing world and which firms (or countries) thrived *within* the industrial world is less easily explained. Five to ten years after trade opened up in the large industrial markets, trade in the high-value-added segment scarcely existed.

Government regulation was the primary driver of the direction of trade and investment. In a world where governments closely regulate domestic sales and production, decisions by one government produced unforeseen incentives for firms in other countries. The early opening of the telecommunication market in the United States—for terminal equipment in 1968 and for network equipment in 1984—gave all major competitors in the world of the necessary scale an incentive to target this market. NEC, Siemens, Ericsson, and Northern Telecom all focused on the United States; the only ones that did not, Alcatel and Bosch, believed they had adequate scale without a U.S. presence.[77] Had Europe or Japan (truly) opened first, the flow of trade and investment would have been much different.

The sequence and structure of deregulation had further consequences for the players' strategies and their long-run ability to compete. While Japan and then Europe officially opened their markets in the late 1980s, vestiges of regulation continued to influence the direction of trade and investment. This barrier led North American firms (AT&T and Northern Telecom) to focus on the extremities of Europe and Asia, but not France, Germany, or Japan, European firms to focus on Europe or the United States, but not Japan, and Japanese firms to focus on Asia and the United States, but not Europe. Even so, equipment exports (especially CO switches) from the home base to customers in these developed markets remained all but impossible. Despite better economies of direct exports, firms were forced to produce locally to satisfy their customers' political demands. Direct investment superseded trade, despite global-scale economies.

Finally, performance results during this transition have not simply followed either political or economic advantage. Three firms with broadly integrated product strategies, protected home markets, and U.S. entry investments—NEC, Fujitsu, and Siemens—fared rather poorly. Conversely, firms with less-integrated product strategies, protected home markets, and no U.S. entry investments—Alcatel and, we suspect, Bosch—performed well (measured by recent operating returns on sales and assets in Table 4-2). The two most tightly integrated companies with protected but small home markets and U.S. entry investments— Northern Telecom and Ericsson—also have good results to date. And AT&T, the most broadly integrated firm with the least protected home base, lost money (estimated at $100 million per year) in customer-premise equipment and made some profit in its central-office business. Even though AT&T management reported that its central-office business was self-funding, the results for the equipment businesses paled in comparison with its much larger service businesses.

For the future, the new economics of the industry have created the need for scale and scope economies that are at least regional and more likely global. It appears that worldwide demand for network switches and advanced transmission equipment can no longer support more than six or seven integrated producers. As we've seen, consolidation of the nonintegrated PBX suppliers and the weaker CO switch manufacturers has already begun, and may have a bit further to go. Who will survive this shakeout and how global production and trade will be organized come down to two variables: the ongoing government policy regimes and the administrative success of firms in executing their strategies.

Corporate positioning and execution will be critical because the late 1980s and early 1990s have created a window of contestability, through which global competitors briefly possess an opening to their competitors' marketplaces. While the analogy is highly imperfect, we believe that global telecommunication equipment may be somewhat like the U.S. airline industry after deregulation. When the Civil Aeronautics Board began deregulating U.S. airlines in the late 1970s, the market suddenly came up for grabs. Air carriers rushed to buy other airlines and to reposition their fleets and assets. That repositioning was based on different views of how the postregulatory world would look. By the end of the decade (grossly oversimplifying the analysis), firms that invested heavily in nationwide hub-and-spoke systems won; those who did not lost. By 1990 the barriers to entry by domestic competitors were once again very high, and despite the decline of regulation, the market was no longer contestable.

The decline of global regulation in telecommunications has striking parallels. Deregulation began, a flurry of expansion, repositioning, and mergers and acquisitions has occurred, and firms are pursuing different strategies based on different views of the world. Of course, government deregulation in telecommunications will be less sweeping than it was in airlines, and competitive entry will be less simple. But success in the next decade is likely to be determined by how well firms articulate and execute a strategy that takes advantage of the small window of opportunity created by deregulation.

Yet a priori, it is difficult to predict whether NEC's version of C&C or AT&T's version, IM&M, will win—after all, both have similar financial and technical resources, with vertically integrated businesses that extend from semiconductors to computing. While there are obviously big differences between these firms, we believe that their ability to execute their chosen strategies will be fundamental to success. In a world where oligopolists have similar strategies, effective implementation is likely to differentiate performance outcomes. If AT&T cannot better coordinate its enormous resources, financial and technological, then other competitors, like NEC and Alcatel, will reduce America's presence in the telecommunication equipment business. If Siemens cannot better leverage its broad vertical integration into technological or marketing advantages, it, too, faces the prospect of financial or share decline. Similarly, the smaller, more focused firms like Northern Telecom and Ericsson must make immense continuing investments to survive in a business in which technical integration and world presence are essential.

What are the implications of this study for public policy? The primary lessons are related to the style and sequence of regulation and deregulation. In a globally interconnected world, regulatory policy cannot be made in isolation. Policies that might be optimal in an autarkic country, like fostering competition through asymmetrical deregulation, can be destructive in a world of strategic players. To the extent that economies of scale and scope exist, deregulation in one country can be undermined by foreign governments through commission (subsidies or tariffs) or omission (refusing to deregulate).

If foreign governments accommodate higher prices at home, in effect subsidizing the expansion of their "national champions" abroad, they give them enormous strategic advantages. The decision by the United States to deregulate telecommunications, without considering its impact on the international competitiveness of its domestic firms, had precisely this effect: although competition has forced AT&T to cut costs and become more efficient, the transition costs in lost market share and frustrated investments abroad have been very high. AT&T's margins have suffered while the decisions by the Japanese, French, and German governments to delay intense competition at home have subsidized AT&T's competitors. Perhaps government policies in an interdependent world should try to coordinate regulatory and trade moves rather than make those moves unilaterally. If regulatory policies are taken unilaterally, then trade policy should be used to ensure that a level playing field results.

In addition to the sequencing of government policy, the style or substance of regulation should be coordinated. Deregulation has meant different things in different countries: Japan has "privatized" NTT, but NTT was hardly a profit maximizer; Germany has proclaimed the German telecommunication market open, but Deutsche Bundespost remains a monopsonist for central-office equipment; and when the United States divested AT&T of its regional operating companies, it did not allow for free competition, but rather regulated competition that constrained both the Bell operating companies and AT&T from engaging in specified activities. Since the consequences of these differences can be significant, governments improve their policymaking by learning from others' mistakes.[78] The Europeans and the Japanese seem to understand this lesson better than the Americans.

The lessons for firms and firm strategies are equally important. First, when technological disjunctures occur, as they did when switching went from analog to digital (or will if digital gives way to optical), the opportunity for first-mover advantages are so great that they can overwhelm all other competitive forces. Northern Telecom and Alcatel were players of global significance in 1990 only because they moved faster and farther to capitalize on this technology than other firms: had Alcatel and Northern Telecom failed to capitalize on these advantages, France and Canada would probably be comparable to Italy and Australia as forces in the world switch market. Second, firms that try to capitalize on scale and scope economies (defined broadly) beyond the boundaries of their industries have an administrative task so difficult as to undermine their effectiveness. Every firm that has tried to integrate computers and telecommunications, ranging from IBM to Ericsson, has failed at least in part because of the administrative problems of bringing together such diverse technologies. On the other hand, scope economies in telecommunications have clearly been more manageable and successful. Firms diversified in telecommunications did better than single-business firms. Third, in politically salient industries, like telecommunications, dealing effectively with government relations, both at home and abroad, is a prerequisite for success.

NOTES

1. A PBX is a private business system used to route calls among extensions within a private network and to connect a business's internal lines to the outside world.

2. Our research focused on two of the most important segments of the huge world telecommunication market: central-office switches and private branch exchanges. We interviewed government officials in the United States, Europe, and Japan and the largest firms in these segments from around the world, including NEC, Fujitsu, Oki, Hitachi, and Toshiba in Japan, AT&T, Rolm, and Northern Telecom in North America, and Alcatel, Siemens, Bosch, and Ericsson in Europe. Our sample included firms that were vertically integrated across most telecommunication product lines (e.g., AT&T, Siemens, and NEC) and those whose largest telecommunication business was in PBXs (Rolm, Bosch, and Toshiba).

3. From a report prepared by Eurostrategies for the European Commission, "The European Telecommunications Industry."

4. "Time division multiplexing" refers to a technique for merging multiple circuits on the same channel by locating them in different micro–time slots. "Pulse code modulation" refers to a transmission technique of sampling mere fragments of a signal for purposes of carriage, then reconstructing the whole for terminal use. In combination, these two techniques make possible the carriage of thousands of circuits on a single cable or microwave or satellite channel; see AT&T Bell Laboratories, S. Millman, ed., A *History of Engineering & Science in the Bell System: Communications Sciences (1925–1980)* (Murray Hills, N.J.: Bell Laboratories, 1984), 399–428.

5. A third area of technological innovation was transmission media. Traditionally, telephone signals were transmitted over pairs of copper wire. The most recent technology was fiber optics, which entailed transmission of communication signals in a lightwave, through a medium of glass. Fiber optics, in particular, increased the capacity (more circuits or wider bandwidths) and quality of transmission and offered more immense reductions in costs.

6. ISDN is a network management concept that consists of fully digital switches, digital transmission facilities, a common-channel signaling system,

and service control points where distributed databases provide for protocol conversion, routing, billing, and information access. ISDN, moreover, will provide far greater circuit capacity.

7. Authors' estimates based on a number of sources, including NBI, *World Public Switching Market, 1987*, the Eurostrategies report, company annual reports, and company interviews.

8. J. M. Guite, *Telecommunications Equipment: The United States Market* (New York: Salomon Brothers, February 1987), 14.

9. Peter Huber, *The Geodesic Network* (Report to the Department of Justice) (Washington, D.C.: U.S. Government Printing Office, 1987), 14.2, fn. 7.

10. GPT ultimately brought in Siemens as a partner to solve this problem.

11. Digital switch output is usually measured in local lines' worth of switches shipped, rather than units, since the capacity of a unit can vary from 5,000 to 100,000 lines. This figure of 6.5 million is the output of AT&T's Oklahoma City Works for 1987, estimated by Northern Business Information, in *The Telecom Strategy Letter*, March 1989, 32.

12. The total line figure includes analog and digital lines, but is primarily composed of digital shipments in 1989. The figure was calculated from data provided in Ericsson's 1989 annual report and from data obtained in interviews at Siemens.

13. In several plant visits we had a firsthand look at the potential scope economies. AT&T's Merrimack Works is a good example. At this gigantic facility, AT&T developed a flexible, integrated manufacturing system that allows multiple products in small and customized batches to be manufactured, tested, and shipped at the same time on the same lines. Similarly, at NEC's plant in northern Japan, relays, hybrid semiconductors, and circuit boards were manufactured on one line, but inserted into PBXs, digital switches, and other related electronics products. Information obtained from interviews at AT&T, Merrimack Works, December 1989; interviews at NEC, November 1989.

14. The costs to adapt a COS to a foreign market varies by manufacturer: Northern Telecom and Ericsson's switches, which were designed to be more flexible across markets, could be adapted to some nonlocal markets for as little as $30–$50 million; AT&T's 5ESS, which was not designed for markets outside the United States, could cost more than $200 million to adapt for those same customers.

15. The size and cost of this downstream requirement is difficult to isolate, since it cannot be wholly separated from either research or manufacturing. This evidently was the stumbling block for NEC's first foray into the U.S. central-office market in the early 1980s. In the latter 1980s, NEC decided it needed a fully integrated manufacturing, research, and aftermarket service organization to re-enter the United States.

16. See Dekkers Davidson and Richard Vietor, "Economics and Politics of

Deregulation: The Issue of Telephone Access Charges," *Journal of Policy Analysis and Management* 5, no. 1 (Fall 1985): 10.

17. One former AT&T manager suggested that, in the aggregate, PBX suppliers to the Bell System had not made a profit since the mid-1960s.

18. AT&T's Network Systems, Northern Telecom, and would-be foreign entrants devoted immense programming resources to meeting the Bell operating companies' demands for centrex features. Since AT&T downplayed centrex prior to its divestiture, to avoid competing with its own PBXs, it has subsequently been subject to suspicion by its central-office customers. To minimize this, AT&T has completely isolated its PBX research, manufacturing, and sales organizations from Network Systems, which makes the 5ESS switch. Although the suspicion is slowly dissipating, Northern Telecom, which coordinated its development and production of PBXs and the DMS 100 (its central-office switch), avoided this problem by closing down their direct distribution and allowing Bell companies and third parties to sell their PBXs. See Richard Vietor, "AT&T and the Regional Bell Holding Companies" (Boston: Harvard Business School Case No. N2-388-078, 1988).

19. Dataquest Inc., *PBX*, November 1988, 8.

20. NATA, *Telecommunications Market Review and Forecast* (North American Telecommunications Association, 1990), 109. For even larger needs, the integrated companies can sell to a premise customer a central-office switch that serves as a PBX with as many as 50,000 lines. This sort of switching system is often sold to colleges with multibuilding campuses or state governments with similar geographic dispersion.

21. Interviews at ROLM Systems, August 1989.

22. Northern Telecom emphasized the advantages of design; Bosch indicated it gained benefits from understanding the network; NEC saw advantages in its semiconductor technology; and Toshiba reported that it could sell multiple products with its office-automation strategy. Since so many firms viewed PBXs as a subsidiary business, profitability of PBX sales per se was not necessarily unimportant. The same was true even for firms like AT&T, which viewed PBXs as a physical and service "presence" with business customers; in this role, they may facilitate ancillary sales, computer sales, local-area networks, and, especially, enhanced long-distance service.

23. Bell Canada, which was divested from AT&T under an antitrust consent decree in 1956, is likewise privately owned; Northern Telecom, its exclusive equipment supplier, is a 50% owned subsidiary. Other American telephone companies, including nearly 1,500 independent exchange companies, are also privately owned. GTE, which is one of these, was also vertically integrated.

24. *Carterfone* 13 F.C.C. 2d 606 (1968): *Foreign Attachments Tariff Revisions*, 15 F.C.C. 2d 605 (1989); *Second Computer Inquiry*, 77 F.C.C. 2d 384, 390 (1980).

25. In a 1959 decision, the FCC allocated microwave frequencies to large users. In 1969 it allowed MCI to resell private-line services to third parties.

26. *Above 890 Mc.*, 27 F.C.C. 359 (1959); *Microwave Communications, Inc.*, 18 F.C.C. 2d, 953; *MCI Telecommunications Corp. v. FCC*, 580 F.2d 590 (D.C. Cir.), *cert. denied*, 439 U.S. 980 (1978). By 1990 MCI and Sprint, the two leading long-distance competitors of AT&T, had won about 20% market share, helped by the fact that AT&T bore most of the brunt of cross subsidies to local service; Davidson and Vietor, "Economics and Politics of Deregulation." Both also managed to become full-service vendors, expanding as well into international long-distance services.

27. *U.S. v. AT&T*, C.A. No. 82-0192, "Modification of Final Judgment," August 24, 1982.

28. Richard H. K. Vietor, "AT&T and the Public Good: Regulation and Competition in Telecommunications, 1910–1987," in Steven Bradley and Jerry Hausman, eds., *Future Competition in Telecommunications* (Boston: Harvard Business School Press, 1989), 80–93.

29. FCC, Docket No. 85-229, *Third Computer Inquiry*, "Report and Order," June 16, 1986.

30. FCC, *CC Docket No. 87-313*, "Notice of Proposed Rule Making," August 21, 1987; *Communications Week*, March 20, 1989, 1, 52.

31. Ministry of Posts and Telecommunications, *Telecommunications Market of Japan: OPEN*, Tokyo, 1989, 3.

32. Timothy J. Curran, "Politics and High Technology: The NTT Case," in I. M. Destler and Sato Hideo, eds., *Coping with U.S.-Japanese Economic Conflicts* (Lexington, Mass.: D. C. Heath, 1982), 201. A Japanese telecommunication executive claimed that this quote was taken out of context.

33. A private monopoly, Kokusai Denshin Denwa, provided international service.

34. The data we received from different companies were contradictory, but the four firms had roughly equal shares in the mid-1980s, with Fujitsu and NEC typically vying for the top position. The situation in PBXs was similar: the three largest DenDen suppliers controlled 80% of the market, and Oki another 8%. And like COSs, Japan had no significant foreign presence. Rolm, Northern Telecom, and AT&T each sold a few systems through local distribution partners (e.g., Oki and Toshiba), but never established an ongoing business. This pattern suggests significant external barriers, partly economic and technical, partly political (NTT procurement patterns and certification), and certainly cultural.

35. For more detailed descriptions of Japan's telecommunication policies, see Tsuruhiko Nambu, Kazuyuki Suzuki, and Tetsushi Honda, "Deregulation in Japan," in Robert Crandall and Kenneth Flamm, eds., *Changing the Rules* (Washington, D.C.: Brookings Institution, 1989), 147–173; Youichi Ito, "Telecommunications and Industrial Policies in Japan: Recent Developments," in

Marcellus S. Snow, ed., *Marketplace for Telecommunications* (London: Longmans, 1986), 201–230; Jill Hills, *Deregulating Telecoms* (Westport, Conn.: Quorum Books), Chapter 4.

36. For the most careful and detailed description and analysis of this political process, see Chalmers Johnson, "MITI, MPT, and the Telecom Wars: How Japan Makes Policy for High Technology," in Chalmers Johnson, Laura Tyson, and John Zysman, eds., *Politics and Productivity: The Real Story of Why Japan Works* (Cambridge, Mass.: Ballinger, 1989), 177–240.

37. MPT, *Telecommunications Market of Japan: OPEN*; and Datapro Research Corp., *Japan: The Commercial and Regulatory Environment* (Delran, N.J., April 1988).

38. Harumasa Sato and Rodney Stevenson, "Telecommunications in Japan: After Privatization and Liberalization," *Columbia Journal of World Business*, Spring 1989, 31–41.

39. Ibid., 37.

40. In April 1989 an advisory council to MPT issued its report, finding that NTT was still too big for efficient operations or fair competition. It recommended divestiture in one of three forms: (1) separation into one long-distance company and eleven regional, local-exchange companies; (2) separation into several regional but integrated firms; and (3) separation into one long-distance and one local-exchange company; Telecommunications Council to the Ministry of Posts and Telecommunications, "Future Telecommunications Industry Structure," April 1989, MPT English Language Summary, 1–27.

41. In the Eurostrategies database prepared for the EC, Germany held 7.7% of the world telecommunication-equipment market.

42. Prior to 1987, the EC had adopted several resolutions, including establishment of a joint R&D program called RACE, a framework for standardization of telecommunication technologies, common standards for certain satellite broadcasting, and ISDN; and an important directive on the initial stage of mutual recognition of type approval for telecommunication-terminal equipment: Commission of the European Communities, *Green Paper on the Development of the Common Market for Telecommunications Services and Equipment* (Brussels, June 1987), 5.

43. Ibid., 14–16.

44. European Commission, "Commission Directive on Competition in the Markets in Telecommunications Terminal Equipment" (Brussels, July 4, 1988).

45. European Commission, "Commission Directive of June 28, 1989 on Competition in the Markets for Telecommunications Services" (Brussels, June 1989).

46. European Commission, "Proposal for a Council Directive for the Procurement Procedures of Entities Operating in the Water, Energy, Transport, and Telecommunications Sectors" (Brussels, July 14, 1989).

47. Minitel is a system of "dumb" data terminals, originally distributed free by the DGT, through which customers can access literally hundreds of informa-

tion services, all private ventures, with access to the Minitel network. France's early digitization of its network, and the subsidized distribution of terminals, made this success possible.

48. Eberhard White, *Restructuring the Telecommunications System: Report of the Government Commission for Telecommunications* (Heidelberg, 1987).

49. Deutsche Bundespost, "Recommendations in the Witte Report," adoption schedule, 1989.

50. In 1989, for example, AT&T was unable to sell its top-of-the-line DAC products directly to Deutsche Telekom. Subsequently, Siemens, with whom the government evidently felt more comfortable, approached AT&T with an arrangement to buy the DACs and resell them to Telekom as part of its ongoing network provisioning.

51. GPT was a joint venture combining the telecommunication-equipment businesses of GEC and Plessey, which together dominated the United Kingdom market. Siemens and GEC then jointly acquired Plessey outright, with Siemens's stake set at 40%.

52. Extranational statistical data on trade and market share, as we have painfully discovered, are grossly inadequate for any sort of consistent time-series analysis or product-line disaggregation. Product categories are invariably ill defined, and there is no attempt to assess the division of value-added as between parts, software, and completed units. Even national statistics offer little insight to trade by product line, and estimates of market share vary sharply from one analyst to the next. Where market share data are available, moreover, they are usually reported in terms of "lines" rather than switch units or sales revenues. Thus, we have had to construct the data on which the following analysis is based from various sources, with judgments made for disaggregation and comparison across countries and over time. Notwithstanding these efforts, there remain some significant contradictions.

53. It is possible that some transmission equipment, which AT&T does export, has been erroneously subsumed under "switches."

54. Of course, in the short run, such policies are detrimental to consumer welfare. Because of the externalities in an industry like telecommunications, and because of the possibility of improving the terms of trade in a future global oligopoly, however, the short-run welfare costs could be offset by dynamic long-run benefits.

55. As we will describe, in the U.S. market, Northern Telecom and AT&T are at opposite ends of the spectrum, from focus on equipment only to integrating service and equipment; in Germany, Siemens believes it must be global to compete, Bosch believes it can thrive locally; in Japan, NEC and Fujitsu believe they must be in the U.S. market, Oki and Hitachi have different priorities, and so on.

56. Robert Galvin, speaking at Harvard Business School, Colloquium on Global Trade and Competition, December 3, 1991.

57. Many factors make it difficult to analyze COS line prices. First, there are significant economies in price per line associated with larger switches and, as we have learned, switches can vary from 5,000 to 100,000 lines in size. Second, toll/tandem switches are generally more expensive than local switches. The capability designed into a switch in the form of software features can vary widely (e.g., centrex capability). Finally, contract structure and margins can also vary. All these factors combined make it necessary to discuss prices in terms of wide ranges and difficult to look at price data through time. It is also difficult to make cross-sectional price comparisons among competitors, even within one country market.

58. Interview with retired AT&T executive in Tokyo, November 1989.

59. NTT, for instance, offered no detailed billing information on long distance to customers as late as 1990, and it was slow to introduce digital switching and then ISDN.

60. Some analysts believed that inefficiencies in the market for corporate control in Japan allowed firms like NEC to undertake very long-term investments with highly uncertain payback, which would be hard to justify in the American context.

61. Siemens maintained a 35% share of the PBX market in Germany, which rose to 45% with its purchase of Nixdorf in 1990, and about 45% share of the German COS market. Siemens's share of the EC COS market exceeded 25% after its joint venture with GEC gave it 40% ownership in GPT. Market share numbers in Germany, however, may underestimate Siemens's market power. The other major COS producers for the Bundespost, with the exception of Alcatel, were licensees of Siemens's EWSD design.

62. While this strategy looked optimal, there were trade-offs. Decentralized R&D, for instance, reduces potential economies of scale. Furthermore, Siemens was unable to execute successfully its PBX strategy. Thus, despite its development of a digital PBX in the United States, which it planned to export, it could not successfully introduce its "Saturn" PBX in non-U.S. markets. Similarly, its Hicom ISDN switch, developed in Germany, was not successfully introduced in the United States through 1990.

63. Interviews with Siemens executives, January 1990.

64. *New York Times*, February 6, 1990, D-1.

65. Several companies were interested in bidding for Nixdorf's business in Germany, including AT&T and NT. While its product line was weak, Nixdorf had a strong distribution channel in PBXs and computers. According to one of our interviewees, Nixdorf was "not for sale" except to Siemens, which "was instructed" by the big German banks to acquire the company.

66. Of the companies we studied, Siemens may be the most overtly "political." In the bidding for Italtel, for instance, it was rumored that Siemens sought to have the German government intervene. The press suggested that Germany threatened to veto EC approval of huge subsidies to Italy's ailing steel industry

if Siemens was not chosen. *Business Week*, March 13, 1989, 141. Similar stories are heard about the CGCT bid in France.

67. *The General Electric Company plc, Siemens AG and the Plessey Company plc*, a report on the proposed mergers, presented to Parliament by the Secretary of State for Trade and Industry by Command of Her Majesty (London: Her Majesty's Stationery Office, April 1989).

68. In late 1990 there were some indications that Siemens's inability to support the various systems was taking its toll. In the United States, Siemens was trying to convince Rolm customers to migrate toward Siemens's other switches. According to at least one other competitor, this opened competition for Rolm customers, cutting into Siemens's U.S. share.

69. According to estimates provided by Alcatel, NT was fourth in PBXs and third in COSs; our estimates put NT third in COSs and second in PBXs.

70. The best example of how this works to NT's advantage is the sales of centrexes and PBXs. While one division of AT&T sells centrex to the Bell operating companies, another division of AT&T tries to undercut the Bell companies with a PBX. NT avoids the conflict by allowing the Bell companies to distribute NT PBXs; NT makes no direct sales of PBXs to private customers.

71. Northern Telecom, responding to increased pressure in its home area, made a move to build a strong European beachhead in 1990 by acquiring STC, a British telecommunication-equipment company.

72. The merger also gave CGE ITT's strong position in less-developed nations. Today, CGE owns 61.5% of Alcatel, ITT 37%, and Crédit Lyonnais the remaining 1.5%.

73. Interview with a senior executive at Alcatel, 1990.

74. Ericsson made a large move into data-processing and office equipment in the early 1980s. The company's stated strategy was to position itself for the merger of data processing and communications. However, the data-processing group sustained heavy losses from 1984 to 1986 and was divested. The 1987 annual report called the move "an unnecessary mistake." Ericsson has also aggressively pursued the market for mobile radio communications and is the second-largest mobile supplier in the world behind Motorola.

75. The company, which had distributed its products through third parties, began to find it increasingly difficult to sell its new larger-capacity and more complex products through these channels and was forced to develop some direct-selling capability to support its product strategy.

76. Interviews with Bosch management, September 1990.

77. In 1991 Alcatel began focusing increasingly on the U.S. market; however, its efforts were devoted to transmission equipment rather than switching.

78. The Japanese seem the most conscious of this fact: we heard many times in Japan that they did not want to repeat the experiences of AT&T's divestiture. Japan's approach was to study the U.S. approach assiduously and avoid America's mistakes.

5

AUTOMOBILES: FROM IMPORT SUBSTITUTION TO EXPORT PROMOTION IN BRAZIL AND MEXICO

Helen Shapiro

INTRODUCTION

In the early 1950s, representatives of the Ford Motor Company told Brazilian planners that the idea of building a domestic automobile industry was "utopian" and that engines could not be produced in the tropics. Undaunted, the Brazilian government proceeded with its plans to install integrated automobile manufacturing capacity. In 1956 it banned vehicle imports, presenting foreign automobile companies with an ultimatum: either they abandon the lucrative market or they invest to manufacture vehicles with 90–95% Brazilian-made content (by weight) within five years. Despite its protestations, Ford, accompanied by General Motors (GM), Volkswagen (VW), and other firms that had been assembling imported knocked-down cars and trucks, invested to produce motor vehicles for the Brazilian market. These foreign companies came to dominate Brazilian vehicle production, and by 1975 were churning out almost a million cars and trucks a year. In 1962 Mexico followed Brazil's example and issued its own auto plan, which imposed similar, though somewhat less restrictive, conditions on foreign automobile companies. By the mid-1970s, the U.S. Big Three (Ford, GM, and Chrysler), Volkswagen, Nissan, and several Mexican-owned firms were producing over 300,000 vehicles a year with approximately 60% domestic content (by value).

Both the Brazilian and Mexican auto industries were originally established to serve exclusively the domestic market; in the 1970s, neither

I would like to thank Miguel Lengyel, Phyllis Dininio, Antônio Botelho, and Clemencia Torres for valuable research assistance; David Yoffie, Lou Wells, and other members of the World Trade and Global Competition Interest group at the Harvard Business School, as well as José Ferro and Tom McCraw, for their comments; and the many individuals affiliated with the auto industry for sharing their expertise.

country exported more than 9% of the automobiles produced. By the
end of that decade, however, it became increasingly common to find
Brazilian- or Mexican-made engines under the hoods of cars made in
the United States or Europe. These engine exports were soon followed
by finished automobiles. Over the 1980s, Brazil's exports as a share of
car production grew, albeit erratically, peaking at 41% (279,530) in 1987,
and settling at 18% (119,409) of the 663,383 cars produced in 1990. At
the same time, the country was exporting over $220 million worth of
engines; Ford's "tropical" engine, exported from Brazil to the United
States, attained the company's highest-quality rating. By 1990 Mexico
had become the largest exporter of engines to the United States, exporting
211,640 cars, predominantly to the United States and Canada.

The voluminous literature on the automobile industry has focused on
the implications of globalization for the dominant firms and their home
bases in the United States, Japan, and Europe, which account for the
largest markets and the bulk of international trade and investment. (See
Table 5-1.) This chapter attempts to explain the less-heralded but no less
portentous shift in trade patterns between these countries and Brazil and
Mexico, the two largest motor vehicle producers in Latin America. It
documents the shift in the volume and direction of these trade flows in
the 1970s and 1980s and assesses the relative impact of variables relating
to firm strategy, government policies, and underlying country character-

TABLE 5-1
Motor Vehicle Production in Selected Countries (thousands of units)

	1960	1965	1970	1975	1980	1985	1990
Japan	482	1,876	5,289	6,942	11,043	12,271	13,487
United States	7,905	11,138	8,284	8,987	8,010	11,653	9,778
West Germany	2,055	2,976	3,842	3,186	3,879	4,446	4,977
France	1,369	1,642	2,750	2,861	3,378	3,016	3,769
Italy	645	1,476	1,854	1,459	1,612	1,573	2,121
Spain	58	229	536	814	1,182	1,418	2,053
USSR	524	634	916	1,964	2,199	2,232	NA
Canada	398	847	1,160	1,424	1,374	1,933	1,923
United Kingdom	1,811	2,177	2,098	1,648	1,313	1,314	1,566
Belgium	—	167	272	222	260	266	386
South Korea	—	—	29	36	123	378	1,322
Brazil	133	185	416	930	1,165	967	915
Mexico	50	97	193	361	490	398	821
Sweden	129	206	311	367	315	461	410
Poland	36	60	118	257	431	349	NA
China	23	41	87	140	222	443	NA

Note: NA = not available.
Sources: MVMA—A *World Motor Vehicle Data* and Associacão Nacional dos Fabricantes de Veículos Automotores (ANFAVEA)
data.

istics in determining these patterns. Was government regulation behind the shift to exports? Are these examples of infant industries that "grew up" and became internationally competitive? Did firms increase exports to compensate for weak local demand or as part of their global strategies in response to changes in the industry worldwide?

Understanding the changing trade patterns of these particular national industries is important for a number of reasons. They are two of the largest in the periphery, including most of the industry's major transnational players, several of which have subsidiaries in both countries. Brazil has been home to the world's tenth-largest automotive industry. For General Motors, Ford, Volkswagen, and Fiat, which produce virtually all of Brazil's passenger cars, it has also been home to their largest subsidiaries outside the United States and Europe. Volkswagen established its first offshore facility there in 1954, and Brazil is now the only less-developed country in which Fiat has integrated manufacturing capacity. General Motors, Ford, Chrysler, Volkswagen, and Nissan dominate Mexico's automobile industry, which has recently been the world's fastest growing and is becoming increasingly integrated into firms' North American operations. Today Mexico is Volkswagen's only production site in North America and the home of Chrysler's only foreign subsidiary outside of the United States and Canada. (See Table 5-2.) For Brazil and Mexico, the industries are major sources of jobs and foreign exchange. Automotive exports accounted for a large share of both countries' record-breaking trade surpluses in the 1980s. Understanding the sources of this export boom is an important step toward explaining how these countries effected such dramatic structural transformations of their economies more generally. It also sheds light on the potential role of each national industry within regional integration schemes such as the North American Free Trade Agreement or the Enterprise for the Americas.

These case studies also provide insights into the dynamics of world trade and investment that extend beyond Brazil and Mexico. The automobile industry was one of the first global oligopolies in manufacturing, characterized by scale economies, barriers to entry and exit, and learning curves. Firms' investments are discrete and relatively long term. The industry has been considered "strategic" for both reasons described by David Yoffie in his introduction: it generates high profits and positive spillover effects in other sectors, and its dynamics are characterized by strategic rivalry among a limited number of firms and governments. Brazil and Mexico are not unique; governments have intervened to some extent in virtually all national auto industries.

TABLE 5-2
World Motor Vehicle Production by Selected Firm

	1985	1989
General Motors		
Total Production (units)	9,119,148	7,611,447
By Country (%)		
United States	70	63
Canada	9	10
West Germany	10	13
United Kingdom	2	3
Spain	3	5
Brazil	2	3
Mexico	1	1
Australia	2	1
Ford		
Total Production (units)	5,409,954	6,046,514
By Country (%)		
United States	53	52
Canada	12	10
West Germany	9	10
Belgium	5	6
United Kingdom	8	9
Spain	5	5
Brazil	3	3
Mexico	1	2
Australia	3	2
Argentina	1	0
Volkswagen		
Total Production (units)	2,705,364	2,880,892
By Country (%)		
West Germany	67	68
Argentina	1	0
Brazil	13	11
Mexico	4	4
United States	4	0
Spain	12	16
Nissan		
Total Production (units)	2,829,668	3,003,461
By Country (%)		
Japan	90	81
Mexico	2	4
Australia	2	2
Spain	1	3
United States	5	8
Chrysler		
Total Production (units)	1,936,583	2,208,629
By Country (%)		
United States	76	71
Canada	20	22
Mexico	3	7
Fiat		
Total Production (units)	1,508,968	2,157,827
By Country (%)		
Italy	89	88
Argentina	0	0
Brazil	10	10
France	0	0
West Germany	1	1
United Kingdom	0	1

Source: MVMA—A World Motor Vehicle Data.

The Brazilian and Mexican experiences shed light on what may happen to national industries when the domestic and external conditions under which they were originally established change, and how the legacy of previous investment and government policy might influence firm strategy with respect to new investments and global sourcing patterns. Both the Brazilian and Mexican industries were initially established under import-substitution strategies to serve protected domestic markets and not to export. Foreign investment flowed into domestic production at a time when firms remained multimarket rather than globally integrated operations. The conditions that allowed these countries to attract foreign investment have since changed. With globalization, foreign subsidiaries potentially become part of a global strategy and no longer serve only individual unconnected national markets. The industry's structure and the nature of international competition have been transformed. On the domestic front, market stagnation accompanied the debt crisis in Brazil and Mexico, forcing both debtor nations to become net exporters in the 1980s, and reversing recent historical trends.

Owing to the "stickiness" and long-run nature of investment in the auto industry, investments made in one time period affect firms' decisions about exports in the next. Since firms do not automatically view these investments as sunk costs, their subsequent strategies might be different than they would be in the absence of these prior investment decisions. Would firms have chosen Brazil and Mexico as bases for export in the 1970s and 1980s if they were not already participating in the local market from having invested in the 1950s and 1960s?

A comparison of Brazil and Mexico also illustrates how the legacy of specific government policies might influence the manner and extent to which national industries become integrated into global trade flows. Within similar protectionist frameworks, each country initially adopted different policies with respect to domestic content requirements and regulations on foreign ownership and vertical integration. These policy regimes played a role in shaping the ultimate structure of the domestic industries and in determining the types of products manufactured. Therefore, subsidiaries in each country were in a different position to confront the domestic and external changes discussed above.

The differences in policy regimes and domestic economic conditions also had implications on the means by and extent to which each government could influence firm strategy. Unlike many countries that also have considered the automobile industry strategic enough to warrant protection and promotion, both Brazil and Mexico built their domestic industries based on foreign rather than domestic firms. Their experience provides lessons about the potential constraints imposed on their domestic industries by firms' global operations, particularly with respect to exports, and about the conditions that provide host governments greater leverage on these firms. The chapter briefly covers the experience of South Korea, which built its industry primarily on the basis of domestic firms and which focused on exports at a very early stage. Although, for a variety of reasons, the South Korean strategy was not an option for either Brazil or Mexico in the 1950s and 1960s, a comparison of the two approaches highlights the challenges presented to latecomers to the industry and the trade-offs involved with respect to each.

Finally, the oligopolistic nature of the industry has methodological implications for this study as well. A rigorous test of the various hypotheses for the shift to exports is beyond the scope of this chapter. Nevertheless, an analysis of macro-economic variables and industrywide indicators such as revealed comparative advantage may not be sufficient to explain, and may even obscure, the underlying story behind the nature and direction of Brazilian or Mexican automotive exports. Intrafirm transactions account for a large percentage of global trade. In the Brazilian and Mexican context, the industry involves a handful of firms making decisions in the face of heavy government regulation and their own global options and strategies. The governments have enforced firms' export commitments, regardless of price and exchange-rate fluctuations. Factor costs alone cannot account for the different strategies with respect to export product and destination taken by firms in the same country. Moreover, industry-level data could be misleading when a single firm (Fiat) is responsible for one half of a country's car exports (Brazil) and ships almost half of them to one country (Italy). Under these conditions, exports may reveal less about a country's competitiveness than about firms' export decisions, which are based on their existing production locations and may be difficult to change in the short to medium run. I therefore integrate both macro-economic and industry phenomena with government policy and firm strategy to explain the emergence of automotive exports from Brazil and Mexico.

The chapter begins with a brief overview of the industry's changing global structure from World War II to the present. This is followed by an account of the process by which the Brazilian and Mexican industries were established in the 1950s and 1960s. After a brief comparative summary, I analyze the major trends in the two industries since 1973, with special emphasis on firm strategies. The chapter ends with some concluding remarks and a brief comparison of the Brazilian and Mexican experience with that of South Korea.

COMPETITION AND TRADE IN AUTOMOBILES SINCE WORLD WAR II

From early this century, U.S. companies came to dominate the world auto industry through their mastery of mass-volume-production techniques.[1] In defensive reaction, European governments erected tariff walls around their national vehicle and component industries, and in some cases subsidized domestic firms. In response, Ford and GM, which had been assembling imported vehicle kits in Europe since the 1920s, opened integrated manufacturing facilities in both Germany and the United Kingdom.[2] They were denied access into the French, Italian, and Spanish markets, however. As a result of government policies, as well as variations in income and driving conditions, the European market remained fragmented and divided among relatively small-volume producers.

While government protection helped save national auto companies from extinction, the United States and Canada (where U.S. companies dominated) still accounted for 70% of world auto production and about 60% of the world market on the eve of World War II. After the war, North America's share of production rose to 85%. Over the next two decades, European production would not only match prewar levels but would outstrip that of North America.[3]

In the late 1940s and early 1950s, both U.S. and European automobile companies faced sellers' markets at home as a result of the repressed demand that had accumulated during the war. By the mid-1950s, however, when most of this demand had been satisfied, particularly in the United States, domestic and international competition intensified. Profits on domestic operations fell. Firms in the United States and Europe placed greater emphasis on overseas expansion, either through exports, expanding existing subsidiaries, or creating new ones. In the United States, changing market conditions bankrupted the few independents that had survived the Great Depression, leaving GM, Ford, and Chrysler in control of 95% of the car market by 1955.[4] In Europe, the creation of the European Economic Community (EEC) and the gradual reduction of tariffs on imported vehicles created pressures additional to the slowing of demand growth and increased production capacity; the volume of intraregional trade in motor vehicles nearly quadrupled between 1958

and 1965.[5] Although national markets still remained remarkably segmented, with imports accounting for a small share of total sales, this
period witnessed the first cross penetration of producer-country markets;
before the war, most exports had gone to nonproducing countries.[6] The
protected, relatively faster-growing European market also became more
significant for U.S. firms. Ford and GM had particularly aggressive
expansion plans. European firms were therefore confronting new types
of competition but were also becoming larger and more efficient as a
result of domestic market growth, exports, and the promotion of mergers
and national champions by home governments.

The recovery of the European industry also led to increased competition in the U.S. market. Imports jumped from less than 1% of sales in
1955 to 10% in 1959 as a result of reduced productivity differentials and
European firms' ability to fill the small-car market niche vacated by
the independents. Volkswagen was particularly aggressive in this regard.
Europe's import share would decline when the Big Three introduced
their own compact models in the early 1960s, but would bounce back
to 10% by 1970.[7]

Competition among U.S. and European firms became increasingly
stiff for third-country markets immediately after the war, even while their
domestic markets were booming. European exports began to challenge
the U.S. firms, even in their traditional markets of Latin America. This
in part reflected pressure by the firms' home governments to export as
much as possible despite unmet domestic demand. To ease their increasingly binding foreign exchange constraints, many European countries
provided their recovering auto industries with a variety of financial incentives and with privileged access to imported inputs to promote exports.
The fact that many less-developed countries (LDCs) held reserves of
inconvertible European currencies, the general postwar scarcity of dollars, and the emergence of barter arrangements also helped open the
door to markets previously dominated by U.S. firms. And trade patterns
changed as colonial preferences were eliminated and geographical proximity became less important.[8]

Heightened interest in these markets reflected firms' belief in their
future profitability and attempts to maintain a presence in countries
where domestic manufacture was being considered. In addition to Brazil
and Mexico, many importing countries, including Argentina, India,
Australia, and South Africa, began to restrict auto imports in the 1950s
and 1960s. The intensified competition among firms for foreign markets
and the European challenge to U.S. dominance provided these countries

with relatively more bargaining space in which to force firms to set up integrated manufacturing facilities.

On the eve of the first oil shock in 1973, 39% of the world's automobiles were produced in Europe, as compared with 37% in North America. The European and North American markets were about the same size, but European firms exported a greater share of their production. This was partly because they continued to supply the U.S. market through export as opposed to local manufacture.

While inter- and intra-European trade barriers had begun to fall and trade and investment had increased within Europe and across the Atlantic, national markets and products were still distinct, and national companies still dominated their domestic markets. Firms with production facilities in various countries followed different strategies for these distinct markets. In 1973 imports accounted for 15% of the U.S. market (9% from Europe, 6% from Japan), and Japanese imports accounted for 4% of the market in Europe. Intra-European trade was even more revealing of national market segmentation. While trade among all Western European countries, including those without domestic auto production, came to 26% of European production in 1970, trade among the major auto producing countries came to only 12% of production.[9]

Because of early market segmentation, no one firm dominated product design in Europe as GM had in the United States. European firms differentiated themselves on the basis of product design. Markets remained fragmented because of differences in vehicle taxes (France and Italy differentiated taxes by engine size), population density, and so forth. U.S. firms continued to be protected by two oceans, cheap gas, and highways. No other firms built big cars with tailfins, and no other consumers really wanted them, owing to differences in driving conditions, gas prices, taxes, and incomes.

This international market structure was challenged in the 1970s by rising oil prices and the emergence of powerful new competitors from Japan. While Japan's industry was new to the international scene, it had been an efficient producer of trucks during World War II. Japanese firms had survived the 1930s thanks to protectionist government policies. These measures effectively drove Ford and GM, which had been locally assembling imported knocked-down kits since the 1920s, out of the country. In the 1950s the Ministry of International Trade and Industry (MITI) supported the domestic industry by restricting foreign exchange allocations for vehicle imports, imposing a 40% value-added tax on imported cars, and providing financial subsidies. MITI encouraged Japanese firms to establish short-term agreements with foreign companies so they could assimilate foreign technology.[10]

By the late 1960s Japan's revolution in production technique had produced low-cost–high-quality vehicles suitable for export. While Japanese exports to the United States in the early 1970s had come primarily at the expense of European small cars, that changed as Japanese cars became increasingly competitive and took away market share from U.S. firms. They posed an increasing threat in Europe as well. As a result of the Kennedy Round of General Agreement on Tariffs and Trade (GATT) negotiations, by 1973 the tariff on autos was down to 10.9% in Europe, 3% in the United States, and 6.4% in Japan.

Countries responded to Japan's growing share of world production and trade by imposing caps on Japanese imports. Italy banned Japanese imports outright in the early 1960s, and in 1969 the two countries agreed to allow 1,000 imported cars a year into their respective markets as of 1970; in 1976 the limit was raised to 2,200. In the rest of Europe the rate of growth of Japanese imports was first limited on a country-by-country basis, starting with the United Kingdom and France, then on an EEC-wide basis. The U.S. voluntary restraint agreement went into effect in 1981.

Firms responded in various ways. Many restructured their operations in an attempt to cut costs and downsize their product lines. Some firms focused on automating plants at home, others on relocating production to low-wage, offshore sites. The search for low-cost production sites, combined with the emergence of new product lines, led to a new wave of foreign direct investment in peripheral producing countries such as Spain and South Korea. Spain benefited from its access to the EEC; by 1980 it was producing over a million vehicles a year, 80% of which were exported. This restructuring and globalization process would open new opportunities—and constraints—for Brazil and Mexico as well.

INSTALLATION OF THE BRAZILIAN AND MEXICAN AUTO INDUSTRIES

In the 1950s and 1960s a combination of sector-specific government policies and the dynamics of oligopolistic competition led to the creation of domestic auto production capacity in Brazil and Mexico. Through the installation of domestic productive capacity, both countries hoped to save on the costs associated with imports, which included not only scarce foreign exchange but the rents paid to the importing firms and the positive production and technological externalities associated with the industry. In each case the auto program was part of a general import-substituting industrialization effort in which the industry was to play the role of leading sector by attracting foreign capital and technology and generating linkages to complementary sectors. The government planners also hoped that the transnational firms would transfer technology and skills to the still incipient industrial work force. In effect, they hoped that the auto firms would be forced to *create* the factors that would increase the productivity of their industrial sector as a whole and would attract new investment to the country.[11]

Brazil, 1956–1973

Brazilian planners did not expect firms to invest voluntarily. Even though foreign firms had been assembling completely or semi-knocked-down kits in Brazil since the 1920s, and the Brazilian market was the largest in Latin America, accounting for 25% of the 2.7 million vehicles in circulation in 1955,[12] these firms had resisted Brazilian attempts to increase significantly the domestic content shares of their imported vehicles and move into full-scale manufacturing. The Brazilians concluded that they would do so only if given no alternative but to abandon the market.

A five-year plan was promulgated through executive decree in late 1956 and early 1957. Its basic approach was effectively to insulate the sector by closing the market to finished vehicles and to guarantee it subsidized access to foreign exchange to import necessary components and pay off foreign financing. In return for these foreign exchange and tax subsidies,[13] firms had to meet an exceptionally ambitious domestic content schedule. The requirements increased annually; by July 1960 trucks and utility vehicles were to contain 90% domestic content, jeeps and cars 95%.

Eleven firms ultimately participated in the plan. Three were controlled by Brazilian capital, two were fifty-fifty joint ventures, and six were controlled by, or wholly owned subsidiaries of, foreign firms. Total investment by the terminal sector in imported capital equipment within the five-year program came to $145 million. By 1962, five years after the plan had gone into effect, 191,194 vehicles were rolling off Brazilian assembly lines. By 1961 the share of domestic content in vehicle production had reached 93% of weight and 87% of value.

A disaggregation of the industry's performance reveals that European and U.S. firms initially responded to Brazil's auto program differently. Volkswagen had been assembling vehicles in Brazil since 1954. At the time of the 1956 plan, VW did not have manufacturing facilities anywhere outside of Germany and was financially weak. The company, the market leader at home, was seeking new markets abroad—VW of America, Inc., was founded in 1956 to distribute cars in the United States. The Brazilian subsidiary (in which a Brazilian partner held 20%) submitted plans to produce a minivan and the Beetle. VW do Brasil was the only majority-owned European subsidiary to enter the passenger car market aggressively.[14]

Although U.S. firms had the longest history in Brazil, and had dominated car sales before World War II, the Big Three also opted out of the passenger car market. Chrysler, facing hard times at home, chose to stay out of the market altogether. Despite appeals by the Brazilians, Ford and GM submitted projects to produce trucks but not automobiles; neither felt it necessary to match Volkswagen. Japanese firms also stayed out of Brazil's passenger car market. At the time of Brazil's automotive decrees, Japan was producing fewer than 200,000 automobiles a year and exporting a small number.[15] Toyota submitted a proposal to produce jeeps, which was accepted.

The Brazilian industry entered a period of crisis and consolidation in the early 1960s. Firms had built ahead of demand and the industry was plagued with overcapacity. The market also shrank with the downturn in overall economic activity in 1963 and 1964 and disintegrated when the military implemented an austerity program after the coup of 1964. Smaller, financially weaker firms, which had been able to survive until that point because of protection and market shares rationed through foreign exchange allocations, did not survive these lean years.

By 1968 the original eleven firms had shrunk to eight. Only those controlled by transnational capital remained.[16] It was at this time of consolidation that Ford and General Motors entered the passenger car market through investing in new production facilities and absorbing existing firms. They became the second- and third-largest automobile producers after Volkswagen. They aimed their products at the replacement market for the growing middle class. Production became even more concentrated. In 1960 the four top firms—Willys-Overland, VW, GM, and Ford—produced 78.5% of all vehicles. Three firms—VW, Willys-Overland, and Vemag—produced virtually all passenger cars. By 1968 VW, GM, and Ford controlled 89% of the total vehicle market; VW's share alone was 55%.[17] (See Table 5-3 for production figures.)

TABLE 5-3
Brazilian Motor Vehicle Production and Exports, 1957–1990

Year	Total Vehicle Production (units)	Vehicle Exports (units)	Vehicle Exports as % of Production (%)	Passenger Car Production (units)	Passenger Car Exports (units)	Passenger Car Exports as % of Production (%)
1957	30,542	—	—	1,166	—	—
1958	60,983	—	—	3,831	—	—
1959	96,114	—	—	14,495	—	—
1960	113,041	—	—	42,619	—	—
1961	145,584	380	0.3	60,205	—	—
1962	191,194	170	0.1	83,876	—	—
1963	174,191	—	0.0	94,764	—	—
1964	183,707	57	0.0	104,710	—	—
1965	185,187	129	0.1	113,772	—	—
1966	224,609	210	0.1	128,821	—	—
1967	225,487	35	0.0	139,260	—	—
1968	279,715	9	0.0	165,045	—	—
1969	353,700	25	0.0	244,379	—	—
1970	416,089	409	0.1	306,915	52	0.0
1971	516,964	1,652	0.3	399,863	656	0.2
1972	622,171	13,528	2.2	471,055	6,611	1.4
1973	750,376	24,506	3.3	564,002	13,891	2.5
1974	905,920	64,678	7.1	691,310	47,591	6.9
1975	930,235	73,101	7.9	712,526	52,629	7.4
1976	986,611	80,407	8.1	765,291	62,079	8.1
1977	921,193	70,026	7.6	732,360	56,636	7.7
1978	1,064,014	96,172	9.0	871,170	77,388	8.9
1979	1,127,966	105,648	9.4	912,018	76,486	8.4
1980	1,165,174	157,085	13.5	933,152	115,482	12.4
1981	780,883	212,686	27.2	585,834	157,228	26.8
1982	859,304	173,351	20.2	672,589	120,305	17.9
1983	896,462	168,674	18.8	748,371	132,804	17.7
1984	864,653	196,515	22.7	679,386	151,962	22.4
1985	966,708	207,640	21.5	759,141	160,626	21.2
1986	1,056,332	183,279	17.4	815,152	138,241	17.0
1987	920,071	345,555	37.6	683,380	279,530	40.9
1988	1,056,332	320,476	30.3	782,441	226,360	28.9
1989	1,013,252	253,720	25.0	731,992	164,885	22.5
1990	914,671	187,314	20.5	663,084	120,377	18.2

Source: ANFAVEA data.

The newly structured industry, growing at rates of over 20% a year, led the Brazilian "economic miracle" of 1968–1973. Demand for cars boomed in response to income concentration and new consumer credit instruments; wage compression and the repression of trade unions reduced labor costs. To ensure some price discipline over the increasingly concentrated oligopoly, the military resorted to price controls. A new wave of investment accompanied this growth spurt. The projects approved by the Industrial Development Council from 1967 to 1973 anticipated investments of $1.3 billion, more than half of which was approved in 1973 alone.[18] Exports were virtually nonexistent, amounting to only 2.5% of automobile production in 1973. Firms had invested exclusively to serve the domestic market.

Attracted by Brazil's estimated 1985 market potential of 1.5 million vehicles, Fiat entered the market in 1973 and began production in 1976. While the company had minority positions in foreign joint ventures, Fiat do Brasil was its first wholly owned foreign subsidiary and accounted for its biggest automotive investment outside Italy. Fiat overcame the disadvantages of being a latecomer to the Brazilian market by negotiating an attractive incentive package with the state of Minas Gerais, which had been trying (unsuccessfully) to attract an auto plant since the 1950s. The entire auto complex had been concentrated around the city of São Paulo in São Paulo state. The state government of Minas guaranteed the necessary infrastructure, provided fiscal incentives, and participated in loan offerings to Fiat. The company did receive some incentives from the federal government, but the state subsidies were decisive.

Mexico, 1962–1973

Mexico was motivated by similar foreign exchange and industrialization concerns as Brazil. The two national plans had much in common. Nevertheless, several important differences between the two countries led to some variation in strategy and outcome.

To begin, as the first mover in Latin America, Brazil had established a precedent for the rest of the region. That experiment not only provided valuable data for the Mexican government but influenced firms' strategies in Mexico as well. Second, Mexico's long border with the United States presented the country with different constraints. Unlike Brazil, its import-substitution process took place in the context of macro-economic stability and a fixed and unified exchange-rate regime, which precluded the use of exchange-rate differentials as a means of subsidizing the industry. Third, with a smaller population and per capita income level, Mexico did not possess the market potential of Brazil.

Finally, the starting points of their respective industries were different. On the one hand, unlike Brazil, some Mexican-owned firms had a strong market presence. Fábricas Auto-Mex, for example, had been assembling vehicles under license from Chrysler since 1938. It remained a wholly owned family business until 1959, when Chrysler bought a third of its stock. In 1960 its market share was 25%. On the other hand, the only foreign firms assembling vehicles were from the United States; no European or Japanese firm had yet invested in the market. In general, Mexico took a more nationalistic posture toward foreign capital.

The Mexican automotive decree was issued in 1962. Besides protecting the market from imported vehicles, the government offered such fiscal incentives as exemptions from taxes and import duties on imported equipment and components. Mexico relied more heavily on quantitative restrictions than did Brazil, imposing quotas on imports and production. Automobile manufacturers were exempted from Mexico's standard foreign investment regulations, which restricted foreign firms to minority ownership positions. A requirement of majority domestic ownership was imposed on the supplier industry, however. In addition, firms were restricted to assembling vehicles, machining engines, and manufacturing components that they had produced prior to the decree; further vertical integration was prohibited.

Domestic content requirements were less stringent than those in Brazil. As of September 1964, 60% of a car's value had to be manufactured in Mexico. The power train (the engine and transmission) was to be included in this percentage. By setting domestic content levels at 90–95% of a vehicle's weight, Brazil had ensured that body stamping would be done in the country. In general, the Mexicans were more concerned about relative costs and inflation, and the largest economies of scale are in the stamping process. Also, with so much contact with the United States, Mexican consumers were exposed to the frequent Detroit model changes. A domestic content level of 60% allowed for body stampings to be imported and facilitated frequent model changes. This benefited U.S. firms, which relied more heavily on annual body changes than the European and Japanese firms did at the time.

All together, eleven firms had received permission to produce automobiles by 1964. These included three wholly owned subsidiaries of foreign firms, one joint venture with Mexican majority ownership, and six Mexican firms, one of which was state owned. By 1970 the ownership structure of the industry had changed considerably. The foreign-owned subsidiaries of Ford, GM, and Nissan remained. Of the five privately owned Mexican firms, three had ceased operations, a fourth was bought by Volkswagen in 1964, and the last was divided between American Motors (40% equity) and the Mexican government (60%). The joint venture remained under Mexican control, but Chrysler increased its equity share from 33% to 45% in 1968. As in Brazil, the consolidation and denationalization of the industry resulted from differences in firms' access to financing and technology; in the Mexican case, easier access to imported parts was also a contributing factor.[19] (See Figure 5-1.)

Nevertheless, the Mexican industry had not consolidated to the same extent as the Brazilian manufacturers had by this time. In 1976 the top three firms accounted for 57% of all vehicles produced in Mexico, the top four for 70%. (The corresponding figures in Brazil were 90% and 95%.) The difference was partly the result of the severe recession in Brazil, which exacerbated the cyclic fluctuations in the industry and forced many financially weak firms to shut down or sell out; the Mexican production quotas, which guaranteed firms some market share; and the Mexican government's commitment to prop up domestic firms as counterweights to the foreign subsidiaries.

U.S. companies played an active role in the establishment of the Mexican auto industry. Ford in particular, having been the most intransigent in Brazil, showed an early willingness to begin domestic production in Mexico when it appeared that the government would close the market to imports. In contrast to Brazil, both Ford and GM went into car production in Mexico immediately.

The Mexican motor vehicle industry grew at an average annual rate of 17.6% from 1962 to 1974, almost twice as fast as the manufacturing sector as a whole. In 1973 it exported 9% of the 200,147 cars produced and 7% of total vehicle production. Although these export shares were greater than Brazil's, they were not enough to compensate for the sector's imports, which, due to its relatively low domestic content requirements, increased along with production volumes. A government resolution issued in 1969 tried to address the growing trade deficit by rewarding exporting firms with larger production quotas. While exports showed some growth, reaching 16% of imports by 1975, they came nowhere close to the 50% target set for that date.[20] A 1972 decree reconfirmed the timetable for compensating imports with exports, adding the additional caveat that by 1974, 40% of a firm's exports would have to consist of components provided by Mexican suppliers with 60% Mexican capital. This, too, failed to bring the sector's trade into balance.

Summary

By the mid-1960s both Brazil and Mexico had halted virtually all vehicle imports, and firms that had previously supplied these markets through exports now did so through local production. Their success in attracting foreign direct investment was due in great part to the nature

FIGURE 5-1
Mexican Vehicle Production and Exports, 1970–1989

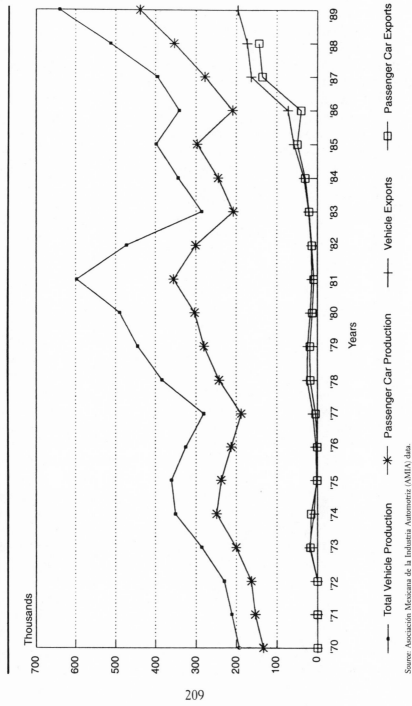

Thousands

Years

Source: Asociación Mexicana de la Industria Automotriz (AMIA) data.

— Total Vehicle Production   —✱— Passenger Car Production   —✛— Vehicle Exports   —☐— Passenger Car Exports

of oligopolistic competition in the industry at the time.[21] Both countries restricted auto imports when competition for foreign markets was intensifying, particularly in Europe; firms responded by following one another to these new markets. Brazil and Mexico would have had less bargaining power vis-à-vis the transnational firms had they faced the virtual duopoly of Ford and GM that prevailed before World War II.

The degree of market fragmentation in the initial stages of these national industries lends credence to the argument that the nature of firm entry was a response to oligopolistic competition. The bunched investments appear as defensive maneuvers rather than strictly a response to short-term profits and therefore financial incentives or subsidies. Vehicle markets, expected to reach little more than 100,000 units by the early 1960s, clearly could not technically support so many manufacturers for some time. Estimates for the optimum scale of an integrated auto plant, or the point at which additional cost savings from increased production taper off, ranged from 300,000 to 500,000 units a year. The optimum varied among processes, with the largest economies of scale in stamping metal exteriors (which therefore set the optimum for an integrated plant), followed by forging and machining engines.[22]

Outcomes were not completely determined by oligopolistic firm behavior, however. Government policy was critical for risk reduction. Subsidies not only significantly reduced the cost of capital investment, but guaranteed a return if the market had not materialized. Most important, these government automotive programs set the timing of firm investment. The extent to which government policy accelerated firm entry is not a trivial point, given the larger objective of jump-starting industrialization and generating productive linkages, rather than protecting domestic firms. In addition, as will be seen, these investments of the 1960s would have ramifications for trade flows in the 1970s and 1980s.

Moreover, structural characteristics unique to each country, combined with distinct industrial policies, led to differences in firm investment strategies and industrial structure, which would ultimately create variation between the countries' trade patterns. Brazil had a more sophisticated industrial infrastructure and, with a larger population, greater market potential. Its trading partners and sources of capital were relatively diverse. Mexico's foreign trade was tied to the United States, and its economy was subject to macro-economic constraints that Brazil evaded. As a result, Brazil was in a stronger position to require firms to build cars with very high levels of domestic content. The market size would allow for greater economies of scale, and the inflationary impact of high-price automobiles could be accommodated, at least in the short run. In Mexico, however, firms were less willing to incorporate such high levels of local content. The government was also more concerned about the impact on prices. In addition, the U.S. firms' proximity to suppliers at home made them even more inclined to fight against higher nationalization levels.

Because of these differences, Brazil built up a larger and more sophisticated supplier network. The auto companies were accompanied to Brazil by many of their suppliers from home. High domestic content requirements, combined with policies that banned the importation of components and parts for which there were domestically produced similars, insulated the domestic industry from the world. As a result, many car models on the street tended to be antiquated, as firms changed models infrequently in order to amortize tooling costs. Mexico's lower domestic content allowed firms greater flexibility in production, particularly by allowing metal stampings to be imported. This was important for U.S. firms, for which frequent model change was an important competitive strategy. On the other hand, Mexico's lower domestic content levels also meant that the sector's trade deficits grew proportionally with the numbers of vehicles produced.

Mexico's microlevel industrial policies also affected the extent to which firms were willing to substitute local production for imports and the way in which firms competed. Firms, constrained from vertically integrating, could be only minority partners in any independent supplier firm. Some U.S. firms claimed that there were some small components that they might have produced in Mexico had they been allowed full control. (Brazil had no limitations on either vertical integration or on foreign investment in the automotive parts sector.) These industrial policies also made U.S. firms even less willing to balance trade by increasing domestic content levels. Mexico's decrees also influenced market structure by allocating production quotas and limiting the vehicle classes firms could enter. This limited a firm's ability to compete and to increase market share through product diversification.

In both countries foreign direct investment had become a substitute for trade. The substitution was more complete in Brazil as a result of government policy and domestic market conditions. In 1973, producing more than 560,000 automobiles and almost 200,000 commercial vehicles, Brazil appeared to be the one less-developed country whose industry had a chance of becoming a global competitor. Mexico's industry was trivial in comparison, producing little more than a third as many cars.

By 1991, however, Mexico's production would rival, and its exports would surpass, Brazil's.

THE SHIFT TO EXPORTS

Brazil

At the time of the first oil shock in 1973, 80% of the oil consumed in Brazil was imported. Concerned with the balance of trade, the government looked to the auto industry as a potential source of foreign exchange. It shifted the incentive structure toward export promotion with the aim of generating a positive trade balance at the industry level.

While some export incentives were introduced in the late 1960s, export promotion gathered steam only in the early 1970s under the Special Fiscal Benefits for Exports (BEFIEX) program, which was not unique to the automobile industry. To qualify for BEFIEX, firms had to commit to targeted dollar values of total exports and net foreign exchange earnings. The incentives they received in return included exemptions from taxes on imported capital goods, parts, components, and raw materials. Every three dollars in exports was worth one dollar of duty-free imports. Federal and state value-added and sales taxes were waived on exports. Firms received a credit equal to these waived taxes that could be used toward taxes due on goods produced for the domestic market. Various drawback schemes were also introduced which allowed firms to import goods that would otherwise be banned for the production of exports. If the export or trade balance target was not fulfilled, firms had to refund these incentives.[23]

The government was motivated primarily by its desire to generate foreign exchange rather than by broader concerns of industrial policy and attaining economies of scale through exports. Increasing exports would be necessary to avoid any import constraint on investment and economic growth. Brazil's general response to the oil shock was to adopt a debt-led growth strategy rather than impose economic austerity. Therefore, the auto industry continued to grow at respectable annual rates, although not as quickly as during the "miracle" years. Total vehicle production topped the magic million mark in 1978, and future domestic demand projections were optimistic.[24]

Each major auto company participated in the BEFIEX program. The most important incentives from the firms' point of view were the cash credits on exports and the ability to import equipment duty free. Access

TABLE 5-4
Brazilian Vehicle Exports, 1970–1990 ($ thousands)

Year	Vehicles	Engines	Components	Total
1970	2,790	534	5,598	8,922
1972	24,935	144	29,067	54,146
1974	118,712	17,386	67,671	203,769
1976	233,579	67,442	84,721	385,742
1978	373,641	132,078	104,689	610,408
1980	729,948	210,620	160,600	1,101,168
1981	1,066,045	188,459	311,911	1,566,415
1982	715,853	188,853	250,128	1,154,834
1983	594,036	293,862	299,160	1,187,058
1984	669,247	350,272	413,931	1,433,450
1985	746,410	407,176	450,153	1,603,739
1986	667,461	280,514	539,585	1,487,560
1987	1,522,382	259,027	671,707	2,453,116
1988	1,645,636	261,714	710,336	2,617,686
1989	1,489,257	304,252	776,500	2,570,009
1990	975,127	220,710	701,647	1,897,484

Source: ANFAVEA data.

to imported parts was important for exports, but the law of similars was still on the books for domestically sold vehicles, and the government demonstrated less flexibility with respect to imported parts after the severe foreign exchange crunch of 1974–1975.[25] (See Tables 5-4 and 5-5.)

Firms adopted different export strategies. Generally the U.S. firms as represented by Ford and GM responded to the challenges of the 1970s by automating in the United States and by adopting "world car" strategies. They sought to increase economies of scale and spread R&D costs over more vehicles by increasing product standardization worldwide and by using low-wage production sites as export platforms for engines and components, whose design changes are less frequent and whose scale requirements are less extreme than for finished vehicles. European firms such as Fiat and VW looked to LDCs such as Brazil as low-cost export bases for finished vehicles to other low-income countries with similar demand profiles. Vehicle exports by all firms were directed primarily to regional markets. Ford and General Motors fulfilled their BEFIEX obligations by exporting engines to the United States. European firms exported both engines and finished vehicles. GM, Ford, and VW each committed to $1 billion in exports over a ten-year period, Fiat to $550 million.[26] BEFIEX participation meant that firms were not able to alter export targets in response to foreign demand, domestic capacity, and exchange-rate fluctuations, but were bound to fulfill export commitments by a given date.

TABLE 5-5
Brazil: Trade Balance in Automotive Industry ($ thousands)

Year	Imports	Exports	Trade Balance
1940–1950	420,547	—	(420,547)
1951	256,846	—	(256,846)
1955	232,403	—	(222,403)
1960	83,505	39	(83,466)
1965	8,256	3,192	(5,064)
1970	69,128	8,922	(60,206)
1972	97,642	54,146	(43,496)
1974	347,947	203,769	(144,178)
1976	235,088	385,742	150,654
1978	292,889	610,408	317,519
1980	524,185	1,101,168	576,983
1981	468,702	1,566,415	1,087,713
1982	318,386	1,154,834	836,448
1983	367,729	1,187,058	819,329
1984	394,618	1,433,450	1,038,832
1985	435,522	1,603,739	1,168,217
1986	656,240	1,487,560	831,320
1987	826,327	2,453,116	1,626,789
1988	695,606	2,617,686	1,822,080
1989	678,110	2,570,009	1,891,899
1990	733,095	1,897,484	1,164,389

Source: ANFAVEA data.

BEFIEX was introduced at a time when firms, with the expectation of rapid growth rates, were investing heavily for the domestic market. Given the lumpy nature of auto investment, exports could also serve as a temporary outlet for excess capacity while the domestic market grew. As a result, investment levels were sustained despite the slowdown in domestic market growth compared to the "miracle" years, particularly in the early 1970s.

Despite their growth in numbers, exports remained a small percentage of production, and the industry continued to focus on the domestic market. The industry's "opening" to world markets was asymmetric in that imported vehicles were still prohibited and imported parts did not grow in tandem with exports. Once the major investment push was complete, the sector generated growing trade surpluses. (See Table 5-6.)

The optimistic projections of internal demand did not materialize in the 1980s as the full impact of the debt crisis hit. Firms looked to exports as an alternative. Brazil's export success in the 1980s depended partly on fortuitous timing. The BEFIEX program had come at a time when new product lines—particularly in engines—were coming on-stream as firms

TABLE 5-6
Brazil: Domestic Market Share for Passenger Cars, 1974–1989 (percentage)

	Fiat	Ford	GM	VW	Chrysler	FNM
1974	—	19.1	20.6	55.6	4.0	.5
1975	—	17.6	20.1	59.2	2.2	.7
1976	—	17.9	20.3	57.9	2.5	.7
1977	9.4	14.4	17.0	55.9	2.2	.5
1978	11.5	15.7	19.3	51.1	1.8	—
1979	12.5	15.8	18.6	51.2	1.5	—
1980	13.6	15.2	21.5	48.7	.8	—
1981	10.5	19.2	24.0	45.9	—	—
1982	10.5	17.5	26.7	44.9	—	—
1983	10.6	19.8	28.0	41.6	—	—
1984	10.4	20.5	27.4	41.7	—	—
1985	13.0	20.6	27.2	39.2	—	—
1986	12.9	19.6	26.0	41.4	—	—
1987	15.3	20.7	28.7	35.1	—	—
1988	11.4	20.4	28.9	39.3	—	—
1989	11.8	19.8	30.6	37.4	—	—

Source: The Economist Intelligence Unit, *International Motor Business,* "Short Term Prospects to the Brazilian Motor Industry," October 1990.

began to downsize. The export capacity was available from investments planned in the 1970s, when projections for internal demand were optimistic and firms made BEFIEX commitments. Rather than building upon a growing domestic market to attain economies of scale, exports came to substitute for, rather than complement, domestic sales for some firms. (See Table 5-7.)

The direction of exports, however, began to shift as Brazil's LDC markets also contracted in response to debt-driven austerity programs and increased protection. In the early 1970s, nearly 90% of finished vehicle exports went to other Latin American countries. By 1984 this share was reduced to 60%, and by 1989, 60% of vehicle exports were being shipped to the United States, Canada, and Europe.[27] As discussed in more detail

TABLE 5-7
Brazilian Export of Passenger Cars by Firm (units)

	1980	1987	1988	1989
Volkswagen	57,137	130,947	96,058	57,049
Ford	2,896	3,931	11,068	7,144
General Motors	16,419	37,132	30,914	17,850
Fiat	38,256	107,520	87,936	82,842
Others	774	—	—	—
Total	115,482	297,530	225,976	164,885

Source: ANFAVEA data.

below, Fiat and VW were responsible for this shift in trade flows. (See Table 5-8.)

Recent data on Brazil's production costs are sketchy. In the early 1970s the cost differential with U.S. automobile production was estimated at 35%, which compared favorably with Mexico's differential of 45% to 53%.[28] The World Bank found, on the basis of implicit tariff calculations, that the prices of Brazilian vehicles (excluding taxes) were below those of similar foreign models and characterized the industry as a successful infant industry on the verge of maturity in the early 1980s.[29]

In the mid-1980s one firm in Brazil found the country competitive in machined castings and forgings because of their high labor content and Brazil's lower wage rates, which offset productivity differentials. It identified Brazil's greatest cost advantage in engines and transmissions, since 70–80% of their content was comprised of such components. Owing to a 50% content of plastic, glass, and other parts in which Brazil was not competitive (and which in this case were also outsourced), it found passenger cars had cost disadvantages. Comparing production costs for small cars in 1988, the company found that ex-factory costs in Brazil compared favorably to those in Spain, unfavorably to those in Japan and Korea, and were about the same as those in the United States. These costs partly reflected the appreciation of the cruzado, as the growth in industry costs exceeded devaluation by 30% from 1986 to 1988, but were also inclusive of export incentives, which came to over $800 per vehicle.

Individual firm strategies.   Ford relied almost exclusively on exporting engines and components to the United States. When originally planned, engine production was considered to be cost-competitive even in the absence of BEFIEX subsidies. Engines were preferred over cars due to lower transport costs and simpler quality control. Also, since the technological sophistication of engine production was embedded in the machines, the production process was less dependent on skilled labor. Furthermore, the domestic supply base for certain car components was not considered to be internationally competitive. The decision to produce engines came at a time when Ford was downsizing and needed new capacity. A more sophisticated, four-cylinder engine of the same family was being built in Lima, Ohio. According to Ford executives, if the engine had not been produced in Brazil, it would have been produced at the Lima plant.

Ford did experiment briefly in the mid-1980s with exporting Escorts to Scandinavia when Ford-Europe was capacity constrained and relative

TABLE 5-8
Brazil Automobile and Utility Vehicle Exports by Firm and Destination (units)

	1989						1988					
	Fiat	Ford	GM	VW	Other	Total	Fiat	Ford	GM	VW	Other	Total
Argentina	23,472	6,049	0	1,341	0	30,862	24,576	9,249	0	12,026	3	45,854
Chile	2,508	694	8,868	7,558	0	19,628	1,756	1,002	6,277	5,607	0	14,722
Colombia	0	0	5,514	0	1	5,515	0	0	7,410	0	18	7,428
Uruguay	3,397	350	2,487	1,359	80	7,673	2,802	649	2,602	2,691	8	8,752
Venezuela	1,488	0	2,899	0	0	4,387	13,873	0	16,316	0	0	30,189
Nigeria	0	0	0	1,815	0	1,815	0	0	4	978	0	982
Canada	0	0	0	3,614	0	3,614	0	0	0	8,783	0	8,783
United States	0	3	0	43,820	10	43,833	4	0	0	52,230	18	58,252
Denmark	161	0	14	0	0	175	246	0	0	0	0	246
Finland	0	0	0	0	0	0	2	0	0	0	0	2
France	8,727	1	0	0	0	8,728	6,910	0	0	10	0	6,920
Italy	77,874	0	0	0	0	77,874	65,356	0	0	0	5	65,361
Norway	0	0	0	0	0	0	0	0	0	0	0	0
West Germany	1,854	0	1	7	37	1,862	5,737	0	0	21	1	5,759
England	2,689	0	0	0	0	2,689	2,747	0	0	0	0	2,747
Sweden	308	0	0	0	0	308	198	0	0	0	0	198
Iraq	0	0	0	0	0	0	0	0	0	6,891	0	6,891
Taiwan	2,288	0	2,026	670	0	4,984	2,779	0	3,602	531	0	6,912
Other	13,064	546	4,540	1,866	115	20,131	11,230	813	10,655	12,098	300	35,096
Total	137,830	7,643	26,349	62,050	243	234,115	138,216	11,713	46,866	101,866	353	299,014

TABLE 5-8
(Continued)

	1987						1986					
	Fiat	Ford	GM	VW	Other	Total	Fiat	Ford	GM	VW	Other	Total
Argentina	18,674	5	0	12,249	0	30,928	10,227	12	0	14,028	0	24,267
Chile	1,629	762	2,361	5,303	0	10,055	648	386	210	707	0	1,951
Colombia	1	0	7,584	0	53	7,638	0	0	6,342	1	16	6,359
Uruguay	4,086	809	3,946	6,033	5	14,879	2,559	134	1,279	3,682	2	7,636
Venezuela	12,195	2,400	21,198	1	0	35,794	8,835	5,952	24,815	0	0	39,609
Nigeria	0	0	0	988	0	988	0	0	0	1,958	0	1,958
Canada	0	0	0	21,123	0	21,123	0	0	0	764	0	764
United States	5	0	0	52,814	56	52,875	4	0	0	1,402	24	1,430
Denmark	1,123	0	0	0	0	1,123	5	400	0	0	0	405
Finland	0	0	0	0	0	0	0	0	0	0	0	0
France	3,272	0	0	0	0	3,272	2,301	0	0	0	0	2,301
Italy	85,287	0	0	0	0	85,287	30,161	0	0	0	0	30,161
Norway	0	0	0	0	0	0	0	0	0	0	0	0
West Germany	1,803	0	0	1	0	1,804	1,698	0	0	0	0	1,698
England	0	0	0	0	0	0	0	0	0	0	0	0
Sweden	0	0	0	0	0	0	0	0	0	0	0	0
Iraq	0	0	0	28,885	0	28,885	0	0	0	29,413	0	29,413
Taiwan	1,418	0	0	227	0	1,645	320	0	0	31	0	351
Other	8,566	512	9,283	9,320	118	27,799	7,483	135	9,510	4,604	59	21,791
Total	138,059	4,488	44,372	136,944	232	324,145	64,241	7,019	42,156	56,559	106	170,071

	1985						1984					
	Fiat	Ford	GM	VW	Other	Total	Fiat	Ford	GM	VW	Other	Total
Argentina	8,113	0	0	9,452	0	17,565	9,216	0	0	11,305	0	20,521
Chile	53	121	410	183	2	769	126	41	277	129	0	573
Colombia	2	0	5,038	0	23	5,063	0	1	4,630	3	2	4,636
Uruguay	1,685	739	1,345	1,170	0	4,939	1,079	1,600	906	1,108	7	4,700
Venezuela	6,240	5,004	22,061	0	0	33,311	6,242	8,161	19,301	0	0	33,704
Nigeria	0	0	0	15,565	0	15,565	0	0	0	13,576	0	13,576
Canada	0	0	112	0	0	112	0	0	0	7	0	7
United States	2	0	1	41	23	67	0	2	1	17	20	40
Denmark	1,375	8,016	0	0	0	9,391	2,849	2,995	0	0	0	5,844
Finland	0	1,194	0	0	0	1,194	0	4,940	0	0	0	4,940
France	4,980	0	1	0	0	4,981	5,558	0	0	0	0	5,558
Italy	35,605	0	0	0	0	35,605	42,626	0	1	0	0	42,627
Norway	0	2,835	0	0	0	2,835	0	5,387	0	0	0	5,387
West Germany	2,232	0	0	6	0	2,238	2,375	0	0	0	0	2,375
England	0	0	0	0	0	0	0	1	0	0	0	1
Sweden	0	4,950	0	0	0	4,950	0	8,001	0	0	0	8,001
Iraq	0	0	22	44,845	0	44,867	2	0	1	20,004	0	20,007
Taiwan	200	0	0	39	0	234	160	0	0	15	0	175
Other	4,538	1,972	4,465	3,293	105	14,373	7,345	1,514	2,207	3,171	94	14,331
Total	65,025	24,831	33,455	74,594	153	197,259	77,578	32,643	27,324	49,335	123	187,003

Source: ANFAVEA data.

219

exchange rates favored Brazil over England and West Germany, which had previously been supplying these markets. Ford do Brasil had adopted European product lines in the 1970s because they seemed better suited to the domestic market, and Ford-Europe was generating more attractive model lines while Ford-U.S. was losing market share. The export program was short-lived, since Brazilian Escorts became less cost-competitive when the exchange-rate situation reversed itself, European unions protested, and Ford began to turn its attention to East Asia as a potential export source.[30] Brazil was also chosen as the primary source of the Cargo truck for the U.S. and Canadian markets when Europe was seen as a high-cost production site.

Volkswagen used Brazil as a low-cost production site for finished vehicles to other LDCs, and continued to produce such models as the Beetle, which had been discontinued in Germany. Brazil had always accounted for a larger share of VW's global production than Ford's, and before its investments in Spain, was its primary low-cost production site. When Latin American markets collapsed in the early 1980s, VW do Brasil first shifted its exports to the oil-exporting nations in Africa and the Middle East.

Volkswagen and Ford formed the holding company of Autolatina in 1987, which became the largest private company in South America. The union was formed to overcome financial difficulties in Brazil and to rationalize operations in both Argentina and Brazil, which had begun negotiations for freer trade in automobiles. Ford had suffered consistent losses from 1981 to 1986 and, with Brazil accounting for only 3% of global sales, was reportedly considering exiting from the market altogether. VW's Brazilian operations had dropped from a high of 25% of total sales to only 7%, and needed a partner to regain economies of scale in the face of falling domestic market share.[31] The companies maintained separate brand names and dealer networks.

In 1987 Volkswagen do Brasil introduced the Fox, a compact passenger car, and began to export it almost exclusively to the United States and Canada. VW needed an entry-level product for the U.S. market, and VW do Brasil needed alternatives to its depressed LDC export markets. Although the car received positive reviews when it was first introduced, it quickly lost its competitive edge to Japanese and Korean imports. An increasingly overvalued exchange rate and internal cost increases were critical in its price-sensitive market niche. VW could not raise prices sufficiently to cover its losses. Overall uncertainty in Brazil, as well as an aging product, were also contributing factors.

As a result of the increasing unprofitability of Brazilian exports and the enormous uncertainty of Brazil's economy, by 1990 Autolatina had effectively canceled or was in the process of phasing out all export programs, including the Fox and the Cargo, with no plans to replace them. The millions of dollars in high-quality, four-cylinder engine exports were also scheduled to disappear, since Brazil was not chosen as the production site for the updated model. As the only company that exported finished vehicles to the United States, and for which the United States was practically its only export market, Autolatina was hit especially hard with the overvalued exchange rate. Until 1986 the company's exports had been profitable owing to a combination of export incentives, a favorable exchange rate, and a good mix of export products. Starting in 1986, it would have incurred losses on exports if not for BEFIEX incentives, and in 1988 it did suffer losses on exports. Acording to the firm's calculations, its exports would have been profitable if the cruzado had remained at its 1985 parity with the dollar.

After General Motors began its first "world car" program in the mid-1970s with the introduction of the "J" car series (Chevy Cavalier, Opel, and Monza), GM do Brasil (GMB) lobbied Detroit to introduce the J car in Brazil. The subsidiary needed a new product line to compete in the Brazilian market, and there was no competition in the market niche that the J car would fill. However, the domestic market could not justify the large investment needed to build the J cars new engine, which had to be manufactured in Brazil to comply with domestic content requirements. It was decided that GM do Brasil would provide the family two-engine for the U.S. Pontiac division as well as for the domestic market.

Although producing engines in Brazil was cost-effective for GM, even without BEFIEX, the company did not need to build a new plant. It could have supplied them from its engine plant in New York state. GM do Brasil was also not held in high regard in Detroit. The subsidiary had suffered financial losses in the late 1970s in its nonautomotive activities, which were sold off. Capital infusions from the parent were necessary. Roger Smith, the CEO at the time, considered Brazil a black hole.

Nevertheless, domestic market considerations drove the decision to produce J cars and to export engines, according to GM managers. In 1979–1980, the 1990 forecast for domestic demand was 2 million vehicles. Exports would absorb the excess engine capacity while the Brazilian market grew. Brazil's case for the J car was assisted by the liability suits GM was facing from having shut down its operations in Argentina; exiting the market could have been costly, and staying in required new product lines. Although domestic considerations predominated, BEFIEX export incentives helped sweeten the deal. The import duty exemptions on imported capital equipment were particularly important in reducing the investment costs.

Engine exports were important to GMB's financial health in the 1980s when the domestic market stagnated. It remained cost-effective to export engines from Brazil, although the margins shrank as a result of rising domestic costs and exchange-rate appreciation. In 1990 Brazil exported engines to GM-Opel for the first time. Until then, the firm's global sourcing strategy had assigned the U.S. market to Brazil and the European market to Australia. GM was forced to grant Brazil access to the European market, since demand was down in both the Brazilian and the U.S. markets as a result of economic recession. Otherwise, GMB would not have been able to meet its export commitments, upon which its import strategy was dependent.

GM do Brasil never considered exporting vehicles to either the United States or Europe. The U.S. market had a short product cycle, which made competition very stiff. Like the overall industry, GM's product line was antiquated. There was no pressure from imports to make frequent model changes, which would have been costly given Brazil's small production volumes. In addition, Brazilian models had followed European product lines since 1968, with a lag. German models, smaller and based on similar gasoline pricing, were considered more appropriate for the Brazilian market.

GM divided the world by region: Australia served the Pacific, Opel served Europe, and Brazil served South America. The cars that were exported from Brazil went to GM assembly plants in other Latin American countries, particularly Venezuela, Colombia, and Chile. Recently, these subsidiaries have been clamoring for cars made by GM's Japanese partners.

In the late 1980s, looking toward the day when it could no longer depend on engine exports, GMB proposed a plan to export minivans to Pontiac. The subsidiary also wanted to reduce its dependence on the domestic market. The project would have been self-financed, partly through an intricate debt conversion plan. Contributions made by the parent would have been repaid through a transfer-pricing mechanism. Although the plan received preliminary approval, currency appreciation in the late eighties and the Brazilian government's termination of debt swaps killed the project.

As of 1991, GM do Brasil had no new approved export proposal, although it continued to export engines. Like Autolatina, it planned to invest to remain competitive in the domestic market in the face of potential market liberalization, but was capital-constrained; all funds had to be internally generated. In June 1991 GM announced that it was relocating its Latin American headquarters from São Paulo to Miami. The company insisted that the move was motivated by other factors, but many Brazilians interpreted it as a sign of GM's diminishing commitment to their country.

Fiat initially considered exporting cars to other Latin American countries from Brazil. Its Brazilian product was always akin to that produced in Europe, so when Latin American markets collapsed in the 1980s, it was able to shift its exports to Italy. Fiat do Brasil exported the Uno, which, as the smallest and cheapest car of its product line, complemented Italian production. These exports were made feasible with BEFIEX incentives; without them, according to company spokespeople, they would not have been cost-competitive.

In most years since 1982, exports accounted for 40% to 50% of Fiat's annual production, most of which went to Italy. This export performance made Fiat Brazil's largest private exporter. Fiat do Brasil benefited from rapid growth of the Italian market and Fiat-Italy's capacity constraints. The company's expectations of Brazil's domestic market growth did not come to fruition, but because its vehicles were introduced practically at the same time in both Brazil and Italy, it was easy to integrate its operations. Since Italy was a captive market, the company could smooth out cycles in the domestic market through exports.

In the face of increasing costs, Fiat's export performance would be hard to maintain in the 1990s. Nineteen ninety-one promised to be more problematic for exports. The Italian market was recessed and exports amounted to only 30% of production. Exports of Unos were being phased out.

Mexico

Mexico's difficulties in adjusting to the oil shock led to increasing economic disequilibrium and a balance-of-payments crisis. In 1976 the peso was devalued for the first time since 1954, by 50%, and austerity measures were adopted. The domestic recession hit the auto industry particularly hard. The discovery of vast oil reserves at the end of 1977, and with it easy access to foreign loans, promised to eliminate any balance-of-payments constraint on future economic growth. With real GNP growing at an annual average rate of 8.4% from 1978 to 1981, prospects for the domestic auto market brightened considerably.

It was in this context that the government issued the 1977 automotive decree. The decree marked the first serious attempt to leverage firm access to the domestic market for increased exports, since new investments would be required to make existing capacity more competitive and to initiate new export projects. It mandated firms to eliminate their trade imbalances by 1982 by increasing either domestic content levels (set at a minimum of 50%) or exports. Firms' import bills were broadened to include the imported portion of domestically purchased parts and components, as well as royalty and interest payments abroad. In an attempt to modernize the domestic supplier industry, at least 50% of a firm's export requirement had to be supplied by local auto parts producers. Firms that failed to balance their trade would sacrifice various subsidies and tax exemptions and risk loss of market share through reduced access to imports.

Although the auto firms did not respond immediately, they all ultimately complied with the decree by building new engine capacity for export.[32] After first increasing exports of wire harnesses from a *maquiladora* plant on the border, GM announced its plans to build a new engine plant and a new assembly plant in 1979. By 1988 the plant was exporting 412,000 engines to GM subsidiaries around the world, making GM's Mexican subsidiary the largest engine exporter in Latin America.

Defensively, the other automobile producers followed suit. Altogether, the plants increased Mexico's annual productive capacity in engines to almost 2 billion units.[33] With the exception of VW, which concentrated all facets of production in its Puebla facility, the firms built their engine plants in north or north-central Mexico, far away from their manufacturing operations near Mexico City. All the engines were aimed at the U.S. market, except for Nissan's, which were to be divided equally between the United States and Japan.

The motivating factor behind these new investments was the automotive decree, in the absence of which none of the firms would have built new engine capacity. An increase in exports was required to protect or increase domestic market share in Mexico, which at the time of the decree was booming. While each firm was in a slightly different position, all of them needed the additional capacity as they restructured their global operations, a necessary condition for the decree's efficacy. Mexico had no evident cost advantage as a production site, although it was not clear that it had a serious cost disadvantage; in fact, these plants proved to be both cost- and quality-effective.[34]

The position of individual firms also helps explain their responses. (See Tables 5-9 and 5-10.) Without the decree, GM and Ford would probably have built the engines in the United States by increasing capacity at existing facilities. Potential, yet uncertain, cost advantages did not drive their decisions. Labor and political volatility, in their view, was still a mitigating factor against using Mexico as an export base. GM also needed additional capacity for its Mexican operations. Although Ford in particular cited United Automobile Workers (UAW) pressure at the time, the fact that the U.S. market was growing made the Mexican investment less controversial. Additionally, Mexican-made engines, hidden under the hood, were less conspicuous than finished vehicles.

The Chrysler Corporation, struggling to survive, was in the process of closing down many subsidiaries in the late 1970s. Its Mexican subsidiary was its only Latin American operation that was not a financial drain. In fact, at the time of the decree, the subsidiary was exporting capital to support the parent. Therefore, it was important for Chrysler, despite its financial weakness, to protect its Mexican operations. As in the cases of Ford and GM, the alternative production site would have been the United States rather than a third country.

Volkswagen was in a unique position. Until the 1970s, it produced a single passenger car model, which facilitated reaching high levels of domestic content. Unlike the U.S. firms, it started stamping in Mexico even before building engines. The distance from its parent company also worked in favor of higher domestic content. Since its vehicles had higher local content levels, VW's trade deficit was not as severe as that of U.S. firms. However, the company also had a harder time adapting to export promotion because it did not have easy access to its primary market, as did the U.S. firms. In 1974, VW stopped producing Beetles in Germany, and in 1977 started exporting them from Mexico. Germany was no longer an economical production site and European demand was small. (When Brazil stopped production in the mid-1980s, Mexico became the only remaining producer of the Beetle in the world.)

In 1974, in response to the appreciation of the German mark and intensifying competition from the Japanese, VW built a plant in Westmoreland, Pennsylvania, to supply the U.S. market. At the time, Mexico was not considered as an alternative site because of poor infrastructure, low domestic volumes, and country risk. To comply with Mexico's export

TABLE 5-9
Total Exports by Company, Mexico, 1981–1989 ($ millions)

	1981	1982	1983	1984	1985	1986	1987	1988	1989
Chrysler	70.9	121.4	229.6	486.1	584.7	851.7	990.0	825.6	842.3
Ford	3.1	12.8	34.4	142.9	172.4	283.7	721.8	860.7	555.7
General Motors	38.1	159.7	344.7	477.8	566.7	736.1	709.9	1,252.5	1,348.3
Volkswagen	104.8	99.4	140.3	145.1	227.0	268.6	222.1	228.4	428.8
Nissan	23.0	13.4	9.1	29.2	90.3	106.1	NA	NA	NA
Renault	0.4	—	4.1	1.5	28.3	30.9	101.1	164.4	224.2
Vam	0.2	3.8	3.5	4.7	—	—	—	—	—
Dina	42.3	NS	0.3	6.9	—	—	—	—	—
Totals	282.8	410.5	766.0	1,294.2	1,669.4	2,227.1	2,746.0	3,331.6	3,399.3

Note: NS = not significant.
Sources: Juan Carlos Moreno Brid, "Structural Change in Mexico's Motor Vehicle Industry," in *Industry on the Move*, edited by Gijsbert van Lient (Geneva: International Labour Organization, 1992), p. 270.

TABLE 5-10
Passenger Car Domestic Sales and Exports by Company, Mexico, 1986–1990 (units)

	1986		1987		1988		1989		1990	
	Domestic Sales	Exports	Domestic Sales	Exports	Domestic Sales	Exports	Domestic Sales	Exports	Domestic Sales	Exports
Chrysler	27,666	15,499	23,464	41,037	48,952	28,495	56,952	45,643	52,580	55,355
Ford	19,516	—	16,524	51,773	32,001	66,361	47,801	39,580	52,352	88,604
General Motors	11,365	18,672	14,444	32,272	15,284	36,389	22,876	39,536	32,351	40,993
Nissan	43,291	5,965	49,064	10,325	60,247	12,319	69,855	17,228	80,502	18,737
Volkswagen	54,865	80	50,631	74	53,802	456	77,021	23,057	134,823	46,232

Source: AMIA data.

requirements, however, an engine plant was built to supply engines to the U.S. plant and to provide needed capacity in Mexico. VW needed the new engine capacity to supply its U.S. plant as well as its Mexican operations. As the other producers found, the engine plant proved to be cost-effective and of good quality. With fewer production sites worldwide or in the Americas, and facing higher transport costs, VW began to integrate Mexico into a North American strategy before Ford and GM did.

While all firms wanted to protect their domestic market position in Mexico, it is unlikely that any would have complied with the decree if the additional capacity had not been necessary. In effect, the decree did not really test the importance of the Mexican market to these firms, as no existing facilities elsewhere had to be shut down in order for them to comply. In interviews, industry executives made clear that they would not close a facility if its product still had a viable market. Even with accelerated depreciation, the financial hit of closing an operation can be significant. Exit costs include not only the losses posted on the firm's balance sheet, but contractual arrangements with workers, as well as union and community opposition. VW was subject to German laws that forbade firms to relocate production abroad if it resulted in layoffs. The decree did demonstrate that at the margin, the Mexican government could compel firms to choose Mexico over alternative sites when building new capacity.

While this new export capacity was coming on-stream, the sector's overall trade deficit skyrocketed along with domestic sales, hitting $2.1 billion in 1981. This represented 58% of the total trade deficit and made the automotive industry the largest private sector contributor to Mexico's trade imbalance.[35] The government responded in 1981 by insisting on stricter compliance with the 1977 decree, but to little avail.

The automotive decree of 1983 was an attempt to rationalize the industry and to improve its overall balance-of-payments position. By 1987 firms would have to generate their own foreign exchange to cover all imports and service payments. They would also have to reduce their product lines to one make and five models. Additional makes would be allowed only if they were self-sufficient in foreign exchange. Self-sufficiency could be accomplished by exporting either half the units produced or the equivalent value of components used in their manufacture. Moreover, production of V-8 automobiles for the domestic market was prohibited, as were imported components for luxury cars. Some flexibility was allowed with respect to domestic content, especially for makes that were self-sufficient in foreign exchange. The decree hit U.S. firms especially hard, since it placed severe limits on their ability to compete via product diversification. In addition, their fastest-growing and most profitable lines had been in luxury and sports cars during the oil boom.[36]

Unlike the 1977 decree, the 1983 decree was announced during a time of deep economic recession. The debt crisis had exploded in Mexico the previous year. Car production had fallen by 15% in 1982 and would fall another 30% in 1983. Several firms had built up large dollar-denominated debts during previous expansion plans, and the maxi-devaluation of the peso was financially catastrophic.[37] At least Ford and GM seriously considered pulling out of the Mexican market altogether. Although the Mexican subsidiary was a small part of GM's total operation, its losses were severe enough to have a negative effect on the company's overall income statement for 1982.

In 1986 production was still 43% less than in 1981. One estimate of industry losses over these years was $1.5 billion.[38] The French firm, Renault, gave up and pulled out of the Mexican vehicle market in 1986. Growth resumed in 1987, when the domestic economy began to recover. In the years from 1985 to 1987, the industry's performance would have been even poorer if not for the growth in automobile exports. Nevertheless, while growing in percentage terms and as a percentage of total production, only a small number of vehicles were exported. Moreover, Ford's new Hermosillo plant was responsible for the bulk of them. With that notable exception, the government did not succeed in getting firms to invest in major new export projects. Nor did it succeed in getting firms to substitute vehicle for engine exports; the engine plants still generated the lion's share of sectoral exports.

From 1983 to 1988, the industry overall showed a trade surplus for the first time, due initially to the reduced demand for imports in the face of severe contraction in domestic vehicle production and subsequently to export growth (see Table 5-11). Auto companies became the country's biggest private exporters and importers. After PEMEX, the state-controlled oil company, GM and Chrysler switched top billing for exports and were the most outwardly oriented of the auto firms, with exports accounting for 45–58% of sales from 1983 to 1985. Exports as a share of sales grew in importance for all firms in 1986 owing to the steep drop in the domestic market. During these years GM and Chrysler maintained positive trade balances, while Ford and VW had more scattered performances and Nissan showed perpetual deficits. In 1986 the auto industry

TABLE 5-11
Mexican Motor Vehicle Industry Trade Balance ($ millions)

	1970	1975	1977	1980	1981	1982	1983	1984	1985	1986
Exports										
Total	26.4	122.0	253.5	404.4	377.8	483.1	674.9	1,492.9	1,518.9	1,855.5
Passenger Cars	0.1	4.7	12.2	98.5	70.1	66.9	72.4	119.1	116.6	187.3
Trucks	—	4.0	17.8	30.1	39.5	14.3	11.7	26.7	24.4	29.4
Parts	26.4	55.3	95.9	209.4	165.0	131.4	152.2	270.2	240.7	374.5
Chassis	—	1.9	.9	1.0	1.5	.4	.05	.01	.1	.06
Engines	—	35.4	82.5	30.5	61.5	214.2	395.4	982.7	1,039.7	1,152.7
Other	—	20.7	44.1	34.8	40.4	55.9	42.9	94.1	97.3	111.6
Imports										
Total	256.7	750.3	638.8	1,903.2	2,265.2	1,206.2	349.7	684.7	904.0	737.8
Trade Balance	−230.3	−628.3	−385.3	−1,498.9	−1,887.5	−723.1	325.2	808.2	614.9	1,117.7

Source: Juan Carlos Moreno Brid, "Mexico's Motor Vehicle Industry in the 1980s," World Employment Programme Research Working Paper No. 21 (Geneva: International Labour Organization, August 1988).

229

accounted for 20% of Mexican exports, the most important sector by far after oil (54%), and registered a trade surplus of $13.7 billion.[39]

In 1989 the new Salinas government issued its own automotive decree, which mirrored more general moves to liberalize the economy. Restrictions were removed on product lines, and for the first time, the government allowed auto firms manufacturing in Mexico to import finished vehicles.[40] A firm had to generate a trade surplus of 2.5 dollars for every dollar spent on imported vehicles. Over time, the ratio would be reduced. In an effort to build up the local supplier industry, 36% of a car's value-added would have to include parts and components supplied by the domestic parts sector. After the decree was issued, the domestic market unexpectedly boomed, and firms had trouble meeting demand.

Individual firm strategies.   The 1983 decree would have forced GM to reduce its passenger car offering to one product line unless the company introduced a new export project. In retrospect, company executives insisted that GM would not have created a new export niche simply to add an additional line to maintain domestic market share. (For firms' domestic market shares, see Figure 5-2.) Conveniently, the Chevrolet El Camino and the GM Caballero pickup were being phased out in the United States. The vehicle on which they were based was defunct, and production was shifted to Mexico until market demand disappeared altogether. The Ramos Arizpe assembly plant, which had been built along with the new engine plants to assemble A body cars for the domestic market, had extensive excesss capacity. Small runs of these vehicles were assembled there, sourced almost exclusively from the United States. As low-volume-niche vehicles, they could be handled cost-effectively in Mexico.[41]

In 1987 GM de Mexico moved from the International group to the Chevrolet-Pontiac Canada group within the corporation. GM also announced its intention to shift some production of certain A cars from the United States to its Mexican plant. In response to UAW complaints, the firm claimed that these cars would eventually be phased out and that 95% of their components would be imported from the United States. As of late 1991, the assembly plant was operating with two shifts, but for ten years had operated at 20% capacity. According to top management, it would never have been built without government pressure.

By 1991 GM products in Mexico and the United States were updated at the same time. The cars produced for the domestic market were virtually the same as those produced for export, except for domestic content

FIGURE 5-2
Mexico—Domestic Market Share for Passenger Cars

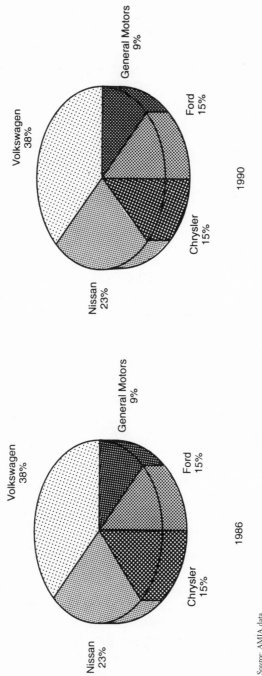

Volkswagen
38%

General Motors
9%

Ford
15%

Chrysler
15%

Nissan
23%

1990

Volkswagen
38%

General Motors
9%

Ford
15%

Chrysler
15%

Nissan
23%

1986

Source: AMIA data.

TABLE 5-12
Mexico Motor Vehicle Exports by Destination, 1981–1990 (units)

Year	North America	Central America	South America	Africa	Asia	Europe	Total
1981	3	697	4,144	1	385	9,198	14,428
1982	623	711	56	—	845	13,584	15,819
1983	203	3,600	133	1,520	269	16,730	22,455
1984	13,448	3,645	624	—	798	15,120	33,635
1985	47,197	6,845	1,129	—	99	3,153	58,423
1986	60,466	8,419	2,490	—	707	347	72,429
1987	145,658	12,621	4,047	—	377	370	163,073
1988	153,040	11,187	8,513	92	4	311	173,147
1989	170,270	9,698	14,443	125	717	746	195,999
1990	251,350	10,641	12,735	289	1,445	399	276,859

Source: AMIA data.

levels. GM was Mexico's leading truck manufacturer; its domestic truck sales continued to dominate domestic car sales, and engine exports swamped car exports. Nevertheless, despite rapid growth in domestic car sales, GM sold about 25% more of its car production abroad than it did in Mexico in 1990 (see Table 5-12). In the early 1980s, GM had studied the costs of exiting the Mexican market. In 1991 the Mexican subsidiary was its most profitable in the Western Hemisphere.

Ford was the last auto firm to respond to the 1977 decree, and its engine plant in Chihuahua came on-stream in 1983, when the domestic market was depressed and the company was considering whether or not to stay in Mexico. In 1986 it opened a plant in Hermosillo to assemble Mazda-designed Mercury Tracers for export to the United States and Canada. In Japanese fashion, it was the first Ford plant to house stamping and assembly operations under one roof and Ford's only stamping facility in Mexico (which, according to Ford executives, would remain the case). Since the plant was devoted exclusively to export, the government did not object to the fact that 60% of the vehicles' content was sourced from Japan, 30% from Mexico, and 10% from the United States. What's more, the government provided the project with financial and infrastructural support.

Ford built the Hermosillo plant to fulfill the government's foreign exchange requirements. Only afterward did it use the plant to negotiate government approval to introduce the Taurus line to the domestic market. Some have speculated that the prime motivation for building the plant in Mexico was to evade U.S. constraints on Japanese imports. This seems implausible, since the vehicle, though sourced from Mazda in

Japan, had been assembled in Taiwan and would not have been considered a Japanese import.

The Hermosillo plant closing for six months in 1989 to retool for a new Escort/Tracer negatively influenced Mexico's vehicle exports for the year. Eighty percent of the new model's content would be sourced from the United States. The reason behind the model switch evidently had to do with U.S. regulations. Owing to U.S. Corporate Average Fuel Efficiency regulations, which required firms to calculate separate fuel efficiency averages for imported versus domestically produced (75% U.S. or Canadian value-added) vehicles, the original Tracer was counted as an import because of its low U.S. content. Fortuitously, the appreciating yen lessened the pain of the switch by raising the relative cost of Japanese sourcing.

Hermosillo was still a relatively small-scale assembly plant, but production had been growing; 89,000 Escorts and Tracers were exported in 1990, helping Mexico's total car exports grow by more than 50% compared to 1989. Like GM, Ford's car exports dominated domestic sales. Still, because of the sluggish demand for automobiles worldwide, the plant was not running at its full capacity of 170,000 vehicles a year. Ford-Mexico considered using the plant to source the more buoyant domestic market, but was concerned about running into foreign exchange problems. Furthermore, it was more profitable for the company to export small cars and to sell luxury cars in Mexico.

Chrysler began to export small volumes of vehicles to Puerto Rico in 1983, making use of its excess capacity. In 1985, in response to capacity and financial constraints in the United States, the company started to produce K cars in Mexico for export. As of 1991, except for local content, Mexican products were the same as those manufactured in the United States. Certain models were produced in Mexico exclusively. Within Mexico, the company had reduced its product offering, which cost it market share but, according to company spokespeople, not profits. The only firm in Latin America to produce automatic transmissions, it no longer produced cars with manual transmissions in Mexico. As of 1990, Chrysler's trading pattern came to resemble that of the other U.S.-based companies when passenger car exports came to dominate domestic sales.

Volkswagen closed its Westmoreland, Pennsylvania, plant, which had been running at only 30% capacity, in 1988. While the Mexican plant was not doing much better, projections for increasing cost efficiencies and volume growth in the medium term were better for Mexico than for the United States. Although Mexican production involved other risks, exporting to Mexico's protected market was not an option, while exporting to the United States was. VW also was a market leader in Mexico, while its already small market share was declining in the United States. According to VW management, the decision was completely dictated by Mexican trade policy; closing the Mexican plant would have meant abandoning the Mexican market, yet the same was not true for the United States.

In 1991 VW announced a $1 billion, five-year investment program to modernize and expand capacity in Mexico, where production for all of North America was now concentrated. The stamping equipment from the South Carolina plant that previously supplied Westmoreland had been relocated to Puebla. (In contrast to the U.S. firms, VW had not located any of its operations at greenfield sites in the north.) The domestic product line was broadened to include Golfs and Jettas. Mexico was to supply the U.S. market with both these cars, which had been produced at Westmoreland. By 1991 about 500,000 engines a year were being exported to Germany. Unlike the United States, Canada bought only Golfs from Mexico and Jettas from Germany. Starting with the 1992 model, both were to be supplied by Mexico.

The primary reasons for shifting production to Mexico from Germany were the lack of capacity in Europe and the need to reduce exchange-rate risk. VW's market share in Europe had grown, so it needed Mexican capacity to meet North American demand. The weak dollar had also hurt VW sales in North America; it competed in a price-sensitive market niche. Unlike their effect on U.S. firms, exchange rates helped shape VW's trade strategy. VW tried to balance trade with Europe by exporting engines and increasing local content. At 1991 exchange rates, Mexican production was cost-competitive with Germany's.

VW showed the fastest growth of all the Mexican auto producers and controlled almost 40% of the Mexican passenger car market in 1990. Car exports climbed from practically nothing in 1988 to more than 46,000 in 1990. Nevertheless, unlike the U.S. Big Three, domestic sales dwarfed exports, and VW sold more cars in Mexico than in the United States.

Along with VW, Nissan benefited from the economic crisis and government tax policies that expanded the relative importance of the popular car segment of the market. Nissan's sales increased in 1982 even as total industry sales declined. Although the firm was able to balance its trade in 1982, its export markets in Latin America evaporated. Despite relatively high levels of domestic content (75% in cars and 70% in commercial vehicles), Nissan had a trade deficit for the next five years and, in 1984, showed the largest trade deficit of any Mexican firm.[42] In response to the loss of market share resulting in part from capacity constraints, in 1990 the company announced a billion-dollar investment plan for new production facilities. (For firms' exports, see Table 5-13.)

CONCLUSION

Import Substitution Reconsidered

The nature of automobile production would not lead one to expect the industry to operate in the manner of a strictly defined competitive industry. The additional factor of ubiquitous government intervention makes it even less likely that trade and investment flows in the industry could be predicted by models that assume free trade and unregulated markets. While an oligopolistic structure has prevailed since the industry's early years, the introduction of new technologies and new entrants has meant that the nature of oligopolistic competition has changed over time and that the relative impact of government policies, firm strategy, and country-specific characteristics on investment and trade flows has varied as well.

Brazil and Mexico were able to take advantage of the shake-up occurring in the industry after World War II. Even if their industrial infrastructures, administrative capacities, and domestic markets had been as developed before the war, it is unlikely that similar policies could have induced either Ford or GM, the industry's giants, to invest in domestic manufacturing. Brazilian and Mexican attempts to increase exports in the 1970s were also coincidental with another shake-up in the industry, as U.S. and European firms were forced to restructure and reduce costs in response to the oil shock and the Japanese challenge.

Nevertheless, structural changes in the industry were a necessary, but insufficient, condition for these outcomes. Government policy shaped the timing and nature of firms' investment strategies in both instances. In the 1950s and 1960s, import-substitution policies forced firms to replace vehicle exports with domestic investment; without these policies, firms would not have invested in manufacturing capacity at that time. In the face of government export-promotion policies in the 1970s and 1980s, firms' options were constrained by the existence of these prior investments. Firms were forced to consider not only the need to protect access to these markets but to protect their past investments, which they did not

TABLE 5-13
Mexico Motor Vehicle Exports by Firm and Destination (units)

1990					
	Chrysler	*Ford*	*GM*	*Nissan*	*VW*	*Total*
---	---	---	---	---	---	---
North America	75,604	88,604	40,993	156	45,993	251,350
United States	73,080	88,604	40,993	—	35,594	238,271
Canada	2,524	—	—	156	10,399	13,079
Central America and Caribbean	78	—	—	10,563	—	10,641
South America	1	—	—	12,734	—	12,735
Chile	—	—	—	9,664	—	9,664
Africa	—	—	—	289	—	289
Asia	—	—	—	1,201	—	1,201
Japan	—	—	—	5	—	5
Guam	—	—	—	1,096	—	1,096
Europe	41	—	—	358	—	399
West Germany	—	—	—	—	—	—
Spain	—	—	—	300	—	300
Iceland	3	—	—	—	—	3

1989					
	Chrysler	*Ford*	*GM*	*Nissan*	*VW*	*Total*
---	---	---	---	---	---	---
North America	67,620	39,580	40,292	3	22,789	170,285
United States	61,701	39,580	40,292	—	21,413	162,967
Canada	5,919	—	—	3	1,363	7,285
Central America and Caribbean	147	—	—	9,507	40	9,698
South America	—	—	84	14,145	214	14,443
Chile	—	—	—	13,030	199	13,229
Africa	—	—	—	112	13	125
Asia	64	—	—	653	3	717
Japan	—	—	—	3	—	3
Guam	—	—	—	650	—	650
Europe	9	—	—	713	22	744
West Germany	—	—	—	—	16	16
Spain	—	—	—	713	—	713
Iceland	—	—	—	—	—	—

1988					
	Chrysler	*Ford*	*GM*	*Nissan*	*VW*	*Total*
---	---	---	---	---	---	---
North America	50,249	66,361	36,389	—	41	153,040
United States	46,655	64,932	36,389	—	41	148,017
Canada	3,594	1,429	—	—	—	5,023
Central America and Caribbean	59	—	—	10,445	389	11,187
South America	—	—	117	8,135	11	8,513
Chile	—	—	117	7,400	3	7,520
Africa	—	—	—	80	12	92
Asia	—	—	—	1	3	4
Japan	—	—	—	1	—	1
Guam	—	—	—	—	—	—
Europe	84	—	—	210	17	311
West Germany	—	—	—	—	8	8
Spain	—	—	—	210	—	210
Iceland	62	—	—	—	—	62

Source: AMIA data.

treat as sunk costs. As a result, the Brazilian and Mexican governments had more leverage, and received commitments to new export projects that they otherwise would not have gotten.

Indeed, the findings of this study indicate that auto companies do not randomly survey the globe in search of low-cost production sites, despite the images conjured up by the notion of a "world car strategy." While this may be an accurate portrayal of firm strategy in labor-intensive industries that can be easily relocated to exploit low wages and government incentives, it is less so for industries like automobiles, which require large fixed investments, distribution networks, industrial infrastructures, skilled labor, and a domestic market. Firms were reluctant to close a plant until it had been written off or its product was obsolete. Given the large investments and long time horizon in the industry, as well as government-imposed export targets, trade and investment strategies do not change immediately in response to variation in relative costs. While internationally competitive production costs might be a necessary condition for a firm to begin exporting from a country, it is not a sufficient one.

The fact that firms were forced to consider these countries as production sites, when they otherwise might not have, speaks to a successful dynamic outcome of import-substitution policies, which have recently come under such sharp criticism. Once the initial investments were made, firms took these sunk costs seriously. Moreover, these investments increased costs for new entrants or for those firms which might consider re-entry after leaving the market, increasing the risk of temporarily opting out of a potentially growing market. The example of Volkswagen in North America provides an extreme case of how trade policies can influence investment decisions. VW de Mexico not only built capacity to export engines, but became the sole location of all North American production as a result of Mexican trade policy. While this study does not attempt to calculate the full domestic resource costs of these national industries, its findings about firm behavior do raise questions about how best to assess costs and benefits. They suggest that the initial investment's impact on future investment, foreign capital flows, and exports must be considered in the calculation.

The Impact of Sectoral Policies on Trade and Investment

While these general findings apply to both Brazil and Mexico, a comparison of the two countries reveals how differences in policy regimes and macro-economic performance affected the way in which their respective industries were integrated into world trade and the degree to which their governments could leverage access to the domestic market in exchange for exports. Consequently, the study indicates that the overall regulatory regime, and not simply trade policies, must be included among other country-specific factors such as location, macro-economy, and market size as potential influences on the nature and direction of trade in particular industries.

In the cases of the Brazilian and Mexican auto industries, different domestic content requirements influenced the type of products that were manufactured and subsequent trade patterns. The fact that Mexico could produce more up-to-date vehicles that were based on international standards made it easier to increase exports and integrate into global production plans. High domestic content policies left a problematic legacy in Brazil not only because they isolated the industry and led firms to have longer production runs, however. By moving to high domestic content levels so quickly, the Brazilian government sacrificed trade policy as an instrument with which to shape firm behavior. Since firms had invested to produce at 95% domestic content levels, preferential access to imports was not an issue. When Brazil wanted to promote exports, it could offer only subsidies and a limited drawback scheme as "carrots," but had virtually no "sticks" to discipline firms for not participating. Access to the domestic market was unaffected, since vehicle components were domestically supplied. To force firms to export and/or to become more competitive, the government must threaten to open the market to finished vehicles and risk reductions in employment. Moreover, reducing domestic content levels would be politically difficult because the supplier network that arose to support the industry would be affected, as would the auto firms that built relatively integrated facilities.

Mexico, on the other hand, was in a weaker bargaining position vis-à-vis the transnational auto companies and originally adopted lower domestic content requirements. It was able to use access to imports, however, as a way both to structure the industry and to force firms to export. Given the changing nature of oligopolistic competition, policies that were adopted out of weakness were turned into a strength.[43]

Firm strategy with respect to vehicle type was also a factor in positioning these two national industries. Ford and GM in Brazil started producing European-designed car models in the late 1960s and early 1970s. These cars had little relationship to those sold in the United States. VW also produced different vehicles in each country. Autolatina did not produce Golfs and Jettas, but cars of its own design. VW de Mexico, like the U.S. subsidiaries, took its product lines from the parent. Autolatina's Fox was in a category slightly different from the Golf and Jetta. As a result, Mexico and Brazil did not compete for the same export markets, even if they were the largest producers in Latin America.[44] Brazilian exports would face tough competition in the European market from other low-cost producers such as Spain, where GM, Ford, and VW also have subsidiaries. If trading blocks were to form around locational proximity and common currency, Brazil would be in a difficult position.

The two countries have seldom competed as potential sites for investment in new capacity. When U.S. export programs were canceled in Brazil, they were relocated to the United States. The alternative to engine production or vehicle assembly in Mexico was also the United States. This was true for GM and Ford, which had many alternative sites, as well as for Chrysler, which had far fewer.

The Centrality of the Domestic Market

This study also underscores the importance of a country's domestic market in explaining its export performance and in determining its leverage over foreign firms. Cost and locational considerations alone are not sufficient to induce investment for export in the absence of domestic market potential. As the 1990s began, firms in Mexico focused on satisfying domestic demand while they looked for ways to rationalize production in North America in anticipation of a North American Free Trade Agreement (NAFTA). It was the domestic market potential that kept firms in Brazil and would determine Brazil's future role in international trade.

Brazil's initial success in attracting foreign investment was based on the rapid growth of its domestic market. At the beginning of the 1980s, the Brazilian auto industry appeared to be on the verge of maturity, but was confronted with domestic market contraction and macro-economic uncertainty. The nature of the industry and Brazil's position within firms' global strategy made it difficult for the auto firms to find sustainable alternatives to the domestic market and the traditional LDC export markets. Virtually no capacity was added over the 1980s.

As long as foreign firms decide to maintain a presence in Brazil despite stagnant demand, they will make marginal investments to maintain their competitive position in the domestic market. As long as the market remains relatively protected, the sector will continue to balance trade and even generate a surplus. In the absence of domestic market growth, even if the market is opened, it is unlikely that firms will commit new capital inflows, as they have recently done in Mexico.

Alternative Strategies: Latin America and South Korea Compared

While this study shows the conditions under which government policy can influence the investment and trade decisions of transnational firms, it also shows how the reliance on foreign firms generates constraints as well as opportunities. Firms worry about sunk costs and market access only up to a point. Occasionally they carry out their threats to leave, as evidenced by Fiat and GM in Argentina and Renault in Mexico. It is unlikely that they will subvert operations in their primary markets for less important ones, and they often limit export opportunities for subsidiaries.

The South Korean government also provided privileged access to critical imports in exchange for exports but, in contrast to Brazil and Mexico, promoted domestic firms. As a result of their respective political economies, different financial constraints, and different historical starting points, building national industries with domestic firms was never seriously considered in Brazil and was not sustainable in Mexico. Moreover, the Korean government's control over imports and access to cheap financing gave it considerably more leverage over domestic firms. Nevertheless, a comparison of the national industries illustrates some of the trade-offs associated with each strategy.

South Korea followed a Japanese approach toward its auto industry by promoting domestic firms and the development of an extensive supplier network.[45] In the early 1960s the government banned the importation of built-up vehicles and began to tie foreign exchange allocation to domestic content levels. The government abandoned a gradual approach to reaching 100% domestic content levels in response to the 1973 oil shock and promoted heavy industry. The 1974 Long-Range Automobile Industry Promotion Plan banned imported kits and forced firms to move quickly into integrated manufacturing. Passenger car production soared with the overall economy, growing from about 9,000 units in 1974 to more than 112,000 in 1979. After the devastating economic impact of the second oil shock, government policy shifted once again, encouraging industrial consolidation and tying low-cost financing and import licenses to a firm's export performance. Vehicle production skyrocketed, reaching 387,000 units in 1985 (57,200 of which were passenger cars), 602,000 in 1986

(457,400 cars), 980,000 in 1987 (793,100 cars), and topping a million by 1988. This growth was export led. In 1985 exports comprised 45% of car production; by 1988 they were 65%, shipped primarily to the United States and Canada.

Three companies were responsible for the impressive growth rates in passenger car production. They included Kia Motor Corporation, which had suspended passenger car production as part of the government's consolidation efforts in 1981. It resumed in 1986, when Ford purchased 10% of its capital, Mazda 8%, and C. Itoh 2%, and began to export Ford Festivas to the United States.

Hyundai Motor Company began assembling cars in 1967 with licensing agreements with Ford, but it consciously diversified its sources of technology among different countries and firms. It responded to the government's 1979 export policies by licensing more technology, opening its own R&D center, and attempting to design and produce a subcompact specifically for export. To help in this endeavor, it sold 10% of the company to Mitsubishi in exchange for technological assistance, but retained managerial control and the rights to import parts and technology from Mitsubishi's competitors and to compete in the same foreign markets. Hyundai became the largest producer and exporter by far. In 1988 it was responsible for over 60% of total production and 70% of total exports.

The third passenger car producer was Daewoo Motors, which formed a fifty-fifty joint venture with General Motors in 1972. In 1986 Daewoo started producing Opel's Kadett to supply GM in the United States. It also produced the Pontiac Le Mans.

The South Korean government was successful in working with large industrial conglomerates to export automobiles. Hyundai and Kia, firms dominated by Korean capital, produced cars of uniquely Korean design and were more inclined to develop technological capacity than Daewoo, which did relatively little to develop domestic technological capacity or product designs and seemed to follow the strategies of foreign subsidiaries in Brazil and Mexico with respect to technology transfer and export strategy. Hyundai was also the only one of the three main firms to develop its own distribution networks abroad; the others relied on their foreign partners. While alliances with transnational partners could in theory allow Korean firms to save on the costs associated with building new sales networks and provide them with broad name recognition, they may also restrict access to some foreign markets. Kia exported to Japan through Mazda and Ford. However, GM would not sell other Daewoo products in North America, and the company was dependent on GM's sales network.

There are potential difficulties in being able to sustain a "national champion" strategy based on exports and to repeat Japan's success, however. South Korea's extreme dependence on the world market, and on the United States in particular, may be risky. As Amsden has pointed out, Japan developed its industry under more favorable international economic conditions, and competition in the industry has since intensified, especially in the U.S. market. Moreover, Korean exports accounted for a larger share of production from the industry's early days, while exports did not reach 15% of Japanese production until 1968, over a decade after full-scale passenger car production had begun. Japan also started to export when its industry was running at full capacity. By 1968 15% of Japanese production came to 600,000 vehicles. The relatively small size of Korea's domestic market on which to build mass production is potentially problematic.

The pace of technological change has also quickened, necessitating greater resources. The South Korean auto firms are heavily dependent on foreign technology and components; official calculations of domestic content levels are 90%, but experts claim that the actual levels are closer to 50%.[46] Accessing capital and technology through licensing and forming minority joint ventures may become more difficult. Yet South Korean firms will need to upgrade and develop new products even more as its wage rates increase and it faces competition from other East Asian countries attempting to follow in its footsteps. From 1987 to 1989 labor costs in the industry doubled in domestic currency and rose even more in dollars with the appreciation of the won, all but eliminating any cost savings.[47]

In order to increase volume and reduce costs, the industry is going forward with plans to build additional capacity and introduce new models in the face of a recessed U.S. market and against the wishes of its transnational partners. The government is promoting local R&D, a challenging and costly strategy that many established firms in the United States and Europe have been forced to abandon in the context of today's competitive environment.

Mexico's and Brazil's strategy of relying on foreign firms to build up national industries does create the possibility of accessing capital, technology, and markets. Mexico's strategy of reducing domestic content, increasing imports, and integrating its domestic industry more closely with that in the United States does carry some risks, however. The industry is currently showing a trade deficit. Even if the North American Free Trade Agreement is finalized, it provides an adjustment period in which the sector will still have to meet balanced trade requirements. With the domestic market growing at such a rapid clip as compared to the U.S. slump, there is the risk that future growth in the industry (as for the economy as a whole) could become foreign exchange constrained. U.S. firms may be less willing to export from Mexico at the expense of U.S. production. Slow growth in exports may also slow down the importation of finished vehicles to Mexico. Market share per dollar is cheaper for domestic vehicles than for imports, for which 2.5 dollars in additional exports must be generated. On the other hand, Mexican facilities could benefit from a consolidation of the U.S. industry, as was seen in GM's 1992 restructuring. While Mexico may have had less ability to regulate the behavior of transnational firms than it would have had over domestic firms, the integration of the North American economies under a NAFTA would blur these national distinctions.

Moreover, Mexico, which saw real wages drop precipitously during the 1980s and allows for 100% foreign ownership, could benefit at South Korea's expense. Facing difficulties in South Korea, firms such as Ford and GM may focus more on Mexico and take advantage of its geographical proximity to the United States, its increasingly secure investment climate, and its buoyant domestic market. The outcome will depend in part on the impact of the NAFTA. Brazil for the near future will be dependent on its own domestic market potential and that of its South American neighbors.

NOTES

1. The following section draws heavily on Rhys Owen Jenkins, *Transnational Corporations and the Latin American Automobile Industry* (Pittsburgh: University of Pittsburgh Press, 1987); Daniel Roos and Alan Altshuler, codirectors, *The Future of the Automobile* (Cambridge, Mass.: MIT Press, 1984); and Lawrence J. White, *The Automobile Industry since 1945* (Cambridge, Mass.: Harvard University Press, 1971).

2. Ford and General Motors adopted different strategies. Ford opened new plants in England and Germany, while GM entered both countries by acquiring existing firms.

3. Roos and Altshuler, *The Future of the Automobile*, 19–20. Until 1965, North America and Europe accounted for over 90% of world production.

4. Jenkins, *Transnational Corporations*, 29.

5. Douglas C. Bennett and Kenneth E. Sharpe, *Transnational Corporations*

versus the State: The Political Economy of the Mexican Auto Industry (Princeton: Princeton University Press, 1985), 58.

6. Tariffs on passenger cars, which had fallen slightly after the war, still averaged over 30% in 1960 except in Germany, where they were 13–16%. By 1968 tariffs within the EEC were eliminated and had fallen to 17.6% in the United Kingdom. Vehicle trade among the major auto-producing countries in Europe was 6% of production in 1950, 7% in 1960, and 12.3% in 1970. Trade within Western Europe as a whole was 18.1%, 18.8%, and 25.8% of production for those same years (Roos and Altshuler,*The Future of the Automobile*, 17, 22).

7. Ibid., 25.

8. The loss of imperial preference was particularly important for the United Kingdom. In combination with Australian import restrictions, it led to Germany's surpassing the United Kingdom as the world's largest exporter of finished vehicles, a position it maintained from 1956 to 1973 (George Maxcy and Aubrey Silberston, *The Motor Industry* [London: George Allen and Unwin, 1959], 16–18). It should be noted that the aggregate import figures by country of origin mask firm nationality and hence exaggerate the inroads made by European-owned companies. After the war, for example, Ford, facing supply bottlenecks at home, shifted its export base to its European subsidiaries.

9. Roos and Altshuler, *The Future of the Automobile*, 22–25.

10. For more on the Japanese industry, see Michael Cusumano, *The Japanese Automobile Industry* (Cambridge, Mass.: Harvard University Press, 1985).

11. As strategic trade theorists have shown, economic rents are not competed away through free trade in oligopolized industries such as automobiles, which are characterized by economies of scale and other barriers to entry. See Paul Krugman, ed., *Strategic Trade Policy and the New International Economics* (Cambridge, Mass.: MIT Press, 1984). The existence of such market imperfections may justify government protection of domestic industries. Given the nature of motor vehicles and the political economy of Brazil and Mexico, domestic production was to be controlled by foreign rather than domestic capital, as is typically assumed in the literature on strategic trade. Therefore, the issue would not be simply rent distribution between nations, but the internal distribution between the firms and the state. For more on this aspect, see Helen Shapiro, *Engines of Growth: The State and Transnational Auto Companies in Brazil* (Cambridge: Cambridge University Press, forthcoming).

12. Eduardo Augusto de Almeida Guimarães, "Industry, Market Structure and the Growth of the Firm in the Brazilian Economy," Ph.D. diss., University of London, 1980, 173. The next-largest markets of Argentina, Mexico, and Venezuela each had only 200,000 vehicles in circulation.

13. For more on the Brazilian incentive system and its costs in general, see Joel Bergsman, *Brazil: Industrialization and Trade Policies* (London: Oxford University Press, 1970); Albert Fishlow, *Foreign Trade Regimes and Economic*

Development: Brazil, n.d.; Lincoln Gordon and Engelbert L. Grommers, *U.S. Manufacturing Investment in Brazil: The Impact of Brazilian Government Policies 1946–1960* (Cambridge, Mass.: Harvard University Press); on the auto industry in particular, see José Almeida, *A implantação da indústria automobilística do Brasil* (Rio de Janeiro: Fundação Getúlio Vargas, 1972), and Helen Shapiro, *Engines of Growth*.

14. Simca's automobile project never really got off the ground, Germany's Auto-Union was only a minority holder in Brazilian-controlled Vemag, and Alfa Romeo licensed technology to the state-owned National Motor Factory (FNM). Other European companies that participated in the program, Mercedes Benz, for instance, restricted their production to commercial vehicles. For more on VW's history, see Simon Reich, *The Fruits of Fascism* (Ithaca, N.Y., and London: Cornell University Press, 1990).

15. Cusumano, *The Japanese Automobile Industry*, 4. As a result of their late arrival on the international scene and their reluctance to source major components from offshore sites, Japanese firms have stayed out of the Brazilian car market to this day. Toyota continues to produce several thousand jeeps a year.

16. Already a minority shareholder, in 1966 Chrysler bought 92% of Simca in France, gaining control of Simca in Brazil, which had originally been 50% Brazilian owned; Chrysler also purchased International Harvester's truck facility. (In 1981 Chrysler discontinued automobile production and sold its truck operations to Volkswagen.) Volkswagen took over Vemag, which had been controlled by Brazilian capital, first through its acquisition of Auto-Union, a minority holder, then through purchasing the remaining shares. In 1967 Ford gained control over Willys, another firm that had been predominantly Brazilian owned, through its purchase of a controlling interest in Kaiser, and Alfa Romeo took over the previously state-owned firm, FNM.

17. Although Ford and GM were allowed to enter the passenger car market in 1968, Ford had been submitting proposals for passenger car production since 1958, all of which were rejected for not meeting government specifications or for competing with projects already under way. It is likely that the company underestimated the Brazilian government's willingness and capacity to prevent its entry into passenger cars in the initial years of the plan and the resultant costs of the delay. Ford's (and GM's) absence from the Brazilian market in these years allowed VW to redefine and capture the Brazilian car market. Subsequent interviews with Ford managers at the time indicate that they view Ford's late entry as a mistake. In contrast, Ford immediately entered into passenger car production in both Argentina and Mexico. For more detail on Ford in Brazil, see Helen Shapiro, "Determinants of Firm Entry into the Brazilian Automobile Manufacturing Industry, 1956–68," *Business History Review*, Winter 1991; Elizabeth Bortolaia Silva, *Refazendo a fábrica fordista* (São Paulo: Editora Hucitec, 1991); and Mira Wilkins and Frank Ernest Hill, *American Business Abroad: Ford on Six Continents* (Detroit: Wayne University Press, 1964).

18. Eduardo Augusto de Almeida Guimarães, "A política governamental e a indústria automobilística," World Bank Paper, October 1988, 5.

19. Bennett and Sharpe, *Transnational Corporations versus the State*, 128.

20. Juan Carlos Moreno Brid, "Mexico's Motor Vehicle Industry in the 1980s," World Employment Programme Research Working Paper No. 21, International Labour Office (ILO), Geneva, August 1988, 6.

21. For a discussion of the dynamics of foreign direct investment, see Richard E. Caves, *Multinational Enterprise and Economic Analysis* (Cambridge: Cambridge University Press, 1982); Stephen Hymer, *The International Operation of National Firms: A Study of Direct Foreign Investment* (Cambridge, Mass.: MIT Press, 1976); Frederick T. Knickerbocker, *Oligopolistic Reaction and Multinational Enterprise* (Boston: Division of Research, Harvard Business School, 1973); and Richard Newfarmer, ed., *Profits, Progress and Poverty: Case Studies of International Industries in Latin America* (Notre Dame, Ind.: University of Notre Dame Press, 1985).

22. Relevant estimates for optimum plant size vary. Bain estimated 300,000 (Joseph Bain, *Industrial Organization* [New York: John Wiley, 1968], 284–287). Baranson shows production costs per unit leveling off at 120,000 for assembly, 240,000 for engines and other power train parts, and 600,000 for body stampings (Jack Baranson, *Automotive Industries in Developing Countries*, World Bank Occasional Staff Papers, No. 8 [Washington, D.C.: World Bank, 1969]). Maxcy and Silberston (*The Motor Industry*, 75–98) estimate optimum capacity at 100,000 for assembly, 100,000 for casting, 400,000 for machining engines, and up to 1 million for body pressings, even though the rate of cost savings decreases as volumes grow. The economies of scale available to an individual firm differ from an individual plant. A firm can spread preproduction costs across plants and products, and a multiproduct mix allows some interchange of components. Measurement is difficult owing to the nonhomogeneity of product and the variety of cost allocations used by firms. Maxcy and Silberston estimate that technical economies are exhausted at 1 million units, while most of the substantive gains are made at the 400,000 mark. Optimum production for the industry as a whole would take into account the economies of scale available to suppliers as overall auto production increases. These estimates are all related to automobile production of the 1950s and 1960s. As a result of technological and organization innovations, similar calculations for today's industry would differ.

23. In response to complaints from GATT, the original export subsidy of 26% was reduced to 15%. After 1989, export subsidies disappeared altogether, except for old contracts that were grandfathered.

24. The domestic auto industry had negative repercussions on the balance of payments through its contribution to Brazil's oil-import bill. In order to reconcile the potentially contradictory goals of market growth and import reduction, Brazil implemented an ambitious gasohol program. Subsidies were offered

to sugar growers in the field and consumers at the pump. The production of gasohol-engined cars began in 1979. By 1982, 95% of new cars sold ran on gasohol.

25. Gesner Oliveira Filho, "Comissão para concessão de benefícios fiscais a programa especiais de exportação (BEFIEX) 1973–81," master's thesis, University of Campinas, Brazil, 1984.

26. Kenneth Mericle, "The Political Economy of the Brazilian Motor Vehicle Industry," in *The Political Economy of the Latin American Motor Vehicle Industry*, edited by Rich Kronish and Kenneth S. Mericle (Cambridge, Mass.: MIT Press, 1984).

27. Bernhard Fischer et al., *Capital-Intensive Industries in Newly Industrializing Countries: The Case of the Brazilian Automobile and Steel Industries* (Tubingen: J. C. B. Mohr, 1988), 25, and ANFAVEA, *Statistical Yearbook* (São Paulo: ANFAVEA, various years).

28. Fischer et al., *Capital-Intensive Industries* (citing CEPAL), 55.

29. World Bank, *Brazil: Industrial Policies and Manufactured Exports*, World Bank Country Study (Washington, D.C.: World Bank, 1983), 116.

30. Silva, *Refazendo a fábrica fordista*, 89.

31. *Business Month*, December 1988, 27.

32. For detailed accounts, see Bennett and Sharpe, *Transnational Corporations versus the State*, and Barbara C. Samuels II, *Managing Risk in Developing Countries* (Princeton: Princeton University Press, 1990).

33. James P. Womack, "Seeking Mutual Gain: North American Responses to Mexican Liberalization of its Motor Vehicle Industry," prepared for the forty-fourth Annual Plenary Meeting, Mexico–U.S. Business Committee, Orlando, Florida, November 9, 1989, 19.

34. These observations are based on extensive firm interviews. Samuels and Womack come to similar conclusions on the motivations behind firm entry. On the quality- and cost-effectiveness of Mexican production, see Harley Shaiken, *Mexico in the Global Economy* (San Diego: Center for U.S.–Mexican Studies, University of California, 1990), and Shaiken with Stephen Herzenberg, *Automation and Global Production* (San Diego: Center for U.S.–Mexican Studies, University of California, 1987).

35. Samuels, *Managing Risk*, 128.

36. It is worth noting that while the rest of the economy was being substantially liberalized under President Miguel de la Madrid during the 1980s, the auto industry was still protected from import competition.

37. The Mexican Central Bank eased firms' debt burden by allowing them access to dollars at a subsidized rate.

38. *Automotive News*, February 9, 1987.

39. Moreno Brid, "Mexico's Motor Vehicle Industry," 60.

40. According to The Economist Intelligence Unit, the large investment commitments by Nissan and VW were rewarded with prohibitions on imports

of subcompact cars until the 1993 model year (*Mexico's Motor Vehicle Industry, Prospects to 2000* [London: Business International Ltd., 1991]).

41. GM was also the leader in setting up automotive *maquiladora* plants. In 1986 it relocated almost all its wiring harness and upholstery cut-and-sew operations for its North American assembly operations to the Mexican border, and by 1990 had thirty plants. Ford and Chrysler have also set up border plants, but to a lesser degree. See James P. Womack, "A Positive Sum Solution: Free Trade in the North American Motor Vehicle Sector," in *Strategic Sectors in Mexican–U.S. Free Trade*, edited by M. Delal Baer and Guy F. Erb (Washington, D.C.: Center for Strategic and International Studies, 1991).

42. According to The Economist Intelligence Unit, Nissan's weak export performance was due in part to premature efforts to ship components to Japan at the urging of the Mexican government in the late 1970s and in part to the delicate trade situation with the United States. While Nissan is the only company that does not export vehicles from Mexico to the United States, it has begun to interchange components between its Mexican subsidiary and its transplant in Smyrna, Tennessee (*Mexico's Motor Vehicle Industry*).

43. This emphasis on the legacy of government and firm policies does not mean that locational considerations are unimportant. Mexico's location on the U.S. border allows U.S. firms to integrate Mexican facilities into their North American operations and centralize management. Ford's export plants even report directly to the U.S. division. Transport costs are a factor as well. Easy access to the U.S. market certainly influenced VW's decision.

44. One minor exception was a case of a four-cylinder marine engine produced by GM in Mexico and Brazil. Both subsidiaries competed for the U.S. market of about 30,000–40,000 units a year. According to GM de Mexico, Brazil's BEFIEX subsidies put GM do Brasil in a preferential position.

45. The following discussion is based on Chuk Kyo Kim and Chul Hee Lee, "The Growth of the Automotive Industry," in *Macroeconomic and Industrial Development in Korea*, ed. Chong Kee Park (Seoul: Korea Development Institute, 1980); Alice Amsden and Linsu Kim, "The Role of Transnational Corporations in the Production and Exports of the Korean Automobile Industry," in *Management Behind Industrialization: Readings in Korean Business*, eds. Amsden and Kim (Seoul: Korea University Press, 1989); Gary Gereffi, "Big Business and the State," in *Manufacturing Miracles: Paths of Industrialization in Latin America and East Asia*, edited by Gary Gereffi and Donald L. Wyman (Princeton: Princeton University Press, 1990).

46. *Far Eastern Economic Review*, January 18, 1990.

47. Ibid; *The Wall Street Journal*, March 2, 1990, and Womack, "A Positive Sum Solution."

PART II
Oligopolistic Competition

6

BEARINGS: THE VISIBLE HAND
OF GLOBAL FIRMS

David J. Collis

BEARINGS, LITERALLY, PLAY a pivotal role in most manufactured goods that involve moving parts. But beyond its importance for industrial production, the bearings industry is also a fascinating laboratory in which to study international trade and investment, because over the past forty years the industry has evolved into a classic global oligopoly, dominated by a handful of firms from Europe, Japan, and the United States. With large global companies now holding such a significant position, a study of the bearings industry can shed light on the relative importance of firms versus countries as determinants of the pattern of international trade.

While this study found that country factors continue to have a significant influence on trade and capital flows,[1] the research found evidence of the direct impact firms can have on trade.[2] The accumulation of strategic decisions by firms was critical in producing either virtuous circles of success and the earning of oligopolistic rents, or vicious circles of failure when the inability of a firm to build a competitive position precluded it (and its nation) from playing an ongoing role in global competition.[3] By examining the mechanisms by which firm-specific factors systematically produced variance in the pattern of trade from that predicted by comparative advantage, this chapter concludes that in the bearings industry a managerial visible hand has come to play a vital role in international trade.

This chapter has benefited greatly from discussions with participants in the World Trade Project and the Strategy Interest Group at Harvard Business School, most particularly with David Yoffie. I wish to acknowledge the research assistance of Nancy Donohue, Dianna Magnani, Masahiro Tanaka, Timothy Sorenson, and Toby Stuart and the financial support of the Harvard Business School Division of Research.

THE BEARINGS INDUSTRY

Economics of the Industry

Bearings,[4] or as they are more formally and accurately described, antifriction bearings, reduce friction between two moving surfaces and so are found in almost any product with moving parts, from computer disk drives and VCR heads to machine tools and autos. There are two kinds of antifriction bearings—ball and roller[5]—each of which accounted for about half the estimated world output of $15.5 billion in 1988. However, each kind is divided into different products—ball bearings into annular and thrust bearings, roller bearings into tapered, cylindrical, spherical, and needle bearings—and these products are differentiated according to international standards by size, precision level, and technical specifications like single/double row and sealed/unsealed. There are estimated to be more than 200,000 different bearings produced to stock, while an additional 30% of output is customized. Ball bearings tend to be standardized, while most roller bearings are customized and produced in smaller quantities.

Buyers of bearings cover the range of manufacturing industries. After the automobile industry, which purchases between 30% and 40% of bearings output in the United States, other important end-use industries are industrial machinery 10%, aerospace 6%, consumer electronics 3%, and office automation. This mix of end-users has not changed much over the years, although important shifts have occurred, such as the switch from tapered roller to double-row ball bearings in autos with the advent of front-wheel drive, and the rise in demand for miniature precision bearings accompanying the growth of computers and consumer electronics. The composition of demand in a country differs according to its industrial structure. In Japan, for example, the auto industry accounts for just over half of demand, and consumer electronics is a larger consumer of bearings than in the United States.

Primary demand for bearings is relatively price inelastic because bearings are a producer good. This factor, exacerbated by the procyclical inventory policies adopted by purchasers (delivery lead time at a market peak can reach two years), makes demand extremely cyclical. Output in the United States fell by 40% in real terms between the cyclical peak in 1979 and the cyclical trough in 1983 (see Figure 6-1).

The two main distribution channels for bearings are direct OEM sales (about 70%) and through distributors to smaller OEM customers and the replacement market (about 30%). Customer concentration can be quite

FIGURE 6-1
U.S. Bearings Production and Capacity Utilization (in 1982 dollars)

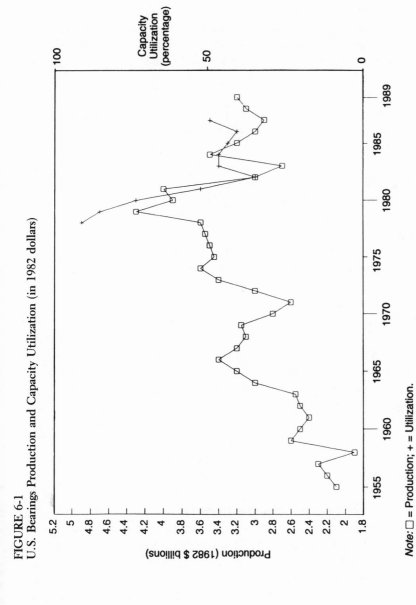

Note: ☐ = Production; + = Utilization.

Source: U.S. Bureau of the Census, "Business Trends."

high, particularly for firms that focus on the auto industry. The largest single customer may account for 10% of a bearings company's output. Increasingly these are global customers, such as car companies, which prefer the same supplier worldwide.

Buyer purchase criteria center on performance characteristics and price. Each type of bearings has different attributes and therefore different uses. Ball bearings are generally preferred in high-speed applications, roller bearings for heavy load applications. Moreover, since small design differences lead to big differences in such important performance characteristics as longevity, vibration, weight, and temperature sensitivity, careful applications engineering is required to meet customer specifications. This need for a close design link between manufacturer and customer provides a competitive advantage to manufacturers with long-established customer relationships and pushes companies to establish not only marketing but also design and production facilities in countries where they sell.

A nationwide network to service OEM machines wherever they fail has some value but, once the specification for a bearing is set, price becomes the major purchase criterion for OEM customers. This is particularly true for large-volume purchasers of standard bearings. Indeed, manufacturers often bemoan the commodity nature of their industry, notably when overcapacity in a recession leads to fierce price competition.

In this context, competitive success in the bearings industry comes from an appropriate choice of scale, scope, and international presence. Consistent positioning on these dimensions enables manufacturers to accommodate customer needs while remaining cost-competitive.

Scale is necessary to minimize production costs. Cost structures vary enormously according to the size and type of bearing (see Figure 6-2), as well as with run length and the degree of vertical integration. In general, about 30% of manufacturing cost is fixed, 50% is material content, and 20% is direct labor cost.

Given this cost structure, manufacturers can achieve substantial economies when they have sufficient volume of a particular size and type of bearing to automate production. At very high output levels of a single bearing (more than 300,000 ball bearings per month)[6] mass production on a highly automated line is possible. Such modern facilities now produce bearings from bar steel almost untouched by human hands. Operators perform only inspection, quality control, and material handling. For medium volumes (30,000–50,000 per month), companies use a "chan-

FIGURE 6-2
1988 Manufacturing Cost Structure (percentage)

Percentage

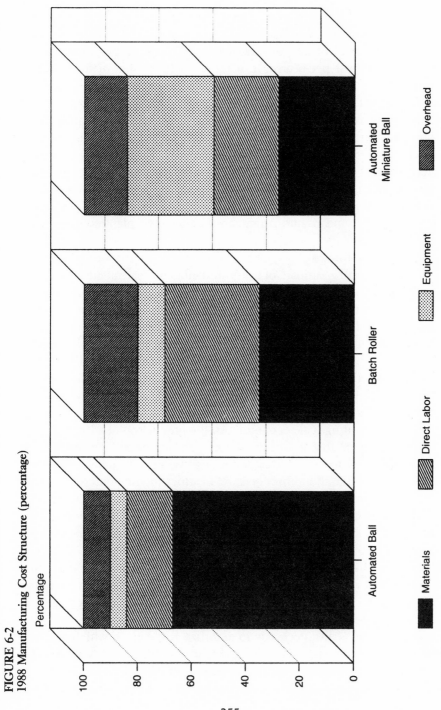

Materials   Direct Labor   Equipment   Overhead

Sources: Automated ball: NSK; batch roller and automated miniature ball: SKF estimates.

nel concept" of linked material flows between separate machine groups. This technique increases labor content by about 25%.[7] At very low volumes (batch sizes of one to several thousand), piece production is the rule and the cost per bearing can be seven times that of high-volume output.[8]

As manufacturing scale economies reside at the line level, a bearings plant today is specialized both for a particular type of bearing (ball, tapered roller, or needle, for example) and for a limited range of sizes (often between ten and forty). This is a change from the 1950s, when a factory would produce the full range of bearings consumed in its domestic market. Indeed, focusing factories on a limited product range was an important strategic advantage that the Japanese exploited in the 1960s, forcing the Europeans and Americans to alter their plant configurations in the 1970s.

Scale economies at the plant level, in contrast, are not particularly important. A 1975 estimate of minimum efficient scale at 800 employees (with an 8% cost increase for a one-third-size plant) has not needed substantial altering.[9] Industry estimates suggest that a minimum efficient scale ball bearings plant today costs $70 million, employs about 500 people and produces 3 million units a month on ten final assembly lines.[10] Increasing factory scale beyond this size usually involves adding product varieties. This increases the complexity of an operation, as half the labor force consists of indirect workers, more than enough to offset further plant overhead economies.

While exploiting scale economies in the production of a limited product line suggests that a narrow scope is an appropriate strategy, broad scope has come to be a source of competitive advantage in the bearings industry. This situation arises because bearings production cost is driven by accumulated experience, which to some extent can be shared across products. The industry experience curve is estimated to follow a 75% slope.[11] The process and machinery improvements that lie behind the experience curve have also acted as an effective entry barrier. No viable competitors have emerged in the last decade from the newly industrializing countries (NICs) or less-developed countries (LDCs). Even the South Korean and Taiwanese bearings manufacturers are only junior partners in local joint ventures with foreign companies.

Broad scope is also necessary to amortize R&D costs, which at 2% of sales value are an important determinant of strategic position. Mostly, however, broad scope is necessary because of the need to maintain an efficient service and distribution network and to effectively serve customers who are aware of the substitution possibilities between bearings types. As the distinction between uses has blurred over time—auto manufacturers, for example, can now use ball, tapered roller, and needle bearings, as well as integral hub units, in car axles—offering a full line has become a necessity. Of the largest fifteen producers today, none is a pure specialist, and only three—Minebea (miniature ball), NDH (integral hub units), and Timken (tapered roller)—generate more than 70% of their revenues from a single bearing type.

The need for scale and scope and the growing globalization of customers favor bearings producers with substantial international sales. These also allow firms to access the technological developments in bearings and in the consuming industries in different countries. Because manufacturing cost is quite sensitive to capacity utilization, international sales also allow bearings manufacturers to offset the domestic cycle and maintain capacity utilization, which can drop as low as 50% in a recession (see Figure 6-1).

Since transport costs across a hemisphere vary only from 2–7% of sales value according to size, international sales theoretically allow a firm to exploit line-scale economies by centralizing world production of each bearing in a single plant. At one time or another many firms experimented with this centralized production configuration. However, the need for close customer relations to coordinate design and guarantee supply compelled manufacturers to locate production facilities in the markets they served. This pressure, plus the absence in LDCs of the requisite infrastructure and machinist skills, made bearings unsuitable for production in low labor cost countries, notwithstanding their relatively high labor content. Only Minebea, which has moved the highly automated production of its standard miniature ball bearings to Southeast Asia, has located in low labor cost countries. Instead, the major producers have moved to adopt a "Triad" production configuration, with plants inside each of the world's three major economic regions—Europe, the United States, and Southeast Asia.

Country Performance

The pattern of country performance in the bearings industry since 1955 that emerges from the production data (see Figure 6-3) shows the rapid rise of Japan, the gradual decline of the United States, the continuing strength of West Germany, the deteriorating performance of the other European nations, and the recent emergence of a few NICs (notably

FIGURE 6-3
Share of Largest Eight Countries' Production (percentage)

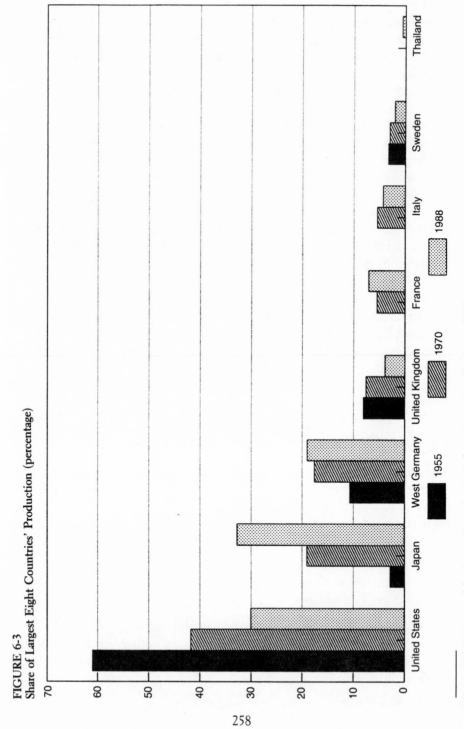

Sources: U.S. Bureau of the Census; Japan Bearing Industry Association; Torrington; FAG.

Thailand). Even if we abstract from the immediate postwar period of readjustment[12] and examine the years 1970–1988, the trend is the same (although some care has to be taken in examining annual data because of volatile exchange rates and imperfectly correlated business cycles).

World production of $15.5 billion is now roughly divided among Europe (one-third), United States (one-fourth), Japan (one-fourth), and the rest of the world, including the Eastern bloc. As a single entity Western Europe is, and has been since 1970, the largest producer of bearings in the world.

The data on shares of world exports, which better represent the "competitiveness" of a country's industry (because production shares are highly correlated with domestic market size), confirm the pattern (see Figure 6-4). While the level of world trade in bearings has gradually expanded— the share of world output exported has increased since the 1960s from 11% to 33%—the U.S. share declined from nearly a quarter in the early 1960s to its most recent low, in 1987, of 6.5%. The Japanese share of world exports more than doubled in twenty years from less than 10% in the early 1960s to over 20%. It is important to note, however, that this share peaked in the early 1970s and has since declined somewhat. Export-led growth stopped for the Japanese bearings industry in the mid-1970s, to be replaced by foreign direct investment. West Germany has consistently maintained a 25% share of world exports. The decline of the United Kingdom and Sweden is also more starkly observed in these data. Finally, the emergence in the 1980s of Thailand, which together with Singapore accounts for nearly 7% of world exports (almost exclusively from Minebea), stands out.

The bearings trade balance of each country completes the performance picture. With a combined surplus of $1.25 billion, West Germany and Japan are the only substantial net exporters (see Table 6-1). The United States, which slipped into deficit in 1972, now has a $400 million trade deficit that represents 19% of its consumption. Of the other European countries, only Sweden (home of world leader SKF) has a consistently positive trade balance. Thailand now boasts the fifth-largest bearings trade surplus in the world.

Company Performance

There are now about two hundred bearings manufacturers worldwide, of whom only fifteen have world market shares above 1%. (See Table 6-2, which identifies *only* a company's sales of bearings by excluding

FIGURE 6-4
Share of World Exports (percentage)

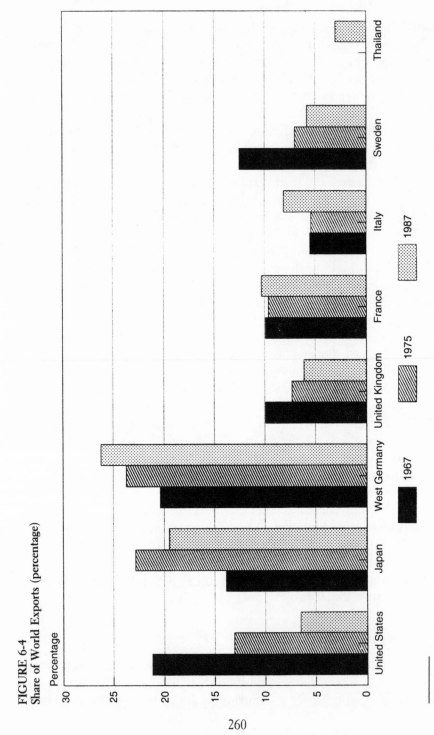

Percentage

Sources: ITC; OTA; Japan Bearing Industry Association; U.S Bureau of the Census; UN Trade
Statistics.

260

TABLE 6-1
International Trade

Trade Balance ($ millions)	United States	Japan	West Germany	United Kingdom	France	Italy	Sweden	Thailand
1955	24	1	NA	NA	NA	NA	NA	NA
1960	46	6	NA	NA	NA	NA	NA	NA
1965	48	39	48[a]	15[a]	(5)[a]	1[a]	48[a]	NA
1970	31	126	84	9	(25)	(17)	48	NA
1975	16	365	242	2	NA	(28)[a]	47	NA
1980	(60)	497	470	36	12	(82)	88	NA
1985	(322)	530	366	(18)	57	45	69	1
1987	(383)	749	553	(34)	112	(4)	80	77
Share of Production Exported (percentage)								
1971	8.6	30.4	34.3	28.1	38.3	32.1	76.2	NA
1987	9.1	29.5	57.8	77.9	65.1	76.0	120.6	190.5
Share of Consumption Imported (percentage)								
1971	7.2	1.9	17.3	22.1	40.9	27.7	45.9	NA
1987	19.5	7.2	43.2	80.0	59.0	78.6	131.8	NA

[a]Adjacent year (deficit).
Note: NA = not available; ( ) = deficit.
Sources: UN Trade Statistics; U.S. Bureau of the Census; Japan Bearing Industry Association.

TABLE 6-2
Company Sales of Bearings Worldwide ($ millions)

	1950	1955	1960	1965	1970	1975	1980	1985	1987
Japanese Companies									
NSK	3	11	31	44	134	243	521	683	1,079
NTN	NA	NA	33	42	159	330	499	704	1,058
Koyo	3	6	28	61	154	300	349	478	781
Nachi-Fujikoshi (NF)	1	3	14	22	48	98	163	185	263
Minebea	—	0.1	0.3	1	9	28	79	210	360
European Companies									
SKF	124	202	326	540	733	1,300	2,151	1,755	2,615
FAG	15	55	100	150	233	627	965	805	1,293
INA	NA	45	67	NA	86	173	396	408	845
SNR	NA	NA	NA	NA	60e	139e	100e	200e	150e
RHP	—	—	—	77	96	124	178	114	156
U.S. Companies									
Timken	95	123	150	120	270	570	966	775	826
Torrington	<34	<44	<68	<93	86	<376	240	480e	610e
Federal Mogul	25	<100	<133	86	94	114	205	242	195
New Departure Hyatt	NA	NA	NA	NA	240e	NA	400e	475e	450e
Kaydon	NA	NA	NA	NA	NA	NA	NA	NA	<133
Barden	NA	8e	15e	21	25e	35	50e	NA	69
Fafnir	NA	15e	71	103	120e	NA	NA	240	—
Hoover	NA	<20e	<50e	29	44	—	—	—	—
MPB	NA	5e	10	12	25e	47	70e	NA	100
New Hampshire Ball Bearing (NHBB)	NA	2	8	7	13	21	44	59	—
Marlin Rockwell	NA	NA	40e	NA	NA	NA	NA	100	—
Brenco	NA	NA	NA	NA	20e	NA	25e	NA	<33

Note: NA = not available; e = estimate from adjacent year; < = reported as part of a larger group; — = not in existence.
Sources: Annual reports, company estimates.

revenue from other products, and Table 6-3, which, reasonably accurately, interprets those data as world market shares.) Of these, Japanese firms have dramatically increased their world market shares since the 1950s. U.S. firms have dramatically lost world market share, and European companies have held their market shares. As with the country share of production data, this trend holds for the post-1970 period as well as for the immediate postwar readjustment.

Of the nine largest bearings producers today, three are European (SKF of Sweden and FAG and INA of West Germany); three are Japanese (NSK, NTN, and Koyo), and three are U.S. firms (Timken, Torrington, and New Departure Hyatt [NDH], which is General Motors' in-house supplier). In contrast, in 1955, five of the nine largest producers were U.S. firms and four were European. Since that time, the only U.S. firm to gain market share has been Torrington, which did so by acquiring Fafnir (while continuing to lose combined share). Indeed, six of the larger U.S. companies from the 1950s are no longer in business, having been acquired by other competitors (MPB was bought by Timken, and Barden by FAG in 1990). In Europe, the success stories have been SKF, which has retained its world leadership position, FAG, and INA. The French manufacturer SNR (owned by Renault) and the English manufacturer RHP (acquired by NSK in 1990) have both lost world market share. Each of the five Japanese firms has grown steadily throughout the period, although Koyo (20% owned by Toyota) had serious problems in the late 1970s and lost ground to its two main rivals.

The data on world market shares hide a wide variance in company shares across countries (see Table 6-3). All manufacturers possess much higher domestic market shares than foreign ones. Even NSK and NTN, each of which has about 30% of the Japanese market, hold less than 5% share of markets outside Japan, and only SKF holds a greater than 10% share anywhere outside its home region. The result is that concentration levels in a country are much higher than world market shares suggest.[13] In West Germany, for example, SKF (30%), FAG (28%), and INA (17%) dominate the market. In both France and Italy, SKF has approximately a 67% market share. Concentration levels in individual product categories are also much higher because of the product focus strategy of several major bearings manufacturers. In the United States, for example, Timken holds roughly a 75% market share in tapered roller bearings, Torrington a 50% share in needle bearings, and Minebea a 90% share in precision miniature ball bearings.

The major players today sell between one quarter and one third of

TABLE 6-3
Company Market Share[a]
(percentage)

	World Share			1987 Regional Share		
	1955	*1970*	*1987*	*U.S.*	*Japan*	*Europe*
Japanese Companies						
NSK	1.4	4.8	10.0	3	31	2–3
NTN	1.6	5.7	9.8	4	30	3
Koyo	0.8	5.5	7.3	2–3	21	1
NF	0.4	1.7	2.4	1–2	8	1
Minebea	0.0	0.3	3.3	2	5	2
	4.2	18.0	32.8	13	95	10
European Companies						
SKF	25.6	26.4	24.3	10–12	0.3	35
FAG	7.0	8.4	12.0	4	U	17
INA	2.5	2.1	6.0	2	U	10
SNR	2.5	2.2	1.4	U	U	2
RHP	3.8[b]	3.5	1.5	U	U	2
	41.4	42.6	45.2	17	1	66
U.S. Companies						
Timken	15.6	9.7	7.7	14	U	4
Torrington	3.8	3.1	5.7	14	U	1
Federal Mogul	4.4	3.4	1.8	5	U	U
New Departure Hyatt	19.0	8.6	4.2	10	U	U
Kaydon	1.3	2.7	0.9	3	U	U
Barden	1.0	0.9	0.7	2	U	U
Fafnir	1.9	4.3	—	—	—	—
Hoover	1.9	1.6	—	—	—	—
MPB	0.6	0.9	0.9	3	U	U
NHBB	0.3	0.5	—	—	—	—
Marlin Rockwell	3.2	2.9	—	—	—	—
Brenco	1.3	0.7	0.2	1	U	U
	54.3	39.3	21.5	52	U	5
Total identified			89	82	96	81
Concentration Ratios						
C3	60	45	46	40	82	62
C6	75	64	71	55	99	72

[a]Share of identified companies' sales.
[b]Estimate of combined predecessor company sales.

Note: — = not in existence; U = unknown, but almost certainly <1%.
Sources: Annual reports; company estimates.

their volume overseas (see Table 6-4), and most have manufacturing sites around the world (see Table 6-5).

As a consequence of this globalization of firms' activities, country and company performance have diverged. Figure 6-5 illustrates that whereas in 1966 there was some foreign-owned production in all countries, the United States was the only country whose firms performed proportionately better than their home base. By 1986 the picture had reversed. One

TABLE 6-4
Overseas Involvement, 1989[a]

	Overseas Sales (percentage)	Overseas Production (percentage)		Founded
NSK	26	11	Since 1972	1914
NTN	29	12	Since 1971	1918
Koyo	29	5	Since 1973	1921
NF	32	11	Since 1972	1939 (bearings)
Minebea	43	98	Since 1971	1951
SKF	37	21	Since 1911	1907
FAG	25	15	Since 1936	1883
INA	27	13	Since 1958	1943 (bearings)
SNR	NA	0	—	NA
RHP	28	8[c]	Since 1989[c]	1969 (merged)
Timken	38	36	Since 1920	1904
Torrington	25 (45)	16 (39)	Since 1961	1886
Federal Mogul	25	7	Since 1969	1899
New Departure Hyatt	<5	0	—[b]	1892
Kaydon	8	0	—	NA
Barden	NA	15	Since 1959	1942
Brenco	29	0	—	NA

[a]European firms defined as outside Europe.
[b]Facility opened in 1991.
[c]In continental Europe.
Note: NA = not available; ( ) includes joint ventures.
Sources: Company estimates.

fifth of U.S. output was coming from foreign-owned facilities (up from 13% in 1980 and 16% in 1985)[14]—indeed, ten of the fifteen largest bearings producers in the United States are now foreign owned—while American firms' worldwide sales were less than total bearings output in the United States. Conversely, because of their extensive international production facilities, both Japanese and European firms enjoy world market shares greater than the production share of their home countries.

Thus, the pattern of postwar and recent performance is straightforward. Japan and Japanese firms in particular have performed remarkably well, initially by exporting but since the early 1970s by establishing global facilities. European firms, already well established around the world, have maintained their share of world production. The United States, and disproportionately its firms, has declined.

Patterns of Trade

It is this combination of country and company performance that creates the pattern of trade (Table 6-1 and Figure 6-6). The U.S. export

TABLE 6-5
1988 Bearings Manufacturing Facilities

	North America	Asia	Europe	Other
Japanese firms				
NSK	2	9	1	1
NTN	5	6	1	—
Koyo	1	5	—	1
NF	1	5	1	1
Minebea	3	6	1	—
	13	31	4	3
European firms				
SKF	12	—	24	9
FAG	2	1	11	2
INA	4	1	8	2
SNR	—	—	5	—
RHP	—	—	6	—
	18	2	54	13
U.S. firms				
Timken	7	—	3	4
Torrington	11	3	6	3
Federal Mogul	4	—	1	—
New Departure Hyatt	2	—	1*	—
Kaydon	<9	—	—	—
Barden	2	—	1	—
Brenco	4	—	—	—
MPB	4	—	1	—
	<43	3	13	7

*Planned.
Note: Numbers include parts of facilities. U.S. firms include joint-venture facilities.
Sources: Annual reports; company interviews.

share of production barely increased between 1971 and 1988 from its already low level of 9%, while the U.S. import penetration ratio nearly tripled to 19%. Over the same period the destination of U.S. exports stayed constant—more than half of U.S. exports went to Canada and Latin America (primarily Mexico)—as did the composition of its imports—one-half from Japan, one-third from Europe.

The Japanese export share of production peaked in 1975 at 39% and has declined slightly since then. The destination of those exports has changed little—one-half to the United States, one-fifth to Europe, and one-third elsewhere. Japanese imports do, however, tell an important story about the role of firms in determining trade patterns. While the overall import penetration level has nearly quadrupled (at 8% it is still the lowest of any industrialized nation), the mix has shifted dramatically: two thirds of Japanese imports now come from Southeast Asia. These are imports from facilities established in Southeast Asia by Japanese firms, notably Minebea. In fact, the import penetration ratios from the

FIGURE 6-5
Share of Production by Domicile of Manufacturer (percentage)

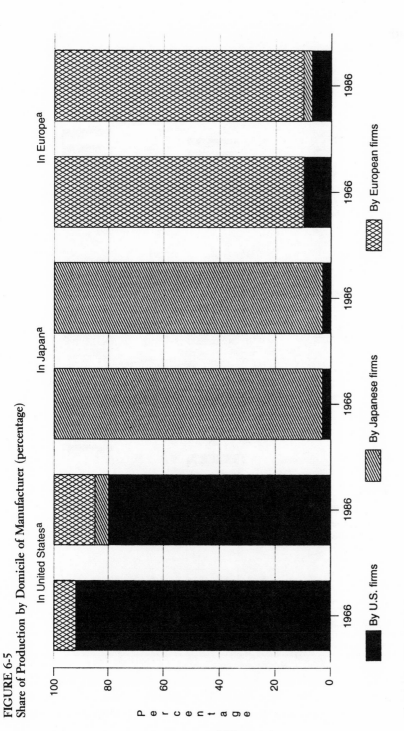

aIncludes joint ventures

Source: Author's estimates from interviews.

FIGURE 6-6
Trade Patterns

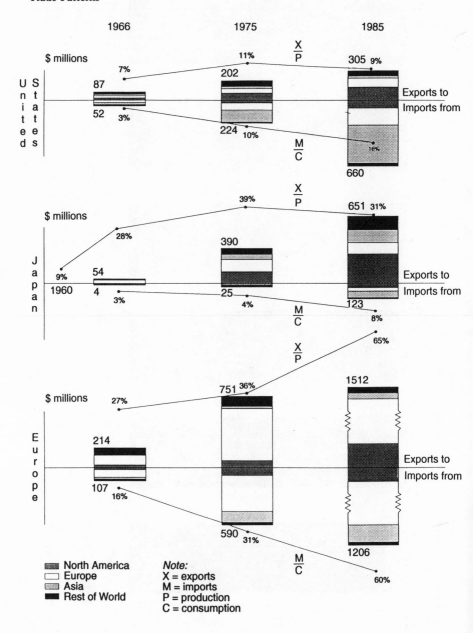

Sources: UN Trade Statistics; U.S. Bureau of the Census; Japan Bearing Industry Association; FAG.

United States and Europe have changed very little since 1971, rising from 1.2% to 1.4% for the United States and from 0.7% to 0.9% for Europe. In Japan, exports stopped growing (as a share of production) because Japanese firms moved production to Europe and the United States, while imports rose only because firms shifted production for the domestic market to Southeast Asia. Japanese firms' strategies have therefore directly affected the pattern of Japanese trade.

In Europe, company strategies (notably of SKF) also explain developments in trade patterns. Both export and import shares in Europe have risen dramatically as nations there have become more intraregional traders. Intra-European trade has increased from less than half of all European trade to more than two-thirds. This trend followed directly from SKF's decision in the early 1970s (later imitated by other European companies) to change from producing in one country all the products to be sold in that country to having a single plant supply each product Europewide.

This pattern of Japanese and European trade is evidence for the important determining role of company strategy, at least since the 1970s emergence of a global oligopoly. The next section more fully explains to what extent these trade patterns resulted from the influence of firms.

DETERMINANTS OF TRADE PATTERNS

A Model of Trade

The framework proposed to demonstrate how firms mediate the relationship between country variables and trade patterns contains four elements (see Figure 6-7).[15] Two are country based, two company based.

The first country-based element is the domestic incentive structure for firms in an industry. This is created by the combination of a country's industry structure,[16] related and supporting industries,[17] demand structure,[18] traditional factor endowments (defined at a fairly disaggregated level to include "advanced factors"), and government policy that Porter has recently termed the "diamond."[19] These structural forces influence firms' strategic choices, either directly by creating demand-side opportunities or indirectly by facilitating access to the supply of a particular factor of production. In turn, those strategic choices will determine the success of domestic firms in international competition.

The second country-based element is the locational advantage a country may possess for the performance of particular activities. The same

FIGURE 6-7
Country and Company Determinants of the Pattern of World Trade

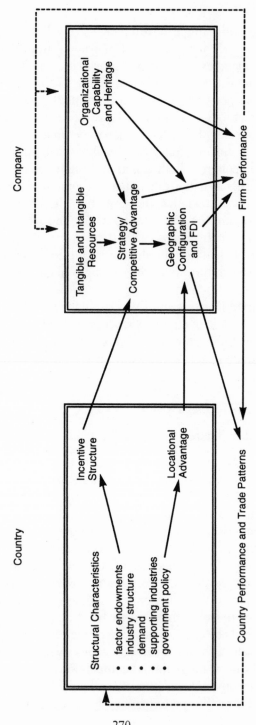

forces that shape economic incentives also determine locational advantage. This time, however, they affect the location of each activity a firm performs, not its basic choice of strategy.[20] Thus, while the structural characteristics of Thailand may not support the pursuit of a low-cost strategy to serve the aerospace industry by an indigenous Thai firm, they may allow a Japanese bearings company to locate the production facilities for such a strategy in Thailand. The overall incentive structure need not be present for a single activity to be performed in a country.

The two company factors that affect the pattern of world trade are those that Dunning identifies as necessary for the existence of the multinational.[21] The first is the set of unique tangible and intangible resources a firm possesses, such as brand name, technical know-how, and physical plant. Recent theoretical developments in strategic management suggest that these resources provide firms which choose appropriate strategies with sustainable competitive advantage in product markets.[22]

The second company factor—organizational capability and heritage[23]—is analogous to Dunning's internalization advantage. For a company to justify foreign direct investment rather than contracting for the performance of an activity or, conversely, licensing firm-specific assets, there must be an institutional advantage to retaining the transaction within the hierarchy.[24] Typically, this is attributed to the existence of a market failure such as accompanies the transfer of information[25] or asset-specific investments.[26] However, such an analysis ignores the cost of administering the transaction within the firm.

If the internal administrative cost is extremely high, whether because of opportunity costs in the use of scarce organizational skills or because firms lack international management experience, the hierarchical solution will fail, irrespective of the level of market transaction costs. As internal organizational costs are reduced, the number of activities that can be retained inside the multinational increases. This explains why firms generally enter a foreign market by exporting through a third-party distributor, then establish their own marketing activity, and later replace the distributor with its own sales force. At each stage the reason for increasing the scope of the firm has nothing to do with the market transaction costs, which stay the same throughout, and everything to do with the decreasing cost of internal coordination.

The implication is that successful multinational firms which seek to realize the economic potential inherent in a dispersed geographic configuration[27] must possess the organizational capability required to coordinate multicountry activities. This capability does not emerge full-blown at the birth of the enterprise, but rather grows as the organization's international experience accumulates and its stock of firm-specific human resources expands.[28]

We can now assemble the model in which both company and country factors play a role in the determination of trade patterns from its constituent parts. The first causal link, which recognizes that country factors have no direct influence on trade patterns but are always mediated by firm behavior, is from a country's endowments or characteristics to the incentive structure that leads domestic firms to choose particular strategies. However, a country's endowments create only an incentive structure. They do not mandate firms to pursue a particular strategy. Indeed, voluntaristic action to transcend the domestic incentive structure or exploit a desirable foreign "diamond" is the essence of strategy formulation.[29] While a powerful influence on strategic choice, and hence on success in international competition, the effect of domestic structural forces is mediated by those firm-specific elements—resources and organizational capability—which must be present to explain why one firm rather than another succeeds in a particular country.

The second causal link is from the locational advantages of a country to a firm's geographic configuration. Again, country factors do not directly determine configuration decisions. Those are determined jointly with the firm's strategy—only companies pursuing a particular strategy will want to exploit a specific country's locational advantage—and by the firm's current organizational capability—whether it has accumulated the experience and resources to effectively coordinate a geographically dispersed configuration. These decisions lead to foreign direct investment, which then produces the divergence of company and country performance.

In this framework firm performance is determined by the interaction of each firm's resources and organizational capability with its choice of strategy and geographic configuration. Finally, country performance and, most important for this chapter, patterns of world trade, are the outcome of firms' performance and the geographic configuration of those firms. Feedback loops then exist from country performance to endowments as, for example, factor costs alter in response to varying factor demands or government policy changes to remedy elements of country performance. Similarly, a feedback loop from firm performance to firm strategy and organizational capability exists as firms accumulate resources and international management expertise. These feedback loops make the framework dynamic and so introduce a role for history.

In this framework, trade patterns can be identified as the joint outcome of the nationality of successful firms and the location of their activities. This chapter therefore evaluates the role played by firm-specific factors in the determination of trade patterns in the bearings industry by their influence on those two separate outcomes.

However, the relative importance of firm factors is theoretically, and was found empirically, to be dependent on the industry structure. Under conditions of perfect competition, firms' freedom of action is constrained. Competitive pressures imply that only firms which have made the cost-minimizing investments survive. If, for example, the optimal location is in country A, the additional transaction costs for a firm in country B (however small) of relocating or managing activities in the foreign country by themselves prevent the firm from successfully superseding its domestic constraints. The invisible hand is indeed superior to the visible hand.

In contrast, in an industry that features oligopolistic (imperfect) competition among multinational firms—the structure that predominates in the trade of manufactured goods—such aberrant behavior is permitted because of the "slack" available from the receipt of oligopolistic rents and because the threat of entry is minimal. "Suboptimal" decisions merely reduce the profit stream; they do not endanger a firm's long-term viability. Thus the ability of firms either to choose a strategy that overrides the constraints of the domestic incentive structure in order to be internationally successful or to locate an activity in an inferior country, i.e., to play an independent role in determining the pattern of world trade, is conditional on the structure of competition in the industry.

Nationality of Successful Firms

The framework's feedback loops (which represent the effect of path dependence) suggest that one must examine each firm's history to understand its success, because a large part of the explanation of why a firm is successful today is that it was successful yesterday. In doing this, one observes that the relative importance of firm-specific factors in determining the nationality of successful firms alters over the company's life.

Founding. In the start-up phase, firms are unlikely to escape their domestic constraints (not in the least because the industry structure tends to perfect competition). The immediate concern is establishing viability, and the obvious context for pursuing the entrepreneurial opportunity is the domestic market. To imagine serving the foreign market before the domestic market or to obtain financing for a venture whose success, tenuous in the best of circumstances, is contingent on additional uncertainties, such as exploiting advanced factors in foreign countries, is extremely unlikely. For a new venture, which is distinguished by a scarcity of resources of all types (capital, information, and labor), the costs incurred in violating domestic constraints are practically insurmountable.[30]

SKF, for example, was founded in 1905 by Sven Wingquist, a maintenance engineer at a Göteborg textile plant. Frustrated by the poor quality of imported ball bearings used in the shafts connecting the central steam engine to the spinning machines, Wingquist decided to "make the bearings in Sweden from Swedish steel."[31] The move was a success, as "the home-made ball bearing proved to have many times the life of its imported counterpart."[32] In 1907 Wingquist achieved a major technological breakthrough when he designed a unique double-row self-aligning ball bearing to solve the problem of friction and premature wear in the bearings "when rain softened the clay foundations of the textile plant [causing] buildings to settle and lineshafts to bend."[33] Realizing the value of the product, "but because of low sales potential in Sweden,"[34] Wingquist himself (at the time SKF had fifteen employees) spent three months in Europe that year visiting one hundred potential customers. By 1910 SKF had sales offices in France and Germany, sales agents in, among other places, Australia and Finland, and two subsidiaries in the United States and the United Kingdom.

I recount this story in some detail to make two points.[35] The first is the importance of country factors in the establishment of new enterprises. Sweden in the early twentieth century was renowned for high-grade iron and steel made from its deposits of iron ore with low phosphorus content. Using these steels, the country had developed a sophisticated metalworking industry. These two elements—Swedish steel and engineering skills—fostered development of Wingquist's first product. Arguably, climate led to his second breakthrough, but it was clearly limited domestic demand that pushed SKF to become a global competitor within five years of its founding. A combination of country factors, therefore, created the conditions, or an incentive structure, that were ripe for exploitation. But—and this is the second point—it was an entrepreneurial vision and technical competence that took advantage of that opportunity. Country factors may be a necessary condition for the establishment of a particular type of enterprise, but they are insufficient to identify which company or individual will succeed.

Elsewhere in Europe it was primarily country factors that influenced the establishment of other bearings firms. The predecessor company to FAG was founded in 1883 in Schweinfurt (the home of the German bearings industry ever since) as a manufacturer of grinding machines that could produce small balls of reasonable quality in factory quantities for use in bicycle bearings. The domestic demand pull from this new industry—based in Germany because of its expertise in metalworking and transportation—therefore created the incentive for the invention of the ball grinding machine.[36] INA developed its breakthrough caged needle bearing in 1949 to meet demand for small light bearings for use in compact German cars. Ransome Hoffman Pollard (RHP), the United Kingdom's only domestically owned bearing manufacturer of note, was formed by a merger of the three largest U.K.-owned bearings manufacturers in 1969. This amalgamation was engineered by the Industrial Reorganization Corporation (IRC), a body created by the Labour Party to revitalize British industry, with the explicit goal of consolidating the fragmented U.K. bearings industry structure.[37]

In Japan, domestic incentives also predominated in the founding of bearings manufacturers—notably the need for a domestic source of bearings to support the war effort. NSK was founded in 1914, NTN was founded in 1918 by an ironworking company to meet war demands, and Nachi-Fujikoshi (NF), an existing manufacturer of cutting tools and specialty steels, began bearings production in 1939.

Government policy and the domestic demand structure also influenced Japanese firms in their renaissance after World War II. In 1956 the government designated bearings as a "specified machine" to benefit from four programs—formulation of modernization plans (five-year plans enforced by annual working plans); joint cooperation unrestrained by the antimonopoly law; establishment of a council to deliberate "important" matters; and access to Japan Development Bank (JDB) loans.[38] Although cooperation was limited to allocating particular types of specialty bearings to individual companies (perhaps 5–6% of output) while maintaining "free competition" in standard bearings,[39] and although JDB loans to the bearings industry totaled only ¥275 million through 1961,[40] the emphasis placed in the Ministry of International Trade and Industry's (MITI's) modernization plans on the development of the machinery industry as a whole encouraged bearings firms to invest to serve that rapidly growing domestic industry.

An exception to the importance of country factors in the establishment of Japanese firms is Minebea. It was founded in 1951 to supply the aircraft industry with precision miniature ball bearings, when Japan had no domestic aircraft industry, and when the industry itself acknowledged that the quality of even its standard bearings was perhaps only 80% of U.S. quality.[41] The overriding vision of Minebea's maverick Chairman Takami Takahashi was the sole reason for Minebea's establishment,[42] demonstrating that company-specific factors still matter at this stage of a company's development.

In the United States, country factors also predominated in the origins of the industry. Fafnir was founded in 1911 to serve "the infant automobile industry's need for precision ball bearings."[43] Under Alfred Sloan's leadership, Hyatt (the predecessor company to NDH) also aggressively developed its sales to automobile manufacturers. Sloan himself, for example, wrote to Henry Ford asking for his business in 1899, when Ford was still experimenting with autos and had yet to commit himself to the business.[44] Persistence in establishing early contacts with the hundreds of automobile companies being organized at that time paid off as Hyatt acted as their consulting engineers on the design of the rear axle and transmission and so were able to specify Hyatt bearings. Such a close customer relationship was possible only for a domestic firm.

The importance of domestic demand in the formation of enterprises in the United States is also illustrated in the more recent establishment of MPB in 1941, Barden in 1942, and New Hampshire Ball Bearing (NHBB) in 1946 to supply the defense and aerospace industries.

During the establishment of an industry, country factors largely determine when corporations are founded and what products they develop. Only Minebea appears to have overridden its domestic incentive structure at the date of its founding. Firm-specific factors, notably entrepreneurship, explain which individuals or companies respond appropriately to those incentives, but in the more perfectly competitive industry structure that accompanies an industry's emergence, they play a limited role in determining in which countries firms become established.

Growth.   Many more bearings companies than the ones described above emerged over the years, yet few achieved sales of any magnitude in their own country, let alone globally. To succeed during the growth phase, firms must make the appropriate first-mover investments[45] or commitments[46] and achieve cross-functional consistency.[47] The real issue at this stage is therefore to what extent a firm's choice of strategy is determined by its home base and to what extent by voluntaristic company behavior. If country factors predominate, we would expect to see most firms in a country pursuing similar strategies. If firm-specific factors matter, we should see strategic choices reflecting those intrinsic firm differences.

Japanese firms best exemplify how country factors affect strategic choice, since they all became internationally prominent by pursuing essentially the same strategy. This was the "typical" Japanese low-cost strategy of high-volume production of a limited product range, emphasizing manufacturing process technology improvements to raise quality, and aggressive capacity expansion and investment in new equipment.[48]

To implement this strategy, and partly as a result of the "cooperation" agreement, each bearings firm's product range was restricted. Although all produced the standard lines, the big four emphasized either roller bearings (NTN and Koyo) or ball bearings (NSK and NF). Today, while NSK's production is 65% ball bearings,[49] NTN's is only 45%.[50] The Japanese combined such specialization with recognition of the value of line scale, not factory scale, as the crucial determinant of cost by exploiting economies of scale in focused plants. They were also prepared to invest ahead of demand in customized machinery that improved quality and increased automation. In 1963, for example, the capacity of the four main producers represented a 50% surplus over the previous year's output of the entire industry.

Importantly, this low-cost strategy was initially adopted to serve only the rapidly expanding domestic market. Protected by tariffs and exchange control restrictions that effectively prohibited import of "non-necessary" standard bearings,[51] the Japanese industry grew at a compound annual rate of 25% between 1951 and 1961, while the export/production ratio rose only from 7% to 9%.

By 1960 the three largest Japanese bearings manufacturers, although only one-tenth the size of world leader SKF (whose production was fragmented among European plants), were the low-cost suppliers of high-volume standard bearings. At this juncture they turned to develop export markets, leveraging the cost advantage created in their domestic market[52] and making use of various export promotion schemes. In the export-driven decade of the 1960s, exports grew at 28% a year compound (twice the rate of production), and the export/production ratio more than tripled to 30%.

The first country targeted for exports was the United States, chosen for reasons that resonate with Porter's prescription to serve advanced customers (but which he argues can only be accessed if they are domestic).[53] NF spoke of "establishing a reputation."[54] Koyo reasoned that since "auto companies were our biggest customers in Japan, if we wanted to be a first class roller bearing company we had to be in the biggest market in the world."[55]

Initially, the product line sold in the United States through trading companies or distributors was even more limited than that sold in Japan, and it was biased in favor of standard ball bearings. The Japanese imposed this limitation partly because of an inability to offer the sophisticated applications engineering needed to customize bearings without their own sales forces in place and partly because of customer resistance; Hoover, for example, limited its U.S. distribution agreement with NSK to standard ball bearings. However, they also intentionally focused sales to exploit line economies of scale in their Japanese plants. They achieved market penetration by offering substantially (up to 40%) lower prices and much shorter delivery times out of stock to customers, such as auto companies and electric motor manufacturers, from which they could obtain large volumes with single orders.[56]

By 1963 the U.S. industry recognized that "other industrialized countries are frequently able to produce their more limited range of sizes and types of bearings at a lower price" and that "steep increases [in imports] are usually due to a decision by a few big users, such as autos, to import a large volume of certain types of bearing."[57] By 1965, Japan was supplying more than half of U.S. imports (of which over 70% were ball bearings), up from 0.8% in 1958, and in that year the U.S. industry filed the first of many protectionist suits asking for an investigation under the provisions of the Trade Expansion Act of 1962.

In 1969 Japanese imports peaked at 63% of all U.S. imports, while the previous year a peak of 47% of Japanese exports had gone to the United States. By this stage, the range of bearings offered in the United States had expanded as the Japanese reputation for quality was established[58] and as Japanese firms had set up their own sales forces in America. The next stage in Japanese company development would be the opening of manufacturing facilities in the United States.[59]

Postwar growth for U.S. firms was somewhat different but still driven by country factors, primarily the size of the U.S. market and the capital market's encouragement of the sale of bearings companies to conglomerates. Both factors contributed to the choice of inappropriate long-term strategies that ultimately led to the decline of the U.S. industry. Those U.S. firms which have performed well escaped from the constraints of these country factors by proactive managerial decisions rooted in the company's heritage.

The first strategic choice for U.S. bearings firms, which was heavily influenced by their domestic market, was whether to be a specialist or full-line manufacturer. Given the size of the U.S. market, specialization was both feasible and, in the immediate postwar years, probably economic. As a consequence, the major bearings manufacturers retained their specialization after World War II—Timken in tapered roller bearings, Fafnir and Hoover in ball bearings, and Torrington mainly in needle bearings. The newcomers founded during the war also served niches in precision aerospace bearings and railroad bearings that existed only in the large U.S. market. In contrast, the first U.S. firms to buckle under competitive pressure during the 1960s were the full-line competitors, Federal Mogul and NDH.

Federal Mogul, for example, had acquired a complete set of bearings companies (roller, ball, and miniature) by 1960 (see Figure 6-8). Unfortunately, although large overall (among the top five U.S. producers), it was a small player in each product and consequently uncompetitive. After exiting miniature bearings production in the early 1960s, the company gradually withdrew from other product lines until by 1988 it was producing only short-run ball bearings for the auto aftermarket.

While breadth was therefore inappropriate through the 1960s, the strategy of specialization has come back to haunt U.S. firms in recent years as broad scope became necessary to exploit shared learning, amortize sales costs and R&D, and serve full-line bearings distributors. U.S. firms, struggling as specialists, therefore either acquired other specialists to become full line (see Figure 6-8), sold out to bigger, broader (and usually foreign) competitors, or shrank to become true niche players— New Departure Hyatt in integral hub units (70% of all sales); Kaydon in large-size bearings (a 90% market share in bearings over 100″); Brenco in railroad and bronze bearings; and Federal Mogul in short-run ball bearings. Torrington and Fafnir, for example, merged in 1985 "to survive in [rather than] exit roller bearings; to exploit synergies in sales force, overhead and R&D; and to retain access to distribution in the more profitable aftermarket where full-line competitors, like SKF, were 'targeting short line suppliers.'"[60] Even Timken finally recognized the economic need to become a fuller-line manufacturer of bearings when it acquired MPB in 1990.

The size of domestic market also seduced many U.S. producers into ignoring the faster-growing foreign markets to their long-run detriment. Indeed, international activity by U.S. firms, apart from limited exports, was notable for its absence. Federal Mogul never had antifriction bear-

FIGURE 6-8
Mergers and Acquisitions in the U.S. Bearings Industry

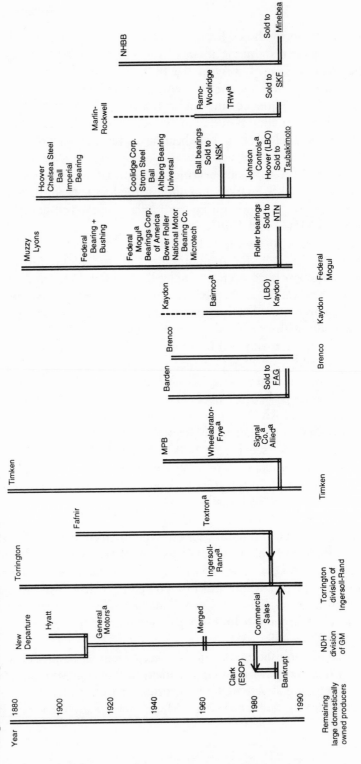

[a]Diversified corporate parent.
Note: Underlined = foreign ownership.

ings facilities outside the U.S. until a recent small Mexican acquisition. Notwithstanding GM's presence outside the United States, NDH had no plant overseas until 1991. Hoover, Marlin-Rockwell, Brenco, NHBB, and Kaydon never built plants abroad.

Cocooned in the world's largest market, U.S. bearings companies felt no pressures to open overseas manufacturing facilities and relied on sales-only subsidiaries or agents for limited export coverage. This severely inhibited their ability to penetrate foreign markets and contributed to their later decline. The only two U.S. manufacturers with substantial long-term overseas presences were motivated by firm-specific factors.

At Timken, the firm-specific factor was simply the Timken family's desire to make their firm international. No economic necessity forced it to become a worldwide competitor. Timken's first overseas activity was to license Vickers in 1909 to make bearings under the name British Timken. A U.K. manufacturing facility was established in 1920, and in 1927 Timken bought a majority share in British Timken. Timken then used this subsidiary to spearhead penetration of the European market via sales offices in France (1928) and elsewhere. After World War II, Timken quickly expanded overseas with plants built in Canada, South Africa, Australia, France, and Brazil. Even by 1960, Timken's foreign production accounted for about 30% of total output. The family commitment to make the company a worldwide competitor pushed it to escape the bounds of its domestic market.

For Torrington, the only other American bearings manufacturer with any substantial overseas presence before World War II, the firm-specific factor was its resource as the dominant supplier (90% world share) of needles for Singer sewing machines. Even so, bearings sales were exports piggybacked onto the (inappropriate) sewing machine needle sales force, and Torrington had only one overseas bearings facility until the 1980s (although it had operated sewing needle facilities overseas since 1895).

The third country factor affecting U.S. bearings manufacturers' strategies was the capital market. For many years this rewarded unrelated diversification and the transfer of resources within a conglomerate's portfolio of businesses from those perceived to be low potential to those whose returns and growth were believed to be easier. Hoover, for example, grew by acquisition in the 1950s to reinforce its presence in ball bearings and ball production. But it then diversified aggressively, acquiring nineteen companies between 1964 and 1977 in fields as diverse as farm equipment, modular homes, and springs to become a conglomerate. Corporate management then limited reinvestment in bearings, believing that because Hoover depended for half its bearings sales on the electric motor industry (1959 data)—precisely the target of the Japanese—other businesses offered higher returns.[61] By 1965 bearings accounted for less than 25% of Hoover's sales, and its strategy of gradual segment retreat culminated in the sale of all bearings assets to NSK in 1975.

This corporate strategy was unfortunately typical of other specialty bearings producers that were acquired by conglomerates in the 1960s. Textron, the archetypal conglomerate, acquired Fafnir in 1963. Bought "off the books" as a well-run profitable company that met Textron's (ROI) criteria,[62] Fafnir suffered from "no reinvestment because of ROI criteria" and "a lack of leadership as Textron management did not know the business."[63] After years of segment retreat to "viable niches" and "just making ROI targets with lots of effort and struggle,"[64] Textron sold it to Torrington. While recognizing that Textron support helped Fafnir over a period when it might otherwise have failed, remaining management argued that "in the long haul it would have been better to be an NYSE company than in Textron."[65]

Similar placement of the bearings business in the corporate portfolio of Marlin-Rockwell at Ramo-Woolridge and then TRW, and MPB at, successively, Wheelabrator-Frye, Signal, and then Allied, almost certainly hindered the performance of those companies (see Figure 6-8). Only at Ingersoll-Rand, which ran Torrington as an operating company, was conglomerate ownership not perceived as a drawback.[66]

The exception to this pressure from the domestic capital market was Timken. Its heritage as a largely family-owned and -managed corporation with an aversion for debt led it to reinvest steadfastly in the bearings industry over the years. For example, having invested $500 million in 1985 in the first integrated steel mill to be built in the United States in twenty-five years, Timken committed another billion dollars in 1989 to the bearings industry, despite an average aftertax return on equity of only 10.4% between 1965 and 1988.

In Europe country factors had the opposite effect from that in the United States. In particular, small domestic markets drove bearings manufacturers to grow by becoming full-line suppliers and opening overseas markets. RHP, for example, was created by the IRC specifically to exploit the scope and scale economies that the three independent specialist companies could not achieve alone. SKF was a full-line supplier of ball and roller bearings by the mid-twenties. FAG was a full-line supplier by the thirties. SNR made both ball and some roller bearings for its parent Renault. Even INA, which remains a needle bearings specialist (about

60% of its bearings sales), added cylindrical roller and ball bearings to its product line after 1960. It recognized that its strategy was "applications engineering for customers' bearings needs, not a particular product or technology."[67]

Similarly, the need for economies of scale provided an initial impetus to become internationally active. It is clear, however, that the successful European firms extended their international activities well beyond that needed to exploit scale economies at a time when most production still took place in the consuming country. Having developed a competitive advantage domestically, firm-specific factors led European firms to choose to replicate that advantage in other countries. No domestic incentives and, at that time, no industry economic pressures compelled them to become such substantial international competitors.

SKF, for example, had by 1918 established eight foreign plants. This desire to build a global presence continued between the wars as SKF built its foreign network, most importantly by acquiring seven German companies in 1929 to become the largest bearings manufacturer in Germany. After World War II, as the world leader in bearings, SKF willingly accepted invitations by autarkical governments to establish facilities in Brazil, Spain, Holland, and Canada. As early as 1960, therefore, 90% of SKF sales and two thirds of its production were outside Sweden.[68] SKF therefore chose to translate its initial technical breakthrough into becoming the largest worldwide producer of bearings by locating plants in many countries. Any of the pioneer bearings companies could have exploited these first-mover advantages; SKF under Wingquist merely pursued it first and most aggressively.

FAG's story is similar. Like Timken a family-owned company[69] (FAG went public only in 1986), its simple desire to be internationally successful carried FAG into overseas markets. In 1914, 60% of FAG's sales were exports,[70] and it maintained that share at 50% during the 1930s, notwithstanding the enormous domestic demand growth under the Nazi military buildup. After the decimation of World War II (Schweinfurt was the prime Allied strategic bombing target), and while accommodating the enormous growth in domestic demand under the German "economic miracle" of the 1950s, FAG still had the vision and prior experience to rebuild its international activities. FAG built a Canadian plant in 1953 to serve the U.S. market, acquired a Swiss plant in 1957, and built Brazilian and Indian plants in the 1960s. Indeed, by the early 1960s it was recognized at FAG that "we had to go overseas if we wanted to grow and build the Schweinfurt economy."[71] As with SKF, it was the company's broad horizon and desire for growth rather than economic incentives that pushed FAG to aggressive development of its overseas network.

During a company's growth, therefore, it appears that both country and company factors are at work in the important strategic choices of scale, scope, and international presence.

Global Oligopoly.   All industries need not become global oligopolies; whether they do depends on their underlying economics. Although worldwide concentration in bearings was high in 1955 (see Table 6-3), this was mainly because of the wartime destruction of the industry in Japan and continental Europe. Concentration declined through the mid-1970s as those economies recovered, but began to rise after that date as firms exploited the benefits of scale and scope discussed earlier. By the mid-1970s the oligopoly in its current form was more or less in place.

In this stage, company factors gain importance as determinants of success for three reasons.[72] First is the importance of multimarket competitive interaction—the initiation of competitive moves, such as attacking a rival's domestic stronghold, in one country because of their repercussions in other countries. As a consequence, how firms play the competitive game across all markets—a skill that in no way depends on country factors—becomes a key to success. Second, possession by firms of resources (both tangible and intangible) acquired over decades of operations,[73] and the "freedom" of an oligopolistic industry structure allows them to be successful regardless of whether domestic country factors favor them. Conversely, those firms which lack necessary resources are unlikely to succeed unless management makes a conscious decision to change strategy. Third, accumulated international experience gives a firm the capability to configure itself in whatever way is necessary, including relocating headquarters,[74] to maintain a competitive advantage. Thus the ability to coordinate a geographically dispersed configuration and exploit locational advantages wherever they occur becomes more important to competitive success than the incentives or characteristics of the home country.

As illustration of the first explanation, the struggle among bearings firms to reach minimum efficient scale in each region has become central to international competition since the 1970s. All players recognized that to be successful in the global oligopoly they had to have a sufficient market share in each region of the Triad to justify a local facility. As a result, Japanese and European firms, for example, have been prepared to invest for market share in the United States. As SKF observed about its ability to shift production to the United States: "We have 12% of the market so we can afford to do this. Had our share been 1%, we'd never have been able to think along these lines."[75] In the last five years foreigners have made seven major acquisitions in the United States, halving the number of large U.S.-owned bearings manufacturers. Similarly, investments in greenfield plants in the United States are made "when local demand justifie[s] financially viable local production and when the firm ha[s] human resources to staff it,"[76] but the definition of financial viability includes the "long-term investment value of a foothold for overseas production."[77] Indeed, most plants are unprofitable for a while after their start-up. According to NSK, after fifteen years of foreign production "it is difficult to maintain a fair profit on overseas production facilities."[78] Confirming this, an International Trade Commission (ITC) survey of the performance of domestically owned and foreign-owned operations in the United States reveals the much lower profitability of the latter group.[79]

Bearings companies also recognize the need to invest for market share in the Far East. SKF accepts that it currently has a major strategic problem because of a "wrong decision" not to market aggressively there in the past, which has resulted in its market share being below that needed to justify local supply.[80] FAG established a Korean joint venture to "get a base for sales in the Far East,"[81] and INA, after a period of European expansion when it was "not aware of global aspects,"[82] saw the need to push sales in Japan after NTN unilaterally dissolved its license agreement in 1987.

Torrington and INA, the two major needle bearings manufacturers, are, however, perhaps the best example of how competitive interaction with a global rival affects international trade. In 1980 Torrington's overseas activity consisted primarily of a most successful Japanese joint venture for the production of needle bearings. Only about 10% of its U.S. output was exported, and an additional 5% of sales was manufactured overseas.[83] Two factors, the sale of the sewing machine needle business in 1980, which took away the infrastructure supporting the export of bearings to many countries, and INA's aggressive expansion in the United States in the late 1970s, which was explicitly designed to attack Torrington in its home market,[84] prompted a change in strategy.

After failing in a bid for Nadella, the French needle bearings manufacturer, and being unable to build share through exports, Torrington resorted to acquisition. This enabled it to build market share and local production in order to challenge INA in its home territory while "sav[ing] the trouble of a start-up"[85] for a company with limited international expertise. In 1982 Torrington bought a share in an Italian spherical bearings manufacturer. Then, in 1984, in a joint venture with SNR, Torrington acquired Nadella's needle bearings business, which its new owner was spinning off. This became the core of Torrington's European activities, to which it added Fafnir's international operations after its acquisition in 1985, although these were "in disarray, a hodgepodge of country-by-country deals."[86] By 1989, valuing the joint ventures at its 50% share, Torrington's overseas sales were up to 45% of total company sales, and its all-important needle bearings market share in Europe was about 25%.[87] Had Torrington not responded this way to INA's aggressive moves in the United States, it is unlikely it would have been as successful, even in the United States, as it has been.

Competitive interaction like this has nothing to do with country factors—the domestic incentive structure for a company is irrelevant. It is a corporate response to the state of global competition. In a mature global oligopoly, successful competitors must transcend domestic factors and become strategic players in the global marketplace.

The second reason firm-specific factors gain importance at this stage of the industry is that successful firms have in place the accumulated investments or resources which afford them protection against newly established or poorly positioned competitors even if they are located in more attractive countries. Timken, for example, has maintained its worldwide strength in tapered roller bearings by building off its unique accumulation of know-how and experience in their design and production. Its decline in world market share is due to the declining share of tapered roller bearings in world output, not to declining relative position.

In contrast, those firms which have not yet acquired adequate resources become victims of their history. For example, those firms which had failed to go international by the 1970s subsequently lost world market share because they lacked the ability to become Triad players. RHP, for instance, attempted to become a global competitor in high-volume lines immediately following its creation in 1969, but failed because its world market share was only 3%. As a consequence, the company decided to diversify out of the bearings industry. As its CEO said in 1973, "The next step for RHP is to diversify into industries which are countercyclical to bearings. After all, we are here to look after the shareholders, not to look after the bearing industry."[88] Used as a "cash cow" with limited reinvestment, RHP's performance gradually deteriorated until it was sold off to a leveraged management buy-in team in 1987. Renamed United Precision Instruments (UPI), the company was turned around by focusing on a limited range of specialty bearings—notably outside the auto market[89]—before it recognized its inevitable fate and sold out to NSK in early 1990 to gain access to global markets and superior resources.[90]

Other companies coming into the 1980s with weak resources were also vulnerable. Profitable only because of generous Renault transfer prices, SNR was reputedly up for sale in 1990. Koyo, which ran into trouble in the 1970s (slipping from first to third in Japan between 1965 and 1980), had to sell off overseas facilities and required an injection of Toyota management and capital to prevent a worse fall in market share. The future viability of the surviving domestic-only U.S. manufacturers Federal Mogul, Brenco, and Kaydon—with 7%, 0%, and 0% production outside the United States, respectively—must also be questioned because of the weak position they inherit. Sale to one of the remaining twelve global oligopolists seems almost inevitable, and their global rivals, not country factors, will determine the fate of these companies.

For the two poorly positioned firms that were able to turn themselves around, NDH and Torrington, it was insightful strategic thinking, not country factors, that contributed to their viability. New Departure Hyatt transformed itself during the 1980s because of management's long-term commitment to develop the integral wheel hub, even though the U.S. auto industry was in decline. NDH saw its only viable role as a manufacturer of a limited range of high-value products in which it had technological and design leadership.[91] Developing the third-generation wheel hub offered this opportunity, and NDH, with support from GM, invested perhaps $0.5 billion in the design of and highly automated manufacturing facilities for such a product.[92] The strategic foresight of NDH executives in the mid-1970s to bet the company on Generation III ("without Generation III, we would not be around today"),[93] has led to a rebound in its performance. Sales of the new hub unit are growing fast, market share is expanding, sales to other auto companies have recommenced, and in 1991 NDH opened its first overseas manufacturing facility in Spain. Its performance demonstrates that a company's strategic resolve can lead it to break the constraints of its history and domestic country factors.

Torrington also exemplifies how a leader's drive can outweigh the country constraints that had inhibited performance. Its parent, Ingersoll-Rand, acted as little more than Torrington's banker until it sent Tom Bennett to be president in 1981. Bennett's strategic changes included the acquisition of Fafnir in 1985, to make it the United States' only full-line producer, as well as its shift to a global configuration described earlier. Both moves remedied the strategic failings that domestic factors had previously produced.

Merely choosing to become a global competitor will not enable companies to achieve that goal. They must also possess the organizational capability to effectively manage those multinational activities and multimarket competitive interactions. Organizational capability is, therefore, the third critical firm-specific element that determines competitive success in the global oligopoly.

Minebea demonstrated its organizational capability when it established its first Thailand plant and reconfigured itself to LDC production. The vital task shifted from merely maintaining "absolute cost competitiveness"[94] to transferring Minebea's production capability to a new environment and coordinating dispersed production sites. Although Minebea essentially replicated its Japanese facilities in Thailand, keeping all component production in house and building its own infrastructure, there was still a need for close communication and physical linkages with existing plants, particularly for new product development. To achieve this successfully (Thai plant productivity is now better than that of the Japanese mother plant, and production cost is a quarter that of Japan),[95] Minebea flew its own 707 shuttle between production facilities, extensively trained Thai workers in Japan, and created new staff experts who oversaw certain functions, such as cutting, worldwide.[96]

Similarly, SKF has had to transform itself twice in the last twenty years to meet evolving global competition. While the main thrust of those transformations was to reconfigure production facilities (see below), each change was accompanied by a major reorganization that severely tested its managerial capabilities.

Through the 1960s, SKF allowed its overseas subsidiaries a "measure of local autonomy."[97] In practice this meant that each country subsidiary serviced its domestic market. When Japanese imports began to threaten SKF's European dominance in the late 1960s, the need for a more tightly coordinated production network became apparent. SKF therefore initiated a number of "progressive moves to streamline administration, to increase international cooperation and overall awareness of group policies, and to eliminate production duplication and bottlenecks."[98] In 1967 the company set up in Göteborg a group headquarters with the authority to make supranational decisions. Next, plant scheduling was coordinated to even out the utilization of European facilities. Finally, in 1974, SKF rationalized European production. Coordinating the new production configuration was a Brussels office, which ran a sophisticated computerized global forecasting and supply system (GFSS) with the objective of "internationaliz[ing] the production and distribution of bearings on a European and modified worldwide basis."[99]

The second transformation occurred in line with the move to a Triad configuration in the late 1980s. SKF organized into three global businesses corresponding to its three main customer groups—OEM, distribution, and specialty. These businesses set strategy around the world and have wide authority, for example, to decide on the location of new plants. This was intended to make "the group more customer driven."[100] While SKF still identified its number one problem as "adapting to a new organization structure because we all have to change,"[101] the resilience of an organization with eighty years of international activity behind it in adapting to an ever-changing competitive and economic environment is apparent.

In contrast, while Torrington has enhanced its competitiveness with its recent international moves, it is still constrained by its limited organizational capability overseas. Partly because of the joint-venture structure of two thirds of its overseas activities, and partly because of its more limited expertise there, Torrington is the only major producer to organize its overseas activities around an international department. In Europe, for example, Nadella handles all sales activities at transfer prices negotiated through the international department. But Torrington maintains its own warehouse in West Germany to handle the distribution of all Torrington-made bearings and maintains an independent applications engineering and marketing center in Paris. This ungainly structure, the heritage of Torrington's late international moves, inhibits effective coordination and will continue to impair Torrington's performance far more than the fact that it is domiciled in the United States.

SKF, however, remains the best example of the minor role played by country factors in a global oligopoly in determining the nationality of successful firms. Sweden accounts for less than 7% of its production. Its largest manufacturing facility is in Schweinfurt, literally across the street from FAG's home plant. Its central R&D facility is in Holland, and its global production coordination office is in Belgium. Its corporate language is English. Although it is still headquartered in Göteborg, SKF's rivalry is with global competitors, not with nonexistent Swedish rivals.

SKF is a Swedish firm, but to view its future success as predicated on Swedish country factors rather than on the resources and organizational capability it has accumulated would be a mistake.

Location of Activities

The benefits of superior customer service create a bias toward local production in the bearings industry. Historically, import substitution was therefore the main driver of location, and country output tended to follow demand as manufacturers established plants in each country they served. In 1916 SKF, for example, built a plant in the United States so that delivery would not depend on the slow and hazardous ocean transport of imports.[102] The company constructed its French plant to take advantage of wage and material costs that were lower at that time (1917) than in Sweden.

In the 1970s this assumption about the appropriate production configuration was challenged by the success of the Japanese producers. Their demonstration of the value of line-scale economies forced companies to recognize the benefits of coordinated global product flows from specialized plants. Consider the case of SKF. In the late 1950s all its plants—except Sweden, which exported 70% of its output—were self-contained, selling on average 80% of their output domestically.[103] Indeed, in 1970 three new European plants came on-stream in as many countries with no coordinated planning and no product swaps arranged between facilities. To remedy this failing, and as part of a £250 million investment plan, SKF closed six of twenty-two plants and focused production in five large facilities, each of which would supply a limited product range to the entire European market. The result was a 20% cut in production costs as run lengths increased by a factor of five and the work force was reduced by 25%.[104]

By the mid-1980s, however, SKF found that this reorganization did not solve the trade-off between the benefits of local production and global scale economies because of changes in the external environment. Protectionism was on the increase: European countries penalized Japanese imports, and the United States was to impose dumping duties on European and Japanese imports in the late 1980s. Exchange rates had demonstrated enormous volatility since 1972. And Japanese firms were no longer exporting just to the United States and Europe—they now had manufacturing facilities in both regions.

To accommodate these new pressures, SKF, like other firms, reorganized to a Triad configuration. The justification for this configuration, and the choice of specific countries for plants inside each Triad region, reflected four firm-specific biases—risk reduction, history, personal preference, and reaction to government policy—which can lead to a systematic divergence in location from that justified by factor endowments.[105] The result of these firm-specific locational decisions is that the pattern of trade is influenced by the "visible hand" of firms, as well as by the invisible hand of market forces.

Risk reduction. The first firm influence on location is risk reduction. The optimal location for a new plant is uncertain because although investments are long-lived, future economic conditions are unknown. As a consequence, firms choose to reduce the risk associated with plant location in two ways: the first by adopting a Triad configuration,[106] the second by mimetic behavior,[107] or copying competitors' locations. The former hedges the risk of differential economic performance between blocs by placing the firm as an "insider" in each of the three economic blocs—Europe, the Americas, and Asia.[108] Indeed, a Triad configuration capitalizes on the option value that the uncertainty about future economic conditions in each bloc creates.[109] The latter reduces risk because, in an oligopoly with no external threat from new entrants, the relevant performance measure is relative to existing competitors. By matching competitors' locations a firm can remove all risk of poor performance, even if at the same time guaranteeing that it will never dramatically outperform competitors. The combination of these risk-reducing strategies has led the major bearings firms to follow one another toward a Triad configuration.

SKF, for example, replaced global production with "currency zone production" in the late 1980s.[110] Setting the dollar, Deutschemark, and yen as the three currency zones, the company decided that "what is sold in each zone [would] be made in that zone."[111] In Europe, therefore, each European country's sales force would take output from the one European factory that was the designated supplier for each product. By adopting this Triad configuration, SKF accepted the impossibility of fully exploiting global-scale economies. However, management believed that the risk of protectionism and exchange-rate fluctuations would expose customers to too much price volatility if they were supplied by a plant outside the currency zone, particularly when competitors had factories in each zone. Within a currency zone, in contrast, a factory in one country could effectively supply the region with a particular range of products because intraregional transport costs were lower and currency alignments, such as the European Monetary System (EMS), would "by and large" produce currency stability.[112]

SKF therefore set self-supply goals within each currency zone. Europe would reduce its exports from 20% to 5% of output. Self-supply in the United States would rise from 80% to 90–95%, and in the Far East from 10% to 80%. Only protected markets, like Brazil and India, would remain outside the currency zones, served by inefficient local production facilities.

Since the early 1970s, the Japanese (with the exception of Minebea) have also pursued essentially the same configurational strategy as a way to reduce risk and accommodate economic pressures on the industry. What is more, although the Japanese ostensibly built plants overseas when "local demand justified it,"[113] the fear of losing ground to their Japanese rivals led to mimetic behavior. All five Japanese firms built their first U.S. plants within two years of one another (see Table 6-4).

For Japanese firms, centralizing production carries with it "too high a risk of exchange-rate and wage-rate fluctuation."[114] "Trade friction problems,"[115] with their resulting protectionist and local content requirements, also compel companies that sell globally to manufacture globally. In their view, to make centralized production work would require "totally free trade and stable exchange rates."[116]

Given this situation, the philosophy of the four major Japanese producers is "to be in the three markets where demand exists"[117] and to "have a plant in each area to meet demand for that area."[118] Other than in a few self-contained countries like Brazil, the goal is usually to have a plant in each region making the higher-volume products for that region, while importing the remaining lower-volume lines from specialized plants in Japan.[119] NTN is typical in this respect, making high-volume auto bearings in three regions and keeping production of lower-volume industrial machinery bearings in Japan. As a consequence, NTN recognizes that "15–20% of U.S. sales will always be Japanese exports."[120]

Currently NSK produces overseas 43% of what it sells overseas;[121] Koyo 20%;[122] NTN 40%, but 60% in the United States;[123] and Nachi-Fujikoshi 30%,[124] but the goal for all is substantially higher. At the same time, these companies plan to maximize local content in overseas plants. Even with respect to R&D facilities, Japanese firms plan a gradual evolution to a global configuration as their organizational capabilities develop. Currently, only NTN, with the largest market share outside Japan, has a basic R&D facility in the United States. NF and NSK have technical service centers in the United States (and NSK in the United Kingdom) that are more liaison and test/redesign facilities than basic research. But each envisions these developing as their overseas presence and capability grow.

The other global competitors are also adopting a Triad configuration. FAG is moving from "a worldwide concept of production," with European plants specialized by product to supply the world—such as a Portuguese plant for miniature ball bearings—to a Triad configuration. This will have "three basic production facilities in Europe, the United States, and the Far East supplying within the region"[125] to reduce its logistics, currency, and protectionism risks.[126] INA also perceives three basic production areas, Deutschemark, dollar, and yen, and a need to have products sold in each area made in that area because of "currency reasons."[127] Within an area, however, INA also tries to balance exports and imports among countries although it recognizes that in Europe, "if the [EMS] snake were permanent and stronger we would not need to do this."[128]

The sole exception to this Triad configuration is Minebea. Its precision miniature ball bearings made in high volume in automated facilities are perhaps the only products that are economic to produce in a low labor cost country. They tend to be sold out of stock, have low transportation costs (<1% of value to ship from Singapore to the United Kingdom),[129] and still retain a high direct labor content (more than 10% of manufacturing cost even in Thailand). Even so, Minebea's move to produce miniature ball bearings in Thailand in the early 1980s shocked the Japanese industry. Others doubted the value of LDC production of high-volume items, pointing out the irony that automation, which makes the work appropriate for a less skilled work force, drives down the labor content. The specter of missed deliveries (Minebea carries three months of finished inventory[130] compared with NSK's two weeks),[131] inadequate quality output from an unskilled labor force, and a weak infrastructure in an LDC also made the move "a very risky decision" and "a philosophy of production not for everyone."[132]

History. The second firm-specific influence on location in an oligopoly is the effect of history, both in terms of a firm's past physical investments and its accumulated organizational capability. The latter constrains location because firms can manage dispersed geographic locations only when they have accumulated a suitable organizational capability. Koyo, for example, explained that it did not open a U.S. facility on entering the market in 1958, because it "needed experience of the U.S. market," and recognized that it could go to full local content only when it had developed "the required internal HRM infrastructure."[133] NSK spoke of overseas expansion being held back by "limited human resources in Japan" and the "need to learn a market and the culture of its people."[134]

Past physical investments constrain a firm's configuration because the sunk costs associated with many physical asset investments deter firms from continual reoptimization in response to changing economic conditions. Instead, firms only occasionally change their production network, and then often subject to the constraint of retaining existing facilities. Thus the heritage of past location decisions biases current production away from the cost minimizing location that a new entrant would choose. FAG, for example, explained why each plant made a particular product range as "historical accident."[135] NDH's first European plant will be in Spain simply because GM had spare capacity in a facility there.[136]

The impact of history is, however, clearest in the case of SKF. In the 1970s SKF rationalized European production facilities on the understanding that "the plant that volunteered for a product line stood the best chance to get it."[137] The resulting allocation of products among facilities was therefore based less on cost optimization than on existing product mix and other historical factors. The German plant, for example, inherited the production of cylindrical bearings for machine tools because of the historic strength of the German machine tool industry. The Göteborg plant management was emotionally attached to spherical roller bearings because that product had been invented in Sweden.

When SKF built a $20 million R&D facility in 1972 as a joint undertaking of the five largest European subsidiaries, it chose Holland as the site because of its "neutrality."[138] Even though SKF management believed that this was neither the best place to recruit engineers or communicate with the European marketing and production subsidiaries nor the low-cost location, the company selected it because there was no SKF subsidiary with a plant there that could usurp the independence of the new facility. The same justification had led to the decision to place the GFSS facilities in Brussels a few years earlier.

Less tangible aspects of a firm's history can also have important and long-lived repercussions. SKF suffered for thirty years because the consent decree of an antitrust suit settled in 1953 compelled SKF to compete with SKF Industries, its own subsidiary, in the United States. SKF Europe, for example, was obligated to operate its own sales force in the United States! As a result SKF could not build the U.S. market share it viewed as optimal. A poor working relationship with SKF Industries management, which guarded its independence, was "distant" to European management, and "lived their own lives," hindered attempts to market in the United States.[139] Only after 1983, when the decree had expired, did the parent company take over the running of SKF Industries, consolidate plants, integrate America into its worldwide production planning, and transfer know-how from Europe. These changes encouraged the group to invest funds in the United States (including acquiring Marlin-Rockwell), allowing it finally to establish the market share it had long needed to secure its global market position.

Personal preference. The third systematic bias in firm location decisions is individual preference. Again, because it is often impossible to determine an optimal location, the final choice from among a list of roughly comparable locations can be influenced by strictly noneconomic criteria. Personal factors, such as the nationality of the commercial director's wife (Spanish), which led RHP to consider Spain as a possible site for its new plant,[140] is one of these influences. More understandably, it was the "strong leadership"[141] of the company's founder and chairman, Takami Takahashi, that led Minebea to take the risk of producing in Thailand over much internal opposition.

FAG also illustrates the effect of individual preference. As a family-owned company with "a sense of obligation to the Schweinfurt facilities,"[142] FAG has tried to retain employment there. Currently 70% of the company's worldwide output comes from its West German facilities clustered around a single 10,000 employee Schweinfurt plant.[143] The bias remains, even though "it matter[s] to have a local plant, so that we have a poor market share in France because we have no plant there."[144]

A cultural preference for German employees also strongly influenced FAG's international expansion. For example, FAG chose Stratford, Canada, as the site for its first North American plant in 1953, notwithstanding the poor transportation links to Detroit, because skilled German workers lived nearby.[145] German-speaking Switzerland and Austria were the next sites for expansion abroad. Even as the Schweinfurt plant ran out of space and workers had to be bused in from as far as 100 kilometers away, the company retained its commitment to Schweinfurt, dividing the one site into multiple profit centers in an effort to overcome the complexities of managing a huge facility. As a consequence, FAG's move to Triad production was hindered by the family's commitment to its Schweinfurt work force.

Japanese bearings companies' locational decisions are often affected by the need to minimize demands placed on their human resources and organizational capabilities. Less than 3% of NTN's overseas personnel, for example, are Japanese.[146] As a consequence, the purely economic variables of local demand, labor costs, parts availability, and so forth, are often "outweighed"[147] by noneconomic "hidden"[148] factors like a preference for the English language (Nachi-Fujikoshi, NSK), a cultural difficulty in dealing with Latins (NSK), or the availability of qualified middle- and top-level managers in the country (Koyo). Thus national or cultural prejudices that reflect language differences, historic and political linkages, or more underlying racial and ethnic prejudices, i.e., the Chinese antipathy to the Japanese, can affect locational decisions in a systematic way.

Government policy.   In the past, government policy as a country factor clearly influenced locational decisions. SKF, for example, built a plant in the United Kingdom in 1911 because production had to be commenced within four years of filing a patent for it to be legally valid at that time.[149] SKF's post–World War II foreign plants were responses to government invitations to open facilities behind protectionistic barriers. Similarly, in 1954, INA built its first plant outside Germany, in the Saar, to circumvent French tariffs.

More recently, protectionism continued to affect location decisions. Japanese foreign direct investment, for example, was usually triggered by government action. Minebea acquired SKF's U.S. production facility for miniature ball bearings in 1971 because of the Department of Defense prohibition that year on purchases of non-U.S. manufactured bearings. Koyo's construction of a U.S. plant in 1973 was directly caused by the "Nixon shock," when the yen exchange rate appreciated from ¥360 to ¥248. NSK's first U.K. plant, built in 1976, was "partly in response to the EEC dumping suit."[150]

In more recent instances, FAG moved aircraft bearings manufacture to Canada in response to the antidumping duties imposed in 1989 by the United States on European imports. At the same time, INA accelerated the transfer of production to the United States. Protectionism today is therefore seen as accelerating the move by foreigners to produce in the protected country,[151] and at best to offer domestic firms a "breathing space"[152] of higher short-term prices.

However, supportive government policies can also influence location. Although governments cannot affect their country's factor costs in the long term (because it would involve an infinitely long-lived subsidy),[153] known and certain short-term benefits can, given future uncertainties, influence firms' decisions. Thus, when choosing among what appear to be comparable long-term locations inside a Triad region, short-term government incentives—whether tax breaks, labor subsidies, assistance on plant investment, or direct grants—can make the difference for some firms.

To NSK, government incentives "were a big reason that we went to the United Kingdom at that time."[154] Minebea ostensibly went to Thailand "primarily for the government incentives; only coincidentally was it for low labor cost."[155] In contrast, Koyo management viewed things differently, arguing that "government incentives can be a big reason for location, but they are short-term profit. You need a long-term vision of the best place to be."[156]

A concern for government support can, however, be of paramount importance. INA management prefers to export to Japan from the United States rather than from Europe because it is "politically easier."[157] Executives of both NSK and Nachi-Fujikoshi said that the prospect of being the only Japanese bearings manufacturer in a country affected their choice of location. This move not only ensured better treatment for the firm but also bestowed greater political leverage in multinational bodies (like the EEC) when they had to decide issues (such as dumping suits) concerning the Japanese industry.

CONCLUSIONS

Both country and company factors determine the nationality of successful firms and the location of their activities, and hence the pattern of world trade. The debate is really about the relative importance of each and how that changes over time. Without country factors, for example, firms would never adopt a dispersed production configuration. Without company factors we could not explain how firm A does better in the United States than firm B.

Isolating the relative contribution of country and company factors is difficult, particularly since sufficient backward iteration can always introduce a role for country factors, however strained the argument becomes. Minebea's adoption of an LDC production strategy, for example, can be attributed to shortages of land and labor in Japan rather than Chairman Takahashi's personal inclination. This problem is particularly acute when company and country performance are closely correlated.

The real opportunity to discriminate comes when company and country performance diverge because of substantial foreign direct investment.

With respect to the relative contribution of country and company factors to the determination of the nationality of successful firms, the conclusion is that the influence of the firm increases over time. At the founding, country factors predominate by creating the domestic opportunity set for the entrepreneur. Company factors, notably the entrepreneur's ability to mobilize the resources necessary to exploit the opportunity,[158] determine which individual or firm actually makes the breakthrough. But country factors explain why such a firm emerged in one country and not another.

During a company's growth phase, strategic choices of scale and scope determine firm success. Those choices can be attributed to both country and company factors. In the bearings industry, the influence of country factors on investment (capital markets), the definition of the served market as global or domestic (domestic demand), and the choice of generic strategy between specialized or full-line (domestic demand, government policy) was readily apparent, particularly because of the striking similarity of strategies adopted by different firms within a given country. Nevertheless, firm-specific factors were also found to shape important choice decisions at this stage. In particular, a firm's ownership structure and its corporate scope appeared to have substantial influence. Timken's family ownership gave it the commitment to long-term investment and international expansion in the bearings industry. FAG and INA's family ownership had similar results. NDH's ownership by GM made it a broad-line producer, while its role as component supplier to in-house car divisions inhibited its cost competitiveness.

When a firm becomes a global oligopolist, it is mainly company-specific factors that determine performance.[159] This is not to say that all industries attain this structure. But if, as in the bearings industry, the underlying economics produce broad-scope competitors engaged in global oligopolistic rivalry, firms themselves, not their domicile, determine their fate.

The domestic incentives that result from factor endowments, the structure of demand, domestic rivalry, supporting and related industries, and even government policy have been made less relevant as firms supplant the constraints of their home environment by locating activities overseas to capitalize on those incentives in other countries. The advanced structure of U.S. aerospace bearings demand, for example, is no longer a factor that favors U.S. firms, since of the five large U.S. producers of aerospace bearings only two, Torrington and MPB (now owned by Timken), are American owned.

The only country factor that seems of importance in the global oligopoly is the capital market, because ownership of bearings firms remains concentrated in their home base. As major firms become listed on foreign stock exchanges, even this factor should decline in importance. If Timken, say, pursues a long-term investment strategy that Wall Street dislikes because of its damage to short-term earnings, then in principle (if capital markets really are fundamentally different) a Japanese investor would buy the stock instead. What then might remain of country factors are the cultural and philosophical attitudes toward business held by executives, who today remain mostly nationals of the home base. As with stock ownership, however, even the composition of executive teams is becoming more cosmopolitan.

In the place of country factors, firm-specific factors assume importance in determining the nationality of successful firms. The physical resources each firm has in place around the world as a result of its past strategies, as well as its accumulated organizational capability become the determinant of global strategic position. The nationality of successful firms then emerges from the struggle between almost "stateless" corporations to optimize their geographic configuration in response to global oligopolistic interaction. The fact that such firms tend to resemble one another as they all adopt a Triad configuration only reinforces the conclusion that firm-specific factors, notably organizational capability, will differentially determine their future success.

Finally, at any stage, firm factors can outweigh country factors as determinants of the nationality of successful firms. The founding of Minebea, Timken's single-minded pursuit of the tapered roller bearings business on a worldwide basis, and FAG's dependence on Schweinfurt, for example, can be explained only by company-specific factors.

Industry structure determines the relative importance of firm-specific factors on the location of activities. In particular, with imperfect competition, oligopolistic rents can be used to support suboptimal locations. In this case, systematic biases away from the current cost-minimizing location will be introduced into the geographic configuration of successful firms. The uncertainty surrounding the identification of an optimal location, coupled with the limited consequences of incorrect location, permit risk reduction, history, personal preference, and reaction to government policy to influence, within broad bounds, the choice of location.

Taken together, these conclusions suggest that, in mature global oligopolies, the visible hand of trade is a powerful determinant of the pattern of world trade. The nationality of successful firms and the location of their activities are influenced by firm-specific, as much as by country-related, factors.

Implications

In advocating policies in this environment, it is unwise to look only at the partial equilibrium outcome in the single industry under study, particularly because no attempt was made here to examine the welfare consequences, for example, of Japanese government policy toward the bearings industry. Nevertheless, in an industry that has become a global oligopoly, and wary of advocating these as policies for industries with other structures, the implications for trade policy are fourfold.

The first is that, except in an industry's infancy, when protection (if combined with domestic rivalry) can create appropriate incentives for the establishment of firms, measures designed to shore up uncompetitive domestic enterprises are unlikely to have value. The imposition by the United States of antidumping duties on Japanese and European imports in 1989, for example, had two main consequences: a jump in prices, estimated to average 11%, and an acceleration of the plans of all manufacturers, American and foreign alike, to expand production in the United States. Protection merely confirmed to foreigners the need to reduce their dependence on imports to North America. The additional flexibility this move affords them will in fact increase, not decrease, their competitiveness in the long term and will only produce overcapacity in the United States in the medium term. The most protection can offer domestic firms is temporary breathing room for change, but no more.[160]

However, what *can* be valuable in an oligopolistic industry, as strategic trade theory has shown, is denial of access by the home country of a successful global competitor to both imports *and* foreign direct investment. Restricting access to a market prevents competitors from increasing scale or capturing the option value of a presence in an important market.[161] It also allows the domestic firm to fund investments in other countries out of domestic profits. If competitive advantage comes from exploiting a global presence, denying that presence to foreign firms helps already successful domestic companies capture the industry's rents. While this is true for one country, if all countries attempt the same beggar-thy-neighbor policy, world welfare is reduced. The second important policy implication is therefore not to adopt such a policy but rather to ensure access to all markets for both goods and capital.

In the bearings industry, the one market that remains relatively closed is Japan. The cause is not overt protectionism but the close ties between bearings manufacturers and consumers. How to open the market is more problematic—after all, thirty years ago U.S. customers were notable for their close ties to bearings manufacturers, and it took 40% price discounts to attract their attention to Japanese imports.[162] Perhaps European and U.S. firms have to resolve to invest in production facilities in Japan in advance of demand (which none have) in order to establish their credentials as true insiders.

The third policy implication is to encourage foreign direct investment when domestic firms have failed. At least in the context of a Triad industry, such investment represents the securing of economically beneficial activities for a country. In true Triad industries the only difference between the presence of domestic and foreign firms is the flow of earnings. Firms are not merely exploiting factor cost differences, they are becoming complete insiders locating all activities inside each leg of the Triad. When domestic firms have stumbled, the second best solution is therefore for foreign firms to locate in the country, and governments should adopt supportive industry policies without regard to the nationality of firms active there.[163]

While some policies that make a country receptive to and attractive for foreign direct investment, like language and culture, cannot readily be altered, others can be altered without prostituting the country. Because the prospect of limited but guaranteed short-term benefits often sways a firm's locational decision, the inducement required to attract foreign firms need not overly distort the domestic economy. However, this prescription also runs the risk of degenerating into an international zero-sum game of bidding for foreign direct investment, such as the competition between countries in Europe for automobile plants. The solution has to be international agreements on what is permissible support for foreign direct investment.

The last policy implication, again in the context of a global oligopoly, is to ignore domestic antitrust requirements. SKF, for example, has had an overwhelming share of the Swedish bearings market for decades without harming its performance, because its real rivalry is in the West German market. In global oligopolies, worldwide concentration and competitive interaction are drivers of industry performance, not market shares in any one country. If having a single domestic firm dominate the home market benefits its global competitiveness, then regulators should leave it alone.

The implications for managers, who, unlike policymakers, need not worry about the general equilibrium repercussions of their actions, are somewhat easier to identify. The first is a mandate to understand the evolution of the industry's global structure. This requires a fundamental understanding of industry economics and involves looking beyond the immediate constraints of the domestic market.

Second, a strategy should be premised on reinforcing competitive advantage by locating activities to take advantage of country-specific factors. Whether these advantages are low labor costs or the presence of an advanced set of buyers, choosing the appropriate geographic configuration of activities becomes a critical strategic variable.

Third, the competitive arena should be seen as the world, and the competitive benchmark should be global, not domestic, competitors. In this context, understanding and managing the multimarket competitive interaction among global rivals become vital.

Fourth, the analysis of the bearings industry suggested that a Triad configuration was justified by uncertainty and risk reduction. For firms in other global oligopolies, these forces are also powerful reasons to adopt a Triad configuration.

Finally, the firm must not only plan globally but also act globally to build an organizational capability that can successfully coordinate a geographically dispersed strategy.[164] The real challenge for multinationals is organizational. The objective should be to transcend the home base, not only with respect to production facilities but also with respect to management philosophy and style. Only then can a firm build a truly successful global strategy.

NOTES

1. See the treatment in any standard text, e.g., R. E. Caves and R. Jones, *World Trade and Payments* (Glenview, Ill.: Scott Foresman, 1990).

2. Recent trade theory, incorporating imperfect competition and increasing returns to scale, has sought to explain this phenomenon. See, for example, E. Helpman and P. R. Krugman, *Market Structure and Foreign Trade* (Cambridge, Mass.: MIT Press, 1985).

3. W. B. Arthur, "Self-reinforcing Mechanisms in Economics," in P. An-

derson, K. Arrow, and D. Pines, eds., *The Economy as an Evolving Complex System* (Reading, Mass.: Addison-Wesley, 1988).

4. Additional data on the industry are available in a longer version of this chapter, D. J. Collis, "Country and Company Determinants of the Pattern of Trade in the Global Bearings Industry," Harvard Business School Working Paper No. 91-047.

5. A third type—a plain sleeve or journal bearing—is a friction bearing, which is not included in the study.

6. A high-volume automated roller bearing line may produce only 100,000 units a month.

7. I. Magaziner and R. Reich, *Minding America's Business* (New York: Vintage Books, 1982).

8. F. Aguilar, "Ransome Hoffman Pollard Limited," Case No. 374-043 (Boston: Harvard Business School, 1973).

9. F. M. Scherer et al., *The Economics of Multiplant Operation* (Cambridge, Mass.: Harvard University Press, 1975).

10. Roller bearings factory minimum efficient scale has been estimated at 60–70% of ball bearings output, with a capital cost of $50 million.

11. SKF and The Boston Consulting Group, "Perspectives on Experience," Boston, Boston Consulting Group, 1975.

12. J. S. Nye, *Bound to Lead: The Changing Nature of American Power* (New York: Basic Books, 1990).

13. Concentration in Japan and Europe is exceedingly high (see Table 6-3). In the United States, concentration is substantially lower *and* declining. Estimates suggest that while C6 in 1963 was 75%, by 1988 it was 55%. C8 declined from 64% in 1984 to 58% in 1987 (U.S. Department of Commerce, 1988). As foreign bearings companies build market share in the United States at the expense of once dominant U.S. producers, concentration decreases. This development has set up a race by all remaining players to gain U.S. market share in anticipation of the industry's consolidation into a structure comparable to that elsewhere.

14. U.S. Department of Commerce, "The Effects of Imports of Anti-Friction Bearings on the National Security," July 1988.

15. This model is a description of the causal relationships among the five elements that the broader research project recognized as determining trade patterns: country endowments, government policy, industry structure, firms, and history.

16. J. A. Schumpeter, *The Theory of Economic Development* (Cambridge, Mass.: Harvard University Press, 1934).

17. A. Marshall, *Principles of Economics*, 8th ed. (London: Macmillan, 1920).

18. Following A. B. Linder, *An Essay on Trade and Transformation* (Uppsala: Almquist and Wicksell, 1961), and R. Vernon, "International Investment

and International Trade in the Product Cycle," *Quarterly Journal of Economics*, May 1966, 190–207.

19. M. E. Porter, *The Competitive Advantage of Nations* (New York: Free Press, 1990).

20. P. Hagstrom, "Unshackling Corporate Geography," Geografiska Annaler, Series B, *Human Geography* 72B, no. 1 (1990): 3–12.

21. J. H. Dunning, "Trade Location of Economic Activity and the MNE: A Search for an Eclectic Approach," in B. Ohlin et al., *The International Allocation of Economic Activity: Proceedings of a Nobel Symposium Held at Stockholm* (London: Macmillan, 1977).

22. See the research on the "resource-based" view of the firm by J. Barney, "Firm Resources and Sustained Competitive Advantage," *Journal of Management* 17, no. 1 (1991): 99–120, R. M. Grant, "The Resource-Based Theory of Competitive Advantage," *California Management Review*, Spring 1991, 114–135, and B. Wernerfelt, "A Resource-Based View of the Firm," *Strategic Management Journal* 5 (1984): 171–180. For an application to the bearings industry, see D. J. Collis, "A Resource-Based Analysis of Global Competition: The Case of the Bearings Industry," *Strategic Management Journal*, Summer 1991, 44–69.

23. See C. Bartlett and S. Ghoshal, *Managing Across Borders* (Boston: Harvard Business School Press, 1989), and Y. Doz and C. K. Prahalad, *The Multinational Mission* (New York: Free Press, 1988).

24. O. E. Williamson, *Markets and Hierarchies* (New York: Free Press, 1975).

25. K. Arrow, *Economics of Information* (Cambridge, Mass.: Belknap Press of Harvard University Press, 1984).

26. Williamson, *Markets*.

27. Porter, *Competitive Advantage*.

28. This view of organizational capability mirrors Chandler's description of the historical growth in scope of U.S. industrial enterprise as both requiring and creating a competent managerial function—the "visible hand." The "visible hand of trade" is the geographic equivalent of the coordination required by vertically and horizontally integrated domestic enterprises. See A. D. Chandler, Jr., *The Visible Hand* (Cambridge, Mass.: Belknap Press of Harvard University Press, 1977).

29. Porter, *Competitive Advantage*. See also R. Reich, "Who Is Them?" *Harvard Business Review*, March–April 1991, 77–89, and K. Ohmae, *The Borderless World* (New York: Harper Business, 1990).

30. Porter's account of the diamond creating successful industries in particular countries is therefore biased toward an explanation of the foundation of firms and not of strategic choices made by mature enterprises. See Porter, *Competitive Advantage*.

31. SKF, "The Story of SKF" (Göteborg, 1982), 1.

32. Ibid.

33. Ibid., 2.

34. Ibid.

35. Other instances of this and the other phenomena described in the paper that illustrate a consistent pattern across firms can be found in the longer version of this chapter, Collis, "Country and Company Determinants."

36. See M. Piore, "The Impact of the Labor Market upon the Design and Selection of Productive Techniques within the Manufacturing Plant," *Quarterly Journal of Economics* 82 (November 1968): 602–620, and E. Von Hippel, "Learning from Lead Users," research paper, Harvard Business School, 1983.

37. Aguilar, "Ransome."

38. JETRO, "Japan's Postwar Industrial Policy" (Tokyo: Japan External Trade Organization, 1985).

39. K. Yamayoshi, managing director, NF, personal interview, August 1989.

40. JETRO, "Policy."

41. Yamayoshi interview.

42. K. Kester, "Minebea Company Ltd.," Case No. 287-022 (Boston: Harvard Business School, 1988).

43. Torrington, "Torrington Today—Special Issue," Fall 1985.

44. A. P. Sloan, *My Years with General Motors* (Garden City, N.Y.: Doubleday, 1964).

45. A. D. Chandler, *Scale and Scope* (Cambridge, Mass.: Belknap Press of Harvard University Press, 1990).

46. P. Ghemawat, *Commitment* (New York: Free Press, 1991).

47. K. Andrews, *The Concept of Corporate Strategy* (Homewood, Ill.: Richard D. Irwin, 1971).

48. Magaziner and Reich, *Minding.* For a similar story in the machine tool industry, see D. Collis, "The Machine Tool Industry and Industrial Policy 1955–1982," in A. M. Spence and H. Hazard, eds., *International Competitiveness* (Cambridge, Mass.: Ballinger, 1988).

49. S. Hirano, managing director, NSK, personal interview, August 1989.

50. Y. Suma, president, NTN Toyo Bearing Co., personal interview, August 1989.

51. And protected to a certain extent at this time by relatively low labor rates.

52. As the Japan trade organization perhaps self-servingly states, "Japanese companies first built up domestic markets for their products, achieving economies of scale prior to directing the products to export markets on a full scale." See JETRO, "Policy," 32.

53. Porter, *Competitive Advantage.*

54. Yamayoshi interview.

55. T. Uematsu, executive director, Koyo Seiko Co. Ltd., personal interview, August 1989.

56. The strategy was similar in other industries, such as television sets, with which the Japanese entered the United States through private labeling.

57. U.S. Bureau of the Census, "U.S. Industrial Outlook," 1963.

58. In 1981 the U.S. industry had to admit grudgingly and understatedly that there were "no quality differences with foreigners" (U.S. Bureau of the Census, "U.S. Industrial Outlook," 1981). Today, for example, while U.S. firms use balls ground to a standard 3 or 4, Japanese firms use a higher standard 5. The difference is noticeable in use if not to the naked eye (R. Baty, president, Hoover Precision Products Inc., personal interview, July 1990).

59. In Europe the strategy was repeated a decade later, although limited by EEC protection after the mid-1970s. Japanese imports priced 35–50% below factory levels were concentrated in only 45–100 lines (primarily soundless bearings for electric motors) so that in the United Kingdom in 1975, for example, 70% of Japanese imports were single-row ball bearings <70mm in diameter (*Financial Times*, February 11, 1975).

60. T. E. Bennett, president, Torrington, personal interview, July 1990.

61. Baty interview.

62. R. Ames, former executive vice president, Textron, personal interview, July 1990.

63. S. Martin, president, Fafnir, personal interview, July 1990.

64. Ibid.

65. Ibid.

66. Bennett interview.

67. Dr. L. M. Raith, president, INA, personal interview, September 1990.

68. SKF, "Story."

69. SKF today could also be considered family controlled as the Wallenbergs control 40% of its voting stock.

70. W. Eck, marketing manager, FAG, personal interview, February 1990.

71. Ibid.

72. Since firm maturity and the global oligopoly industry structure are collinear in the bearings industry, this research cannot disentangle the relative contribution of these two causes of the predominance of firm-specific factors.

73. E. T. Penrose, *The Theory of the Growth of the Firm* (New York: M. E. Sharpe, 1959).

74. Porter argues that the occurrence of effective shifts of home base, such as Philips establishing headquarters for lighting in Italy, is "still relatively low" because of cultural and organizational defensiveness. See Porter, *Competitive Advantage*, p. 614.

75. M. Sahlin, interview in *The Wall Street Journal* (Europe), July 5, 1990.

76. Uematsu interview.

77. Yamayoshi interview.

78. Hirano interview.

79. United States International Trade Commission, "Antifriction Bearings." Washington, D.C., #2185, May 1989. An alternative explanation is that U.S. firms have perhaps shown a willingness to retreat to the remaining high-profit market segments. The evidence for this is not complete because of the difficulty in gathering a time series of consistent profitability data across companies at the level of their bearings operations. A gross comparison suggests that U.S. bearings firms were more profitable than Japanese firms in the cycle from 1978 to 1986 with an average operating profit of 7.6% compared with 5.3% (Annual Reports). Moreover, two indicators suggest that this reflects U.S. firms' harvesting the business. First, over that same time period, U.S. bearings industry operating profitability was higher than that for all of U.S. industrial machinery (Robert Morris Associates). Second, the U.S. bearings firms' operating margin actually rose on average from 1968–1977 to 1978–1986 (Business Trends).

80. M. Sahlin, president, SKF, personal interview, February 1990.

81. Eck interview.

82. Raith interview.

83. Bennett interview.

84. Raith interview.

85. Ibid.

86. Ibid.

87. Ibid.

88. Aguilar, "Ransome," 15.

89. A. Bowkett, managing director, UPI, personal interview, February 1990.

90. For more detail on RHP see Collis, "Analysis of Global Competition," and C. Carr, *Britain's Competitiveness* (London: Routledge, 1990).

91. S. Davey, manager, New Departure Hyatt, personal interview, August 1990.

92. Ibid.

93. Ibid.

94. Minebea, "Minebea's Operations in Thailand," November 26, 1988, 1.

95. R. Misukami, director, Minebea Co. Ltd., personal interview, August 1989.

96. For a fuller description, see Collis, "Analysis of Global Competition."

97. SKF, "Story," 13.

98. Ibid., 14.

99. "SKF's U.S. Strategy," *International Management*, June 1986, 40–49.

100. Sahlin interview.

101. Ibid.

102. SKF, "Story," 7.

103. Ibid., 14.

104. SKF undertook this reorganization as the EEC and European countries introduced protectionist measures against the Japanese after 1972. If country

factors are solely important, this development should have removed SKF's incentive to act.

105. They also lead to divergence from location in larger countries with exports to smaller countries, which recent trade theory incorporating imperfect competition and transport costs suggests is the efficient configuration. See Helpman and Krugman, *Market Structure*, 197.

106. K. Ohmae, *Triad Power* (New York: Free Press, 1985).

107. F. T. Knickerbocker, *Oligopolistic Reaction and Multinational Enterprise* (Boston: Division of Research, Harvard Business School, 1973).

108. The trend to harmonization of economies within each bloc means that the choice of country within a bloc is unlikely to affect performance dramatically.

109. B. Kogut, "A Note on Global Strategies," *Strategic Management Journal* 10, no. 4 (1989): 383–390. Note that in perfect competition this type of risk reduction through geographic diversification is infeasible. The firm that happened to locate in the country which turned out to be the optimal location would always beat the geographically diversified firm.

110. Sahlin interview.

111. Ibid.

112. Ibid.

113. Yamayoshi interview.

114. Ibid.

115. Hirano interview.

116. Uematsu interview.

117. Hirano interview.

118. Yamayoshi interview.

119. Uematsu interview.

120. Suma interview.

121. Hirano interview.

122. Uematsu interview.

123. Suma interview.

124. Yamayoshi interview.

125. Eck interview.

126. As it moved away from centralized production somewhat late, FAG was seen, in the United States particularly, as the maverick, disrupting prices to maintain utilization in dedicated European facilities.

127. Raith interview.

128. Ibid.

129. Misukami interview.

130. Ibid.

131. Hirano interview.

132. Ibid.

133. Uematsu interview.

134. Hirano interview.

135. Eck interview.

136. Davey interview.

137. Sahlin interview.

138. Ibid.

139. Ibid.

140. Bowkett interview.

141. Misukami interview.

142. Eck interview.

143. Twenty-seven percent of FAG's German work force has more than twenty-five years of tenure with the company.

144. Eck interview.

145. Ibid.

146. Uematsu interview.

147. Hirano interview.

148. Yamayoshi interview.

149. SKF, "Story."

150. Hirano interview.

151. Baty interview and F. Musone, president, Chassis Products, Federal Mogul, personal interview, August 1990.

152. Bennett interview.

153. Not only is it uneconomic for governments to offer long-term incentives, governments cannot even credibly commit to offer long-term incentives because of the dynamic consistency problem. Once a firm has located in their country, governments have an economic interest (barring the reputation effect) in curtailing those incentives.

154. Hirano interview.

155. Takami Takahashi, speech at Harvard Business School, April 1988. Mimeographed.

156. Uematsu interview.

157. Raith interview.

158. See, for example, articles by J. A. Timmons and H. H. Stevenson in J. J. Kao and H. H. Stevenson, eds., *Entrepreneurship* (Boston, Mass.: Harvard Business School, 1985).

159. I would, for example, take issue with Porter's statement as it applies to SKF that "some Swedish and Swiss companies are risking their capacity to maintain positions as innovators, for example, by failing to invest in their home environments: in a desire to 'go global.' " See Porter, *Competitive Advantage*, 607.

160. Protection will not restrain the strategic pricing policies adopted by foreign firms to gain share in the U. S. market, as these are driven by a desire to enhance competitive position in the one leg of the Triad where consolidation has yet to occur.

161. See P. Krugman, ed., *Strategic Trade Policy and the New International Economics* (Cambridge, Mass.: MIT Press, 1986), and J. A. Brander and B. J. Spencer, "Export Subsidies and International Market Share Rivalry," *Journal of International Economics*, 16 (May 1984): 227–242.

162. When this was pointed out to U.S. firms, a typical reaction was "but at 30% lower prices we still wouldn't get the business in Japan." Musone interview.

163. Reich, "Who Is Them?"

164. Bartlett and Ghoshal, *Managing Across Borders.*

7

CONSTRUCTION EQUIPMENT: FROM DOMINANCE TO DUOPOLY

Michael G. Rukstad

ALTHOUGH COUNTRY-BASED DETERMINANTS like the changing volume of demand and government policies on trade and exchange rates in recent years affected the $30 billion construction equipment industry, the competitive upheavals following the oil shocks in the 1970s have been the galvanizing force behind change. The worldwide recession that ensued in the 1980s altered the nature of competition among the chief producers and the patterns of trade supplying the end-users. Production became more concentrated, more global, and more cost conscious.

Principal players shifted into and out of prominence. Caterpillar, Inc., lost its long-held grip on the world construction equipment market in the face of challenges by contenders, mainly Komatsu. From the end of the 1970s to 1990, Caterpillar's world market share slipped one-third, from 46% to 30%, while Komatsu's rose from 11% to 20%. International Harvester, the world's second largest producer at the start of the 1970s, was obliged to sell its operation to Dresser Industries a decade later. While J. I. Case maintained a strong market position, Clark Equipment, Dresser Industries, and Fiatallis declined inexorably and had to be rescued by alliances. Hitachi and Liebherr scored notable successes in the 1980s. (See Figure 7-1 on the market share trends of the major producers.)

Even so, in recent years the world market has often appeared to be a contentious duopoly between Caterpillar and Komatsu. Responding to

I received many useful comments from the participants in the World Trade and Global Competition seminar at the Harvard Business School, especially David Yoffie and Benjamin Gomes-Casseres, and from a seminar at the Center for International Affairs, Harvard University. Julia Horn and Masao Ogawa provided excellent research assistance. In addition, Masao served as translator for my interviews in Japan. Finally, I would like to thank the many executives and industry observers I interviewed for this project for their cooperation, in particular Satoru Anzaki, Glen Barton, Bill Foley, Tom Gildehaus, Karl-Friedrich Goluecke, Frank Manfredi, Leo McKernan, Raymond Mellor, Jim Mezera, Robert Nardelli, Ryuichi Seguchi, Pietro Sighicelli, Hiroshi and Yasuo Tadano, and Shiro Umemoto. All opinions expressed in the chapter—and any errors—are mine.

FIGURE 7-1
World Market Shares
Construction Equipment Producers

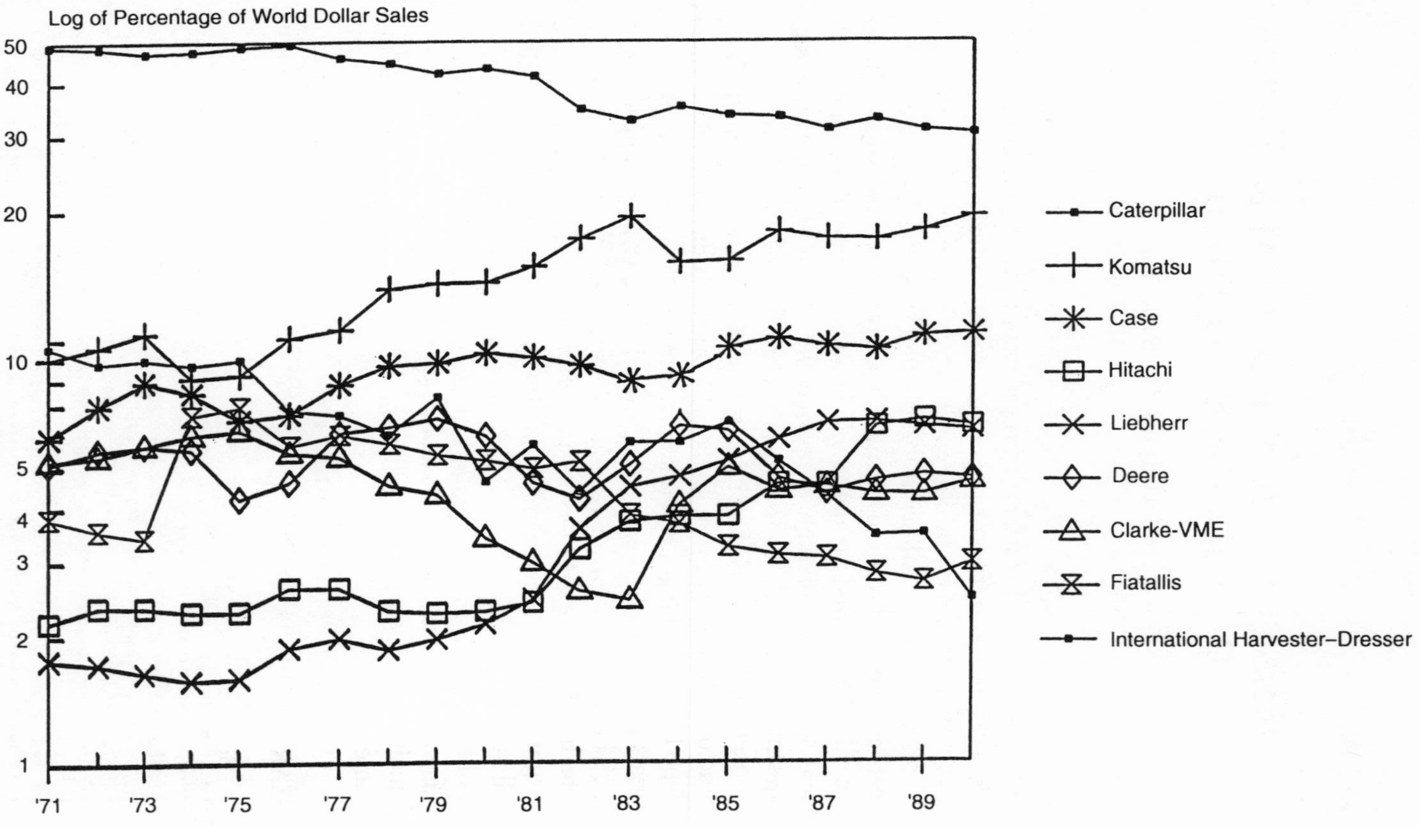

Log of Percentage of World Dollar Sales
50
40
30
20
10
5
4
3
2
1
'71
'73
'75
'77
'79
'81
'83
'85
'87
'89
Caterpillar
Komatsu
Case
Hitachi
Liebherr
Deere
Clarke-VME
Fiatallis
International Harvester–Dresser

this rivalry and trying to offset their own organizational shortcomings, other competitors took steps to seize more influence. They have included consolidation and rationalization of operations, globalization strategies, segmentation of products and markets, and strategic alliances. These moves toward a reversion to oligopoly have had a significant bearing on trade.

Speaking from a national point of view, the United States' share of units produced fell from about one third of the world market in 1975 to less than half that share by 1989. In the meantime, Japan bolstered its production from about 20% to more than half of the world output, and Europe declined from one-quarter to about 20% (see Figure 7-2). The export share of the United States generally fell over this period, while the portions of Japan and Europe rose.

Of course, one can't lump all types of construction equipment under one heading; the products range from small front-end loaders to giant crawler tractors and cranes and include specialized items like pipelayers, mixers, log skidders, and tunnel-boring equipment. (See Figure 7-3 for a sample of products in this industry.) The six largest product lines, ranked by units sold in 1990, are hydraulic excavators, wheel loaders, tractor backhoe loaders, track-type tractors, off-highway trucks, and track-type loaders. Figure 7-4 shows the sources of world production in three years of the past decade.

The majority of the units of construction equipment sold in the world are hydraulic excavators, and their distribution pattern, illustrated in Figure 7-4, not surprisingly bears similarity to the global distribution of all such equipment. As the figure makes plain, however, that does not hold true for all the others. While Japan still produces the preponderance of wheel loaders and track-type loaders, the Japanese concentrate on small models and have traditionally left production of large units to the Americans and Europeans.

EARLY COMPETITION

Before the late 1970s, trade and competition in the industry was carried out largely as standard country-based economics would dictate. The United States boasted huge endowments of capital and technology, thriving agricultural and construction industries, and the world's largest markets with vigorous demand growth in peacetime and in wartime. Caterpillar (Cat) and a few other big American firms, particularly International Harvester (Harvester) and Allis-Chalmers, held significant positions.

FIGURE 7-2
Distribution of World Production
Construction Equipment

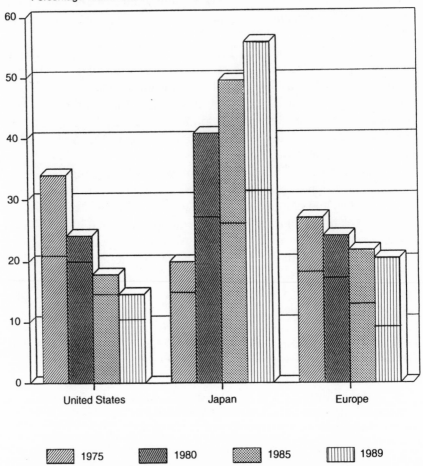

Percentage Total World Production (units)

Legend: 1975   1980   1985   1989

Note: Upper portion of bar is exports, lower portion domestic sales.

Sources: Manfredi; company interviews.

FIGURE 7-3
Representative Products in the Construction Equipment Industry

Track-type Tractors (TTT) or Bulldozers

Off-Highway Trucks

Track-type Loaders (TTL)

Articulated Dump Trucks

Wheel Loaders (WL)

Pipelayers

Motor Graders

Compactors

Wheel Tractor-Scrapers

Hydraulic Excavators

Hydraulic Shovels

Source: Caterpillar.

FIGURE 7-4
Distribution of World Production

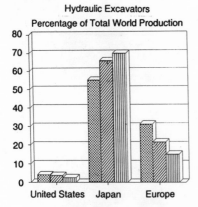

Hydraulic Excavators
Percentage of Total World Production

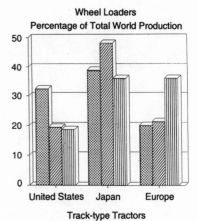

Wheel Loaders
Percentage of Total World Production

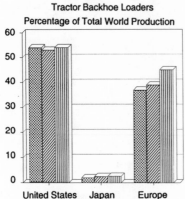

Tractor Backhoe Loaders
Percentage of Total World Production

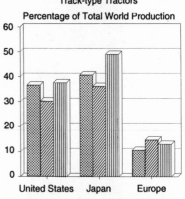

Track-type Tractors
Percentage of Total World Production

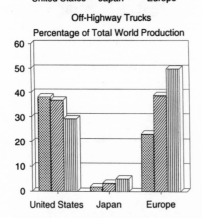

Off-Highway Trucks
Percentage of Total World Production

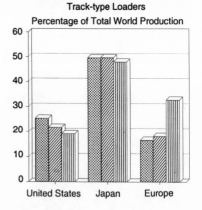

Track-type Loaders
Percentage of Total World Production

▧ 1980   ▨ 1985   ▥ 1989

Sources: Manfredi; company interviews.

With this strong competitive base and with ready access to capital, they exported to the world. If they encountered restrictions in assaulting a large foreign market, they usually reverted to licensing, followed by direct investment.

Some of the major U.S. producers, like Cat and Harvester, started as agricultural or tractor manufacturers, or both. That was also true of other companies, including Fiat in Italy, Hanomag and Lanz in Germany, and Komatsu. Some companies entered from other heavy equipment businesses, like Allis-Chalmers and Clark in the United States, Orenstein & Koppel (O&K), Demag, and Atlas in Germany, and Hitachi and Sumitomo in Japan.

At the end of World War II, however, a few large national producers existed, led by Caterpillar, along with a fragmented fringe of concerns making specialized products, like pipelayers, and serving regional or national markets. During the global construction boom that followed the war, U.S. concerns were the main beneficiaries because their production facilities were still intact. Growing scale economies in new-product R&D, in production, and in dealer, service, and parts networks opened up a potential for globalization—in which rivals' strategic positions in a certain market are affected by their worldwide positions—but the potential remained fully unrealized until the late 1970s.

Caterpillar, by far the largest exporter, was the first company to locate overseas, building a plant in Leicester, England, in 1950 to supply replacement parts.[1] Cat expanded quickly, followed by Allis-Chalmers and, after the advent of the Common Market in 1957, by others, too. The choice of locations was often in the same country as that chosen by the first mover. The leaders competed also on dealer strength and product innovation. Steady, at times spectacular, economic growth in the 1960s in the United States, Europe, and Japan stimulated demand for every kind of construction device and lured into the business newcomers like Case, Deere, and Fiat, leaders in agricultural equipment manufacture. Besides the international companies, many regional producers, e.g., Liebherr, Hanomag, and Komatsu, prospered mightily. Some, like Komatsu, ventured into foreign markets in the late 1960s and early 1970s.

In the recesssion after the first oil shock, in 1973, demand for equipment for the usual infrastructure projects dwindled in the industrialized nations. Ironically, the industry was kept afloat largely with demand from the source of its problems at home—the cash-rich, development-hungry members of the Organization of Petroleum Exporting Countries (OPEC), as well as from the credit-rich, development-hungry less-developed countries (LDCs). At this time Japanese producers established themselves as important exporters; their overseas volume tripled from 1973 to 1975.[2]

As the recession waned, orders boomed once again and factories ran at near capacity. In fact, capacity was becoming the critical factor in competing for OPEC wealth. Throughout most of the 1960s and 1970s, orders routinely exceeded capacity, and all U.S. dealers were "on allocation." In the late 1970s all major producers expanded their facilities greatly, thereby creating overcapacity that plagued the industry for the next decade. Instead of taking inefficient plants off the market, manufacturers tended to incorporate them into their global configurations. One of these companies was Allis-Chalmers, which by 1974 could not sustain the volume to justify continued economic production of its large-size equipment. It could not match the investments in R&D and distribution systems that its main rivals were making at the time.[3] So Allis-Chalmers formed a 65-35 joint venture with Fiat, which incorporated Fiat's three plants in Italy and Allis's factories in the United States, England, and Brazil.

CHANGE IN THE INDUSTRY

The recession caused by the second oil shock, in 1979, alone would have retarded sales of construction equipment. But government action added to the industry's woes: policymakers in many countries cut expenditures, including purchases of equipment, and monetary authorities pushed up interest rates to halt the double-digit inflation. The high interest rates affected dealers and contractors, which typically financed their equipment purchases, as well as developing countries, whose ability to borrow for large projects had withered. Retrenchment and high interest rates also sent exchange rates into prolonged deviations from their historical norms.

The depth and duration of the 1980–1982 recession affected every element of the value chain: end-users, dealers, producers, and suppliers. As residential and commercial projects were scaled down or eliminated, contractors got fewer contracts; governments reduced plans in line with the new fiscal austerity; equipment rental agencies responded to the slowdown by postponing purchases and lowering prices on their underused goods. Rather than replace machinery, users tended to prolong its life with extended maintenance. Serviceability, reliability, and—with energy costing more—fuel efficiency and versatility became the most valued characteristics of equipment.

The search for cost efficiency led to a rise in the popularity of smaller machines; their portion rose 10 percentage points in the 1980s. Demand for hydraulic excavators, whose cost efficiency was better than that of other machines on a load-per-horsepower basis, soared until in 1989 they accounted for more than half the units sold worldwide.[4] (Wheel loaders had the second largest world share, nearly 20%, but it was declining.) Hydraulic excavators had already been in wide use in Japan and Europe because of space constraints on construction sites in urban areas, but not in America. Marketing efforts by Japanese makers contributed in large part to a rise in sales in the United States from 2,000 units in 1980 to more than 8,000 in 1990, although annual U.S. production totaled fewer than 3,500 during the period.

By 1989 some 89% of construction equipment sold went to Japan, North America, and Europe. The nonindustrial world had the very cheap labor to perform construction tasks cost-effectively and, following the third-world debt crisis, also lacked the funding for large-scale development projects. Japan was by far the largest consumer of equipment as it strove to build its infrastructure and add to its housing stock. That country alone bought 41% of the units sold worldwide in 1989, compared with 32% in 1980. During the decade the North American market dropped from 26% to 21% and the Western European rose from 21% to 26%.

The steep prolonged downturn in the early 1980s made customers much more price sensitive. They were mostly general contractors—75% of equipment purchased was used for construction of buildings, infrastructure, and similar big projects—while mining companies were important buyers of certain larger machines. As the number of new projects declined, the remaining work tended to be maintenance programs. These required less equipment and were often bid business, for which bidders were prone to shave margins. So contractors had an incentive to stretch out the useful life of equipment.

The manufacturers, in contrast to their dealers, were large and often had their own dealer networks to supply aftersales service and support; their dealers' customers were small and fragmented. The typical contractor bought a piece of equipment every seven years, depending heavily on the dealer for parts and service and in some cases technical advice. Often the cost of maintenance and repair over the life of the machinery exceeded its purchase price.

Gradually leasing and renting spread as an alternative to buying, particularly with big seldom-used items like bulldozers and scrapers. This practice varied a good deal by country; the rental business ("plant hire" in the United Kingdom) prospered in the United States, the United Kingdom, and Japan, but was almost nonexistent in continental Europe.

The sales slump in the early 1980s severely pinched dealers; North American dealers' average net profit slipped from almost 7% in 1974 to less than 1% in 1982 and 1983.[5] Those dealers lacking a large installed base in their business areas to give them parts and service income endured especially difficult times. Used-equipment sales became more important; dealers' ratio of new-to-used sales fell from 4:1 in 1974 to 2:1 in 1983.[6] During those years it became increasingly important for manufacturers to meet their dealers' needs for dependable products, not only to maintain their financial health but also to protect the investment in the dealer network.

COMPETITORS' REACTIONS

Long-lasting shifts in market share took place at this time, revolving around a battle for the customer on two fronts: the distribution system and price reductions. The strongest players were those which achieved a first-mover advantage in the dealer network in a particular targeted market or those which had the resources to make the necessary investments to overcome this considerable barrier. The scope of the product line was essential to dealer strength.

The second battlefront was on price reductions made possible by lowering costs. Since product innovations were often short-lived and usually not revolutionary, competitors fought it out on costs. Because the operating and repair costs were large, the price battle hinged on more than just the purchase price. Consequently all major manufacturers focused on quality and reliability. Manufacturing operations had to achieve efficient scale, and product introductions designed-in cost reductions.

In the 1980–1982 market downturn, Komatsu fired the first salvo in the push for lower costs and prices. In 1980 Komatsu bought its way out of licensing agreements with troubled International Harvester and Bucyrus-Erie, thereby freeing itself to ship its products to the United States. Other Japanese companies also had the opportunity to pursue aggressive exports of hydraulic equipment targeted at the United States, since they too had bought out of their licensing agreements during the late 1970s and early 1980s,[7] and some unfettered competitors, such as Hitachi and

Mitsubishi, even had market power similar to that of Komatsu at the time (a market share of approximately 20%). However, it was Komatsu that seized this opportunity since it was consistent with its explicit corporate strategy of challenging Caterpillar worldwide and in all major product categories.

Hydraulic excavators having gained a small, but increasing, market acceptance in the United States, Komatsu was now more attractive as a complementary line for the narrow-line dealers that pieced together products from a variety of specialized producers. As the dollar appreciated and the yen depreciated, Komatsu approached dealers of Clark, International Harvester, and Deere equipment and offered them its products without requiring them to drop other product lines. Aided by the low value of the yen, Komatsu lowered prices as much as 40% below the competition. The low prices for the continually improving Komatsu products and the riskless appeal to dealers translated into a rapid increase in Komatsu's market share in the early 1980s.

As the other producers sought to gain scale in their production lines and scope in their distribution systems in order to match the price cuts, the smaller, less efficient producers were forced to merge or go out of business. Before 1979, mergers occurred at a rate of less than one per year; since that time, the annual rate has exceeded five. In 1960 the leading eight firms accounted for 40% of world sales, but by 1990 they made up more than 75%, with Caterpillar and Komatsu dominating the competition. See Table 7-1 for a summary of the major consolidations and alliances.

In the mid-1980s Komatsu's production costs had been estimated by various managers to be between 10% and 40%, depending on the particular product, below the Japanese production costs of Cat, its major competitor. One of the most important factors explaining Komatsu's low-cost position was the efficiencies it achieved in its production process through economies of scale. The minimum efficient scale for hydraulic excavators, for example, rose significantly—with increases in design costs and production process technologies—from approximately 2,000 units per year about 1980 to almost 10,000 units per year at the end of the decade. That cost advantage relative to Japanese producers was eroded as rapid domestic demand in Japan in the 1980s afforded scale economies to more competitors. The fierce domestic competition in Japan motivated companies to undertake other production process changes, such as FMS and robotic welding, in order to reduce parts and work-in-progress inventories. Komatsu and some of the smaller, more specialized firms like

TABLE 7-1
Construction Equipment Firms

Firm (Year Committed to Construction Equipment Industry)	Country	Buyer/Alliance	TTT	TTL	WL	SC	MG	HE	TBL	OHT	CR
Caterpillar (Cat) (1904)	United States		O	O	O	O	O	P	O	P	
Shin Caterpillar Mitsubishi (1963)	Japan	SCM JV (1963)	O	O	O			O			
Mitsubishi (1963)	Japan	Cat JV (1963)	O	O	O			X			
Larsen & Toubro (1963)	India	Cat JV (1982)	O	O	O						
P. T. Natra Raya	Indonesia	Cat JV (1982)	O	O	O						
Eder-Sonnebogen-Zeppelin	Germany	Cat JV (1991)						X			
Komatsu (1921)	Japan		O	O	P	P	P	P		P	
Bumar	Poland	Komatsu JV	O								
Hyundai	Korea	Komatsu JV	O								
Samsung (1987)	Korea	Komatsu Lic.		O	O		O	O			O
FAI	Italy	Komatsu (1988)							X		
Hanomag	Germany	Komatsu (1989)	X	X	X						
Moxy	Norway	Komatsu (1991)								O	
Komatsu-Dresser (1988)	United States		P	P	P	P	P	P		P	
Dresser	United States	Komatsu JV (1988)	P	P	P	P	P	P		P	
Jeffrey Gallion Co.	United States	Dresser (1973)					X	X			X
Marion Power Shovel	United States	Dresser (1977)						X			
International Harvester (IH) (1928)	United States	Dresser (1982)	X	X	X	X		X		X	
Frank G. Hough (1939) "Payloader"	United States	I-H (1952)			X			X		X	
Heil Co.	United States	I-H (1953)				X					
Yumbo	France	Dresser (1983)						X			
Wabco (American Standard) "Haul Pak"	United States	Dresser (1984)		X		X	X			X	X

Company	Country	Acquisition										
J. I. Case (1957)	United States		X	O	O	O	O	P	O		P	O
American Tractor Co.	United States	Case (1957)		X	X	X	X	X	X			
Drott Manufacturing	United States	Case (1967)				X	X	X	X			
Poclain	France	40% Case (1977)						X				X
VME (1985)	Belgium					P	P	P	P		P	P
Volvo (1975)	Sweden	VME JV (1985)	X	X	X	X	X	X	X	X	X	X
Clark (1953)	United States	VME JV (1985)	X	X	X	X						X
Ross Carrier "Michigan"	United States	Clark (1953)				X						X
Euclid (1931)	United States	Clark (1984)								X		
Melroe "Bobcat"	United States	Clark (1969)			O	O			O			
Zettlemeyer	Germany	VME (1990)			X	X			X	X		
Akerman	Sweden	VME (1991)						X	X			
Hein-Werner	United States	Akerman (1981)						X	X			
Hitachi (1968)	Japan	JV	X	O	O	O	O	O	O		O	
John Deere (1966)	United States	JV	O	O	O	O	O	O	P		P	
Fiatallis (1965)	Italy	JV	O	X	X	X	X	X	P		X	P
Allis-Chalmers (AC) (1928)	United States	Fiatallis (1974)	X	X	X	X	X	X	X		X	X
Tractomotive	United States	A-C (1959)	X	X	X	X	X	X				X
Benfra	Italy	Fiatallis (1975)	X	X	X	X	X	X	X			
Fana	Italy	Fiatallis (1975)										
Simit	Italy	Fiatallis (1975)				X	X	X	X		X	
Richier	France	Fiatallis (1983)	X	X	X	X	X	X	X		X	
Benati	Italy	Fiatallis (1990)	P	P	O	O			O		O	
Ford-New Holland	United States	Fiatallis (1990)			O	O			X	O	O	
Daewoo (1987)	Korea	Hitachi Lic.			X	X			O			
Terex (1968, renamed 1987)	United States	IBH (1980)	X	X	X	X	X	O	O		P	O
I. B. H. Holding (1975)	Germany	Many (1984)	X	X	X	X	X	X	X		X	
Massey-Ferguson	Canada	IBH (1982)	X	X	X	X	X		O		O	

(continued)

323

TABLE 7-1 (Continued)
Construction Equipment Firms

Firm (Year Committed to Construction Equipment Industry)	Country	Buyer/Alliance	TTT	TTL	WL	SC	MG	HE	TBL	OHT	CR
Koehring	United States	Terex (1986)									X
Ishikawajima Heavy Ind. (IHI)	Japan	Koehring (1989)						X			
Japan Steel Works	Japan	IHI						X			X
Bucyrus-Erie	United States	Terex (1986)						X			
Unit Rig	United States	Terex (1986)								X	
Dart	United States	Unit Rig (1984)			X					X	
Northwest Engineering	United States	Terex (1986)						X			
Rimpull	United States	Terex								O	
Liebherr (1949)	Swiss		P	P	P			O			O
Orenstein & Koppel (1949)	Germany	O&K (1985)			P		P	O		P	X
Faun-Frisch	Germany	Faun (1975)			X		X			X	
Trojan	United States	Faun (1983)			X						
Kaelble	Germany	Faun (1983)			O					X	
Furakawa	Japan	Faun (1990)	O	O	O						
J. C. Bamford (1945)	United Kingdom				P			P	O		
Sumitomo (1963)	Japan							O			O
Linkbelt (FMC) (1906)	United States	Sumitomo (1986)						O			O
Kobe Steel (Kobelco)	Japan							O			
Kawasaki	Japan				X						
MDI/Yutani (Mitsubishi)	Japan	Kobelco (1982)			O		O				
Harnischfeger-P&H	United States		X	X				X			

Company	Country	Notes	TTT	TTL	WL	SC	MG	HE	TBL	OHT	CR
Atlas-Weyhausen	Germany				O						
Laltesi	Italy				O						
PMI	Italy				O						
Mannesmann Demag	Germany				X						
Hy-Hoe	Canada				O						
Hydromac	United Kingdom				O						
Kato	Japan				O			O			
Gradall (Warner & Swasey)	United States	Pacific Am. (1983)			X			X			
Badger	United States	Pacific Am. (1983)						O			
Insley	United States				O			X			
Hyster	United States	Bomag (1990)			X			X			
Radano (1948)	Japan				X						
Grove	United States	Grove (1981)									O
Lima Cranes	United States	Grove (1984)									O
Cole Cranes	United Kingdom										X
Champion	Canada						O				
Huber (A-T-O)	United States						X				
Marathon/Le Tourneau	United States						X			O	
Aveling Barford	United Kingdom						O			X	
Ingersoll-Rand	United States									O	
Kubota	Japan			O	O			O			
Toyo Umpanki (TCM)	Japan			X	X			X			
October .14	Yugoslavia		X					X			
Tractor Export	Former USSR		X					X			
Cline	United States									O	
M-R-S	United States									O	

325

Sumitomo, were also increasing the amount of purchased materials in their cost structures in order to bring more flexibility and fewer fixed costs.

Another opportunity for cost reduction lay in achieving scale in the design of new products. Moreover, the product designs themselves helped reduce costs via design improvements for ease of manufacturing, material reduction, parts inventory reduction, and improved serviceability and reliability. In the early 1980s, designs incorporating microcomputer controls were introduced, enhancing product quality. Despite the scope of these innovations, the product was mature, and any improvements made by one manufacturer were quickly copied by another. One manufacturer estimated that the average life span of an innovation before copying offset the gain was six months to a year. The net result was an increase in the costs of staying competitive in product development without a commensurate long-term gain in competitive advantage. Only those companies with large production volumes and broad product scope could spread out the increasingly large R&D commitments and deliver the higher-quality product to the customer at a competitive price.

Part of the explanation of the shift in market share positions is the timing of the introduction of new models. For example, in competing models of excavators, Hitachi had pre-empted Komatsu on the last two introductions of the 1980s. The differences in features between Hitachi's Landy series and Komatsu's Advance series were not highly significant. It appears, however, that pre-emptive model introductions were a significant factor in explaining the large increases in market share for Hitachi during this period. These two competitors usually introduced new models with lower prices, while Caterpillar usually raised prices when bringing out new models. The pricing difference can be attributed to a difference in design philosophies among competitors. Caterpillar promoted value-oriented design improvements, whereas many of the Japanese competitors championed cost-oriented improvements. For example, the lower cost design philosophy stressed commonality and reduction of parts—in some cases as much as 20% fewer parts—with a full consideration of robot welding capability. Faster development times for new products allowed manufacturers to get the cost and price reductions to the marketplace before competitors. Komatsu and Hitachi had succeeded in getting the development time for new models down to one to two years, which was considerably faster than Caterpillar in the early 1980s.

As competitors responded to the increased cost pressures during the early 1980s, production in this industry spread around the world. Cat was among the first American producers to move to a more global structure, though it proceeded slowly in this direction in the early 1980s in response to the collapse of the U.S. market and the appreciating dollar. Cat (and other American producers) had typically priced products sold overseas in dollars; consequently, it was seriously affected by the appreciation of the dollar. This promoted worldwide dealer harmony by minimizing the resale of Cat products by entrepreneurial brokers buying products at a discount in weak-currency countries and reselling them in a strong currency country. Komatsu, on the other hand, had traditionally priced its overseas products in the local currency according to local market conditions. But after July 1985, pricing products in local currency became more difficult. In that month the European Community slapped a dumping charge on the Japanese construction equipment manufacturers: 26% duties for Komatsu, 12% for Hitachi, 22% for Mitsubishi, and 33% for Kobe. Komatsu later raised its prices and appears to have set them in yen thereafter, making it more vulnerable to exchange-rate fluctuations.

To *endaka* (the yen appreciation after 1985), Komatsu responded first by expanding export markets to generate volume even if the exports were not profitable. Komatsu targeted U.S. markets with the wheel loaders and hydraulic excavators to compensate for a decline in sales to the Middle East.

Komatsu also anticipated the turn in the exchange rate before the dollar peaked in 1985 and launched a program of cost reductions. Initially this involved product redesigns initiated to trim materials and manufacturing costs. By the end of 1986, when the yen had reached 150 yen to the dollar, Komatsu instituted a target 30% cost reduction in manufacturing and overhead.

In addition, in 1985 Komatsu set up 100% local production in the United Kingdom and the United States to avoid anticipated trade barriers and to take advantage of expected currency changes. It had already reached optimal scale in Japan for its products, so the focus was on locations for the incremental plant capacity. Even as local production was starting up in the United Kingdom and the United States, Komatsu was proceeding with further plans for accelerating it. By the end of 1987, with the yen at 130, Komatsu was enjoying an upsurge in domestic demand and planning to cut off unprofitable exports and supplant them with local production. In 1988 the company established a fifty-fifty joint venture with Dallas-based Dresser Industries to strengthen its production and distribution in the United States. In 1989 Komatsu bought Hanomag, a large German construction equipment firm.

After the dollar fell in 1985, Cat decided to drop prices in an effort to hold market share (and not sacrifice dealers). It closed plants, cut costs, and sliced margins. Its American competitors tried to maintain profits on smaller market shares. Beginning in 1985 Cat has embarked on a $2 billion (later scaled back to $1.5 billion) modernization and reorganization program, known as Plant With a Future (PWAF), to raise its efficiency. PWAF's goal was to reduce costs 20% through, among other things, consolidating production facilities around the world and driving business decisions lower in the organization. Caterpillar had been globalizing its production since the rise of the dollar in the first half of the 1980s, but by the end of the decade its global operations were in need of rationalization and consolidation. From 1982 to early 1987, non-U.S. production of Caterpillar products grew from 19% to 25% and sourcing of parts overseas increased fourfold. From 1985 to 1987, for example, imports of crawler loaders doubled as Caterpillar shifted manufacture of this machine from its U.S. plant to European operations in an attempt to rationalize production.

JOINT VENTURES

In addition to the necessity for all competitors to adopt strategies to lower costs, any long-term global competitor must develop a strong dealer network. Dealers require competitive and reliable products, frequent innovations, and a broad range of products to meet customers' varied and specific needs. Some competitors sought acquisitions, but increasingly more firms were entering into joint ventures in order to compete with the industry giants. The examples of Dresser, Hitachi, Deere, and Fiatallis illustrate how the strategic and organizational requirements of the joint ventures determined management decisions affecting the pattern of production and trade.

Dresser tried to solve the product scope problem in the 1970s and early 1980s through acquisitions. In 1973 it bought the Jeffrey Galion Company in Columbus, Ohio, which produced motor graders, compaction equipment, mining equipment, and a few cranes. Four years later Dresser purchased Marion Power Shovel to expand its already large mining business. The most significant move, however, came in 1982, when Dresser bought International Harvester's construction equipment division in Melrose Park, Illinois, for $100 million. With this purchase the firm added wheel loaders, crawler tractors and loaders, and motor scrapers to its expanding product line; but more important, it acquired a worldwide distribution network that was especially strong in North America. Two years later Dresser made its final significant purchase when it acquired Wabco from American Standard. Wabco produced Haulpak trucks, which are huge off-highway mining vehicles.

Dresser management at this point faced the task of rationalizing its distribution and marketing networks to compete with Cat. Dresser had neither the economies of scale to support the R&D and capital investments to upgrade its product line nor the scope of products to keep its dealers satisfied. Dealers need a broad scope of products within the categories of use: earth moving, mining, and lifting. Dresser dealers with many products in each of these areas, but no broad product line within any one, were forced to acquire complementary lines, which reduced Dresser's influence over them. Therefore Dresser sought a major joint-venture partner to remedy these deficiencies.

In 1988 Komatsu and Dresser entered a fifty-fifty joint venture to produce a dual line of products, under both the Komatsu and the Dresser trademarks, for sale in the United States. The partners, finding only a 30% overlap in customers served by their dealers, reasoned that after some rationalization they would not cannibalize each other's sales. In the deal, Dresser got a broader product line and an injection of capital for product R&D and plant upgrading. Komatsu got access to Dresser's distribution channels as well as some of Dresser's existing production facilities in America. Dresser sold to Furakawa of Japan its wheel loader plant in Germany and its hydraulic excavator plant in France. The joint-venture charter prohibited Komatsu-Dresser from shipping certain of its products worldwide. Much of the Komatsu-Dresser production under the Komatsu trademark was to be used to replace Komatsu exports from Japan to the United States.

In the mid-1980s Hitachi faced many of the problems that confronted Dresser—a narrow product line (hydraulic excavators for the Japanese market), an undeveloped local distribution system, and competition from larger, broad-line competitors. Instead of following Dresser's plan of small-company acquisition, however, Hitachi developed global alliances to give it a market presence. Overseas Hitachi built up momentum after a slow start caused partly by the antidumping charges and endaka. It set up alliances with Deere in the United States and Fiatallis in Italy for the purpose of cooperation in product development and production. Hitachi was to handle sales in the Asia-Pacific area, Fiatallis in Europe and Africa, and Deere in North and South America. The agreements also called for local production to supplant competing exports.

Deere had failed to penetrate the European market in the late 1970s and early 1980s despite great expense, and it failed similarly in Asia, though on a smaller scale. Deere, like all competitors, was also hard hit by the collapse of the global equipment market in the early 1980s. In its move to alliances, it was reacting to Caterpillar's and Komatsu's moves.

The partners developed the global alliance in three steps, the first a joint venture on hydraulic excavators. Deere, like other American competitors, was slow to recognize the importance of the hydraulic excavator in the world market and designed its first model only in the late 1970s. Instead of building its own model, Deere decided to sign a supply agreement with Hitachi, which led the American and Canadian markets. The small excavators were to be sold under the Deere brand name and the large ones under Hitachi. The main body of the excavators would be constructed in Japan and the boom and arms would be assembled in the United States. Deere also purchased Hitachi's North American marketing operations.

The second step was the joint design and production of wheel loaders for the world market. Medium-size wheel loaders were to be produced in the United States, and the small models would be produced in Japan. The final step was the provision of a full line of products to Hitachi for marketing in Asia. The 1990 results for Deere were as follows: some $1.4 billion in construction equipment sales; of that amount, $55 million represented exports from the United States to South America (including about 10–15% parts); and approximately $300 million was for hydraulic excavators and wheel loaders (including $15 million in engines and $20 million in parts) from the United States to Japan.

Deere also arranged a joint venture with Fiatallis in Italy regarding backhoe/loader tractors, crawler tractors, and wheel loaders. The backhoes were to be licensed to Fiatallis and made in Europe for the European and African markets instead of being exported from America. Crawler tractors would be jointly produced in the United States and Italy for sale on their respective continents. Finally, the crawler loaders were to be manufactured in Italy and supplied to the United States. In addition, Fiatallis arranged a separate agreement with Hitachi to manufacture 90% of the value-added of hydraulic excavators in Italy, branded Fiat-Hitachi and sold in Europe. (In the United States, Deere-Hitachi is one of several manufacturers to set up or expand production of hydraulic excavators, causing a significant drop in imports of this machine to America. Others involved include Komatsu, Kobelco, Link-Belt—owned by Sumitomo Heavy Industries—and Koehring.)

With this Triad strategy, Hitachi, Deere, and Fiatallis segregated the world markets, avoided duplicate engineering costs, and established more efficient production facilities. In contrast to Komatsu and Dresser dealers, these three competitors believed that they could be kept together only by respecting one another's marketplace.

CONCLUSION

In this chapter I have highlighted three themes:

1. Traditional country-based explanations adequately explicate competition and trade patterns in the first three decades after World War II. In the dominant oligopoly structure of the industry during this period, the major international players led by Caterpillar tended to supply foreign markets by exports when they were free to do so, and by foreign direct investment when faced with restrictions on their access to those markets.
2. The macro-economic shocks of the late 1970s and early 1980s transformed the structure of the construction equipment industry, giving rise to opportunities for an aggressive rival, Komatsu in this case, to gain a competitive advantage that would alter patterns of trade. The industry shifted from a stable dominant oligopoly to a rivalrous duopoly between Caterpillar and Komatsu.
3. As all competitors responded to the more intense rivalry between the dominant players and confronted their own organizational shortcomings, they took action to return to a more stable oligopolistic structure. These included consolidation and rationalization of operations, globalization of strategies, segmentation of products and markets, and strategic alliances. Such moves, based not on country factors but on the necessities of competitive interaction and their own organizational limitations, significantly affected trade.

The strength of domestic demand is one of the strongest variables among the country-based factors for explaining the rise of Japan as the world's largest producer and exporter of construction equipment. The Japanese domestic economy grew faster than either the European or the North American markets during the postwar years. This phenomenal growth boosted all Japanese producers, but especially those seeking the volume necessary to compete on a global scale. In addition, the appreciation of the dollar supplied the catalyst for a foreign-based competitor with a quality product, like Komatsu, to expand its global market share.

Following the worldwide recession in the early 1980s, customers became more cost conscious and demanded more flexible and efficient machines. The industry was already poised for globalization because of the large and increasing economies of scale in design and production, which gave manufacturers with scale far lower production costs. An aggressive pricing strategy, aided by the exchange rate, allowed a competitor to assail the formidable distribution barriers to entry.

Other competitors, lacking the scale and scope of Caterpillar and Komatsu, were forced, like VME and Dresser, to acquire firms or, like Hitachi, Fiatallis, Deere, and again Dresser, to form joint ventures to share design, production, and marketing costs. Caterpillar diversified its production worldwide, accounting in part for the decline of U.S.-based production. As companies gravitated to a strategy of production in each of the three largest markets, a decline in the importance of Japan as a production base followed. A decline in the volume of trade in finished products in this industry was expected, as well as a rise in the trade of scale-sensitive parts.

NOTES

1. William L. Naumann, *The Story of Caterpillar Tractor Co.* (New York: Princeton University Press for the Newcomen Society in North America, 1977), 12.

2. Data compiled from Japan Tariff Association, *Japan Exports and Imports: Commodity by Country*, December 1973, December 1975.

3. Walter F. Peterson, *An Industrial Heritage: Allis-Chalmers Corporation* (Milwaukee: Milwaukee County Historical Society, 1978), 402.

4. The quantitative market estimates in this section come from the consulting firm of Manfredi & Associates. See, in particular, *Machinery Outlook*, November 6, 1990.

5. North American Equipment Dealers Association, *Equipment Dealers' 1983 Cost of Doing Business Survey*, 1983, 1.

6. Ibid., 5.

7. In 1976 Kubota dissolved its agreement with Atlas of Germany; in 1977 Mitsubishi terminated its agreement with Yumbo of France; in 1979 Kobe Steel ended with Liebherr of Switzerland; Komatsu's actions followed in 1980; in 1981 IHI ended its agreement with Koehring of the United States; in 1983 Yutani ended with Poclain of France; and in 1986 Sumitomo dissolved its agreement with Linkbelt (FMC Corporation) of the United States. Kobe Steel's and Nippon Steel's technical agreements with P&H of the United States and O&K of Germany, respectively, were terminated in their separate reorganiza-

tions of 1982. Among the major Japanese hydraulic excavator manufacturers only Hitachi, Kato Works, and Furakawa had developed their own technology. See the Japanese Construction Equipment Association (Nihon No Kensetsu Kikai Sangyo), *Digest* (Tokyo: Kensetsu Kikai Shinpousha, 1989), 2.

BIBLIOGRAPHY

Allis-Chalmers Manufacturing Company. 1930. *Works and Products*. Bulletin No. 146. Milwaukee: Allis-Chalmers.

Broehl, Wayne G., Jr. 1984. *John Deere's Company: A History of Deere & Company and Its Times*. New York: Doubleday.

Caterpillar Tractor Company. 1954. *Fifty Years on Tracks*. Peoria, Ill.: Caterpillar Tractor Company.

Chakravarthy, Balaji S., and Peter Lorange. 1991. "FiatGeotech and Hitachi," Chapter 10 in *Managing the Strategy Process: A Framework for a Multibusiness Firm*. Englewood Cliffs, N.J.: Prentice-Hall.

Chandler, Alfred D., Jr. 1990. *Scale and Scope: The Dynamics of Industrial Capitalism*. Cambridge, Mass.: Harvard University Press.

Dataquest, Inc. *Japanese Industry News Bulletin*. Various issues.

Hasegawa, Fumio, and the Shimizu Group FS. 1988. *Built by Japan: Competitive Strategies of the Japanese Construction Industry*. New York: John Wiley.

Hippoh, Yasuyuki. 1983. *The Construction Industry in Japan: A Survey*. Tokyo: Asian Productivity Organisation.

Japanese Construction Equipment Association (Nihon No Kensetsu Kikai Sangyo). 1989. *Digest*. Tokyo: Kensetsu Kikai Shinpousha.

Japan Tariff Association. *Japan Exports & Imports: Commodity by Country*. Tokyo: Japan Tariff Association. Various years, 1973–1989.

Kirsher, Bernard. 1981. "Komatsu on the Track of Cat," *Fortune*, April 20.

Laing, Scott. 1979. *Concentration and Diversification of the Self-Propelled Heavy Machinery Industries in the U.S.A.: On- and Off-Highway Trucks, Agricultural Vehicles, and Construction and Earthmoving Equipment*. London: Economist Intelligence Unit, August.

Manfredi & Associates. *Japanese Machinery Outlook*. Various issues.

———. *Machinery Outlook*. Various issues.

———. 1986. *Off-Shore Sourcing: Problem and Opportunities*. October.

Marsh, Barbara. 1985. *A Corporate Tragedy: The Agony of International Harvester Company*. Garden City, N.Y.: Doubleday.

Morgan, Lee L. 1978. *Needed: A National Policy for U.S. Exports*. An Address to the 29th Annual Meeting of the Detroit Section of the Society of Automotive Engineers, White Sulphur Springs, West Virginia. October 13.

———. 1980(a). *Sustained U.S. Export Growth: An Imperative for the 1980s*. An Address to the International Business Council. September 17.

————. 1980(b). *Change in the Air: Free Trade and Economic Growth in the 1980s*. Remarks before the National Foreign Trade Convention. October 20.

Naumann, William L. 1977. *The Story of Caterpillar Tractor Co*. New York: Princeton University Press for the Newcomen Society in North America.

Nelson, Phillip. 1970. "Information and Consumer Behaviour." *Journal of Political Economy* 78:311–329.

North American Equipment Dealers Association. Various years. *Equipment Dealers' Cost of Doing Business*. St. Louis: North American Equipment Dealers Association.

Payne, Walter A. 1982. *Benjamin Holt: The Story of the Caterpillar Tractor*. Stockton, Calif.: University of the Pacific.

Peterson, Walter F. 1978. *An Industrial Heritage: Allis-Chalmers Corporation*. Milwaukee: Milwaukee County Historical Society.

Porter, Michael E. 1980. *Competitive Strategy: Techniques for Analyzing Industries and Competitors*. New York: Free Press.

————. 1990. *The Competitive Advantage of Nations*. New York: Free Press.

Quain, Mitchell I., and Barbara McQueen. 1985. *Caterpillar Tractor and the Earthmoving Equipment Industry*. New York: Wertheim & Co., Machinery Group Study, November.

Tirole, Jean. 1988. *The Theory of Industrial Organization*. Cambridge, Mass.: MIT Press.

U.S. Council of Economic Advisers. 1991. *Economic Report of the President* and *Annual Report of the Council*. Washington, D.C.: U.S. Government Printing Office, February.

U.S. Department of Commerce. 1966. *Construction Statistics: 1915–1964*. Washington, D.C.: U.S. Government Printing Office, January.

————. *Value of New Construction Put in Place*. Washington, D.C.: U.S. Government Printing Office. Various issues.

U.S. Department of Commerce, International Trade Administration. 1984. *A Competitive Assessment of the U.S. International Construction Industry*. Washington, D.C.: U.S. Government Printing Office, July.

————. 1985. *A Competitive Assessment of the U.S. Construction Machinery Industry*. Washington, D.C.: U.S. Government Printing Office, February.

————. 1989. *A Competitive Assessment of the U.S. International Construction Industry*. Washington, D.C.: U.S. Government Printing Office, February.

Woolfson, Charles, and John Foster. 1988. *Track Record: The Story of the Caterpillar Occupation*. London: Verso.

8

MINERALS: ERODING OLIGOPOLIES

Louis T. Wells, Jr.

INTRODUCTION

Economic Models and Actual Trade

The great copper mines of Katanga, Zaire, used to ship their output largely to Belgium. Yet Belgium is a small country that consumes little copper. It is no closer to Zaire than are large consumers like Great Britain and France, and hardly closer than Germany. Zaire's export of its copper to Belgium appears to have been an outcome of Belgium's colonization of the Congo and encouragement of its capital to exploit the local mines; economic factors obviously cannot explain that trade flow. Although Zaire is now independent and Belgian companies no longer control the Katanga mines, traces of the old colonial and ownership ties remain in the shipments of Zairian copper.

Other trade flows in minerals are puzzling at first glance. Ghana is the site of a world-class aluminum smelter owned by Kaiser of the United States. The ore feeding it comes all the way across the Atlantic from Jamaica, where Kaiser mines bauxite, even though Ghana mines bauxite and nearby Guinea not only mines bauxite but also converts it to alumina for feeding smelters. At various times Ghana has exported its bauxite to Great Britain, the United States, and Eastern Europe. Some of Guinea's bauxite is converted to alumina and smelted elsewhere on the African coast; much of Guinea's bauxite moves to North America and Europe for conversion and smelting in facilities owned by the same companies that have invested in Guinea's mines. These long trans-Atlantic cross hauls of bauxite continue even though each conversion step (bauxite to

I thank Krista McQuade, who assembled the trade data in the tables and carried out the linear programming analysis, and the several managers who provided information and insights concerning the three mineral industries on which this chapter reports.

alumina, and alumina to aluminum) cuts the weight to be shipped by half, and local processing facilities can demonstrably be made economic.

Peru is another surprise. As one might expect, Peru concentrates and smelts much of its copper ore for shipment to industrialized countries. The volume transported is therefore much lower than if Peru shipped bulky copper ore or copper concentrates. Even so, in spite of the proven economic feasibility of processing in Peru, that country ships large quantities of bulky copper concentrate to distant Japan for smelting there.

In Indonesia the destinations of exports from the major state-owned mining firm vary widely from year to year. At the same time the exports of Inco, a major private international firm, flow from Indonesia to the same destination year after year. Moreover, both firms export nickel from similar ore from the same island, but in different processed forms. No explanation for these differences between the two firms emerges readily from simple trade theories that ignore risk.

Minerals have all the characteristics of commodities, for which the locations of various processing steps, in the simplest economic models, would be a function of production and shipping costs, and directions of trade would be determined by efforts to minimize transportation costs. The patterns of trade I have described, however, and many other observed patterns, are not those which such a simple analysis would forecast.

Other researchers have noted the inadequacies of simple economic models to explain mineral trade. Of particular importance, John Tilton's early 1960s econometric study of mineral trade found that transportation costs had little power to explain directions of trade.[1] Rather, Tilton claimed, foreign investment patterns were the principal determinant of the destination of exports. Shipments from producing countries moved disproportionally to facilities owned by the same firms that owned the mines. Since the time of the Tilton study, much has changed in mineral industries. New entrants have weakened oligopolies, governments have shifted policies, and so on.

To examine the effects of change in industry structure on trade patterns, I have chosen to examine three minerals: copper, aluminum, and nickel, for which change from 1962 to 1987 has proceeded at different rates. For example, nationalizations have dramatically changed the structure of the copper industry during the period: the major mines of Zaire, Zambia, and Chile were nationalized by the 1960s and 1970s. In contrast, until recently aluminum and one segment of the nickel industry have been almost immune to change.

The Data

A warning to the reader is in order at the outset: world trade data for minerals are quite confusing and surprisingly incomplete. The data have not been easily assembled and sources disagree sharply on volumes, directions of trade, and even classifications of intermediates. Equally important, published data disagree with widely available qualitative descriptions of trade flows. Thus, the most widely cited source for mineral trade fails to report the movement of alumina from Jamaica to Ghana. But the companies involved make no secret of the huge flows and in fact furnish measures of the flows when asked.

Some problems with the data remain unresolved. Although later in the chapter I use aggregate data as published (for nondominant nations only) to avoid introducing new biases, results based on published data should be viewed as shaky. But most of the story I tell here does not rely on such data.

The complexity of the published data causes another problem. In particular, the multiplicity of minor exporters and importers of most minerals makes the tables of trade difficult to interpret at first glance. So the only exception to presenting the data as published is the elimination of minor trade flows.

To cut through the maze of data, and to escape minor anomalies, I focus on the most important producers of the three minerals, for which trade is significant and data, though not always consistent, are available from a number of sources. Thus I first present a noneconometric examination of trade from some of the major producing countries. In each industry, I describe changes in the major suppliers and the resulting shifts in trade flows. I use the matrices of trade flows (see the tables) from published sources in the econometric analysis presented in the Appendix. The results are somewhat reassuring, since they are consistent with the story as told, but the reader should not take the econometric analysis alone very seriously, given all the flaws in the data and the weaknesses in the methodology.

ALUMINUM

The Industry

Although aluminum-bearing materials are abundant on the earth's surface, bauxite is the cheapest aluminum-bearing ore to mine and turn into metal, and it accounts for virtually all production of aluminum.

TABLE 8-1
Bauxite: Actual Trade Patterns, 1962 (metric tons)

Exporter	Australia[a]	Ghana	Guinea[b]	Guyana[b]	Indonesia	Jamaica	Surinam
Importing country							
Canada	30,963	11,836		889,310			277,729
Japan					480,452	3,132	
Netherlands		18,882					
United Kingdom		250,116		32,857			
United States					514,106	6,082,764	2,968,900
Total	30,963	280,834		1,436,273	480,452	6,082,764	3,249,761
World exports	30,978	291,401	166,649	1,632,099	480,452	6,082,764	3,254,301

a1961.
bGuinea exported bauxite primarily to Czechoslovakia, Hungary, and Poland. A small amount also went to Italy and Japan.
Sources: U.S. Bureau of Mines (BoM). Metallgesellschaft (M-G).
Australia: 1961, M-G. 1962 not representative of other years.
Ghana, Guinea, Indonesia, Jamaica, Surinam: BoM.
Guyana: 1961, BoM. 1962 not available as a complete year.

In 1962 bauxite was mined principally in the Caribbean area, but by 1987 other sources had eclipsed traditional suppliers. After being washed, crushed, and dried, bauxite passes through a process that turns it into alumina. The chemical process of conversion, called refining, separates impurities from dried bauxite to produce a white powder, which contains approximately 50% aluminum by weight. A single efficient refinery, say 800,000 tons of capacity, which generally supplies several smelters, could cost more than $1 billion. While a ton of bauxite is valued at around 3% of the value of a ton of aluminum metal, a ton of alumina is worth about 10% to 15% of the same base.

In the past, little refining took place in the bauxite-producing countries. Compared with nickel and copper ores, the metal content of bauxite is fairly high, about 25%. Yet by reducing the weight by about half, refining promises savings in shipping that only partially offset higher handling costs of the powdered product, alumina.

At the next stage a smelting process converts alumina to aluminum, usually in the form of ingot. Because this electrical process is highly energy intensive, smelting facilities tend to be located near low-cost sources of energy. The construction of aluminum smelters requires a large amount of capital: in 1991 some $1.5 billion, plus the huge costs of hydroelectric facilities usually required to generate the power to feed a smelter.

A few vertically integrated firms once controlled most of the world's smelting capacity.[2] They included three U.S. companies (the Aluminum Company of America, or Alcoa, Reynolds Metal Company, and Kaiser Aluminum and Chemical Company), one Canadian company (the Aluminium Company of Canada, or Alcan), one Swiss company (Alusuisse), and one French company (Pechiney). In 1960 these six firms accounted for 77% of the world's smelting capacity outside the centrally planned economies (and, in 1965, 85% of all bauxite mining and 89% of all alumina production).[3]

The strength of these companies derived mainly from control of processing, in contrast to copper and nickel, for which control of rich ore deposits has been decisive. The large capital costs, the technology, and the need for access to a low-cost energy source have made aluminum smelting a difficult stage of the business to enter.

To protect against nationalization or increased taxes, in the 1960s these companies were extremely reluctant to locate smelting facilities, even refineries, in the developing countries where they mined. Putting all the critical components of the industry in one developing country

TABLE 8-2
Alumina: Actual Trade Patterns, 1962 (metric tons)

Exporter	Canada[a]	Guinea	Guyana[b]	Jamaica
Importing country				
Brazil				30,416
Canada			108,884	386,042
Cameroon		99,780		
France		118,215		
Norway		88,537	13,246	184,420
United States	3,514	71,641		
Total	3,514	378,173	122,130	600,878
World exports	3,514	457,653	122,090	637,719

[a]1963
[b]1961.
Source: U.S. Bureau of Mines.

would, they feared, increase "country risk" drastically: an aggressive host government could nationalize mine, refinery, and smelter in one stroke and thus own a viable business. On the other hand, a government that nationalized a large bauxite mine without acquiring the associated processing facilities at the time would probably have found itself unable to market its bauxite or alumina, since the international aluminum giants would refuse to put nationalized alumina or bauxite through their processing facilities, and independent buyers were exceedingly scarce.

Policies of governments in consuming countries, which encouraged the location of smelters at home, reinforced the tendency of companies to separate smelting from mining. Tariffs supported siting in the industrialized countries. Japan, for example, admitted bauxite without duty, but charged duties of around 15% on alumina (and aluminum). The European Community imposed a duty of about 6% on aluminum, and lower duty, or none at all, on bauxite and alumina.[4] Encouragement by local power authorities, which almost universally offered breaks on energy prices, supplemented border protection.

Smelters produce ingot, much of which is then rolled or extruded to produce sheet or extrusions, which are in turn fabricated into products: window frames, siding, cans, and so on. Some is also made into cable or castings. The big international aluminum companies play a larger role in this stage than mining firms have played in similar stages of the other industries in this study. At home, the large firms often owned extrusion and, particularly, rolling mills and power transmission cable facilities. Abroad, where other firms controlled markets (as in Japan), where governments insisted on local participation, or where the risk seemed high, the major firms often had downstream facilities through joint ventures. Thus, Alcan owned many of its own facilities in Europe, through its British subsidiary, but had a joint venture with VAG (a German aluminum company) in Germany and with Nippon Light Metals for Japan.

Since fixed costs are very high in smelting, downstream investment tends to keep throughput in a firm's smelters more stable than it would be without captive markets. Controlled customers can be counted on in times of surplus capacity; independent customers may go to competitors. Further, especially in the case of rolling mills, downstream investment provides some price stability in times of low prices. Prices of sheet products have been more stable historically than those of aluminum ingot, falling less sharply in periods of low demand for aluminum.

The power obtained by aluminum firms through control of refining and smelting, and the protection gained through separation of mining and processing facilities, paid off for them during the nationalization of large mining operations in other industries in the late 1960s and early 1970s. Guyana is the sole bauxite-exporting nation to have nationalized its mines, acquiring Reynolds and Alcan's holdings in the early 1970s. But Guyana was a special case: a large part of its bauxite was used for refractory products, not for producing metal, so it did not depend on access to smelters for a market. India and Indonesia control very small bauxite operations. During the years of widespread nationalization of mines across the third world, other producing nations generally chose to take only participatory roles in the vertically integrated aluminum industry. The heady days of producer cartels in the 1970s generated the International Bauxite Association (IBA). But the main impact seems to have been only to increase the importance of nonmember countries—Australia and Brazil, in particular—as sources of bauxite.

Change in the Aluminum Industry

By 1987 the vertically integrated companies had lost some market share, but their shares were still large. Yet changes were starting to generate a sharp restructuring of the industry, the impact of which has become visible in recent years.

By the late 1980s large Japanese producers and other entrants had appeared on the scene. Some of them were firms from other metal industries that were diversifying their holdings (a phenomenon we will observe later in the nickel industry); some were state-owned enterprises. Most were not vertically integrated, at least not to the extent that the older firms were. While some outsiders entered the industry, cross-market investment grew rapidly. Alusuisse and Pechiney, for example, bought interests in new smelters in the United States. Mitsui gained a foothold in the U.S. market by acquiring facilities from Amax. U.S. companies took positions in Canada (particularly through Reynolds's control of British Aluminium, which had Canadian operations), Japan, and throughout Europe. Many of these investments were joint ventures among the major companies.

The most important changes came in processing locations. Shifts in smelting operations were the most notable, the result of sharp hikes in energy costs. Higher energy prices in the 1970s made smelting in some market countries simply too costly. In recognition of the high costs, policies in some of the consuming countries, particularly Japan, moved away from protection of processing, and companies, both old and new, responded to the new economics by erecting smelting plants in countries that offered lower energy costs.

In the 1970s Japan enjoyed more than 10% of world smelting capacity. After the 1973 oil crisis, however, the Ministry of International Trade and Industry (MITI) concluded that domestic smelting was becoming too costly and decided to encourage the phaseout of smelting in Japan and the construction and purchase of Japanese-tied smelters abroad. MITI accompanied the new policy with incentives, including tariff-free imports of aluminum for firms that would close capacity, and loans to make investments in smelting overseas.[5]

Mitsui quickly responded to the new energy prices and policies by buying capacity from Amax in 1974. Other Japanese firms acquired overseas smelting capacity through consortia, for example, in Sumatra, Indonesia. Where control of foreign plant eluded the Japanese, they provided small amounts of equity, larger amounts of debt finance, and offers of technology to other smelters, like Venalum in Venezuela, in return for long-term contracts to supply the Japanese market.

By 1991 the Japanese were said to have only 35,000 to 40,000 metric tons of smelting capacity, down from the peak of 1.2 million in 1977. The tied arrangements abroad and the facilities owned overseas at least partly offset the decline of Japan as a location for smelting and left the Japanese free of dependence on the vertically integrated foreign firms. They had established themselves as major players in the industry, with diversified sources of supply.

Low energy costs within their borders, and oil revenue or Japanese financing, enabled state-owned firms in certain developing countries to establish their own smelters outside the control of multinationals. The availability of technology from new sources—from Japan and the Eastern bloc countries—also helped new players gain entry.

The rise in energy costs slowed expansion by the traditional producers; they invested mostly to replace plant that no longer complied with environmental regulations. By the 1980s private entry and expansion in the industry had virtually stopped because capacity was adequate. But state-owned firms were least restricted. Governments on the Persian Gulf, in Bahrain and Dubai, for example, built smelters to take advantage of low-cost gas. Other countries, like Venezuela, entered or expanded to draw on hydro power. By 1986 state-owned smelters accounted for an estimated 40% of world capacity.[6]

Flush with cash from oil production, Venezuela first built a smelter (with technology bought from Reynolds), then an alumina plant (technology supplied by Alusuisse), and finally in the late 1980s opened its own bauxite mines. One of its smelters (at 400,000 tons) is the largest in the Western world.

Although Venezuela was unique in building an independent vertically integrated industry, other state-owned enterprises became important. Brazil, Guinea, Surinam, Egypt, and Ghana all formed state-owned firms that were active in some stage of the industry. With money (from oil and bank loans) and technology (from Japanese companies and others) now available to governments, smelting slipped out of the hands of the old private firms. Smelters were being built wherever energy was cheap.

Where alumina was refined changed as well. While formerly the bulk of bauxite was shipped to industrialized countries to be refined into alumina and smelted, by 1987 much of the bauxite was being converted to alumina in the extracting countries. There were particularly large new facilities in Australia. The shift in siting of refining resulted largely from the relocation of smelting operations to mining countries, the influence of transportation economics, and the pressures of governments in the extracting countries for local value-added. The movement of both smelting and refining gained momentum from the erosion of tariff protection for processing in the industrialized countries–an outgrowth of concerns over the environment and energy costs, and of the various GATT trade rounds. Complex consortia reduced the exposure of any one company in a single nation.

For the major firms there was now little point in separating processing from mining to reduce risk, if control over processing was already lost. There was no point anymore in shipping bauxite to the United States or Japan for refining if the alumina was to be smelted elsewhere. Gradually the location of refining came to be driven more by efforts to reduce shipping costs and by pressures from governments in mining countries for local refining. New bauxite mines tended to have refineries located nearby. Refining capacity in consuming countries began to shut down; it fell more than 50% in the United States between 1975 and 1987.[7] (European refining capacity continued to grow, as governments subsidized plants to keep them open.)

The instability wrought by these changes still affects the industry. Nonvertically integrated suppliers of bauxite or alumina are seeking to reduce market risk, sometimes diversifying their markets; similarly, users of bauxite or alumina look for ways to diversify their sources of supply if they do not control them, or firms consider replicating the integrated structures of the traditional companies. These old-line multinationals struggle to determine the balance in capacity they should maintain. The standard policies of vertical balance are in question as unintegrated suppliers and users emerge.

The six vertically integrated firms that accounted for 84% of the world's alumina capacity and 77% of the world's primary aluminum capacity in 1960 accounted for 66% and 54% of the respective capacities in the 1980s (and 51% of smelting capacity in 1985). The declines in share can be ascribed mainly to the emerging strength of Japanese firms and mineral firms elsewhere that were diversifying into aluminum, including copper producers whose future in their traditional business was bleak.

By 1991 the vertically integrated firms no longer controlled the industry. The London Metal Exchange (LME) had begun to trade aluminum in 1978 and grew to become something more than a marginal market serving as a reference price for transactions. Significant quantities of metal were said to be traded over the market. An independent firm with surplus aluminum could find a market for large quantities on the LME. Further, bauxite and alumina found markets directly among unaffiliated parties. Firms developed to act as middlemen to place surplus bauxite and alumina with buyers that lacked adequate regular sources or had temporary shortfalls.

Yet unintegrated producers can still feel quite uncomfortable in an industry with vertically integrated giants. Even Venezuela's roughly balanced capacities in mining, refining, and smelting do not afford total security. The Venezuelans remain quite dependent on the Japanese market, where buyers appear to act in concert. Almost half the output of one of Venezuela's smelters is sold there. But Japan does not depend similarly on Venezuela, since that country supplies only 10% to 12% of Japan's needs.

To lessen the dependence and ensure markets when aluminum was in surplus, Venalum and Alcasa, the two local smelters, have taken steps to capture downstream outlets, including interests in an American extruder and facilities in Belgium, Puerto Rico, and Costa Rica, as well as in Venezuela itself. Further integration into downstream markets is a possibility. But whether the government enterprise will replicate the structure of a major private aluminum firm to break its dependence on thin, uncontrolled markets is uncertain; government ownership itself imposes constraints on the enterprise.

Aneka Tambang, Indonesia's state-owned mining company, faced even greater dependence on the Japanese market, but it had not integrated forward as had the Venezuelans. Justifying government capital for expenditure at home was tough enough; justifying it for foreign investment seemed impossible. The difficulties of Indonesia's state-owned bauxite mine illustrate the problems of a producer situated outside a vertically integrated chain. The firm annually mines about 1.2 million tons (wet) of bauxite, of which about 750,000 tons go to three Japanese concerns. None of the output is refined into alumina for Indonesia's giant Asahan smelter; the smelter imports its alumina from Australia, where Japanese firms in the Asahan consortium also participate in bauxite mining.

The Indonesian firm has not captured gains from rising aluminum prices. In the years 1986 to 1989, the average value of bauxite shipments ranged between $.012/kg and $.013/kg, and the value in 1989 fell slightly below that in 1986. During the same period, the average value of a kilogram of aluminum from Asahan moved upward from $1.11 to $2.33.[8]

Since Aneka Tambang did not have the resources (or the bauxite) to support its own smelter and had no associated refinery, it tried to reduce its dependence on a small number of key buyers by diversifying its customer base. In 1987, through Norsk Hydro, its Norwegian marketing agent, it sold a trial shipment of bauxite to the state-owned smelter in Venezuela. But there was no repeat order. At the same time, Aneka Tambang began shipments of bauxite to Reynolds on the U.S. Gulf Coast. By 1989 sales to this market made up about one quarter of Aneka

Tambang's bauxite shipments. But this contract will expire in 1994, and in interviews management expressed worry that the Gulf smelter will curtail its production because of energy costs and environmental demands in the United States, leaving Aneka Tambang once more dependent on a few Japanese buyers that seemed to act together and anyway were decreasingly interested in bauxite. Success in attaining security through diversification has eluded this unintegrated firm.

Trade in Aluminum

In 1962 the directions of trade were determined primarily by ownership patterns. By 1987, however, that situation had changed as unintegrated firms entered the market, the locations of processing shifted, and independents tried to diversify their sources of supply or their markets.

In 1962 the three largest exporters of bauxite were Jamaica, Surinam, and Guyana. All of Jamaica's bauxite went to the United States, where its principal mine owners, Reynolds, Alcoa, and Kaiser, were headquartered and owned refineries. The bulk of Surinam's bauxite, from Alcoa's and Reynolds's mines, was also shipped to the United States. Most of Guyana's bauxite went to Canada, home of its mine owner, Alcan.

Ownership similarly drove alumina trade. One authority calculated that about 90% of alumina went to related parties in 1964.[9] According to 1962 figures, Jamaican alumina moved largely to Canada, from an Alcan refinery to Alcan smelters, and to Norway, where Alcan also owned smelters. Guyanan alumina went overwhelmingly to Alcan in Canada.

Significant exporters of aluminum in 1962 were Canada, France, Norway, and the United States. Mining and aluminum smelting were almost totally separated. By 1987 processing had shifted closer to the mines, making alumina more important compared with bauxite. In 1962 trade in alumina represented only one tenth, by weight, of the trade in bauxite; by 1987 alumina trade was close to half that of bauxite.

In 1987, however, ownership still dominated in determining directions of trade. The bulk of Jamaican bauxite still moved to the United States. The largest part of Surinam's bauxite also still went to the United States, although Venezuela had become an almost equally important destination. Guinea had become a significant bauxite exporter—to the United States, the home of Alcoa and Noranda, members of the consortium, and to Spain and Ireland, where Alcan, another consortium member, owned or controlled refineries. Australian bauxite went largely to

TABLE 8-3
Aluminum: Actual Trade Patterns, 1962 (metric tons)

Exporter	Canada	France[a]	Japan	Norway[a]	United States
Importing country					
Argentina		2,513			4,654
Australia	20,536				12,104
Belgium/Luxembourg	10,440	39,182			3,558
Brazil	14,124				4,410
Denmark				4,704	
Hong Kong	5,392				
India	4,774				8,923
Israel		1,875			
Italy	12,963	5,077	1,000	12,506	5,861
Japan	6,921				2,164
Republic of Korea			749		7,462
Mexico	8,240				6,967
Netherlands		6,706			2,556
New Zealand	4,709				
South Africa	13,754				
Spain	8,318				
Sweden	10,638			14,437	
Switzerland		1,332			1,962
United Kingdom	152,246			50,458	34,035
United States	192,323	30,463	3,628	49,867	
West Germany	19,768	11,382		29,298	14,799
Total	485,146	98,530	5,377	161,270	109,455
World exports	522,726	105,189	5,493	171,690	137,164

[a]Includes alloys.
Source: Metallgesellschaft.

Japan and the United States, where the owners or financiers of the mines were based, and to West Germany, from which the material could enter the processing system of Alusuisse (with interests in the Gove mine) and the European facilities of American equity holders. Brazilian bauxite moved largely to Canada and the United States, reflecting the offtake commitments of Alcan and Reynolds, with 24% and 5%, respectively, of the equity. Another large portion went to Surinam, where Alcoa had a refinery. Sierra Leone's bauxite, controlled by Alusuisse, was exported principally to a West German port and from there presumably to Swiss-owned facilities.

These shipment patterns continued even though some of the extracting nations had local refineries by this time. When the refineries were in the hands of companies other than those operating the mines in question, bauxite usually was exported rather than refined locally. For example, shipments of bulky bauxite continued from Guinea to a range

TABLE 8-4
Bauxite: Actual Trade Patterns, 1987 (metric tons)

Exporter	Australia	Brazil	Ghana	Guinea	Guyana	Indonesia	Jamaica	Sierra Leone	Surinam
Importing country									
Argentina					3,145				
Belgium/Luxembourg					7,445				
Brazil					1,001				
Canada	33,000	435,000		493,000	363,429		7,000	347,000	52,000
France	154,000			466,000	8,448				
Ireland				1,300,000					
Italy	495,000	3,000		812,000	26,808				
Japan	1,120,000				11,967	484,000			
Republic of Korea					7,532				
Morocco					3,521				
Netherlands					4,451				
New Zealand					1,014				
Peru					855				
Spain	4,000			1,566,000	37,166				11,000
Surinam	28,000	297,000							
Sweden	12,000				4,799				
United Kingdom			36,000		6,107				13,000
United States	1,173,000	452,000		4,140,000	372,805	67,860	3,472,000		108,000
USSR				3,095,000			912,000		
Venezuela					440,271	32,040			105,000
West Germany	808,000			1,174,000	57,311			721,000	
Yugoslavia	12,000			70,000					
Total	3,839,000	1,187,000	36,000	13,116,000	1,358,075	583,900	4,391,000	1,068,000	289,000
World exports	3,839,000	1,187,000	36,000	13,116,000		583,900	4,391,000	1,068,000	289,000

Sources: International Bauxite Association, Metallgesellschaft, United Nations.
Guyana: UN 1987 inverted data.
Indonesia: UN/M-G.
Others: IBA.

348

of destinations even though a French-led consortium had established a refinery in Guinea. Jamaica, Australia, Surinam, Brazil, and other countries continued to send bauxite overseas in spite of the local presence of refining facilities.

State-owned bauxite could follow various routes. The state-owned Guinean mine sent its bauxite to the Soviet Union, even though there was a local refinery; there was no Soviet ownership, but the technology had come from the USSR, and the country had agreed to take the bauxite in barter. Bauxite from the (state-owned) mining firm in Ghana was by 1987 being shipped to the United States, even though there was a major smelter in the country. The construction of a local refinery for the output of the mine was not attractive, since it would have had to operate at a scale too small for efficiency if fed only with Ghanaian bauxite. But the bauxite could have been refined in nearby Francophone African countries, where alumina plants existed. But those facilities, controlled by major international aluminum companies, appeared to have no interest in Ghanaian bauxite. In 1991 bauxite from Ghana was reportedly going to Eastern bloc countries.

By 1987 new entrants in alumina meant that trade with related parties had declined somewhat in percentage terms. About two thirds of alumina was traded among affiliates.[10] While Jamaican alumina still moved from an Alcan plant in large part to Canada, it also went to Alcan's smelters in Western Europe. Large shipments from Jamaica also proceeded to Ghana, where Kaiser, a mine owner in Jamaica, controlled a smelter. Surinam was shipping alumina from Alcoa's and Billiton's refineries to the United States and the Netherlands. Further, some alumina went to Norway, where Alcoa owned smelting capacity. Guinea was shipping much of its alumina from a refinery operated by a Pechiney-led consortium to the (formerly French) Cameroon, where French interests operated a smelter.

Construction of smelters had produced a big shift in aluminum trade. The significant exporters were Australia, Brazil, Ghana, Indonesia, and Canada. With its cheap power, Canada was the sole survivor from the 1962 list. Indonesia, Persian Gulf countries, Venezuela, Brazil, and Surinam were joining the list of aluminum exporters. Export destinations for these countries were also dominated by ownership or sources of debt finance.

The efforts of independent suppliers to diversify markets are evident in the trade patterns. In 1962 Indonesia's state-owned mining company shipped all its bauxite to Japan, but by 1987 it was selling bauxite to the

TABLE 8-5
Alumina: Actual Trade Patterns, 1987 (metric tons)

Exporter	Australia	Brazil	Canada	Guinea	Jamaica	Surinam
Importing country						
Argentina	296,000	669				
Australia		196				
Bahrain	354,000					
Brazil					50,000	184,000
Cameroon				127,000		
Canada	893,000				503,000	12,000
China	225,000			25,000		
Dubai	302,000					
Egypt	248,000					
France				24,000		
Ghana	90,000					
Iceland	170,000					
Indonesia	409,000					
Iran	47,000					
Italy	8,000			176,000		
Japan	18,000					
Republic of Korea	30,000					
Netherlands	1,000				316,000	272,000
New Zealand	470,000					
Norway	345,000	17		21,000	142,000	480,000
Peru		20,908				
Poland				25,000		
South Africa	340,000					
Sweden					40,000	31,000
Switzerland	122,000					15,000
United Kingdom			1,000	67,000	154,000	
United States	3,361,000	20,073	50,000	13,000	90,000	332,000
West Germany	330,000				229,000	20,000
Yugoslavia				25,000		13,000
Other	169,000					
Total	8,228,000	41,863	51,000	503,000	1,524,000	1,359,000
World exports	8,228,000	41,863	51,000	503,000	1,524,000	1,359,000

Sources: International Bauxite Association, Metallgesellschaft, United Nations.
Brazil: UN.
Others: IBA.

United States and Venezuela, as well as to Japan. From its nationalized mines, Guyana shipped to seventeen nations in 1987. Historical ties meant that some quantity still moved to Alcan, but diversification appeared to be a major goal. In 1962, when Alcan and U.S. interests had controlled Guyana's bauxite, its exports went only to Canada, Alcan's home, in very small quantities to the United Kingdom, where Alcan had a wholly owned subsidiary, and to the United States.

There were more players in the industry by 1987, but ownership still

TABLE 8-6
Aluminum:[a] **Actual Trade Patterns, 1987 (metric tons)**

Exporter	Australia	Brazil	Canada	Ghana	Indonesia	Surinam
Importing country						
Austria		1,000				
Belgium/Luxembourg			7,000	4,000		
China	17,000		5,000			
Colombia			2,000			
Finland		1,000	2,000			
France	1,000	6,000	21,000			
Hong Kong	9,000		15,000		799	
India					7,000	
Indonesia	7,000		2,000			
Israel			9,000			
Jamaica			1,000			
Japan	441,000	221,000	129,000		138,513	
Republic of Korea	85,000		40,000		2,694	
Lebanon			2,000			
Malaysia	14,000		5,000		400	
Mexico			3,000			
Netherlands	1,000	2,000	11,000	3,000		2,000
Norway		9,000	1,000			1,000
Other Asia					2,099	
Philippines	6,000					
Portugal			5,000			
Singapore	13,000				11,833	
Spain		2,000				
Sweden			12,000			
Switzerland		4,000				
Taiwan	81,000		19,000			
Thailand	23,000		8,000			
Turkey			32,000			
United Kingdom		5,000	2,000	1,000		
United States	13,000	68,000	919,000	92,000		
West Germany	3,000	31,000	1,000	40,000		1,000
Total	714,000	350,000	1,253,000	140,000	163,338	4,000
World exports	714,000	350,000	1,253,000	140,000	163,338	4,000

[a]Includes alloyed metal.
Sources: International Bauxite Association, United Nations.
Indonesia: UN.
Others: IBA.

played a major role in trade patterns. The new players had not yet established vertically integrated systems to match those of the old international firms. The constraints imposed by state ownership made it difficult for some recent entrants to build vertically integrated systems. Firms without captive outlets or captive suppliers faced risks in an industry whose independent customers and suppliers were few, and much of the industry was vertically integrated.

The old-line multinationals meanwhile were struggling with decisions about the appropriate degree of vertical integration. Bargains in bauxite and alumina presented themselves from time to time when supply exceeded demand; complete vertical integration closed off these opportunities. The upstream part of the industry had clearly become a competitive commodity business. Some firms, like Pechiney, appeared to see their future downstream from smelting, in more differentiated products. Alcoa decided in the mid-1980s to build strengths in aerospace and other engineering-oriented end-use areas. But simultaneously it began an effort to diversify into nonmetals industries.[11]

As a result of the changing structure, the aluminum industry appeared to be in a state of disequilibrium in 1991. It was unclear whether vertical integration would once more rule the industry, but this seemed unlikely. On the other hand, it seemed equally unlikely that the industry would soon become dominated by open spot markets. For the foreseeable future, the industry, it appeared, would wind its way between these extremes, forcing difficult choices on managers.

COPPER

The Industry

Rich veins of copper are scarce compared with, say, aluminum-bearing ores. In the 1960s six countries held some 70% of known world copper reserves: Chile, Peru, Zaire, Zambia, the United States, and the Soviet Union. The cost of mining depended heavily on the richness and accessibility of ore, and the value of a deposit varied according to its by-products, such as gold, silver, and cobalt.

Copper ore is usually concentrated near the mine until it contains some 20% to 25% metal. Smelting converts concentrate in furnaces to make blister copper, which is 97% to 98% pure. The copper smelting business is relatively easy to enter, especially in comparison to aluminum processing. Technologies are readily available and the entry cost is not overwhelming. In 1980 a smelter of optimal scale (about 150,000 tons annual capacity) cost about $350 million to build.[12]

The barriers to entry in copper smelting being rather low, international firms did not hesitate to locate smelters near the mines. Separating the stages of production would have given them little protection against nationalization, since a host country could establish its own smelter or sell concentrates to independent processors elsewhere. In locating smelters

TABLE 8-7
Copper Ore: Actual Trade Patterns, 1962 (metric tons)

Exporter	Australia	Canada[a]	Chile[a]	Mexico	Peru[a]	Philippines	Zambia
Importing country							
Belgium/Luxembourg		1,900					
Japan	80,156	46,200	16,100		9,266	181,184	1,469
Norway		17,200					
Sweden			300		446		6,466
United Kingdom		1,800			44		
United States		20,700	800	7,022	7,730	9,185	
West Germany		5,000	6,500		319		
Total	80,156	92,800	237,000	7,022	17,805	190,369	7,935
World exports	80,250	95,500	25,200	7,022	17,805		

[a]Short tons.
Sources: U.S. Bureau of Mines, Metallgesellschaft.
Australia, Philippines, Zambia: M-G.
Canada, Chile, Mexico, Peru: BoM.

in producing countries, firms reduced their shipping costs; metal was less bulky to ship than ore or concentrates. There was little cost penalty for locating smelting in the mining country, except perhaps inadequate infrastructure in a third-world nation. Therefore, processing locally often made sense from the viewpoints of simple economics and business strategy. That is to say, local processing made sense as long as governments of consuming countries did not intervene with tariffs or other trade restrictions that differentiated by the degree of processing of an imported mineral. Such intervention persisted through 1987, primarily in Japan.

The refining process is electrolytic, and the technology is widely available. In 1980 investment costs amounted to about $130 million for a plant of 150,000 tons annual capacity. This stage also provided no major barrier to entry to the industry. The transportation savings were, however, not great, since the impurities removed in refining made up a small percentage of the material. So refining could be located near the mine or near the market.

Finally, of course, copper is fabricated into many products, like electrical wire and coins, by a wide range of manufacturers. Few are owned by the operators of smelters or refineries, and overwhelmingly they are located in the industrialized countries, near consumers.

Change in the Industry

The copper industry underwent dramatic changes in the period under study. Ownership of the large mines in the third world changed hands. By 1987, moreover, several large new mines had come on-stream, some operated by new entrants.

In the early 1960s, large foreign mining firms controlled production in the major extracting countries. Production in Chile was largely in the hands of Anaconda and Kennecott of the United States. The mines of Zaire (formerly the Belgian Congo) were owned by Union Minière, a Belgian company, while Zambian (Northern Rhodesian) copper was produced by the Roan Selection Trust (controlled by the Anglo-American Corporation of South Africa, 42% owned by American Metal Climax). Marcona and Southern Peru Copper, two U.S. companies, controlled production in Peru.

The late 1960s and early 1970s witnessed much nationalization. Zaire seized the Katanga mines of Union Minière in 1967; Chile took over Kennecott's and Anaconda's properties in stages from 1968 to 1971, eventually placing three quarters of its industry in state hands;[13] Zambia

TABLE 8-8
Copper Metal (Unrefined): Actual Trade Patterns, 1962 (metric tons)

Exporter	Chile[a]	Mexico	Peru	Zambia
Importing country				
Belgium/Luxembourg	8,618		15,496	12,294
Brazil				
India				2,025
Italy		1,494		8,107
Japan			347	152
Netherlands				2,439
South Africa				318
Sweden	2,104			49
United Kingdom	44,841		18,190	42,269
United States	228,771	22,247	64,114	11,505
West Germany	39,358	694	21,030	46,637
Total	323,692	24,435	119,177	133,863
World exports	323,692	24,435	119,185	133,863

[a]Short tons.
Sources: Metallgesellschaft, Bureau of Mines.
Chile: BoM.
Mexico, Peru, Zambia: M-G.

took 51% control of its mines in 1969;[14] Peru nationalized Marcona in 1974. These takeovers accounted for at least two thirds of the capacity of the developing countries.

Meanwhile, new mines were opening via financing and ownership arrangements that differed from those of the past.

In Peru and in Mexico state-owned enterprises launched new mines. In Papua New Guinea and other locations Japanese interests supplied much of the financing, which was tied to long-term sales contracts that committed the bulk of the concentrate produced to Japanese users. Operators of the mines included newcomers like Freeport Minerals (a U.S. sulfur company) and BHP (an Australian company) as well as old hands like Kennecott.

Outside the third world there was change, too. While the mines of the advanced countries remained untouched by nationalization, those in Australia were nevertheless affected by the increasing importance of Japanese finance. There the Japanese sought additional sources to satisfy their fast-growing demand.

Recent years have seen a small reversal of the trend toward state ownership of copper in the third world. The governments of Peru and Chile have permitted new majority-owned foreign investment in their copper industries. But, as on the southwest rim of the Pacific Ocean, companies

TABLE 8-9
Copper Metal (Refined): Actual Trade Patterns, 1962 (metric tons)

Exporter	Australia	Belgium/ Luxembourg	Canada	Chile[a]	Zaire	Mexico	Peru	Zambia
Importing country								
Belgium/Luxembourg			4,491		184,500		4,571	406
Brazil						3,972	5,840	3,922
EEC	6,856							
France		86,238	12,625	11,501	34,000			32,801
India			3,121		1,700			9,154
Italy		9,997	1,959	36,018	40,100			49,551
Japan	6,183		2,665		1,800			6,685
Netherlands		15,335	102	55,716	800		25	3,302
South Africa					6,000		8,608	18,545
Sweden		12,361	4,877	25,695				17,853
Switzerland		13,665	102					5,289
United Kingdom		1,680	84,997	64,337	2,800		12,333	193,081
United States			69,405	883		657		5,084
West Germany	3,103	49,263	10,802	40,294				37,459
Total	16,142	188,539	195,156	234,444	271,700	4,629	31,377	383,132
World exports	16,762	210,123	202,342	264,798	295,400	5,009	36,804	411,039

[a]Short tons.
Sources: Metallgesellschaft, U.S. Bureau of Mines.
Australia, Belgium/Luxembourg, Canada, Zaire, Mexico, Peru, Zambia: M-G.
Chile: BoM.

involved in new third-world investments have generally not been the traditional copper companies. Chile, for example, sold Cia. Minera Disputada to Exxon in 1978.

Even with the return of private companies to the third world, the industry of the 1980s differed fundamentally from that of the early 1960s. The original four American multinationals (Kennecott, Phelps Dodge, Anaconda, and Newmont) owned few remaining interests in the developing countries. Of the important copper firms of the past, only Rio Tinto Zinc remained a major third-world producer.

The processing sites also have shifted considerably. For the most part, ore extracted by majority-owned government enterprises is smelted by those firms domestically. Chile, Peru, Zaire, and Zambia smelt and refine a large part of their copper. Consequently, most shipments consist of metal, the major exception being those to Japan.

The new producers, largely Japanese financed, lagged behind the old mining countries in building processing facilities. Papua New Guinea and Indonesia, which were not extracting copper in the 1960s, were still exporting all their copper in the form of concentrates in the 1980s (almost all of it to Japan).

Further change was evident over the twenty years as many of the old major copper companies disappeared through acquisition. Kennecott was acquired by Standard Oil (Ohio) in 1981. Atlantic Richfield acquired Anaconda in 1977, and, as noted, Exxon acquired Cia. Minera Disputada of Chile. Two small U.S. copper firms were also taken over: Standard Oil (Indiana) took over Cyprus, and Louisiana Land & Exploration took over the Copper Range Company. The oil companies, flush with cash, saw copper as an industry in which their skills in managing government relations, establishing logistical systems, and processing bulk commodities would lead to success. They were to be disappointed, since the firms they acquired could no longer control the market.

As a result of these changes, the copper industry emerged in the late 1980s as the least vertically integrated and least concentrated of the three industries in this study.

Trade in Copper

The directions of trade in 1962 largely reflected ownership patterns. Shipments of unrefined copper from Chile went principally to the United States, home of the owners of Chilean copper production—Anaconda and Kennecott in particular. Unrefined copper from Zambia, not surpris-

TABLE 8-10
Copper Ore: Actual Trade Patterns, 1987 (metric tons)

Exporter	Australia	Chile	Indonesia	Mexico	Papua New Guinea	Peru	Philippines
Importing country							
Belgium/Luxembourg	857						
Brazil	15	235,876		10,000		53,235	
Canada	241	42,635	8,076	20,110		21,500	
China				62,100		21,000	27,608
Finland	20	32,774		9,750			
Hong Kong	12						
Japan	145,964	235,959	229,256	40,000	264,239	115,376	316,603
Korea, DPR				61,509			
Republic of Korea		55,115		20,500	166,409	10,500	17,283
Malaysia	2						
Netherlands	40						
New Zealand	30						
Other Asia		10,395					
Singapore	21						
Spain		147,966		64,785	54,646	3,035	
Sweden	18	17,071				5,556	
Switzerland		11,985					
United Kingdom	752	21,240			1		
United States	2,749	25,540		9,000			
West Germany	20			69,625	191,003	17,107	
Total	150,741	836,556	237,332	367,379	676,298	247,309	361,494
World exports	150,742	836,554		367,379		247,308	361,494

Sources: United Nations, Metallgesellschaft.
Australia, Chile, Mexico, Papua New Guinea, Peru: UN.
Indonesia, Philippines: M-G.

ingly, went in significant quantities to the United Kingdom, where Anglo American had ties.

Even when refining was done in the mining country, the refined copper metal often was shipped not to end markets but to its traditional destinations. Zairian refined copper went overwhelmingly to Belgium, home of Union Minière, and Zambian refined copper went mainly to the United Kingdom, where Roan Selection Trust was located. To be sure, not all metal trade went according to ownership. Most of Chile's refined metal, for example, was sold in Europe instead of going to the United States, where its owners were located.

Ore trade was not directed by ownership in the same way as metal trade. A significant part of Chile's, Peru's, Zambia's, and the Philippines's ore went to Japan, which protected its smelting industry.

By 1987 some of copper's trade patterns had changed considerably, reflecting new ownership. Zairian refined metal went largely to West Germany and the Netherlands; Zambian metal went to a wide range of countries, with the United Kingdom accounting for only a small percentage of sales. Metal moved directly to what had probably been the ultimate markets all along. The disappearance of foreign ownership meant that trade was no longer routed through parent firms.

Trade in unrefined copper metal had changed less dramatically. Exports of unrefined copper declined in importance as the producing countries did more refining. Zambia, for example, reported no exports of unrefined copper at all. But Zaire, which was exporting unrefined copper in 1987, still depended on Belgium for its market. The old ownership ties seemed to direct unrefined copper to the earlier market, even after ownership had changed. As in Guyanan bauxite, historical ties remained important. On the other hand, Chile's exports of unrefined copper, which had declined, no longer went largely to the United States. The particularly acrimonious nationalization seems to have ended even informal ties.

Although the producing countries expanded their processing, their exports of ore also increased. In 1987 the number of refineries was still limited for the output of mines that lacked their own facilities. Of the former ore suppliers, Zambia had dropped out. With few buyers extant, the principal exporter of unrefined metal, Zaire, had to depend to a degree on its old marketing ties with the previous owners of its mines. Although the producing countries expanded their processing, their exports of ore also increased. The bulk of Philippine ore was still going to Japan, as was most Peruvian ore. The major new entrants, Papua New

TABLE 8-11
Copper Metal (Unrefined): Actual Trade Patterns, 1987 (metric tons)

Exporter	Australia	Chile	Mexico	Peru	Zaire
Importing country					
Belgium/Luxembourg				1,608	227,265
Brazil		13,100			
China		8,900			5,000
East Germany		500		400	
France				3,100	11,476
Italy		7,900			
Japan				26,165	
Netherlands		1,500		4,476	
Portugal				1,186	3,000
Turkey		14,900			
United Kingdom	1,004	17,000		28,624	
United States	2,502	31,700	24,295	8,007	
West Germany		23,600		5,248	7,993
Yugoslavia		11,300			3,595
Total	3,506	130,400	24,295	78,824	258,329
World exports	3,506	139,900	24,295	79,327	259,329

Sources: United Nations, Metallgesellschaft.
Australia, Chile: UN.
Mexico, Peru, Zaire: M-G.

Guinea and Indonesia, were also sending the largest part of their ore to Japan. Chile had become the largest ore exporter by this date, to Europe and Brazil, as well as Japan.

By the late 1980s, copper smelting capacity was disappearing in all industrialized countries except Japan, the result of increasing concern over environmental issues. In the United States some smelters continued to operate, but their capacity was dedicated to U.S. ores rather than to imported ores or concentrates. In fact, the major U.S. companies that had imported concentrates in the past turned protectionist after their mines had been nationalized, seeking tariffs on imported ores or concentrates. Japanese smelters remained the principal market for third-world ore and concentrates.

Although the underlying economics indicates that Japanese processing plants should not survive, the cost penalties for locating copper smelting in Japan are certainly much less than for aluminum smelting, whose economics has caused the relocation of facilities. Nevertheless, growing worry over the environment in Japan may cause these smelters to disappear in the 1990s.

NICKEL

Until recent decades the mining of nickel was largely in the hands of a very small number of companies that held valuable deposits. In the early 1960s a single concern, International Nickel Company of Canada (Inco), whose interests were principally in Canada, accounted for 85% of world sales. Falconbridge, with mine interests in Canada and the Dominican Republic, and the Société Anonyme Le Nickel (SLN), whose mines were in New Caledonia, divided almost all the remaining market between them.

Mining was concentrated geographically as well. In the early 1960s free-world mining was located primarily in Canada (74%) and New Caledonia (15%), with some production (about 4%) in the United States.

Commercially mined ores come in two types: sulfide and laterite. Sulfide ores are generally expensive to mine but not so expensive to process, and they usually contain valuable by-products. They can be concentrated and processed to yield a range of nickel-containing products that can be refined to yield close to pure nickel or used directly in alloys. Laterite ores, however, cannot be concentrated economically. They are either smelted or treated through a leaching process as mined. In Inco's Indonesian operation, for example, lateritic ore is screened and passed through a smelter, which yields "furnace matte," containing around 25% nickel. Then, while still hot, the furnace matte goes through a converter that generates "nickel matte," of 75% to 80% purity. Nickel matte can then be refined to produce high-grade nickel. An alternative, used by the state-owned nickel firm in Indonesia, turns lateritic ores into ferro-nickel, with about 25% metal (the purity varies by source and process), which is then sold directly to the steel industry for stainless steel.

Commercial products are categorized as Class I or Class II nickel. Class II products, which range from 20% to less than 99% nickel, are used for a range of purposes, but particularly by the steel industry for alloys. About 60% of nickel produced is used for making stainless steel, with another 25% or so going into other alloys. Nickel is also used for plating, catalysts, electronic shielding, and batteries. Class I nickel, traded on the London Metal Exchange since 1979, is between 99% and 100% pure. It can be used for purposes for which Class II nickel is appropriate, but also for a wide range of other uses.[15]

Laterite ore generally contains less than 2% metal. If transportation costs $40 per ton (industry estimate for charges from Indonesia to Japan), there is a strong economic incentive to carry out processing close to a

TABLE 8-12
Copper Metal (Refined): Actual Trade Patterns, 1987 (metric tons)

Exporter	Australia	Chile	Mexico	Peru	Philippines	Zaire	Zambia
Importing country							
Argentina	10	50,500		5,914	7		
Australia		1,000					
Belgium/Luxembourg						26,187	35,686
Brazil		81,600		9,388		4,970	
Canada						7,058	
China		18,200			8,291		5,000
East Germany		7,500					
Finland							
France	6,674	90,800		10,470		600	801
Greece		13,800			1,499	100	20,409
Hong Kong		600			2	3,120	18,216
India		1,000					53,990
Indonesia	316	16,700			1,994	21,390	12,452
Italy		122,300		31,746			45,219
Japan	28,421	94,000		24,259	40,512	16,339	167,003
Republic of Korea	2,158	48,000			14,106	2,500	4,300

362

	1	2	3	4	5	6
Malaysia	194					7,511
Netherlands	1,436	11,500	22,698			42,651
New Zealand	998	4,300		18,877		5,155
Other Asia		53,200				
Portugal		6,200				
South Africa		300				
Saudi Arabia		4,000				25,944
Spain		5,400				5,310
Sweden		9,400				5,658
Switzerland		500				
Taiwan			5,224			2,050
Thailand	291	1,500		1,331		17,604
Turkey	29,093	200				
United Kingdom		31,300	32,004		3,137	12,314
United States	41	150,600	27,097	2		30,933
Venezuela		9,400				6,792
West Germany	13,836	105,300			100	65,800
Yugoslavia		3,500				8,208
Total	83,468	942,600	179,194	86,621	3,237	476,405
World exports	83,468	942,600	179,795	86,621	3,237	499,412

Sources: United Nations, Metallgesellschaft.
Australia: UN.
Others: M-G.

TABLE 8-13
Nickel Ore: Actual Trade Patterns, 1962 (metric tons)

Exporter	Canada	New Caledonia
Importing country		
Japan	1,672	596,008
Norway	33,396	
United Kingdom	41,861	
United States	479	
Total	77,408	596,008
World exports	77,410	

Sources: Quin's Metal Handbook, 1965; Bureau of Mines.
Canada: Quin's.
New Caledonia: BoM.

mine, thereby reducing shipping costs. (With nickel valued at $4 per pound, the metal contained in a ton of ore with 2% nickel would be worth some $175 when purified. The cost of transporting the ore at $40 per ton would then exceed 20% of the value of the contained metal, or much more than that figure if one subtracts the cost of processing the ore to extract the metal.) Yet, government policy sometimes leads to the shipping of ores and of unrefined products. Laterite ore cannot be concentrated, but sulfide ore can, so the penalties for shipping are less.

Although exact figures for nickel are difficult to collect, smelting, conversion, and refining facilities for nickel are not overwhelmingly expensive, apparently paralleling the costs of copper. The total value of plant and machinery shown on Inco's 1990 books for its Indonesian mine and smelter, for example, stood at about $275 million (before depreciation). Nevertheless, industry managers state a strong preference for expanding existing facilities over building new ones from scratch. The impact of this preference has had a striking effect on the industry's trade patterns.

Change in Nickel

The nickel industry underwent momentous change during the period under study. Increasing world demand after World War II, as markets expanded annually by some 6%, encouraged new entrants. Holding a price umbrella over other firms, Inco expanded its capacity at a rate slower than the growth in demand. Technological changes, particularly in the early 1970s, further encouraged entry. Extremely large-scale

TABLE 8-14
Nickel Metal: Actual Trade Patterns, 1962 (metric tons)

Exporter	Canada	New Caledonia	Norway
Importing country			
Australia	688		
France		13,771	
Japan	1,052	8,147	
Sweden			3,933
United Kingdom	9,921		
United States	104,577		13,960
West Germany	2,000		5,091
Total	118,238	21,918	22,984
World exports	121,712	22,285	27,680

Sources: Quin's *Metal Handbook*, 1965; Bureau of Mines.
Canada: Quin's.
New Caledonia, Norway: BoM.

equipment for open-pit extraction came on the market. The exploitation of low-grade lateritic ores, generally located in the tropics, became economically attractive as the scale of equipment increased. Firms other than the dominant three opened new mines in countries other than those which had supplied most of the world's nickel.

By the early 1980s the market share of the Big Three had fallen to 59%. By 1991 Inco's portion had declined from 85% to perhaps one third of the Western market.[16] New state-owned companies had emerged as producers in some developing countries, such as Aneka Tambang in Indonesia. Governments owned and operated mines or processing facilities in Finland, Greece (with some interest held by SLN), and Yugoslavia. Elsewhere, state-owned firms participated in production, as in Colombia and the Philippines (closed by 1991). Large concerns that mined other metals also entered the business. An American firm, Hanna Mining, and a Dutch firm, Billiton (owned by Shell), for example, joined the Colombian government in a venture to develop nickel reserves in that country, estimated to be 2% of the world's total. Anglo American opened mines in southern Africa. In 1972 Amax purchased Port Nickel in Louisiana, the largest U.S. nickel refinery, which had been virtually shut down because of the cutoff of Cuban nickel after Fidel Castro's takeover.

By 1987 the market share held by the original producing countries had fallen to 53%. In the early 1980s, Canada was still the largest producer and processor, but mine closures and production cutbacks since the 1982 recession affected Canada deeply. New Caledonia, the largest developing-nation producer (technically, however, a part of France), was second to Canada, with 16% of mine capacity and 9% of processing capacity. As in aluminum, Australia emerged during the period as a significant exporter; by the mid-1980s it ranked third, with 12% of mine capacity and 7% of processing capacity. The Philippines, Indonesia, and the Dominican Republic were medium-size producers, and the United States, Botswana, South Africa, Brazil, Greece, and Yugoslavia were minor producers.

The activities of outside firms led to a follow-the-leader strategy in nickel, as in copper, but the strategy could not counter the outsiders' threat to market control. Inco followed the development of laterite ore deposits by investing in Guatemala through a joint venture with Hanna Mining. Because of high fuel oil costs, however, the operator shut down the facility in 1981, and it has yet to reopen. Inco opened a large laterite mine in Indonesia in the early 1970s. Low profitability there in the early years led the company to press the Indonesian government, in vain, to buy a share in the property. Eventually Inco sold some equity to the public on the Jakarta stock market, and Japanese processors took an interest, adding to the vertical linkage.

Despite the more diverse ownership of mining operations by the late 1980s, the developing countries had few independent markets for products to be further refined into Class I nickel. In 1988 Japan owned 15% of global processing capacity. To feed it, Japan imported nearly all of New Caledonia's ore exports and all the output of Inco's Indonesian mine. But even Japan's processing capacity was linked to major multinationals. Sumitomo Metals, which processed nickel from Inco's Indonesian mine, owned some 20% of the mine in 1991. Five other Japanese enterprises also held equity in the mine. Moreover, Inco of Indonesia held interests in at least two of its three customers in Japan. Thus, at least two (and probably all) of the Japanese buyers of Inco's Indonesian nickel were involved in a vertically integrated chain.

Other refining capacity remained largely in the hands of a few firms. Inco and Falconbridge, which controlled most of the capacity in Canada, held large interests in Taiwanese and Korean refining capacity in response to protection there. Norway and the United Kingdom had each captured 6% of the world's market for processed nickel by the late 1980s, but the old majors also owned the treatment facilities in these countries.

The entrants that were already in mining tended to build their own refining capacity or sell under long-term contracts to the Big Three.

Western Mining, a huge Australian concern with both smelting and refining facilities, shipped matte as well to Sumitomo and to Sherritt Gordon. Sherritt Gordon, in turn, bought from Inco, as did Sumitomo, as noted. Amax and Anglo American mined in Botswana and Zimbabwe, where Anglo owned a refinery that processed some of the output of both countries. For a while Amax processed some of Botswana's product in its own U.S. facilities, but then it shifted to selling that output to Falconbridge.

By the late 1980s Western Mining, Sherritt Gordon, Amax, and Anglo American could be considered to have joined Inco, Falconbridge, and Société Le Nickel as major established international nickel companies. Thus, control by seven such firms still left the Class I part of the industry highly concentrated. Of the three industries examined, this has remained the most oligopolistic. In spite of the entry of new players, producers of new nickel matte either shipped it to affiliates for refining or sold it to large multinational concerns under long-term contracts.

Still, nickel miners had a serious alternative: produce ferro nickel or another Class II product for sale mainly to the steel companies. In this way they could remain independent of the oligopoly dominating production of Class I nickel. Yet managers of major and independent firms viewed this market as less stable than the Class I market. Steel firms were generally hit badly in economic downturns; moreover, in such periods they tended to turn to scrap as a source. Also, the major Japanese steel companies were thought to be closely tied to Japanese suppliers of processed nickel. Japanese firms supposedly would buy from those affiliated suppliers, rather than independents, at prices higher than the world market in downturns and lower than elsewhere in upturns. The cyclicality of the steel industry and the tied nature of the Japanese segment caused the price of ferro nickel to vary more widely than that of Class I nickel.

Given the closed nature of the market to Class I producers, it is not surprising that most of the independent firms chose to supply primarily ferro nickel, even though the market for nickel matte was viewed as much more stable. The state-owned Aneka Tambang mine in Indonesia, Colombia's Cerro Matoso, the state-owned Larco in Greece, Codemin/ Morro in Brazil, and Kosovo and Kavadarci in Yugoslavia all sold ferro nickel.

Of course, an independent firm could build its own refinery to produce Class I metal. A few independents, including some in Finland, the Philippines, and Brazil, followed this route. The Philippine refinery closed in the late 1980s, and Brazil has always been a minor player in world nickel trade. The state-owned Finnish company, however, not only sold Class I nickel successfully, but also sold technology to others. Nevertheless, the Class I market remained almost entirely in the hands of large international mining companies. In 1991 change for Class I producers loomed on the horizon. Demand was stagnant, but increased supplies appeared likely.

One nontraditional source of supply had long held a place in the consciousness of the industry: the vast nickel deposits in deep-sea manganese nodules. But the cost of mining them appeared to be prohibitive. If nickel prices should rise sufficiently, or undersea mining costs decline, new firms with deep-sea mining skills would emerge as important players in the industry. But the prospects of deep-sea mining did not appear immediate.

A more immediate threat to control came from the supplies appearing from the former Soviet Union. Russia's deposits are large and rich. Russian exports in 1991 grew by 50% over the previous year, capturing as much as 25% of the Western market for Class I nickel. These sales threatened to boost nickel supplies dramatically. Western nickel executives hoped that the new Russian government would impose export controls on nickel to help stabilize world prices. Even with such controls, however, Russia, and perhaps eventually Cuba, was expected to increase sales on Western markets.

Trade in Nickel

In 1962 trade was largely determined by affiliate relationships. Japan remained somewhat of an exception to the pattern, importing from unaffiliated suppliers. Government policies—particularly those of France and Japan—affected the location of processing. New Caledonia shipped large amounts of ore to Sumitomo in Japan for processing behind its import barriers; small amounts of sulfide ore also went from Canada to the same company—to become an affiliate of Inco—for mixing with New Caledonia lateritic ore. Nickel matte also went from New Caledonia to Shimura Kako of Japan for refining. New Caledonia shipped nickel metal to France, home of the mining company. The preference for expanding existing plants over building new ones also played a role; major companies expanded plants acquired long before—Inco in Wales and Falconbridge in Norway are examples—and dispatched Canadian shipments of ore to these affiliates despite the shipping costs.

TABLE 8-15
Nickel Ore: Actual Trade Patterns, 1987 (metric tons)

Exporter	Canada[a]	Indonesia[b]	New Caledonia
Importing country			
Australia		80,000	
France			10,377
Japan		892,513	1,083,251
Korea, DPR		20,364	
Norway	30,798		
United Kingdom	25,760		
Total	56,558	992,877	1,093,628
World exports	56,558	992,877	

[a]Includes ores, concentrates, mattes.
[b]Does not include matte.
Sources: Canada: Energy Mines and Resources of Canada.
Others: UN.

Nickel trade in 1987 reflected the emergence of two significant suppliers: Indonesia and Colombia. Inco shipped nickel matte of about 78% purity from Indonesia to Japan, where it was further refined. The location of refining in Japan reflected principally the protection offered by the government to Japanese industry. Nickel of less than 78% or 80% purity entered Japan free of duty; in the late 1980s, nickel of greater purity bore a tariff of about 8%. While the tariff rate may not sound very high, it in fact represented an "effective rate of protection"[17] of more than 36% for the refining stage. In the absence of this tariff, nickel matte would probably have been further refined near the mine, according to industry sources.

The other Indonesian miner was Aneka Tambang, the state-owned firm, which had no vertical links to users. It shipped no nickel matte, only nickel ore and ferro nickel. Aware that it needed sales to Japan more than Japan needed it—70% to 80% of Japan's supplies come from elsewhere—Aneka Tambang has taken steps to lessen its dependence on Japanese buyers. The firm invested in facilities to turn nickel ore into ferro nickel, which it could sell directly to steel firms around the world. It has also sought other buyers for ore.

The results of Aneka Tambang's efforts to diversify its markets for ore are indicated in Indonesian trade figures for 1986 to 1989. The United States took some ore in 1986, but none in 1987. North Korea was a destination in 1987 and 1989. A processing plant in Australia, where

TABLE 8-16
Nickel Metal: Actual Trade Patterns, 1987 (metric tons)

Exporter	Canada[a]	Colombia[b]	New Caledonia	Indonesia
Importing country				
Australia				80,000
EEC	24,050			
Japan		475		892,513
Korea, DPR				20,364
Singapore			879	
United States	54,356			
Other	17,714			
Total	96,120	475	879	992,877

[a]Exports to the EEC are not detailed.
[b]1985.
Sources: U.S. Bureau of Mines, MINEMET, United Nations, Metallgesellschaft.
Canada: MINEMET.
Colombia: BoM.
New Caledonia: UN.
Indonesia: M-G.

local ore was being depleted, began to buy Indonesian ore in 1987. Australia had accounted for roughly 25% of exports in 1988 and 1989, but managers feared it would soon disappear as a market.

Did Aneka Tambang's strategy lead to higher or more stable prices? The average prices realized for sales to Australia and North Korea fell below those for sales to Japan, but Japan was apparently buying the highest grade ore, so one can conclude little about price levels. But prices on sales to Japan fluctuated over the 1986–1989 period more than the prices of Inco's nickel matte, which were tied to London Metal Exchange prices. Aneka Tambang seemed not to have been able to generate much stability.

The predominance of state firm–state firm trading is notable. In North Korea, of course, Aneka Tambang's nickel buyer was state owned. Even in Australia, the customer was a plant largely owned by an Australian state government with a bank that had taken over private interests in the processing plant. Aneka Tambang's efforts to find more diversified markets for its bauxite also included sales to a state-owned smelter in Venezuela. Bauxite from Guyana's state firm went to the same smelter. The frequency of state-state trade is probably not the result of a preference of state-owned enterprises for dealing with similar partners; more likely it is an outgrowth of the lack of vertical integration in general by state-owned mining firms and state-owned processing facilities. As independent firms, they make natural trading partners.

The other part of Aneka Tambang's market diversification strategy, the production of ferro nickel, gave it an opportunity to sell directly to steel companies anywhere in the world, free of dependence on foreign unaffiliated smelting and refining facilities. Billiton served as marketing agent and found somewhat steady markets in the Netherlands and India, but buyers elsewhere remained fickle.

In contrast, Inco had secure, stable markets in Japan for its Indonesian nickel. Meanwhile, for Aneka Tambang, lacking a vertical structure in an industry still dominated by vertically integrated firms, diversification and direct access to consumers to gain price and volume stability remained elusive.

In 1987 nickel matte from New Caledonian metal was still going to France, where the refining industry remained protected. New Caledonia was also shipping ore to Japan to escape the tariff on finished nickel. By that year Colombia had emerged as a new exporter, with ferro nickel going to Japan and to European Community steel companies.

Historical factors and the tendency of major mining companies to capture trade internally have continued to influence trade in the nickel industry. As Inco's dominance declined, the large extraction concerns have also tended increasingly to trade with one another. The smaller outsiders, sometimes state-owned, have behaved as in other oligopolistic mining industries. To reduce their risks, independent unintegrated firms have attempted to diversify their markets and sources. In nickel, that effort has affected the product as well as the destination of exports, as independents have emphasized Class II nickel so that they can sell directly to a less-concentrated market.

COMPANIES, GOVERNMENTS, AND TRADE

In this chapter, I have not, of course, examined every change in the three mineral industries. Growing concerns over environmental effects have limited mining, as well as processing, in the industrialized countries. Slowing demand has meant price declines. Experience with nationalization and renegotiations in the 1960s and 1970s has reduced the interest of private capital in third-world mining investments. Debt problems in major mining countries have limited access to capital by their own firms in recent years, constraining pursuit of strategies begun earlier. As a result, few mines have opened anywhere in the world in the past decade and a half, at least by private hands. Moreover, recycling has grown in importance as a source of metals, stimulating competition.

Ignoring such momentous changes, I have concentrated on the impact of certain corporate and government policies and on historical influences on trade patterns. The evidence supports the claim that factors besides those that appear in simple economic models greatly influence trade patterns in the three industries. Consider trade in terms of three factors:

1. Where are mines located?
2. Where is processing done?
3. Which facility, mine or processing, exports to which market?

Where Are Mines Located?

Economic theory would assert that mining is carried out where the lowest-cost ore bodies are located, subject to constraints imposed by transportation costs and host government demands. The simple theory goes a long way in explaining the locations of mining investments, and even such changes as the increased importance of Australia as its low-cost deposits were discovered and its development encouraged by tax policies elsewhere.

Company strategies have, however, mattered. A follow-the-leader strategy led to increased investment in the southwest rim of the Pacific Ocean for copper and to exploitation of laterite nickel deposits by companies with rich ore sources elsewhere. According to Frederick Knickerbocker, an outsider's move in such oligopolistic industries generates followers, since entrenched firms worry that the outsider's investments will threaten stability.[18] If a newcomer's move turns out to be economic, and traditional firms have no access to the low-cost sources, the entrant may cut prices or otherwise disturb the equilibrium. In defense, other firms are tempted to follow the move, as did Kennecott in Indonesia and Inco in Guatemala. Failure to follow might mean an inability to discipline the newcomer or to match its costs, if the move was a wise one. If the move turns out to have been a mistake, the matching parties will have made similar mistakes and so bear similar costs, which in an oligopolistic industry can probably be passed on in the form of higher prices.

Company strategies may also have affected the location of bauxite mining. The drive of integrated companies to separate mining and smelting as a protection against nationalization has perhaps delayed the opening of certain mines near cheap power that could have been used for smelting operations. For example, Ghana's bauxite deposits have long been known. But Kaiser, with a smelter in the country to exploit cheap power from the Volta River dam, seemingly had little interest in developing them.

With these exceptions that result from company strategies, there is no reason to believe that mines were opened, or not opened, for important reasons beyond the attractiveness of low-cost mines and favorable tax policies.

Where Is Processing Done?

The location of processing facilities is a different matter. Purely economic variables would probably lead to the shipment of most minerals in more processed states than what has been observed, especially in the earlier period I covered. If a mineral is further processed, shipping costs usually decline as a percentage of the value of the commodity, or per unit of contained metal. Thus one would expect that economic factors would push processing close to a mine, everything else being equal.

The only simple economic explanations for the separation of mining and processing would lie in higher capital costs in the mining country, the lack of skilled technicians, or the lack of low-cost energy, particularly for aluminum smelting. The costs of constructing smelting facilities in isolated locations might explain some shipments of concentrates, for example, at Bougainville in Papua New Guinea, and Ertsberg in Indonesia's Irian Jaya. But some industry sources report that smelting costs would not be prohibitively high even in such remote locations. Whatever the circumstances in these particularly isolated places, a number of other countries have shown the feasibility of local processing in the mining countries.

Nevertheless, while such locations as Chile, the Philippines, and New Caledonia have big smelters, large shipments of copper concentrate and nickel ore continue to make their way from there for processing elsewhere. Simple economic factors cannot adequately explain the persistent large movements of copper concentrate and nickel ore in international trade.

Government policies in the industrialized countries have affected these decisions. In several metals, trade restrictions in the industrialized countries have differed according to the degree of processing: higher rates apply to the further processed versions. As a result, processing has started in, and to some extent has been retained in, the industrialized nations. Minerals have almost certainly traveled in a less processed state than they would have in the absence of such government intervention.

Protection for processing in industrialized countries is eroding as energy costs rise and environmental concerns grow in importance. In Japan the aluminum smelting industry was the first to lose protection as oil prices climbed in the early 1970s. Probably for economic reasons more than for environmental concerns, the Japanese quickly switched policy and encouraged the movement of aluminum smelting out of the country. The government has only recently, however, encouraged similar moves in copper and nickel. But the trend is clearly toward processing in mining countries.

Company strategies have affected trade patterns, particularly in the historic separation of mining and processing in the aluminum industry. There the goal was to protect the major international companies' bargaining power. The strategies meant that certain economic processing sites remained undeveloped. In the early 1960s the lure of potential cheap power was insufficient to encourage international companies to build smelters where they were already mining bauxite. Guyana was an example.

In copper and nickel, the barriers to entry have been less significant at the smelting stage. Companies did not fear that locating smelters adjacent to mines would encourage nationalization. Yet the companies appear to have acted to some extent to protect their downstream operations in their home countries. Western companies kept and expanded processing facilities at home and in other industrialized countries by continuing to supply them with concentrates. Management seems to have thought of plants as sunk costs and labor as long-term commitments. Expansion seemed cheaper than new plants elsewhere, regardless of the historic factors that drove the original location decision. Further, country risk seemed low as long as expanding facilities were located in the rich countries. When host governments in the third world took over mines, however, they naturally moved to do more of the processing in the mining country.

Japanese government policies of protection at home have been supplemented by the peculiarly Japanese approach to developing mineral sources abroad through loans, technical assistance, and government aid. The resources have been tied to requirements that the mine supply unprocessed materials to Japanese-controlled markets, leading to trade in concentrates and semiprocessed minerals in spite of the general tendency of these stages of processing to migrate to the mining counties.

On occasion the strategy of an unintegrated company has focused on a process or use that opens a wider market, if that option exists. The result affects what is traded. In this study, the important example is nickel, in which ferro nickel had wider markets than nickel matte. Guyana also seems to be influenced in this manner: the use of its bauxite for refractory purposes frees it from dependence on the major aluminum companies for markets.

Thus, for all three minerals, company strategies, government policies, and past decisions have been variables leading to departures from what simple economic factors alone would suggest about the stages at which minerals trade.

Which Facility Exports to Which Market?

Company strategies have also been important in determining the directions of trade. The large multinationals apparently much prefer running ores from their own mines through their affiliated processing facilities, regardless of the economics of transportation.

Why is this so? Of course, the drive for vertical integration stems from fears that oligopolistic markets will not serve the firms' needs. If a few competitors control sources, they may cut off supplies in times of shortage. The high fixed processing costs make shortages extremely costly. Therefore the processor is tempted to control sources, but controlling markets is also attractive. Captive markets can stabilize throughput in times of surplus. These goals could, in theory, be met through cross-firm agreements for swaps or long-term sales contracts. The paucity of such arrangements could be the result of a number of factors.

One claim has been that processing facilities are set up for inputs of particular characteristics. A smelter may be designed to use the ore of a particular mine. Once the smelter is functioning, conversion to use inputs of different specifications is not easy—according to the story. Since a smelter is particularly likely to be built for a mine whose product is well known to the smelter—a mine that the same firm operates—vertical trade links, once established, persist.

If this was the main reason, one would not expect the sharp shifts in trading patterns over the twenty-five years under study. Facilities are, in fact, converted, and sources changed; there are limits, but those limits seem to allow for a wide range of sources. Further, managers I interviewed indicated that conversion problems were in most cases few, as long as the ores were of the same basic types.

Even without this flexibility, facilities could be designed at the outset to handle the closest supplies, regardless of ownership. International firms could ship to each other, swapping ores. Such arrangements are common in the oil industry to suit the needs of scattered refineries. In the mineral industries, however, rivalries evidently make such swaps rare, except in nickel, whose trade among major firms has been carried out more routinely.

Swaps may have been difficult because of the lack of independent transactions by which imbalances and quality differences could be appropriately priced. With virtually no arm's-length trade in bauxite to provide reference prices, imperfectly balanced swaps or swaps of different grade minerals may be very difficult to arrange.

Further, fears of antitrust enforcement may have made such swaps appear risky. The big North American aluminum companies were in fact born by the division of one company through federal antitrust action. Until the 1980s, fears of antitrust loomed large over the plans of major mining firms. Still, these fears did not stop joint investments in facilities that appeared risky and were very expensive. Fears of antitrust provide an insufficient explanation.

It is also possible (likewise partly because of the small number of market transactions) that companies prefer not to record transactions with unaffiliated parties. Doing so raises the possibility that host governments will find (perhaps inappropriate) reference points for challenging transfer prices on intracompany sales. Disputes over transfer pricing between these parties have been frequent. Whatever the reasons, swaps are uncommon. Companies strongly prefer to process their own ore, leading to trade patterns that differ from what one might expect if simple economic factors had been the rule.

Even so, the penalties for not minimizing the costs of shipping some products are significant. As pointed out, it costs about $40 per ton to ship from Indonesia to Japan. If a ton of copper is worth $2,000 to $3,000, the penalty for shipping twice as far does not seem overwhelming when it is considered as a percentage of the final value. On the other hand, the cost of transporting 25% concentrate is much larger as a portion of the value of the cargo. Since a ton of concentrate is worth from less than $500 to $750, an increase in shipping cost looms much larger as a portion of the value of the product. And, of course, for a ton of material with only 1% to 5% metal, the shipping costs become very important. Although a linear programming model (see Appendix) suggests that the shipping distances for internal trade do not depart hugely from those which would minimize costs, the penalties for some actual shipments are quite high. On occasion firms have been willing to pay large sums to keep their trade internal.

History plays a role in trade patterns. In a number of cases, colonial relationships have helped determine the nationalities of extracting companies, and some residual effects of these old relationships remain. Colonial powers generally made sure that the firm exploiting a mine in a colony was based in the home country. The copper deposits of the Belgian Congo (Zaire) were exploited by a Belgian company, the nickel deposits of New Caledonia by a French company, the bauxite deposits of the Netherlands East Indies by a Dutch company, the copper deposits of Northern Rhodesia (Zambia) by a company from the British empire, and so on. Naturally, the choice of company affected the resulting trade patterns. If the mining company wanted to separate the processing facilities from the extraction site, it would usually establish them in the home country, even though another country might be as attractive from an economic point of view.

Outside the colonized areas, industrialized countries' spheres of influence play a similar, though perhaps less forceful, role. In this way, the major foreign mining companies of Latin America and the Caribbean have come from the United States and Canada. Although proximity might be an equally plausible explanation, a hundred years ago it would not have been at all clear that U.S. companies would emerge as the dominant Latin American mining firms. French companies, for example, were important in the early development of Chilean copper, and British investments were important in many other South American mining ventures. Eventually, Latin America and the Caribbean came under domination by U.S. investment, probably for a mix of geographical and geopolitical reasons.

The influence of ownership on shipping patterns is apparent when ownership changes, especially when government policy dictates them. State ownership of mining firms emerged with a vengeance in the late 1960s and the early 1970s as governments in mining countries saw opportunities to take over existing mines or to open new ones free of foreign equity participation.[19]

Still, old patterns do not die completely. Unrefined Zairian copper still moves disproportionately to Belgium. Imperfect markets persist in unrefined copper, and Zaire needs its old antagonist to handle its marketing. Guyanan bauxite is still shipped to Canada in greater quantities than one might expect, given Guyana's nationalization of Alcan's mines. The government's discovery that all its bauxite cannot easily be moved to firms outside the old oligopoly has obliged the state to sell to its former private partner.

Perhaps the most surprising finding in this study is the fact that nonvertically integrated firms are not driven to minimize shipping costs, even when the legacy of a past does not prevail. As vertical links in an industry weaken, the need to diversify becomes a more important issue for management than minimizing shipping costs. When sellers and buyers are not affiliated, yet limited in number, each shies from reliance on a single partner. Therefore, mining firms that are not vertically integrated, in industries with a great deal of vertical integration, tend to seek many customers, regardless of location. The loss of a single customer, in an industry with few independent buyers, is serious; hence the drive for multiple customers, regardless of shipping costs. Similarly, processors lacking captive mines have sought multiple sources of supply, regardless of location. The processor fears the loss of a source in a market that has few independent suppliers. The need to reduce risk mightily affects trade patterns.

Oligopoly and Trade

To some extent, company and government strategies have influenced the mining industries in ways similar to those described for other industries covered in this book. Yet there are important differences between minerals and the other industries studied. Most of the others have undergone increasing concentration in recent years. Globalization has meant that a smaller number of firms hold larger shares of the world market. The three mineral industries have changed in the opposite direction. They have long been global, but changes in technology, the spread of technological ability, the availability of capital from alternative sources, and the decline of colonial influence have combined to allow new entrants. Although the degree of change has differed in the three industries, in all cases the move has been toward less concentration.

One result of fragmenting concentration has been a weakening of the links between buyer and seller; industries that were vertically integrated across international borders have become less so as new firms entered as suppliers and customers. At least marginal markets have developed.

The behavior of mineral firms suggests that the relation between industry concentration and trade patterns may not be the simple one whereby concentration leads to trade internal to oligopolists and dispersion leads to trade dominated by the economic factors usually considered to explain trade. True, when concentration on the supplier side is high, an independent buyer fears becoming dependent on a small number of sellers. Since there are few suppliers, the buyer tends to develop its own sources. Similarly, when buyers are concentrated, large suppliers drive toward vertical integration. An independent supplier fears that it cannot sell its output, especially in times of surplus.

The historical direction of integration is less important than the fact that a state of few sellers and few buyers leads to vertical integration and a particular set of trade patterns. The result has been vertically integrated networks in those cases where both sources and customers were concentrated—and vertically affiliated firms trade with one another.

When technological change and other factors produce an increase in the number of firms, suppliers and buyers have more options. Vertical integration may not seem to be the only way to ensure reliable outlets or supplies. New firms may enter the industry without captive markets or captive suppliers. Yet dependence by a supplier on a single unaffiliated buyer appears to be foolhardy when few alternative suppliers exist, especially if the dependence is not mutual. Similarly, in the early stages of the breakup of vertical integration, a buyer is likely to fear dependence on an unaffiliated supplier when there are few others around. As a result, suppliers as well as buyers seek diversification if they decide not to establish their own vertically integrated chain.

As this process begins, trade patterns change. In the past, sales were concentrated in the firm. Now new competitors sell to a number of unaffiliated buyers, not necessarily the nearest one. Similarly, the old pattern of purchases from a single affiliated supplier (or a small number of affiliated suppliers) changes to include the practices of new firms: purchases from a number of unaffiliated suppliers, regardless of location. This shift, apparent in the industries I examined, may also be observable in other industries.

What happens when an industry fractionates still more? In the minerals studied here, concentration remains fairly high and vertical integration plays an important role. Consequently, the three cases offer no observations of trade in an industry with a really large number of suppliers and buyers. One might, however, speculate on a hypothetical third level in a ranking of industries by concentration. In the next stage, there would be many suppliers and a large number of buyers. Such an industry would, of course, correspond to the assumptions of the model posited by traditional economic theory. In such a case, one would expect the directions of trade to be driven largely by the need to minimize shipping costs. Neither buyer nor seller would opt for vertical integration, and there would be no need for diversification to avoid reliance on a small number of sources (or buyers), since many alternative suppliers and customers would be on hand should relations with particular ones deteriorate. In this case, trade would be influenced not by company strategies but by production and transportation costs.

In sum, different trade patterns might characterize industries with differing degrees of concentration. In industries with both suppliers and buyers highly concentrated, trade between suppliers and buyers is likely to be driven by firm strategies based on vertical ownership ties. Vertical integration will be sought by companies to reduce risk. As a result, destination of exports are likely to remain stable and reflect investment patterns instead of transportation costs. Moreover, a particular country will supply few markets, and a market will get supplies from few sources. If new entrants at various stages begin to break up the concentration, trade—at least by the new entrants—might be influenced greatly by the buyers', and sellers', needs to avoid dependency in markets with small numbers of independent firms. The resulting diversification would lead to more complex trade patterns as buyers and sellers seek to reduce risk.

Finally, my analysis suggests that an industry with many buyers and sellers will find directions of trade to be determined by simple economic factors. In the case of minerals, trade would be determined by factor costs, tax factors, and the desire to minimize shipping costs.

APPENDIX

Linear Programming Analysis

In a limited way, a linear programming model can measure the extent to which actual patterns of trade differ from an optimal pattern. If company strategies play no role in trade, one would expect shipments of ore, concentrates, and metal to move in patterns that minimize shipping costs. The computational task is simply to determine the supply patterns that match the output of each stage of the process with the input of the next stage and that minimize the distance each product must travel. Then the researcher compares the ton-miles in the optimal trade patterns with the ton-miles in the actual trade patterns. The difference measures the degree to which the directions of trade depart from whatever would minimize shipping costs, with a given set of facilities. This difference

TABLE 8A-1
Differences Between Actual and Minimum Shipping Distances, 1962 and 1987

	Year	
Mineral	*1962*	*1987*
Bauxite	0.1%[a]	8.5%
Alumina	0.6	7.2
Aluminum	8.0	12.0
Copper ore	15.1	28.7
Copper metal (unrefined)	2.7	5.7
Copper metal (refined)	1.6	10.6
Nickel ore	0.0	6.0
Nickel metal	22.9	0.0

[a]Interpret as follows: in 1962, the distances bauxite was actually shipped exceeded the minimum shipping distances by 0.1%. The minimum shipping distances were obtained, as indicated in the Appendix, by the use of a linear programming model.

could be measured against either the "worst possible" set of trade routes or a pattern that would result from random trade routes.

A linear programming model, however, permits examination of only a tiny part of company, government, and historical influences on trade. Most important, one must take the location of mines and processing facilities as given, although industry analyses have shown that location is driven partly by government policies, strategic concerns of firms, and historical factors.

There are, in addition, some important technical limitations to the linear programming approach. For example, I have had to assume that each unit of production—mine, smelter, fabricating facility—is operating at capacity. Moreover, for lack of better data, in the model I have assumed that transportation costs increase monotonically with distance. This is clearly not always the case. Finally, the published data are at best incomplete; they are, in some cases, probably incorrect.

In sum, the linear programming results should be viewed as only a very partial and imperfect test of a few ideas that emerged from the case studies. Nevertheless, in spite of the very severe limitations, the results are of some interest.

Several observations can be made from the overall results that are presented in Table 8A-1.

First, the shipping patterns for the given facilities are not as far from optimal as one might have expected, given the dominance of affiliate trade. Second, there is some evidence that shipping patterns are less optimal the more a mineral is processed—although copper seems to contradict this hypothesis. Third, patterns apparently become less optimal over the period under study. In only one case, nickel metal, has the pattern reduced shipping costs compared with the 1962 patterns, and that is for a declining volume.[20]

Products travel, on average, a little more than 8% farther than a cost-minimizing model would suggest. A greater departure from optimal paths might have been expected, given the influence of affiliate trade. Note, however, that some alternative markets are in fact quite close to each other; the penalty for shipping to Belgium instead of Britain, for example, is slight. Indeed, the figures available for shipping distances often do not even reflect actual differences in shipping distances to markets that are close to each other. Thus, the distance from the west coast of South America to Japan is considered to be the same as the distance from the same point to Korea.

The finding that shipping patterns for more processed products depart from the optimal more than those for unprocessed products should not be a total surprise. As a mineral is further processed, its value per unit of weight increases dramatically. As a result, the penalties for not optimizing shipping patterns become smaller with more processing, if one measures the penalty as a percentage of the value of the product. The real surprise should be the fact that the pattern does not hold for every industry, in particular for copper, whose shipment patterns for ore appear to be quite suboptimal. The odd patterns appear to be the result of the ties of certain mines to Japanese smelters.

The most striking result is the increase in the difference between the optimal shipping patterns and the actual patterns over the twenty-five-year study period. The only case in which the differences have declined is in nickel metal trade, for which shipments have also declined and the data are particularly suspect. One could attribute the general increase in less-optimal shipping patterns to an overall decline in real shipping costs; the penalties for nonoptimization have declined, yet the data suggest another explanation, consistent with the case studies: in partially integrated industries, unintegrated sellers and buyers with a strong interest in diversification had emerged by 1987. The need to diversify sources and outlets appears to have been more important to firms than the need to reduce shipping costs.

In 1962 buyer and seller were generally the same company. Mining companies that owned their own processing facilities felt little need to sell to other processors. They were confident that their own facilities would remain as their future purchasers of minerals; even in times of surplus, their smelters could be counted on to buy from commonly owned mines, for example. Further, at least until the wave of national-izations in the late 1960s and early 1970s, processors probably felt little need to turn to sources beyond those which they owned. Ore sources were secure if owned by the same firm.

The relationships that generated the patterns of trade were shaken as vertical links weakened and as the wave of nationalizations struck in the 1960s and 1970s. As the case studies suggested, an independent supplier could no longer depend on a buyer to continue to use its output; no longer did all firms have affiliated sources. Diversification became im-portant.

NOTES

1. John E. Tilton, "The Choice of Trading Partners: An Analysis of Interna-tional Trade in Aluminum, Bauxite, Copper, Lead, Magnesium, Tin, and Zinc," Ph.D. diss., Yale University, 1966.

2. One of the best sources of information on the aluminum industry is John A. Stuckey, *Vertical Integration and Joint Ventures in the Aluminum Industry* (Cambridge, Mass.: Harvard University Press, 1983).

3. David Morton (chairman and chief executive officer, Alcan), "Viewpoints on the Global Economy," Notes for Remarks to the Twelfth IAFEI World Congress, Cancún, Mexico, November 21, 1991.

4. Lest American readers feel smug, note that the United States developed its downstream industry under rather high rates of protection, based on specific rather than ad valorem duties. Some of the history is reported in George David Smith, *From Monopoly to Competition: The Transformation of Alcoa, 1888–1986* (Cambridge: Cambridge University Press, 1988).

5. The history of Japanese policy on aluminum processing is well docu-mented in Tetsuya Matsuoka, "Strategic Approach to the Primary Aluminum Industry by a Japanese General Trading Firm," M.S. in Management thesis, MIT, June 1985.

6. See S. J. Ross-Macdonald, "Trends in International Alumina Trading," *Journal of the Geological Society of Jamaica*, Proceedings of Bauxite Symposium VI, March 17–22, 1986, 273.

7. Carlton E. Davis, "Regional Alumina Capacity, 1975–1986/87: Some Comments," *Journal of the Geological Society of Jamaica*, Proceedings of Baux-ite Symposium VI, March 17–22, 1986, 243.

8. The data are from Indonesian trade statistics. The pattern of bauxite prices lagging increases in aluminum prices is usual, according to managers in the industry.

9. James F. King, "Trends in the Economics of Alumina and Bauxite,"

Journal of the Geological Society of Jamaica, Proceedings of Bauxite Symposium VI, March 17–22, 1986, 214.

10. Ibid.

11. See Smith, *From Monopoly to Competition*, 421–435.

12. See Bruce McKern and Praipol Koomsup, eds., *Minerals Processing in the Industrialization of ASEAN and Australia* (Sydney, Australia: Allen and Unwin, 1988).

13. See Theodore H. Moran, *Multinational Corporations and the Politics of Dependence: Copper in Chile* (Princeton: Princeton University Press, 1974).

14. See Mark Bostock and Charles Harvey, eds., *Economic Independence and Zambian Copper: A Case Study of Foreign Investment* (New York: Praeger, 1972).

15. A useful source on the industry is Joseph R. Boldt, Jr., *The Winning of Nickel: Its Geology, Mining, and Extractive Metallurgy* (Princeton: D. Van Nostrand, 1967).

16. Source: Company's 10-K report.

17. For the definition of this term, see Malcolm Gillis et al., *Economic Development* (New York: W. W. Norton, 1983), 435–437.

18. Frederick T. Knickerbocker, *Oligopolistic Reactions and Multinational Enterprises* (Boston: Division of Research, Harvard Business School, 1973).

19. The direction of causality is disputed. Although Raymond Vernon (*Sovereignty at Bay* [New York: Basic Books, 1971], Chapter 2) and many others argue that government entry resulted from the breakdown of control by the old firms, Michael Shafer ("Capturing the Mineral Multinationals: Advantage or Disadvantage?" *International Organization* 37, no. 1 [Winter 1983]: 93–119) suggests that government entry *led to* the erosion of price stability.

20. The data for nickel are particularly suspect because of the different categories into which the various products are placed.

PART III
Political Competition

9

INSURANCE: DOMESTIC REGULATION AND INTERNATIONAL SERVICE COMPETITION

John B. Goodman

IN THE 1980s THE ROLE of services in international trade has become a major interest of both business leaders and government officials. Three factors are responsible for this renewed attention. First is the realization, especially in the United States, that services make up a major component of all international transactions. Second, changes in information technology and telecommunications are altering the ways in which services are provided, thereby offering the prospect of dramatic growth in international service transactions. And third, success in reducing trade barriers in goods in earlier rounds of trade negotiations has freed policymakers to turn their attention to newer areas, including agriculture, intellectual property, and services.

Services—particularly those in the financial area which are central to GATT negotiations—differ from the other industries examined in this volume in two critical and combined respects: they are both highly fragmented, and they are subject to extensive government regulation. Underlying the regulation of services are deep-rooted beliefs about the appropriate degree of competition and consumer protection. Not surprisingly, both the type and degree of regulation differ substantially across countries. Multilateral efforts to liberalize trade and permit service vendors

I would like to acknowledge the assistance of the many government officials, as well as senior managers from non-life and reinsurance firms, including American International Group, CIGNA, Chubb, Continental, Engineering Insurance Group, General Reinsurance, and Travelers in the United States; Sumitomo Marine and Fire, Taisho Marine and Fire, Tokio Marine and Fire, and Yasuda Fire and Marine in Japan; and Allianz, AXA-Midi, Lloyd's, Munich Re, Royal, Swiss Re, UAP Victoire, Winterthur, and Zurich in Europe. I would also like to thank Maryellen Costello and Masahiro Tanaka for research assistance, as well as A. R. Beadle, James Bedore, Johann Beginn, Robert Carter, Samuel Hayes, Heather Hazard, Udo Knoke, Henry Parker, Robin Rowland, and the members of the Harvard Business School World Trade and Global Competition Interest Group for many helpful comments.

to compete on a global basis have turned national regulation into an international issue.

This chapter examines how differences in government regulation shape international service competition. To do so, it focuses on the insurance industry. Insurance provides a means to transfer the risk of financial loss resulting from the occurrence of specified (but uncertain) events in exchange for the payment of a set premium. Because of the value of this service, insurance now permeates the activities of individuals and firms throughout the world. During the 1980s, annual worldwide premiums exceeded $1 trillion, making insurance a huge business.

Yet it is a mistake to speak of insurance as a single industry. Insurance actually consists of a number of segments that differ in terms of the level of international activity, the pattern of international competition, and the degree of government regulation. In this chapter I compare two key segments—non-life (also referred to as property and casualty) insurance and reinsurance—to highlight the relationships among these variables.[1] Non-life insurance can be thought of as a retail market in which products are sold to both individuals and firms. Those sold to individuals, referred to as personal or mass risks, include both home and auto insurance; those sold to firms, called commercial or large risks, include catastrophic damage, fire, marine, and third-party liability insurance. Reinsurance can be thought of as a secondary market in which insurance companies seek to spread their own risks. In this market, a reinsurance company provides cover to insurance companies, but not to individuals or (noninsurance) firms.

I begin with a look at the structure of non-life insurance and reinsurance. Second, I analyze differences in the levels of international transactions across the two segments. Third, I explain why some companies and some countries are more active than others in international insurance transactions. Finally, I identify the forces driving change and describe the potential impact on future competition in the industry.

THE STRUCTURE OF INSURANCE MARKETS

The size and structure of non-life insurance and reinsurance markets differ markedly. In 1988 the total volume of non-life premiums (net of reinsurance) amounted to $555.1 billion. The United States, Europe, and Japan accounted for about 85% of this sum (Table 9-1).[2] Premium

TABLE 9-1
World Insurance: Gross Premium Volumes 1988 Non-Life and Life ($ billions)

	Non-Life	Life	Total
United States	254.6	176.8	431.4
Japan	70.5	214.1	284.6
Total EC 12 + Switzerland	144.7	137.1	281.8
West Germany	42.7	36.5	79.3
United Kingdom	28.1	40.9	69.0
France	26.6	25.5	52.2
Italy	15.2	4.8	20.0
Netherlands	7.8	7.3	15.1
Spain	7.5	7.2	14.7
Belgium	4.4	1.9	6.3
Denmark	2.8	2.0	4.8
Ireland	1.4	1.9	3.2
Portugal	1.0	0.2	1.2
Greece	0.4	0.2	0.7
Luxembourg	0.2	0.1	0.3
Switzerland	6.5	8.7	15.1
Rest of World	85.3	87.9	173.3
World Total	555.1	615.9	1,171.0

Source: Sigma, Swiss Reinsurance Company, April 1990.

volume in the United States alone totaled $254.6 billion—over 45% of the world non-life premium volume. As can be seen in Table 9-2, the size of a country's market for non-life insurance (measured in terms of total premiums) usually reflects its gross national product (GNP). National markets differ significantly in terms of their maturity: consumers in some countries purchase more non-life insurance as a percentage of GNP than do others; some buy more insurance on a per capita basis than do others.

Non-life insurance is a highly fragmented business: literally thousands of non-life insurers operate worldwide. As Table 9-3 shows, the world's largest insurers tend to be located in the largest markets; six of the top ten are based in the United States. The four largest firms have a global market share of only 10%. Concentration ratios vary significantly across countries, however (see Figure 9-1). In 1987 the top four firms in the United States, Germany, France, and Italy, respectively, received some 20% of all non-life premiums, while in Japan and Switzerland the top four firms received more than 40% of such premiums.

Globally, non-life insurance accounts for some 80% of all reinsurance business. Since non-life insurers reinsure only 9% of their risks (see Table 9-4), the reinsurance market worldwide is considerably smaller than the non-life insurance market. In 1988 world reinsurance premiums

TABLE 9-2
World Insurance: Non-Life Premiums Per Capita and as a Percentage of GDP, 1988

	Non-Life Premiums					
	(in billions) Per Country	Rank	Per Capita	Rank	% of GDP	Rank
United States	$254.6	1	$1,034	1	5.25	1
Japan	$70.5	2	$575	6	2.43	18
West Germany	$42.7	3	$699	3	3.61	4
United Kingdom	$28.1	4	$493	14	3.36	9
France	$26.6	5	$477	15	2.85	12
Italy	$15.2	6	$264	20	1.84	30
Netherlands	$7.8	10	$526	12	3.44	7
Spain	$7.5	11	$193	22	2.16	24
Belgium	$4.4	13	$447	16	2.93	11
Denmark	$2.8	17	$554	8	2.70	16
Ireland	$1.4	28	$383	18	4.22	2
Portugal	$1.0	31	$94	26	2.43	19
Greece	$0.4	42	$44	35	0.87	48
Luxembourg	$0.2	53	$546	10	2.79	14
Switzerland	$6.5	12	$993	2	3.61	5

Source: *Sigma*, Swiss Reinsurance Company, April 1990.

TABLE 9-3
Largest Non-Life Insurers in the World (1988 premiums in $ millions)

Rank	Company	Domicile	Premiums
1	State Farm	United States	23,254
2	Allstate	United States	13,289
3	Aetna Life & Casualty	United States	10,773
4	Allianz	Germany	10,425
5	American International Group	United States	8,529
6	Zurich Insurance	Switzerland	7,281
7	CIGNA	United States	7,061
8	Tokio Marine & Fire	Japan	6,689
9	Royal Insurance	United Kingdom	5,843
10	Yasuda Fire & Marine	Japan	4,934

Sources: Finance World, September 4, 1990; industry sources.

amounted to $91.9 billion.[3] Not surprisingly, the countries with the largest non-life insurance markets—the United States, Germany, and Japan—place the largest amount of reinsurance. The amount reinsured as a percentage of gross written (non-life) premiums tends to vary by market, however, from 6.6% in Japan to more than 20% in Italy.

Reinsurance is a more concentrated business than non-life insurance. Worldwide, reinsurance firms can be counted in the hundreds rather than thousands. In 1988 the top four reinsurance firms possessed 15% of the world market (see Table 9-5). Apart from the United States, where the top four firms hold about 14% of the market, data on market share in different countries are generally not available, owing to both the practices of national regulators and the significant role of trade in reinsurance.

INTERNATIONAL TRANSACTIONS IN INSURANCE

Non-life insurance and reinsurance differ not simply in their size and structure, but also in the degree of internationalization. In analyzing international insurance flows, it is useful to distinguish between trade (e.g., policies sold by an insurer located in the United States to a client located in Britain) and investment (e.g., policies sold by a British subsidiary of a U.S. insurer to a client located in the United Kingdom). Of the world's reinsurance premiums, reinsurance executives estimate that some 30% to 50% is traded across borders and an additional 10% is received via investment. Non-life insurance, by contrast, is essentially a domestic business. Only about 1–3% of all non-life premiums are traded across borders, while an additional 6–10% is received through investment.[4]

FIGURE 9-1
Distribution of Market Shares in Non-Life Business, 1987 (with number of firms in market noted)

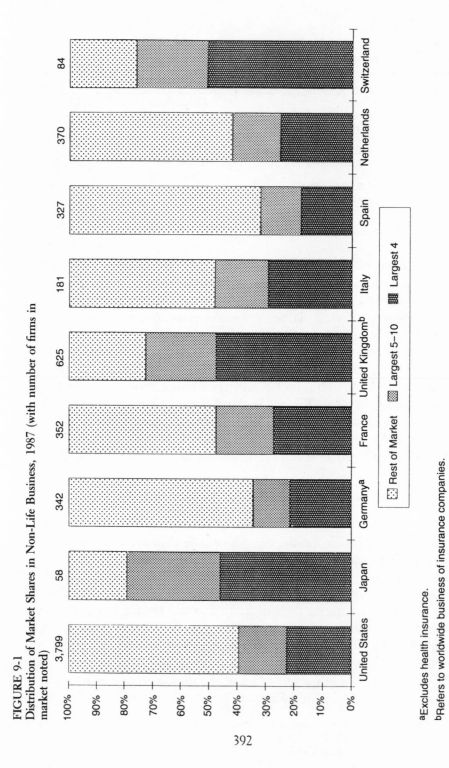

Rest of Market   Largest 5–10   Largest 4

aExcludes health insurance.
bRefers to worldwide business of insurance companies.

Source: *Sigma*, Swiss Reinsurance Company, February 1989.

TABLE 9-4
Reinsurance Demand by Country, 1987 ($ millions)

	Gross Premiums	Reinsurance Demand	Reinsurance as % of GWP[a]
United States	413,267	31,408	7.60
Japan	236,978	15,641	6.60
Germany	81,354	13,749	16.90
United Kingdom	67,372	5,929	8.80
France	50,009	5,001	10.00
Italy	19,764	4,131	20.90
Netherlands	16,396	1,623	9.90
Switzerland	16,005	1,072	6.70
Spain	10,856	1,487	13.70
Austria	6,301	951	15.09
Rest of OECD	63,900	6,608	10.34
Rest of World	49,700	4,300	8.65
World Total (excluding East bloc)	1,031,902	91,900	8.91

[a] Gross written premiums.
Source: Sigma, Swiss Reinsurance Company, May 1989.

The striking contrast in the levels of internationalization of these two segments is explained by differences in the economics of each insurance segment, in the decision-making processes of customers, and in regulation.

TABLE 9-5
The Top Fifteen Reinsurers in the World by 1988 Net Premiums ($ millions)

Rank	Company	Domicile	Net Premiums
1	Munich Re	Germany	6,147.2
2	Swiss Re	Switzerland	4,186.0
3	General Re	United States	1,780.2
4	Skandia International	Sweden	1,219.3
5	Cologne Re	Germany	1,164.4
6	Hanover Re and Eisen & Stahl	Germany	1,151.3
7	Employers Re	United States	1,135.2
8	Assicurazioni Generali	Italy	1,116.9
9	Gerling Globale Re	Germany	1,040.7
10	American Re	United States	976.4
11	M&G Re	United Kingdom	976.4
12	Frankona Ruck	Germany	917.6
13	Tokio M&F	Japan	851.4
14	SCOR	France	759.9
15	Yasuda F&M	Japan	610.9

Sources: Reactions, March 1990; company data.

Industry Economics

The economics of the insurance business suggests three rationales for international expansion: to achieve scale economies, to diversify risk, and to exploit national comparative advantages. Yet the role of these rationales differs greatly for non-life insurance and reinsurance.

Non-life insurance.   Most research suggests that there are relatively low economies of scale in non-life insurance. To understand why, consider the four main activities of the insurance business: underwriting (which involves both the selection of risks and the setting of rates), sales and marketing, claims adjusting and processing (after a reported loss), and investing assets. While sizable scale economies exist in investing and claims processing, they are lower in underwriting, sales, and claims adjusting.[5] Insurance executives note that an insurance company must have a large enough volume of business to attract knowledgeable and skilled underwriters and adjusters. Still, these activities are all labor-intensive and constitute a large proportion of costs. Commissions paid to sales agents, for example, can represent half of a firm's expenses.

The minimum efficient size (MES) of a non-life insurer is generally considered to be small enough that scale economies do not pose a significant entry barrier in large markets like the United States and Japan; that is, MES is small relative to total industry output.[6] Yet even in these markets, there is little evidence that average costs increase with size. While there does not appear to be an economic advantage to the major American or Japanese firms to increase in size, there is no apparent disadvantage either.[7]

Of course, minimum efficient size depends on the scope of an insurer's business. An insurance company offering multiline insurance must be larger (to achieve economies of scale) than a firm exploiting a particular market niche. For multiline business, economies of scale are thought to have been reached by many of the larger firms in the United States and Japan. According to a senior insurance executive of one major U.S. company: "All-state/all-line insurance companies in the United States are capitalized at about $1.5 billion; if you ask these companies if they need to double [in size], they say no."

International expansion, even for firms of this size, would allow a greater geographic diversification of risk—the second rationale for engaging in international activity—but that can also be gained through reinsurance. Thus, from the perspective of size alone, most large American and

Japanese non-life insurers appear to have little incentive (though perhaps no clear disincentive either) to become more international.

In Europe, by contrast, relatively fewer non-life insurers appear to have achieved available scale economies. The segmentation of national markets prevented most firms from becoming as large as their American and Japanese counterparts (see Table 9-3), suggesting that expansion within the European Community makes sense to achieve economies of scale. But a strong case for global expansion cannot be based on the existence of unexploited economies of scale.

Exploiting a national comparative advantage is the third rationale for international expansion.[8] Such advantages do, of course, exist in non-life insurance. Firms located in the more advanced markets enjoy advantages in almost every aspect of the business—from risk evaluation to asset investment. The importance of these advantages shows up in the direction of insurance flows between developed and developing countries. Insurers based in the developed world have been active in the insurance markets of developing countries when not prohibited from doing so by regulation.

Among the advanced industrial countries themselves, such advantages also exist. Firms based in the United States, for example, believe they have developed a greater ability to exploit telemarketing to sell their products. Superior positions may also exist in risk assessment, particularly in niche markets, for instance, insuring art collections. In general, however, comparative advantage plays a smaller role in transactions among the developed countries than between the developed and the developing countries. Moreover, any national advantage must overcome the existence of information asymmetries.[9]

Information asymmetries exist because insurance buyers generally know more about their own riskiness than insurers do. Experience enables insurers to overcome this asymmetry. It looms larger, however, when insurers venture outside their home markets, since the nature of risk, for example, the likelihood of car accidents, product liability suits, or burglaries, varies across countries.

Information asymmetries pertain not only to the nature of risk but also to such other characteristics of foreign markets as customer preferences and distribution channels. Japanese non-life insurers, for example, may lack enough expertise in the U.S. market to know how to tailor an insurance product to meet the needs of American customers. Similarly, Japanese insurers sell policies through direct agents in Japan, but in the U.S. market may operate at a disadvantage because independent insurance brokers play a dominant role. The existence of information asymmetries regarding risk, distribution channels, and customer preferences often leads foreign insurers to be "selected against" when they enter a new market. That is, they cannot discriminate as easily as a domestic-based firm between good and bad risks. Companies that seek to expand quickly into a new market, whether domestic or foreign, will therefore be likely to take on bad risks, which ultimately return in the form of higher losses. Information asymmetries thus reduce the incentive for insurers to compete abroad; when insurers do decide to engage in international activity, such information asymmetries can be overcome more easily by establishing a local brand or subsidiary with underwriters who understand the market.

Reinsurance. In contrast to non-life insurance, there are significant economic advantages in reinsurance to operating internationally. First, scale economies are far more significant in reinsurance than in non-life insurance. Reinsurance is purchased in one of two ways: either directly from a reinsurer or indirectly through a broker. Economies of scale are high through both channels. Reinsurers for whom brokers serve as the principal distribution channel can provide as much cover as either regulation or prudence permits. In this segment of the market, reinsurance is primarily a capital-driven business, which does not require extensive investments in marketing or loss adjustment. As a result, average costs fall per dollar of reinsurance.[10]

The largest reinsurance firms in the world tend to provide cover to non-life insurers directly rather than through brokers. Such direct sales tend to be considerably more profitable because they eliminate the broker's commission. Moreover, direct reinsurers are able to charge higher rates in return for technical assistance—among other things, in the evaluation of risks. Reinsurers, such as Munich Re, Swiss Re, and General Re, all have large staffs of engineers and underwriters who work closely with non-life insurers. For example, Munich Re, the world's largest reinsurer, has at its headquarters a staff of more than 100 engineers who assist clients worldwide. Providing such services requires sufficient market presence and skills, which, according to industry sources, can be accomplished only by the largest firms. So economies of scale are high for these kinds of reinsurers as well.

The advantages of size are particularly evident in the U.S. market. An examination of the underwriting results of U.S.-based reinsurers reveals that larger reinsurers display a better underwriting performance.

Such performance is typically measured by the "combined ratio."[11] The lower the combined ratio, the better the performance. In 1989, for example, firms with premiums of more than $500 million had a combined ratio of 104.9; firms with premiums between $100 million and $500 million had a combined ratio of 107.8; and firms with premiums of less than $100 million had a combined ratio of 112.9.[12] Scale economies have probably been reached by the largest firms operating in the United States, but firms based in smaller markets have to operate internationally to achieve similar scale economies.

Risk diversification also helps explain the greater degree of international activity in reinsurance than in non-life insurance. Reinsurers, whose book of business is spread over a broad geographic area, can smooth out any fluctuations in losses resulting from localized losses. The increase in excess-of-loss contracts, which can expose reinsurers to extremely large liabilities, has made this rationale particularly important.[13] More generally, reinsurance exists because it provides a market within which direct insurers can diversify their own portfolios. Thus, the international expansion of reinsurance can be seen as a substitute for the lack of geographic risk diversification on the part of direct insurers.

Among the advanced industrial countries, international reinsurance appears to be driven more by the existence of scale economies and the benefits of risk diversification than by differences in national comparative advantage. As in non-life insurance, national comparative advantages are offset by information asymmetries that exist in reinsurance, although such asymmetries are less extensive in reinsurance than in non-life owing to the reinsurer's smaller number of customers. Because information is likely to be the most incomplete when a reinsurer enters a new market, reinsurers have also found that they are "selected against" when they first tap foreign markets.

The Customer Decision-Making Process

The decision-making processes of customers have reinforced the way in which economic forces affect international transactions in insurance. The process adopted by non-life insurance customers differs markedly from that adopted by reinsurance customers. Insurance for personal lines or mass risks, such as home fire insurance, is a local business.[14] According to industry executives, individuals or small businesses prefer to buy non-life insurance from a local company (whether foreign or domestically owned), believing that they will receive better advice and service.

Selling insurance to them has therefore historically required a local agent network and postsale servicing contact.

In both Europe and Japan, agents, either independent or "tied" to a single company, represent the principal distribution channel. In the United States, insurers are making greater use of direct marketing for standard products. Even in these cases, however, the sheer volume of postsale servicing requires a local network. As a result, foreign insurers that have sought to enter third markets to cover mass risks have established local branches or subsidiaries.

Compared to individuals purchasing personal lines of insurance, companies that purchase insurance for large commercial risks tend to be more knowledgeable and sophisticated in their purchasing habits. Most large companies use brokers who shop for the best insurance cover for their risks. The largest companies employ their own risk managers, who have enough experience to look beyond their local market. Therefore, in these commercial lines of insurance some coverage is bought from insurers located in foreign markets.

Customers of reinsurance are insurance companies themselves. When buying reinsurance, insurers often look beyond their home borders. The propensity to purchase reinsurance abroad varies by country. In general, cross-border transactions are greater in Europe than in the United States, because the small size of national European markets creates a greater demand for risk diversification.

Whether insurers purchase reinsurance from foreign-domiciled companies depends, in addition, on the two types of reinsurers. Reinsurers whose principal role is to provide financial capacity—that is, to assume risk—can provide such cover without a local presence. In London, for example, brokers bring policies from insurance companies around the world to be reinsured by the various underwriting syndicates at Lloyd's. Direct reinsurers that provide technical consulting services can also provide capacity from abroad, but require greater contact with their clients. Although a local presence might facilitate such contact, it is not necessarily required. For these reasons, the purchasing decisions of customers contribute to the global nature of the reinsurance business.

Government Regulation

Government regulation further reinforces the way in which economic forces influence the level and type of international activity in non-life insurance and reinsurance. Virtually all countries regulate non-life insurance to a greater extent than they do reinsurance. Specifically, most countries require non-life insurers to be locally licensed and established, whereas reinsurers often are not under the same obligation.

There are several reasons for this difference in treatment. First, national regulators generally believe that non-life insurance customers need more protection than do reinsurance customers; underlying this belief is the notion that insurance companies are more sophisticated buyers than firms or individuals who purchase non-life insurance. Second, many governments want to keep non-life insurance premiums within their borders to contribute to economic development. On the other hand, reinsurance serves as a useful mechanism to transfer national risks overseas and protect national insurers from catastrophic loss. Japan, for example, encourages the use of foreign reinsurers by limiting the amount of insurance and reinsurance coverage that can be offered by Japanese firms for earthquake cover. Third, countries often require more insurance capacity than their own non-life insurers can supply. Allowing domestic insurance companies to purchase reinsurance from abroad enables non-life insurers to offer more coverage and to do so at a cheaper price.[15]

The extent of regulation in non-life insurance has reduced the volume of international activity below the level that might be expected simply by examining the economics of the business. In a number of developing countries, for example, governments have completely prohibited the entry of foreign firms, which otherwise would have gained share through their comparative advantage. The effects of regulation can also be seen in the non-life insurance markets of the advanced industrial countries, where entry into some markets has been rendered far more difficult.

SOURCES OF COMPETITIVE ADVANTAGE IN INTERNATIONAL INSURANCE

Not only do the levels of international activity differ between reinsurance and non-life insurance; so too do the sources of competitive advantage.

Non-Life Insurance

Although international activity in non-life insurance has been limited, a few firms, surprisingly, have succeeded in establishing a position in foreign markets. Figure 9-2 provides two measures of the foreign activities of non-life insurance companies. As of 1982 firms based in the United

FIGURE 9-2
Foreign Activity of Domestic Insurance Companies, 1982[a]

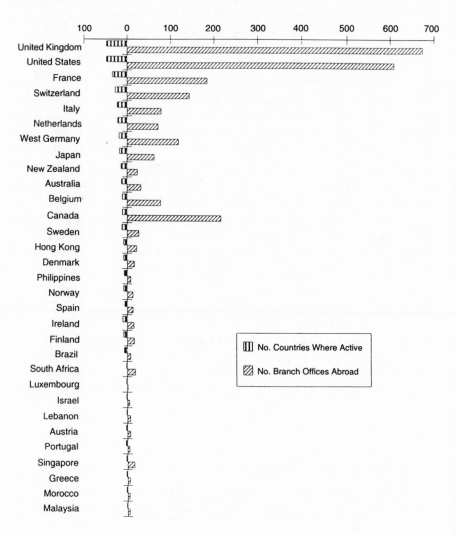

[a]For all countries with at least five branch offices abroad in 1982.

Source: Sigma, Swiss Reinsurance Company, February 1982.

States, the United Kingdom, France, and Switzerland operated in the greatest number of countries and maintained the greatest number of branches abroad.

Figure 9-3 gives the geographic breakdown of business (as of 1988) for a number of insurance companies that operate internationally. The firms with the broadest international networks include Zurich and Winterthur (based in Switzerland); Royal (based in Britain); and AIG and CIGNA (based in the United States). Nationale Nederlanden, a Dutch firm, boasts a large network, but most of this activity is in life insurance. These figures show that the firms which have been most successful operating internationally in the past have been based in the United States, in the United Kingdom, and in Switzerland. Throughout most of the postwar period, German, French, Italian, and Japanese firms, by contrast, have concentrated most of their activities in home or regional markets. The ability of U.S., British, and Swiss firms to overcome the extensive barriers to globalization in non-life insurance can be traced to both country-based advantages and national regulatory regimes.

Country-specific advantages. The most critical determinant of a firm's success in international insurance is the internationalization of its domestic client base. Non-life insurers, like banks, follow their customers overseas. As these customers—whether merchants or manufacturers—engage in foreign trade and investment, they turn to their national insurers to cover the associated risks. National ties between clients and insurers have historically been tight. To manage the overseas exposures of domestic accounts (referred to as home/foreign business), insurers often begin by establishing alliances with foreign insurers. As this business becomes more extensive, however, non-life insurers have an incentive to establish overseas facilities to provide underwriting, survey, claims, and policyholder services. But, as Henry Parker of Chubb Insurance has observed, such "home/foreign business is never sufficient to support a full-scale resident branch and affiliate operation." For this reason, "overseas facilities must compete in the indigenous market to reduce expense overhead."[16] Since most insurers lack good information about the nature of risks in foreign markets, these early efforts often lead to heavy losses. With time, however, many have developed enough knowledge to both evaluate foreign risks and compete effectively against domestic insurers. This process can be seen from the earliest international activities of non-life firms.

FIGURE 9-3
Geographic Breakdown of Life and Non-Life Premiums of Largest International Insurers, 1988

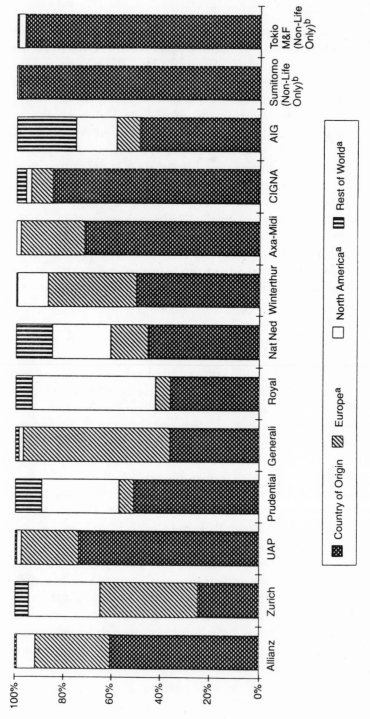

Legend: ■ Country of Origin ▨ Europe[a] □ North America[a] ▥ Rest of World[a]

[a]Excluding country of origin where applicable.
[b]1987 data.

Sources: Annual reports, company data, Oppenheimer Co.

The first insurers to expand overseas, not surprisingly, were British. The United Kingdom's development as an industrial and trading nation gave its insurers an important edge. Initially, international insurance meant marine insurance, and marine insurance meant Lloyd's. Lloyd's began as a coffee house where merchants exchanged information, but by the middle of the eighteenth century it had already established a reputation in marine insurance.[17] Other insurance companies followed Lloyd's; the Royal, for example, was created by Liverpool merchants to provide insurance for their activities.

New international lines of insurance soon developed. First came fire insurance, which became necessary as British merchants set up warehouses overseas. In the eighteenth and nineteenth centuries, marine insurance did not require a well-organized international network. Fire insurance was a different matter. To assess risks and service British clients overseas, insurers found it necessary to appoint agents to represent their interests abroad. These agents also were authorized to insure the risks of foreign nationals. But the lack of knowledge about foreign markets quickly led to heavy losses. In the early 1800s, for example, a number of British insurers began to provide fire insurance in the United States only to exit that market because of mounting losses. Not until the mid-1850s did British insurers reestablish themselves in the United States.

As their business grew abroad, British insurers developed more permanent representation in the form of branches and then subsidiaries. Fire insurance provided the bulk of their U.S. business in the nineteenth century. With strong domestic bases and geographic spread, British firms offered greater financial security than did their American counterparts, and they expanded rapidly.[18] From their base in fire insurance, these firms developed greater knowledge about foreign markets, overcame information asymmetries, and branched out into casualty insurance.[19] The expansion of British non-life insurers continued within the United States, Britain's colonies, and later the Commonwealth. But penetration of continental European markets, especially Germany and Austria, was impeded by regulatory barriers.[20]

The forces driving the international expansion of British insurance operated in other countries as well. In the late nineteenth century, local manufacturers in Switzerland organized the two large Swiss insurance firms, Zurich and Winterthur; as these manufacturers expanded internationally, so too did their insurers. The same pattern can be seen in the histories of large insurance companies in a range of other countries, including Japan, Germany, France, and the United States.[21] In the early twentieth century, insurers from all these industrializing nations followed manufacturers to overseas markets.

World War II disrupted this emerging intercountry pattern of insurance activity. During the war, many insurers were forced to suspend their foreign operations and often found that their assets in hostile countries were either nationalized or liquidated.[22]

The Allied victory helped determine the postwar pattern of international insurance activity. For one thing, it abruptly ended the international operations of insurers from the Axis powers. After the war the Allied Occupation forces barred insurers in Japan and Germany from engaging in foreign business. Even in the absence of such a prohibition, however, the war's destruction virtually ensured that Japanese and German manufacturers would, for the immediate future, remain focused on their domestic markets, thereby depriving their national insurers of a strong overseas client base.

Moreover, the end of the war dramatically strengthened the international position of American, British, and Swiss insurance companies. Swiss insurers, because of their country's neutrality, survived the war with little loss of business, and American insurers found opportunities to expand their operations significantly. AIG, for example, sold insurance to members of the American armed forces stationed overseas; it established a position in Japan, which to this day no other foreign insurer has been able to duplicate because of Japan's stringent domestic regulation.

Of course, the end of the war also had a negative effect on the business of European insurers insofar as it encouraged national self-determination throughout the European colonial system. For British, French, and Dutch insurers, decolonization brought to an end the colonial monopolies they had often enjoyed in earlier days.

National regulatory regimes.   Non-life insurance is one of the most heavily regulated industries in the world, and wide variation exists in the degree of regulation. In the postwar period, differences in national regulation have shaped the ability of firms to benefit from country-based advantages. Broadly speaking, two types of regimes can be distinguished.

In the first, regulation is designed to protect consumers, who are thought to lack sufficient information to assess an insurer's solvency. Consumer protection regulations apply mainly to the level and constitution of reserves held by insurers to pay future claims. In the second type, regulation is intended to prevent disruptive competition. Here, regulations extend to both premium rates and policy content. The rationale for such regulation is that unbridled competition over price or policy content makes it difficult for firms to generate and maintain adequate loss reserves. In practice, however, such regulation also serves to strengthen the position of domestic insurers vis-à-vis foreign competition.[23] Of course, numerous differences in regulatory frameworks exist across countries, so these two regimes should actually be seen as the endpoints of a continuum that runs from less to more regulation.

Regulation in the United States lies closer to the first type. The McCarren-Ferguson Act of 1945 set the framework for U.S. insurance regulation. Under its terms, insurance companies are exempt from federal antitrust law as long as the individual states in which they do business oversee their rates, practices, and solvency. Allowing insurance companies to engage in collusive practices, like collective rate setting, was considered necessary to prevent massive insolvencies. At the same time, state governments were charged with the task of protecting consumers and seeing to it that insurers acted prudently. The actual regulation of insurance was left to the states. Not surprisingly, wide variation developed in the extent of insurance regulation across the United States, although the National Association of Insurance Commissioners has brought some degree of uniformity.[24]

Yet as early as the 1950s, the price discipline that the McCarren-Ferguson Act hoped to promote began to break down. Insurance companies increasingly sought exemptions from the prices established by the various rate-setting agencies. For their part, state regulators also began to view price competition as a desirable goal. Although two thirds of all states still regulate the price of at least some non-life lines (motor insurance being the most common), price competition has become the norm, especially in large states like California and New York.[25] Indeed, in 1990 the Insurance Services Office, the most important rating association, stopped publishing advisory rates altogether.[26]

The ease with which firms (both U.S. and foreign) can enter the U.S. market and set prices makes the non-life business prone to boom-and-bust cycles, especially when financial market returns are high. Large profits attract new capacity. Firms then begin to cut their prices and take on poorer risks to gain premiums to invest. Eventually lower prices prove insufficient to cover rising claims, investment income declines, and insurers are forced to draw on their surpluses to pay claims. As profits fall, firms exit and industry capacity falls. Figure 9-4 traces the cycle in the United States over its last iteration, which reached its trough in 1984–1985.

FIGURE 9-4
Underwriting Results and Investment Income in West Germany, Japan, and the United States

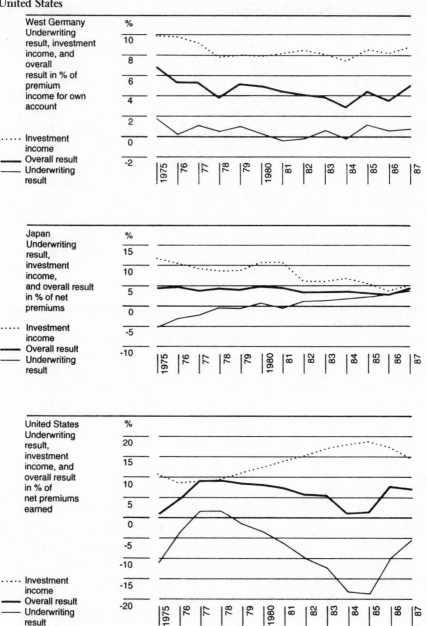

Source: Sigma, Swiss Reinsurance Company, June 1989.

Regulation of non-U.S. firms also varies by state. In general, states generally grant licenses to them on the same terms and conditions as to domestic insurers. Still, many states prohibit the licensing of insurance companies that are wholly or partially owned by a foreign government on the grounds that government ownership provides these firms with an unfair advantage.[27] To operate in the United States, foreign firms must also meet different licensing procedures and solvency rules for each state (which is, of course, also true for U.S.-based insurers). Apart from these direct costs, the sheer volatility of the U.S. market—which is itself partly the result of the relative absence of price regulation—heightens the risks and returns of entry. Foreign insurers are attracted by the potential profitability of the U.S. market on the upswing, but many have learned that operating in the United States calls for deep pockets when the market turns sour, especially in these times of skyrocketing liability awards.

Regulation in Japan, which is far more extensive than in the United States, is designed to prevent excessive price competition. Under the Insurance Business Law, Japan's Ministry of Finance (MOF) regulates the licensing of insurance firms, the types of investments an insurer can make, the rate of premiums, and the terms of contracts. All firms must obtain licenses from MOF before starting business. Licenses are limited in scope; that is, non-life insurers cannot sell life insurance. Furthermore, no new insurance product can be offered without MOF approval. "Premium groups," consisting of the major Japanese insurance companies, generally determine rates, but endorsement by MOF still must be gained.[28] Not surprisingly, Japan's tight regulatory regime has limited the number of insurance companies operating in Japan and guaranteed higher levels of underwriting income than in the United States. It has also all but eliminated the cyclicality of underwriting income (see Figure 9-4) so prevalent in other markets.

Since insurance companies cannot compete on premium rates or policy content, the focus of competition has shifted to both distribution and service. Yet even distribution in Japan is regulated. Under the Insurance Business Law, only insurance firms and agents certified by MOF are allowed to sell insurance. More than 90% of insurance policies are sold through the 400,000 agents all over the country. Independent brokers, who might otherwise supply business to new entrants, are not licensed to engage in domestic Japanese business, since, it is argued, they lack sufficient product knowledge to protect policyholders from losses. Thus, the main source of competitive advantage is control over the distribution channel—specifically, over the number of agents. The need to build a national distribution network to compete effectively has provided significant first-mover advantages.

MOF has used its power to limit entry into the Japanese market, contributing to the high level of concentration. As of 1991, only twenty-three Japanese and thirty-seven non-Japanese firms were providing non-life coverage. Growth in the number of foreign firms is a relatively recent phenomenon, since historically, MOF limited the number of licenses available to foreign insurers. Throughout the 1950s and 1960s, MOF granted licenses to only a few foreign firms, then strictly limited their activities. In the absence of such regulations in the early years of postwar reconstruction, foreign firms would likely have obtained a significantly larger share of the Japanese non-life market in light of their advantages—risk assessment capabilities and financial security—relative to Japanese insurers. By the time MOF did allow an increase in the number of foreign entrants in the mid-1970s, the advantages of foreign insurers relative to Japanese insurers had declined.

The ability of foreign insurers to compete in Japan was also constrained by the low levels of investment of foreign multinationals—their natural client base—in that country. Late entry into the Japanese market has further reduced the ability of foreign non-life insurers to compete for indigenous Japanese business (even though these foreign insurers are not subject to discriminatory capital or solvency requirements). As a result, their share of the Japanese market has remained at 2.8%.[29]

Regulation of premiums and, more specifically, policy content add an additional layer of difficulty for foreign firms in Japan. Foreign insurers report that their applications to MOF to introduce new products have met with long delays, which often have given Japanese insurers time to develop similar products. Even in the absence of regulation, of course, product introduction usually creates no sustainable advantage, since competitors can quickly introduce similar products. But the extent of Japanese regulation on policy content nonetheless has eliminated even any short-term advantage a foreign innovator might enjoy.[30]

Japan's domestic regulatory regime has also influenced the willingness and ability of Japanese insurers to compete abroad. By enabling Japanese insurers to earn higher profits in the home market, Japan's regulatory regime reduced the attractiveness of international expansion.[31] In addition, the stability of prices and income at home has slowed the development of the underwriting skills necessary to compete in more competitive markets. In the 1970s, for example, the major Japanese insurers launched themselves into the U.S. market. But they were not sufficiently knowledgeable about selection, pricing, and differentiation. As a result, brokers, who occupy an important role in the American market, tended not to bring their best business to the Japanese firms. This experience proved particularly costly when the U.S. market turned sour at the end of the decade. Since that time, Japanese non-life insurers have proceeded with great caution in overseas markets and limited their activities to serving their Japanese clients investing abroad.

In the European Community (EC), wide differences exist in national regulatory regimes. Those differences can be seen most clearly through a comparison of insurance regulation in Germany and the United Kingdom. Germany has the strictest regulatory regime among EC members; it includes state control of premiums in many types of insurance, prior approval of the wording of contracts, and standardization of policy clauses.[32] France and Italy have taken a similar approach. By contrast, the United Kingdom (and to a lesser extent the Netherlands) has focused regulatory efforts on ensuring the solvency of companies. The United Kingdom does not regulate contract terms or premium rates and requires no prior approval. Companies are largely free to write any business on any terms they like as long as they establish adequate reserves. Consumers then are left to compare policy terms and prices.[33]

The patchwork of regulation in the European Community has kept national markets largely segmented, creating widely varying product prices across boundaries (see Table 9-6). Differences in national regulatory regimes have also affected the performance of companies in their markets. The more heavily regulated markets tend to exhibit lower cyclicality and better underwriting results than the more competitive markets. These differences, of course, influence the entry calculations of foreign firms.

The stability of underwriting results has made the German market (see Figure 9-4) most attractive to foreign firms. Yet the regulation of both policy content and rates has made it virtually impossible for them to compete on the basis of either price or product innovation. Firms seeking to become a significant player in the German market have to put a distribution network together. This, too, is difficult, since captive agents and company salespeople sell some 80% of all policies. Allianz, the dominant German firm, enjoys a distinct advantage here with its 43,000 agents.

Regulation in the United Kingdom is virtually the mirror image of that in Germany. The dominant role played by brokers makes entry into the British market much easier. With little regulation to stall enterprise,

TABLE 9-6
Insurance Price Comparisons (percentage differences in prices of standard insurance products compared with the average of the four lowest national prices in 1986)

	Life insurance[a]	Home[b]	Motor[c]	Commercial fire, theft[d]	Public liability[e]
Belgium	+78%	−16%	+30%	−9%	+13%
France	+33%	+39%	+9%	+153%	+117%
Italy	+83%	+81%	+148%	+245%	+77%
Luxembourg	+66%	+57%	+77%	−15%	+9%
Netherlands	−9%	+17%	−7%	−1%	−16%
Spain	+37%	−4%	+100%	+24%	+60%
United Kingdom	−30%	+90%	−17%	+27%	−7%
West Germany	+5%	+3%	+15%	+43%	+47%

[a] Life insurance: average annual cost of term (life) insurance.
[b] Home insurance: annual cost of fire and theft coverage for a house valued at 70,000 European Currency Units (ECU); contents valued at 28,000 ECU.
[c] Motor insurance: annual cost of comprehensive insurance for a 1.6 liter car; driver had ten years of experience.
[d] Commercial fire and theft: annual coverage for premises valued at 387,000 ECU and stock valued at 232,000 ECU.
[e] Public liability: annual premium for engineering company with twenty employees and an annual turnover of 1.29 million ECU.
Note: In 1986, 1 ECU = $0.9825.
Source: EC Commission.

competition on both rates and policy conditions is rampant. As a result, many foreign firms have entered the market only to find it difficult to compete profitably. New entrants also run the risk of being selected against, that is, of being offered the worst risks. Hence the share of the British market held by foreign branches or subsidiaries in the 1960s and 1970s remained fairly low.

Competition has made product innovation a hallmark of the British market, and it has provided some advantage to British firms, including Lloyd's, that have developed a reputation as the leading insurers for complex risks.[34] The absence of regulation has therefore strengthened the global position of British non-life insurers built on the base of their domestic clients' overseas operations. As a result, the United Kingdom has become the leading exporter of insurance products in the European Community.[35]

Firm-specific advantages. The importance of the domestic client base and national regulation in structuring international competition has made it difficult for most firms to compete beyond their national borders. Absent access to a particular client base, the key source of competitive advantage is human capital, which is essential to careful risk evaluation, customer service, and investment. If a non-life insurer wishes to compete successfully in foreign indigenous business (that is, if it wishes to enter foreign markets to serve foreign clients, rather than to follow its own domestic clients who have entered the foreign market), it must acquire qualified personnel who are knowledgeable about that market. To do so, foreign firms are likely to have to pay a premium—either directly in the form of salaries or indirectly in the purchase of an entire firm—which places them at a financial disadvantage relative to domestic firms.

Firm-specific advantages do exist, however, in particular segments of the non-life insurance market. These advantages are most apparent in specific niches, such as travel insurance, director's insurance, and especially global protection for multinationals. Providing global services to multinationals requires a network of offices throughout the world. The ability to cover a firm's risks worldwide can enable an insurer to attract and retain multinational business even if its own country-based advantages decline.[36] Such firm-specific advantages, as I shall argue below, are likely to increase in the future.

Reinsurance

In the postwar period the firms that dominate international reinsurance activity have been based in Germany, Switzerland, and the United Kingdom. Of the top three reinsurers in the world (listed in Table 9-5), only Munich Re and Swiss Re receive a large percentage of their premiums from outside their home markets. Approximately 45% of Munich Re's premium income comes from foreign business, while 94% of Swiss Re's premium income comes from foreign business.[37] By contrast, only about 7% of General Re's premium income comes from business outside the United States.

Table 9-4 does not include Lloyd's of London, which has a unique status in the international insurance community. Lloyd's is a market rather than a firm; underwriting syndicates at Lloyd's, composed of individuals (referred to as "names"), provide both insurance and reinsurance for risks around the world. In 1988 the total net premium income received by underwriting syndicates at Lloyd's amounted to $7.6 billion; some observers estimate the amount of reinsurance premiums at approximately $3.8 billion, of which about two-thirds are thought to have come from foreign (i.e., non-British) business.

Why is it that American firms are active in international non-life insurance, but are much less present in international reinsurance? And why are the most international of the European reinsurers based in Germany, Switzerland, and the United Kingdom rather than in other European countries? Part of the explanation lies with country-level factors, particularly the degree of internationalization of the domestic economy and access to capital. The strategies of individual firms have also played a large role. Firm strategies exert a more important influence on patterns of international activity in reinsurance than in non-life insurance because of the significance of first-mover advantages. Those advantages result from the importance of a firm's reputation for financial strength, for which size is often seen as a proxy.

Country-specific advantages.   Country size and capital market development have created important sources of competitive advantage in reinsurance. Country size is important because of the existence of large economies of scale, which result from the fact that reinsurance contracts involve a large volume of business. A reinsurer can substantially increase premium volume without a proportional increase in its costs. As argued above, reinsurers in larger markets like the United States and Japan could achieve greater geographic distribution of risk in their home market than could reinsurers in smaller European countries. American and Japanese reinsurers therefore had less incentive to expand overseas.[38]

Yet country size alone cannot explain why some countries developed internationally oriented—and successful—reinsurance firms while others did not. In Europe the international operations of reinsurers have been strongly affected by the reputation of their domestic capital markets and their domestic currencies. The importance of domestic capital markets stems from the fact that reinsurers must have sufficient capital to back their contracts and to increase the volume of the business they accept. Therefore, minimum capital standards, if not required by the government, are imposed by the market, since direct insurers evaluate the financial stability of reinsurers. Similarly, reinsurers in countries with internationally attractive currencies also enjoy an advantage, as they appear to be better able to pay future claims. These two features distinguish the United Kingdom, Germany, and Switzerland. The development of a vibrant capital market in the United Kingdom contributed to the ability of Lloyd's to bring capacity to the reinsurance market, not to mention the international strength of its financial sector more generally. In Germany and Switzerland, capital availability was historically ensured by close relations with banks; moreover, both the Deutschmark and the Swiss franc have become "strong" currencies in the postwar period. These features have contributed to the financial integrity of reinsurance firms, enhancing their reputation with direct insurers. The dominance of German, Swiss, and British reinsurers relative to, say, French is partly the result of France's decision to nationalize the direct insurers after the war, which in some sense turned the government into the main reinsurer.

Firm-specific advantages.   The advantages of size, capital availability, and currency stability were shared commonly by reinsurers in Germany, Switzerland, and the United Kingdom. Yet in each of these countries, only one major international reinsurer developed: Munich Re, Swiss Re, and Lloyd's. Each of these firms developed specific advantages that underlay its existing position. The development of Lloyd's as a market, rather than a firm, created a significant advantage, for it could combine extensive capacity with flexibility. Lloyd's brokers could place virtually any kind of risk. Much of the success of both Munich Re and Swiss Re, by contrast, lay in the development of close relationships with direct insurers. Munich Re, in fact, helped to establish a number of direct insurers in order to provide it with a steady flow of business, and it now holds a 25% stake in Allianz, which in turn owns an equal stake in Munich Re. More generally, both reinsurers invested heavily in the development of engineering and risk analysis to assist non-life insurers with their evaluation of risks. The ability to offer such services did not create an insurmountable advantage, but it raised the costs of entry for potential competitors considerably.

Moreover, as Munich Re and Swiss Re began to expand within Europe, they added capabilities that gave them two other sources of competitive advantage. First was simply the ability to manage activities across countries. Originally, these two firms did not need to spread their business beyond Europe to achieve scale economies or geographic distribution of risk. But as the economics of the industry changed, giving reinsurers an incentive to become even larger and more global, these firms had more experience than newer entrants or their American counterparts in managing a global network.

Second, early expansion and growth enabled the European reinsurers to develop a reputation for reliability. The importance of reputation derives from the fact that reinsurance essentially involves a *promise* to pay in the future. In purchasing reinsurance, a direct insurer is concerned about price, but also about dependability. In other words, will the reinsurer pay (or be sufficiently solvent to be able to pay) a claim within the span of the contract? Firm size, according to managers of both insurance companies and reinsurance firms, often serves as an indicator of dependability.

THE EVOLUTION OF COMPETITION

Three developments in recent years have led many analysts to predict that competition in non-life insurance will come closer to the global pattern of competition we have seen in reinsurance. First, the rapid change in information technologies, combined with even more rapid financial innovation, is increasing potential economies of scale in the industry and offering the prospect of greater gains through international expansion. Second, a number of manufacturing industries are themselves becoming more global, thus creating demand for global insurance services. Third, the pattern of regulation is changing.

The European Community has become a natural laboratory for observing the effect of regulatory change on the pattern of competition in non-life insurance. The EC's 1992 program is designed to create a single market within which goods, services, capital, and people can flow freely. Already, firms in a multitude of industries have expanded across Europe to take advantage of these new opportunities. Insurance is no exception. A major thrust of the 1992 program is the creation of a common insurance market. Since 1990, non-life insurers in one member state have been able to sell policies to large companies located in another member state, a development that affects 30% of all non-life insurance in the Community. (The Appendix describes the process of insurance deregulation in the European Community.)

The EC's success in dismantling national regulatory barriers and establishing a common insurance market for large commercial risks has led many European non-life insurers to re-evaluate their strategies. In Europe, non-life vendors are quickly seeking to establish positions in other markets to provide better service as their own customer bases become more European. Many insurance executives have concluded that having a "critical mass," or sufficient presence, in the major European markets will become an important source of competitive advantage. This focus on critical mass reflects the need to have a strong local distribution network.

The Second Non-Life Directive (adopted by the European Council) permits insurance for large risks to be sold—i.e., traded—across borders. International trade in insurance products for such risks will increase as large firms make greater use of brokers to shop around for better and cheaper coverage.[39] But international success will still depend on having a strong local presence, since even pan-European clients will demand local service; moreover, many commercial risks and most personal risks will remain a local business. As a result, any company that seeks to compete across Europe will require a pan-European network.

The importance of having a pan-European network also reflects the difficulty of competing on product innovation and quality. Arthur Andersen's recent survey of insurance executives suggests that in Europe, as in Japan, product innovation is unlikely to create a sustainable advantage. Although "a short-lived competitive advantage could be gained by a foreign entrant through the introduction of a new product . . . this would be impossible to sustain as the product was copied by local companies with greater distribution power."[40]

Developing a European distribution network through internal growth is both slow and difficult, especially given the dominant role played by agents in many EC countries. Besides, as we have seen, a company trying to enter a market faces high barriers to entry in the form of information asymmetries. For these reasons, most insurers have sought to grow through acquisition. In the last several years, the European Community has witnessed a vast number of acquisitions, both within and across countries (see Table 9-7). For example, Allianz's acquisitions have included French, Italian, and British companies. In 1989 Groupe Victoire, a major insurer in France, purchased the number two German insurer, Colonia, for a reported $2.5 billion.

Given the cost of such acquisitions, a company's financial strength has turned out to be an important source of competitive advantage. Among European insurers, Germany's Allianz is in an enviable position. This major insurer enjoys the benefits of having both a stable ownership structure (guaranteed in part by its cross holdings with Munich Re) and a dominant position in a previously regulated market. Such stable ownership has helped avoid shareholder demands for high dividend payments. Allianz pays out only 16% of net income in dividends, compared to about 50% for both American and British insurers. As a result, the company has been able to build up significant reserves, which can be used for acquisitions. Similarly, Germany's previous system of regulation made it difficult for new firms to compete in the German market. Thus, Allianz was able to maintain a strong hold on domestic distribution (roughly 16% of the German market), thereby strengthening its capital base and providing resources the company can use to expand internationally.

Allianz's position in the European market has deepened a concern felt by other European insurers about achieving critical mass. Although no insurer has a well-defined understanding of optimal size or reach in the

TABLE 9-7
Insurance Industry Mergers and Acquisitions: Europe

Firm	Acquisition	Year
Allianz (Germany)	Cornhill (United Kingdom)	1986
	RAS (Italy)	1987
	Hungaria Buztosito	1989
	Compagnie Mixte Insurers Ercos (Spain)	1989
	East German State Insurer	1990
	Fireman's Fund	1990
Groupe Victoire (France)	Colonia (Germany)	1989
	La Previsara Hispalense (Spain)	1989
	Prudential Italia (Italy)	1990
UAP (France)	Royale Belge	1989
	Allsecures (Italy)	1990
	GESA (Spain)	1990
UAP Re	SCOR (France)	1990
SCOR	Deutsche Continental Re (Germany)	1989
AGF (France)	Insurance Corp of Ireland	1990
	Assubel-Vie (Belgium)	1989
	Kosmos (Greece)	1989
	Canada Surety	1990
GAN (France)	General Portfolio (United Kingdom)	1990
	Alianza de Seguros	1990
Zurich	Maryland Casualty	1988
Winterthur (Switzerland)	General Casualty of Wisconsin	1990
	Intercontinentale (Italy)	1989
	Transatlantische Allgemeine (Germany)	1989
	Wand AG (Germany)	1990
Bernoise (Switzerland)	Amaya (Spain)	1990
Swiss Re	Lloyd Adratico (Italy)	1989
Royal (United Kingdom)	Lloyd Italico (Italy)	1989
GRE (United Kingdom)	Polaris Vita (Italy), Sipea (Italy), Cidas (Italy)	1989
Minet (United Kingdom)	Anglo-Swiss (Switzerland)	1989
	Essar (Hong Kong)	1990
	Essar (Norway)	1990
Norwich Union (United Kingdom)	Plus Ultra (Spain)	1990
Generali (Italy)	Business Men's Assurance (United States)	1990
	Union Suisse (Switzerland)	1989
Netherlands Re (Netherlands)	Victoria Insurance (United Kingdom)	1990
NV AMEV (Netherlands)	Groupe AG (Belgium)	1990

Sources: Annual reports, newspaper reports.

new market, all are convinced that it is vital to become larger. In this time of uncertainty, in which insurers grope to find optimal size, it is not surprising that they are playing follow the leader.[41] After Allianz bought the Italian insurer RAS, for example, other companies, including Winterthur, UAP, and Victoire, also made significant acquisitions in

Italy. European insurers seem to be seeking to match, as much as possible, the moves made by their competitors to ensure that they do not miss an opportunity. Holding a position in the Italian non-life insurance market, for example, may in fact not be critical to a firm's success, yet no large insurer wants to run the risk of being absent from that market if, in the future, it indeed turns out to be critical—especially if powerful competitors, such as Allianz, have already entered that market.

The evolving pattern of competition in Europe provides some indication of the potential evolution of competition in insurance globally. To be sure, national markets will remain for a vast number of non-life products. But as non-life insurance customers become more global, demand for global insurance services will increase. As a result, competition in non-life insurance will move in the direction of, but probably not reach, the global configuration we have seen in reinsurance.

On the one hand, the competition among global multiline insurers will likely increase. Among the larger non-life insurers, the trend toward globalization has already sparked greater interest in establishing new global networks or enhancing old ones. In 1990, for example, Allianz acquired California-based Fireman's Fund, and French insurer AXA-Midi has taken a major stake in the Equitable. On the horizon are the major Japanese non-life insurers.

In the 1980s foreign business represented a relatively small proportion of the total premium income of Japan's major non-life insurers—Tokio, Yasuda, Taisho, and Sumitomo. As we have seen, this pattern reflected both the profitability of the domestic market and the problems encountered by these firms in foreign markets in the past. Insofar as these four insurers are concerned, all insist that their international activities are based on their desire to serve Japanese clients operating abroad. The continued expansion of Japanese manufacturers into foreign markets should lead these insurers to establish a greater overseas presence, thereby increasing their knowledge about conditions in these markets. With this greater knowledge, their willingness to begin to engage in indigenous business—or, as in Europe, to increase their presence through acquisition—will undoubtedly increase. In this regard, Japan's domestic regulatory regime, like Germany's, has provided its large non-life insurers with a particularly strong capital base. This guarantees the means for future international expansion.[42]

The emergence of strong international insurers from Germany and Japan will create an important test for the existing international insurers. Faced with this new competition, they will need to sharpen their skills to sustain growth. Such skills will involve the creation of better techniques of risk forecasting, marketing, and global management.

More common, and perhaps more successful, than the global multiline companies, however, will be those firms which have the ability to target profitable market niches. Focused niche strategies enable non-life insurers to target those segments of the market in which demand is most homogeneous and therefore where information about foreign conditions is most readily available. Consider Chubb and Hartford Steam Boiler, two U.S. insurers with excellent reputations for service in the home market. Chubb has moved aggressively to develop markets in Europe in those niches with which it was most familiar. In the mid-1980s, for example, it successfully introduced "all-risk" property insurance in the German market. (German insurers had previously provided separate policies for different kinds of risks.) More recently, Hartford Steam Boiler, in a joint venture with General Re, established the Engineering Insurance Group to market its services to European engineering firms.

For both types of competitors—broad market vendors and niche players—the key to success in a world of greater international competition will be an ability to manage a global network. The tension intrinsic to this challenge is between centralizing to derive benefits from the existence of a global network and decentralizing to be responsive to the continuing differences within national markets.

The changes on the horizon in non-life insurance will have repercussions in reinsurance. Most significant is the increase in the size of direct non-life insurers. As insurers grow and develop a more geographically diverse book of business, they tend to reduce the amount of reinsurance they buy. (Figure 9-5 plots the size of non-life insurers against their demand for reinsurance.) Moreover, growth among direct insurers is likely to enhance the value of reputation in reinsurance. Insurance executives and brokers report that large insurance companies have increasingly come to prefer to deal with larger reinsurance firms. These trends suggest that greater concentration in the reinsurance industry is coming. Furthermore, the large direct reinsurers, such as Munich Re, Swiss Re, and General Re, will have to find new ways of providing service to retain their existing client bases.

In a world of greater international competition, insurers, especially in the non-life segment, have an increased stake in establishing a common set of rules. For good reason, all countries regulate their non-life insurance industries. In some countries, such as Germany and Japan, a high

FIGURE 9-5
Correlation between Market Share and Reinsurance Demand of 130 Non-Life Direct Insurers from Nine Countries

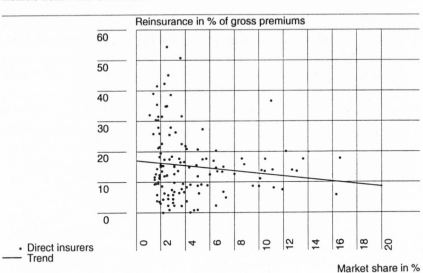

Source: *Sigma*, Swiss Reinsurance Company, May 1989.

degree of regulation has provided financial advantages to the existing firms, albeit at substantial costs to consumers in terms of price and product availability. In others, regulation has been designed primarily to ensure the solvency of non-life insurance firms.

The growth of international insurance transactions calls into question the existing patchwork of regulations. As the world's major corporations continue their expansion across borders, insurers will be compelled to follow. These moves will increasingly create pressure for national regulators to adopt common, or at least similar, rules. Firm strategy and regulation are likely to have a profound effect on the current structure of political competition. For this reason, setting rules for international insurance transactions is rightly on the GATT agenda. A resolution of the GATT round is unlikely, by itself, to have an immediate effect on international insurance transactions in the three major markets of the world. But it is surely necessary to create a framework for the changing pattern of international competition that is occurring as a result of the globalization of the world economy.

APPENDIX

The Creation of a Single European Insurance Market

Insurance has long been seen as an essential element of the Common Market.[43] The Treaty of Rome provided for both freedom of establishment and freedom of services in insurance. (Freedom of establishment is defined as the right of a company in one state to set up branches in another state; freedom of services is defined as the right to market products throughout the European Community without having to establish a branch in every member state.) In 1961 the Council adopted an ambitious program to institute both freedoms in several rapid stages. Both freedoms would first be applied to reinsurance. Second, freedom of establishment would be instituted for both non-life and life insurance. Third would come freedom of services.

In 1964 the Council adopted the first directives relevant to reinsurance. However, since few actual barriers to either investment or trade existed, the directive served primarily to reaffirm the existing situation. Action in the area of direct insurance proved more difficult. Only in 1973 did the Council abolish restrictions on the freedom of establishment in non-life insurance and provide for common standards in setting Community-wide solvency margins. This made it easier for EC insurance companies to enter other EC national markets; but once inside, they still had to meet local regulations. As a result, the EC insurance market remained fragmented.

In 1973 the Commission also proposed a directive to provide for freedom of services for non-life insurance. No progress could be made on this issue, however, owing to strong disagreement among the member states. Support for a more liberal regime came from both the British (who had just joined the Community) and the Dutch; the Germans and the French, on the other hand, resisted efforts to facilitate cross-border insurance transactions.

In the mid-1980s two developments gave new impetus to this initiative. The first was the ruling of the European Court of Justice in a series of insurance cases.[44] The court began by affirming the right to provide services freely across national borders. However, it noted that insurance was a special area, partly due to the lack of harmonization of national insurance laws. Where the need for policyholder protection existed, the state in which insurance services were being provided could still require the insurer to be authorized. But it held that the need for consumer protection was not the same in every case. And where such protection was not required, there was no need for national authorization. The court's ruling left it to the Commission and the Council to determine where consumer protection was required and where it was not. The second development was the signing of the Single European Act in 1985, which introduced qualified majority voting for most of the measures (including those in the area of insurance) needed to bring about a single market.

These two changes gave new impetus to negotiations over freedom of services in non-life insurance, which in 1988 led to the EC Council's adoption of the Second Non-Life Insurance Coordination Directive. The Second Non-Life Directive was a compromise between the advocates and opponents of freedom of services in insurance, which essentially followed the distinction outlined by the court in its earlier ruling. The directive distinguishes between purchasers of cover for large risks, believed to be able to protect their own interests and buy their own insurance, and mass risks, for which national protection by the host state is still considered justified. Large risks are defined as those meeting two of the following three criteria:

Until December 31, 1992:

- 500 or more employees
- minimum of ECU 24 million revenue (about $29 million)
- minimum of ECU 12.4 million assets (about $14 million)

After January 1, 1992:

- 250 or more employees
- minimum of ECU 12 million revenue
- minimum of ECU 6.2 million assets

The directive took effect in July 1990, except for Greece, Spain, Ireland, and Portugal, which were granted a longer transition period. Insurance executives in the Community estimated that the directive would affect approximately 30% of all non-life insurance. Negotiations are now under way to extend freedom of services to all non-life insurance. EC officials and national regulators do not expect that this agreement will be implemented until the mid-1990s.

NOTES

1. The third major segment, which I observed but do not analyze here, is life insurance. Life insurance constitutes nearly half of all world premiums, but has been characterized by little international activity.

2. For this reason, I focus primarily on international competition among the advanced industrial countries, which constitute both the chief providers and the main consumers of insurance products.

3. Reinsurance firms estimate that non-life insurance represents about 85% of their business, while life insurance represents the remaining 15%.

4. Data on international insurance transactions—via trade or investment—are notoriously inadequate. Most countries do not collect or publish trade data, and most companies (if they list premiums obtained from abroad) do not distinguish between trade and investment. Thus, the numbers presented here are my estimates based on interviews with managers of leading international insurance firms and with government officials.

5. For a useful description and guide to the insurance business, see Robert I. Mehr, Emerson Cammack, and Terry Rose, *Principles of Insurance*, 8th ed. (Homewood, Ill.: Richard D. Irwin, 1985).

6. See Randall Geehan, "Economies of Scale in Insurance: Implications for Regulation," in Bernard Wasow and Raymond D. Hill, eds., *The Insurance Industry in Economic Development* (New York: New York University Press, 1986), 148. A 1974 study of the U.S property and casualty industry concludes that MES is only about $30–$60 million in net premiums. See R. F. Allen, "Cross-Sectional Estimates of Cost Economies in Stock Property-Liability Companies," *Review of Economics and Statistics* 56 (February 1974): 100–103.

7. *Sigma*, April 1991.

8. See André Sapir and Ernst Lutz, "Trade in Services: Economic Determinants and Development-Related Issues," World Bank Staff Working Paper No. 480, August 1981, 31; Brian Hindley and Alasdair Smith, "Comparative Advantage and Trade in Services," *World Economy* (December 1984), 369–389; Ken Tucker and Mark Sundberg, *International Trade in Services* (London: Routledge, 1988); Ronald A. Cass and Eli M. Noam, "The Economics and Politics of Trade in Services: A United States Perspective," in Daniel Friedmann and Ernst-Joachim Mestmäker, eds., *Rules for Free International Trade in Services* (Baden-Baden: Nomos Verlag, 1990), 43–87; and Ronald Kent Shelp, *Beyond Industrialization: Ascendancy of the Global Service Economy* (New York: Praeger, 1981), Chapter 4.

9. This is an extension of the argument George A. Akerlof presents in "The Market for 'Lemons': Quality Uncertainty and the Market Mechanism," *Quarterly Journal of Economics* 84 (August 1970): 488–500.

10. Geehan, "Economies of Scale in Insurance," 114.

11. The combined ratio is a standard measure of underwriting performance. It is the sum of the loss ratio and the expense ratio:

Loss Ratio: $$\frac{\text{claims paid} + \text{change in provision for claims outstanding} + \text{claims administrative costs}}{\text{net earned premiums}}$$

$$\text{Expense Ratio:} \quad \frac{\text{expenses}}{\text{net written premiums}}$$

where net premiums (whether written or earned) are defined as gross premiums minus reinsurance costs. Written premiums are all premiums collected during a given period. An entire premium is considered written the day a policy is issued. Earned premiums are the proportional share of each policy's written premium for which the term of coverage has elapsed. Earned premiums are divided evenly over the exposure period of the policy.

12. Data supplied by Reinsurance Association of America.

13. Reinsurance contracts are written either on a facultative basis, where risks are reinsured individually, or on a treaty basis, where the primary insurer agrees to cede a certain share of a pool of risks to the reinsurer. Either contract can come in two forms: (1) proportional, in which a reinsurer pays a fixed portion of any loss in exchange for an equivalent fixed portion of the direct insurer's premium (minus origination fee), and (2) excess of loss, in which a reinsurer agrees to pay all losses above a certain sum and up to a certain limit. Reinsurers may, in turn, reduce their risk exposure by retroceding their policies—in essence reinsuring their own risks.

14. Some trade theorists have argued that services are, by their very nature, not amenable to trade. In this line of reasoning, services are thought to be intangible products that cannot be stored. Production and consumption of services must therefore occur in the same place, which means, in turn, that international trade in these products will necessarily be limited. See T. P. Hill, "On Goods and Services," *Review of Income and Wealth* (December 1977), 377, and more generally, W. Maxwell Corden, *Inflation, Exchange Rates, and the World Economy* (Oxford: Oxford University Press, 1985). To the extent that firms do engage in international transactions in services, Irving B. Kravis and Robert E. Lipsey argue, they will do so by establishing a local presence. See "Production and Trade in Services by U.S. Multinational Firms," Working Paper No. 2615, National Bureau of Economic Research, 1988. For an insightful argument that distinguishes between those services which are tradable and those which are not, see Jagdish Bhagwati, "International Trade in Services and Its Relevance for Economic Development," in Orio Giarini, ed., *The Emerging Service Economy* (Oxford: Pergamon Press, 1987), 3–34.

15. Howard Kunreuther and Mark V. Pauly, *International Trade in Insurance*, S. S. Huebner Foundation for Insurance Education, Wharton School, University of Pennsylvania, Huebner Foundation Monograph 16 (Homewood, Ill.: Richard D. Irwin, 1991).

16. Henry G. Parker III, "A Unified Europe Beckons U.S. Insurers to the Global Marketplace," *John Liner Review* 34 (Winter 1990): 15.

17. On the history of Lloyd's, see D. E. W. Gibb, *Lloyd's of London: A Study in Individualism* (London: The Corporation of Lloyd's, 1972), and Harold

E. Raynes, A *History of British Insurance* (London: Sir Isaac Pitman & Sons, 1950, reprinted by Garland, New York, 1983), Chapter 6.

18. In 1938 more than 70% of the fire premiums received by British firms reportedly came from the U.S. market. Raynes, A *History of British Insurance*, 270.

19. Raynes, A *History of British Insurance*, 274.

20. Ibid., 278.

21. See, for example, William H. A. Carr, *Perils Named and Unnamed: The Dramatic Story of the Insurance Company of North America* (New York: McGraw-Hill, 1967); Michèle Ruffat, Edouard-Vincent Caloni, and Bernard Laguerre, *L'UAP et l'histoire de l'assurance* (Paris: Editions Jean-Claude Lattès, 1990); and *The Tokio Marine & Fire Insurance 1879–1979* (Tokyo: The Tokio Marine & Fire Insurance Co., 1980).

22. Before the war, Tokio Fire & Marine, for example, had earned more than 30% of its total premium income from foreign operations. It suspended many of these operations during the war, although Japan's imperial expansion during the war opened access to the Chinese and Philippines markets. See *Tokio Marine & Fire Insurance*, 114, 147.

23. Kunreuther and Pauly, *International Trade in Insurance*. Less-developed countries have justified further regulatory barriers to protect infant industries and to safeguard domestic capital. On regulatory barriers in the insurance industry, see also Harold D. Skipper, "Protectionism in the Provision of Insurance Services," *Journal of Risk and Insurance* (June–September 1973).

24. The development of insurance regulation in the United States is discussed in Mehr, Cammack, and Rose, *Principles of Insurance*, Chapter 27.

25. See Kenneth J. Meier, *The Political Economy of Regulation: The Case of Insurance* (Albany: State University of New York Press, 1988), 150, 173.

26. Merrill Stevenson, "American Insurance: Survey," *The Economist*, October 27, 1990, 6.

27. James Corcoran, former New York State insurance commissioner, has suggested that state-owned companies be allowed to participate in the U.S. market so long as they do not receive any injection of government funds subsequent to licensing. See James P. Corcoran, "Regulate for a Global Market," *Journal of Commerce*, June 22, 1989.

28. Until 1980 there was only one set premium rate for each product and no room for flexibility for each company. Since 1980 there have been two types of insurance premium settings:

1. Standard premium with 10% flexibility: the rating association recommends the standard rate, which MOF must approve. Each company then may set its own rate within 10% of this figure. In practice, most firms set their premiums exactly at this standard rate. These rates apply to auto, casualty, and fire insurance.

2. Individually approved rates: each insurance company determines this rate, which MOF must approve individually. Hull, cargo, and other insurance covers are determined in this manner.

29. Approximately 2.5% of the Japanese market—nearly the entire share of all foreign firms—is held by AIG, which, as noted above, entered the Japanese market just after the war. Early entry, especially at a time when the Japanese economy was weak and foreign companies enjoyed a strong reputation, enabled AIG (then AIU) to build an agency network, which by the late 1980s numbered approximately 10,000 agents. As of 1991, the company was the sixteenth-largest non-life insurer in Japan.

30. Recently MOF has shown some willingness to speed up the approval process to allow foreign firms to introduce differentiated products. In October 1990, after three years of trying, Chubb & Son, an American insurer long active in international markets, received authorization from MOF to offer director's and officer's liability insurance on the Japanese market for the first time. Chubb, AIG, and Taisho (the fourth-largest Japanese insurer), but no others, won the authorization for a three-month exclusive period. See Henry G. Parker III, "Globalization of the Insurance Industry—Its Consequences for Insurance Markets, Brokers, and Risk Managers," presentation at the Society of CPCU/Colorado Chapter All Industry Day, Aurora, Colorado, November 2, 1990.

31. The rapid growth of maturity-refund insurance (a non-life insurance policy with a savings component) has been especially important to the attractiveness of the home market. Maturity-refund insurance premiums (as a percentage of total written premiums) have risen from 10% of the market in the late 1970s to 40% in the mid-1980s. The Marine and Fire Association of Japan, *Fact Book Fiscal 1988: Non-Life Insurance in Japan*, 13. Writing maturity-refund insurance has been particularly difficult for foreign insurers, given the reserve level required by MOF.

32. Strong similarities can be seen in the German and Japanese approach to insurance regulation, which is not surprising since the Japanese government based its regulatory regime partly on the German model.

33. See Sam Aaronovitch and Peter Samson, *The Insurance Industry in the Countries of the EEC: Structure, Conduct, and Performance* (Luxembourg: Office for Official Publications of the European Communities, 1985), 28–29. For a more detailed description of insurance regulation in the European Community, see Coopers & Lybrand, *International Insurance Industry Guide*, 4th ed. (London: Lloyd's of London Press, 1988).

34. On the importance of domestic rivalry in explaining the international success of British firms, particularly Lloyd's, see Michael Porter, *The Competitive Advantage of Nations* (New York: Free Press, 1990), 265.

35. Approximately 44% of the United Kingdom's net non-life premium income derives from outside its borders. Robert L. Carter, "The United States and the European Community: Insurance," paper delivered to the American

Enterprise Institute's conference, "The United States and Europe in the 1990s," Washington, D.C., March 5–8, 1990.

36. The most prominent example is AIG, which initially served as an underwriting agent for other American insurers in the Far East. With time, its network expanded, and in the 1960s it transformed itself from an underwriting agent to a direct underwriter of insurance around the world. AIG came to be recognized as the leading global insurance company.

37. Both Munich Re and Swiss Re have extensive international networks. Swiss Re, for example, receives 52% of its premium income from Europe, 28% from North America, and 14% from the rest of the world.

38. Of course, to the extent that risk factors are common across many risks within a given country, scale economies cannot be realized within a single country, regardless of its size. I am grateful to Mark Wolfson for this clarification.

39. United States International Trade Commission, *1992: The Effects of Greater Economic Integration within the European Community on the United States, First Follow-Up Report*, USITC Publication 2268, Investigation No. 332-267, March 1990, 5–19.

40. Arthur Andersen, *Insurance in a Changing Europe 1990–95* (London: The Economist Publications, 1990), 15.

41. The dynamics of such behavior are described in Frederick T. Knickerbocker, *Oligopolistic Reaction and Multinational Enterprise* (Boston: Division of Research, Harvard Business School, 1973).

42. On the effect of regulation on the foreign activities of Japanese service firms, see Peter Enderwick, "The International Competitiveness of Japanese Service Industries: A Cause for Concern," *California Management Review*, Summer 1990, 22–37.

43. Discussion in this section is drawn from Bill Pool, *The Creation of the Internal Market in Insurance* (Luxembourg: Office of Official Publications of the European Communities, 1990).

44. The lead case involved a Bavarian insurance broker named Schleicher. Herr Schleicher had arranged for the insurance on his German clients' stocks of furs to be placed through British brokers with London insurers that did not hold an authorization to operate in Germany. Since a condition for such authorization was that the insurers be established in Germany, Schleicher's act violated the German insurance supervisory law. After Schleicher lost his case at the national level, the Commission took the issue to the European Court of Justice. Case 205/84, *Commission v. Federal Republic of Germany* (1986).

PART IV
Implications

10

CONCLUSIONS AND IMPLICATIONS

David B. Yoffie

CHAPTERS 2 THROUGH 9 REVEALED dramatic changes in the structure of global competition and the patterns of international trade over the past several decades. There were rapid shifts in the worldwide positions of both firms and countries as new technologies emerged and governments increasingly intervened. New players and policies were apparent in semiconductors, computers, telecommunications, automobiles, bearings, construction equipment, minerals, and insurance.

In contrast to most conventional thinking, one surprising discovery was that American firms and the United States as a nation continued to dominate most of the industries we studied. American companies retained the number one position in most sectors, and the United States remained the world's largest exporter. Within this larger pattern, however, we found that American firms did lose significant market share. Indeed, many American giants, especially IBM, AT&T, Caterpillar, and General Motors (GM), suffered dearly in the 1980s. The greatest challenge came from new non-American competitors: Japan's Fujitsu supplanted Digital Equipment as the runner-up in computers; FAG of Germany outpaced Timken for the second spot in bearings; NEC and Toshiba replaced both Texas Instruments (TI) and Motorola as global leaders in semiconductors; Alcatel of France emerged as a close second to AT&T in telecommunication equipment; Chile's state-owned enterprise took the top spot over Anaconda and Kennecott as the world's largest copper company. At the country level, Japan became the world's largest producer of bearings, cars, construction equipment, and semiconductors, Japanese companies became significant players in global mineral trade, and Japan was the second-largest exporter of computers, telecommunication equipment, and bearings.

Many observers have argued that this was nothing more than the inevitable shift in relative cost advantage away from the United States to more productive regions of the world. However, our analysis demonstrated that comparative advantage and country factors were insufficient to explain the shift in corporate and national positions. The patterns of trade and investments could be understood only by systematic analysis of all the factors in our framework, including the structure of industries, characteristics of firms, government policy, and historical inertia.

In Chapter 1, we argued that the relative influence of these five factors produced four discernible patterns of international trade based on comparative advantage, oligopolistic competition, regulated competition, and political competition (see Figure 10-1). Our empirical results provided powerful evidence for each pattern.

COMPARATIVE ADVANTAGE

Any explanation of changing patterns of global trade and competition, we found, must still begin with comparative advantage. Evidence that traditional country factors were critical determinants of international competitive success was replete throughout our research. In industries that had few market imperfections and where government's role was modest, the most important drivers of competition were usually relative factor costs, factor endowments, and peculiar features of domestic demand.

Examples from our chapters were numerous. It was hardly surprising, for instance, that we found the largest exporters of copper, bauxite, and nickel came from those countries with the greatest relative abundance and lowest-cost deposits. Many of the strongest exporters of standard low-end electronic products also came from the low-wage countries in Southeast Asia. Regardless of the industry, when products such as telephones, computer boards, disk drives, and televisions approached the status of a commodity, production and trade shifted to low-cost locations.

The early stages of the bearings industry can also be explained with a simple factor-based model that includes unique features of domestic demand. Sweden, well known in the early twentieth century for high-grade iron and steel, as well as sophisticated metalworking expertise, developed a high-grade bearings business; Japan, while gearing up for World War I and World War II, stimulated the growth of its bearings business; and the birth of the automobile industry in the United States required local bearings firms as suppliers.

The role of domestic demand was similarly crucial in the rise of England, Switzerland, and the United States as the home of major global insurance companies: England was one of the first seafaring nations and global empires whose firms needed international insurance; insurance

FIGURE 10-1
Drivers of International Trade

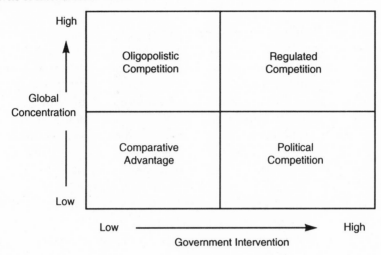

was a logical extension for Switzerland because of its role as a global financial center; and the United States had a naturally high demand for insurance as a large, geographically dispersed market. Most international insurance businesses also followed closely on the heels of the early leaders of international manufacturing. The birth of semiconductors in the United States was partly traced to the availability of general and sector-specific skilled labor, technological, scientific, and engineering capabilities, and a large domestic market. During the 1960s and early 1970s, the ease of entry into semiconductors was facilitated by venture capital, a distinctly American phenomenon. The subsequent rise of Japan can be partly attributed to country factors, such as rapid growth in demand and strong related and supporting industries like consumer electronics.

We also found that country advantages were quite dynamic. While Southeast Asia emerged as an assembly base for many of the industries in our studies—semiconductors, computers, customer-premise equipment in telecommunications, and ball bearings—the region also exhibited something of a snowball effect: once the area became a location for one of these industries, there were externalities that made the region more attractive to the others. Assembly skills for making telephones were relatively easy to transfer to computers; infrastructures, such as roads, power, and airports that were built for a semiconductor plant, made the location more attractive to a television manufacturer, and so forth. In other words, country advantages were not static: low wages helped bring the industries, but the national sources of competitive advantage expanded over time.

When multinational enterprises (MNEs) were involved in these relatively fragmented industries, they usually sought locations that tolerated exploitation of comparative advantages. For instance, Japanese bearings firms became multinational enterprises at a time of relatively intense international competition. Some of the early moves by firms like Minebea, as David Collis pointed out in Chapter 6, were to transfer assembly operations to Southeast Asia in order to lower costs. At the time, bearings had to be produced in low-wage countries to be competitive. The same general pattern appeared in semiconductors in the 1970s: firms moved to low-cost locations in Southeast Asia to minimize costs. In essence, MNEs were using their global flexibility to deploy activities wherever the national environment was most favorable. When MNEs were prominent in fragmented industries, comparative advantages were still critical: the most significant thing that changed was the ownership of production, not where it took place or where it was sent.

Strategic Implications

There are several implications of trade following dynamic comparative advantage in fragmented industries. From the firm's perspective, the critical lesson is *not* that firms must locate production in the lowest-cost country: comparative country costs were constantly changing in the industries we studied. In cars, semiconductors, computers, and bearings, for example, relative cost advantages shifted from the United States after World War II to Japan in the 1960s, to East Asia in the 1970s, to Southeast Asia in the 1980s, and will probably shift again to South Asia, Africa, Latin America, or even back to the United States. Many American semiconductor firms moved assembly and testing offshore to Asia in the 1970s only to discover that capital investment in automation made assembly in the United States just as cost-effective by the 1990s. Only when there are few sunk costs or inherently limited production sites (e.g., sources of certain raw materials), is it clear that firms should chase low factor costs.

The dynamic logic of comparative advantage dictates that most successful firms should make long-term commitments to countries that will act as the best platforms over time for a broad array of activities, beyond pure cost minimization. While initial investments might take advantage of low labor or material costs, the important lesson of trade following comparative advantages in fragmented businesses is the fleeting nature of such advantages. Thus, American semiconductor firms were successful at lowering costs in the short run by moving to low-wage Asian countries, but Japanese firms pioneered automation at home in the 1970s, which increased reliability and quality and ultimately created even lower costs. Especially when firms make large sunk investments to capitalize on a country's comparative advantage, the most productive foreign investments are those which can leverage all the *potential* advantages of a country, from demanding customers to advance infrastructure. Since a firm often makes sunk investments in particular locations, it is critical to recognize that the maximum advantage comes over time. As comparative cost advantages fade, which they inevitably do, firms profit most if they can leverage their sunk costs to capitalize on being close to large domestic markets, new production methods, advanced suppliers of equipment, and so forth.

Policy Implications

From a government's standpoint, there are at least two important lessons to be drawn from the logic of comparative advantage driving trade in certain industries. First, we found that extensive government intervention in relatively fragmented industries was rarely successful. As long as there were numerous firms worldwide, it was difficult for a government to alter long-term global market forces and the international structure of trade or competition. When barriers to entry were low, capital was mobile, and comparative costs were the driving forces behind international trade, government efforts at protectionism, subsidies, and various other forms of direct intervention could not durably influence the country's international trade performance.

Second, it is equally crucial for governments to recognize that when comparative advantage is based on factor costs, that advantage is fleeting. The critical issue for a government becomes expanding the sources of advantage over time. *Relative* costs are not under the control of any given government: if a country grows, which improves the living standard, wages also rise relative to other production locations. In fact, governments should *prefer* that their comparative costs become noncompetitive in certain industries over time. Under these circumstances, the best role for government is to promote a comparatively superior environment for firms to operate in over the long run. This means focusing on areas like improved infrastructure, building the local skill base, and maintaining political and economic stability. As Helen Shapiro found in her study of autos in Brazil and Mexico, even if a country has highly advantageous factor costs, those advantages can be overwhelmed by political and macro-economic instability. Or as Michael Rukstad found in construction equipment, continuous rapid economic growth in countries like Japan can help build an industry's international competitive advantage where few advantages initially existed.

OLIGOPOLISTIC COMPETITION

Among our most important findings was that when industries become relatively concentrated at the global level, industry structure and firm decisions propel export and foreign investment decisions in ways that differ from what one would expect with a factor cost model. The purest examples of such oligopolistic competition in our study were construction equipment, minerals, and bearings; however, autos, computers, semi-conductors, and telecommunications also exhibited many of the features of oligopolistic rivalry. The industries also evolved over time. Some, like autos, computers, and minerals, were highly concentrated industries, but fragmented over time, while others, like telecommunications and bearings, were consolidated in the 1980s. Semiconductors had a fairly constant ratio of approximately ten to fifteen (different) firms dominating the business since its inception. In all these cases we found that varying industry structures had different effects, but strategic and organizational choices by managers were particularly important in determining the location of production and the direction of exports.

Features of Global Oligopolies

Strategic interaction.   A dominant characteristic of all the oligopolies in our research was that firm decisions were heavily influenced by the moves and countermoves of direct global competitors. The first consequence of this strategic interaction was significant cross investment. In fact, *firms invested heavily in competitors' markets, regardless of the profitability of such investments.* Firms aggressively pursued cross investment because they wanted to prevent their competitors from having safe havens, they wished to pre-empt new entrants, or they wanted to create or maintain industry discipline and stability.[1] In a highly competitive market, such strategies would not work. Serving unprofitable markets would drain resources and undermine a firm's global position. But as long as global entry remains difficult, the logic of international trade in an oligopoly becomes a function of maintaining long-run competitive balance, not short-term profit maximization. Thus, Caterpillar invested aggressively in Japan and Europe while European and Japanese construction equipment companies moved into the United States; most large bearings firms, regardless of their home base, pursued "Triad" strategies of locating in the United States, Europe, and Japan in the early 1990s; telecommunication companies from Japan and Europe spent heavily to manufacture in the United States even as they lost hundreds of millions of dollars, while U.S. and Canadian firms aggressively invested in Asia and Europe.

International bragging rights. Part of the reason that strategic interaction was so important was that firms in globally oligopolistic industries were motivated as much, and often more, by international competitors as they were by domestic rivals. "Domestic bragging rights"—the desire to demonstrate superiority over one's neighbor—as Michael Porter has argued, were less important in these industries than international bragging rights. Successful global oligopolists had to make decisions based on their global competitive positions, not their rivalry with the firm down the street. In computers, for instance, IBM executives understood that the threat in 1990 was not just American firms like Compaq and Digital Equipment Corporation (DEC), but Fujitsu and Siemens; when the telecommunication-equipment business developed into a global oligopoly in the 1980s, executives at AT&T quickly realized that they had to worry as much about NEC and Ericsson as Northern Telecom; and virtually all of Komatsu's focus and energy in the 1970s and 1980s were directed toward Caterpillar, with less attention to Hitachi and other local Japanese manufacturers of construction equipment.

Hedge and risk reduction strategies. One of the unique features of firms in global oligopolies was that they had larger scale and/or higher profits (excess rent) than firms in fragmented industries. Our empirical research discovered that this scale and cash flow gave managers the opportunity to buy options for future growth or to buy insurance against competitive, financial, and political risk. In other words, we found that firms often *hedged* their relative positions. The role of such risk reduction strategies was most evident in the highly concentrated oligopolies like minerals. Louis Wells found, for instance, that firms in Ghana ship unprocessed bauxite to smelters in the United States, the United Kingdom, and Eastern Europe, even though Ghana is the site of a world-class smelter, because aluminum firms did not want their entire operation held captive to a foreign government. In semiconductors, Japanese firms invested aggressively in the United States and Europe in the late 1980s and early 1990s because of the *risk* of possible protectionism rather than actual trade restrictions. In some cases, these investments were trade substituting—reducing lower-cost exports from Japan for locally pro-duced goods.

Another manifestation of risk reduction strategies was a consistent pattern of *"follow-the-leader" foreign investment.* One of the greatest fears for firms in oligopolies is that one company may gain an advantage which its competitors will find hard to replicate. If my competitor exports to a new market, does its management know something I do not? If my competitor invests in a new geography, does its management have supe-rior information about demand, costs, available technologies, and so forth? In such situations involving a relatively small number of strategi-cally interdependent firms, second-tier companies tended to follow the market share leader.[2] When in doubt, follow your competitor to overseas markets; if a competitor from the United States goes to Singapore, you go to Singapore—or maybe Penang.[3]

Examples of follow-the-leader behavior were rampant in our studies. When the earlier automobile duopoly of GM and Ford broke down in the late 1950s and early 1960s, American firms followed the leaders to developing countries. Ford, for instance, was reluctant to enter the Bra-zilian market, but was quick to match moves by GM and Chrysler. Several American semiconductor firms followed Texas Instruments to Europe in the 1960s; most American and Japanese firms followed TI and Motorola to Southeast Asia in the 1970s; and the large Japanese semiconductor firms followed NEC, the leading merchant producer, to the United States and then Europe. In construction equipment, Interna-tional Harvester and Deere followed Caterpillar into Europe; and in bearings, all five large Japanese companies built or acquired U.S. plants within two years of one another in the 1970s.

Alliance strategies.   Another feature of global oligopolies was perva-sive alliances. One way to interpret the rapid growth of alliances and joint ventures among firms in oligopolies is a variation of follow-the-leader strategy. Regardless of the economic merit in many of the alli-ances, once a few large firms in an oligopoly built cross-national alli-ances, we observed clear tendencies for other alliances to follow. As the construction industry began to consolidate in the late 1980s, for instance, there was a pattern of firms seeking global alliances among American, European, and Japanese partners that would rationalize global production and carve up global sales. Similarly, when the computer industry began to fragment in the early 1980s, alliances among computer firms of different countries exploded. At least part of the motivation for these alliances was that each major player wanted an insurance policy with a foothold in its competitor markets and potential access to all technologies that might emerge in those markets. Through these alliances, firms hoped to complement their own strengths with those of their competitors.

Implications for Trade and Investment

These follow-the-leader and heavy cross-investment patterns in global oligopolies led us to the following generalization: *As more firms compete head to head in multiple international markets, the more firms (or groups and networks of firms) will gravitate toward similar production locations, trade patterns, and technical and managerial capabilities.* Over time, firms with increasingly similar profiles are likely to emerge: they tend to make similar ranges of products in geographically close proximity and export products to similar locations. If the firms are based in different countries, this reinforces the pattern of substantial cross investment. In addition, if it is impractical for individual firms to replicate their largest competitors, then groups, consortia, and various other alliance combinations may try to create matching profiles. The oligopolies in minerals, particularly aluminum, were perhaps the best example of this pattern. Virtually all the aluminum firms sought comparable cost deposits of bauxite, then all the six leading firms separated mining and smelting operations to minimize the risk of expropriation; as costs exploded, they invested together in consortia. In construction equipment, since individual firms like Hitachi had difficulty matching Komatsu's and Caterpillar's production and distribution systems, they formed alliances in the late 1980s and early 1990s that they hoped would approximate their major competitors' capabilities. The Triad configuration of major bearings competitors also led to increasing similarities among the players.

The implications for trade under these conditions are that export and investment strategies tend to follow the logic of an imperfectly competitive industry and the needs of specific firms rather than the logic of a competitive market. Three firm-level factors played especially important roles in influencing the patterns of trade in our studies: (1) discretionary strategic choices by firms, (2) the role of personnel and organizational dynamics, and (3) national ownership of assets.

Discretionary strategic choices. Major strategic decisions, when managers had a variety of choices available, were critical in many of the industries we studied. For example, it would have been impossible to predict, ex ante, that a French firm, Alcatel, would be one of the world leaders in digital switching equiment in 1990. But senior management at Alcatel, facing problems similar to those of senior management at dozens of other telecommunication companies around the world, made the early decision to invest heavily in digital technology. In industry after industry, we found that the early mover into a market segment—the first to establish a technical standard, the first to make a large investment, and the first to enter a new country—gained huge long-run advantages that often pre-empted competitors. When such early-mover advantages were reinforced with superior execution, our research demonstrated, the effects could last for decades. IBM's dominance in mainframes, the strength of not only Alcatel (and thus France), but also Northern Telecom (and thus Canada) in digital switches, Volkswagen's position in the Brazilian car market, Caterpillar's position in Europe, and SKF's strength in bearings were all examples of advantages gained through early, prescient moves that were sustained for ten or more years. This finding was also consistent with theoretical work by Grossman and Helpman, which found that under particular industry conditions, some first-mover advantages can never be overcome.[4]

Personnel and organizational choices. Individual motivations were also obvious in several cases. In microprocessors, for instance, Israel became the world's second-leading exporter after the United States, despite the fact that Israel had relatively little domestic demand for the product and no indigenous microprocessor firms. The logic of Israeli exports of microprocessors came from the logic of an American firm (Intel) deciding to locate production in Israel.[5] While Israel had skilled labor and some infrastructure to support semiconductor manufacturing, the primary motivation for the plant location was the wish of a senior technical manager to return home. If the company had scanned the world to find the lowest-cost, most-productive, biggest market, or even the largest government subsidy for its product, Israel would have been on the list, but certainly not on top. Various locations in the United States as well as Europe and Asia should have been superior. But given the company's position as the dominant leader in an oligopolistic segment in which it practiced price leadership, any cost penalties associated with locating in Israel were outweighed by the management's desire to retain a valuable engineer and manager.

Similar organizational issues led SKF's management to place its worldwide antifriction bearings R&D facility in an unusual location. SKF had several strong manufacturing operations throughout Europe; the most cost-effective location for SKF's R&D was close to an existing plant in places like Germany or France, where the company could share overhead. Yet internal organizational politics led SKF to an entirely different decision. Fear of giving one of its existing country organizations too much power led it to set up an independent R&D facility in an entirely new country, the Netherlands. Again, given SKF's strong position in Europe, management accepted the cost penalty to maintain organizational peace.

Another example of organizational inertia influencing trade patterns was Inco's early role in world nickel. Inco was a Canadian firm that controlled 85% of the world market for nickel in the early part of this century. Inco's dominant worldwide position allowed it to pursue trade and investment strategies that might seem counter to a classic cost-minimization strategy. Despite the fact that Inco could efficiently process locally mined ore from Canada in Canada, for example, the company shipped unprocessed ore to Norway and the United Kingdom. Since Inco was not under competitive pressure to reduce transportation costs, its managers preferred to utilize plants acquired in the 1920s in Europe rather than expand local capacity.

The sheer administrative capabilities of a corporation also affected international trade and the viability of a country as a platform for production and exports. This was especially true when only one or two firms represented the entire base of a nation's exports in an industry that is difficult to re-enter once a firm withdraws. Under these circumstances, the success or failure of those individual corporations could affect billions of dollars in net exports. In the central-office-switch business, for instance, Richard Vietor and David Yoffie found that the disappearance of England as a major telecommunication supplier and the emergence of Canada can largely be traced to failures of Plessey and the success of Northern Telecom, respectively. There was nothing obvious about the environment in Canada versus England that would predict the foresight of Northern Telecom's management to anticipate the digital revolution in switching equipment. Similarly, AT&T represented half the U.S. market's production of central-office-switch equipment. Even though

AT&T had some of the world's best technology in its segment, AT&T's lack of experience in international competition led to a series of mistakes in Japan, France, and the United Kingdom in its early ventures overseas, which may have cost the United States hundreds of millions or billions of dollars in sales over a five- to ten-year period.

Public and private ownership.   We also found that the ownership of a factory or a mine can affect the direction of trade, regardless of the country of origin. In Chapter 8, Louis Wells found that, in the 1960s, multinational corporations shipped copper concentrates or locally refined copper from countries like Chile and Zambia to their home bases in the United States and Europe. The industry was a tight oligopoly with strong vertical ties from ore to finished products. As long as the industry was tightly concentrated, multinational firms sought to own their sources of supply and refine at home. Over time, however, a looser oligopoly emerged as the industry fragmented and ownership of the mines changed hands. The new owners drove to diversify their markets, leading to a dramatic shift in the direction of trade. Copper from Zaire that went to the United States and the United Kingdom in the early 1960s was shipped to the Netherlands and West Germany in the 1980s. Yet in raw material industries with fewer changes in ownership, like nickel and bauxite, the direction of trade remained comparatively stable.

We observed a similar pattern of ownership influencing the direction of trade in automobiles. During the 1970s Brazil gave incentives to the MNEs in the local market to export products. U.S. firms found that their Brazilian operations were unable to produce highly competitive cars for the world market; as a result, they exported engines and parts. However, Volkswagen and Fiat did attempt to use Brazil as an export base, and Brazil ultimately became a major exporter of cars to *Italy!* Fiat, unlike Ford and General Motors, found that it could sell its Brazilian cars because it had a virtual monopoly at home. While Brazilian cars exported to the United States or Germany faced stiff competition on price and quality, Italy restricted competitive Japanese cars to a few thousand per year. Put simply, if Fiat's manufacturing facilities in Brazil had not belonged to an Italian firm, Brazil would not have shipped 80,000 cars per year to Italy in the mid-1980s.

Finally, we found that the structure of ownership influenced time horizons and investment strategies, which in turn could greatly affect the viability of individual firms and countries. A powerful finding by David Collis in the chapter on global bearings was that firms with substantial private ownership, such as Timken of the United States, SKF of Sweden, and FAG of Germany, were among the most aggressive investors in technology and capacity over long periods of time. While national comparative advantage in bearings may have shifted to Japan, the investment strategies of these three firms differed from those of companies with largely public and largely conglomerate ownership, and the very success of these individual firms (which comprised 43% of the global industry in the early 1980s) was critical for explaining the presence of the United States, Germany, and Sweden in world bearings.

Strategic Implications

Oligopolistic competition has several implications for the formulation of firm strategies. Perhaps the most obvious is that competitive benchmarking must be done against one's global competitors as well as one's domestic rivals. For American managers, in particular, this is a critically important lesson. In many of our industries, U.S. companies recognized the importance of international rivals, but often too late. In construction equipment, Caterpillar was focused on John Deere, International Harvester, and Dresser Industries in the 1970s rather than worrying about beating Komatsu; in the meantime, Komatsu focused all its energy on beating Caterpillar. In semiconductors, American firms followed one another very closely in the 1970s, matching moves and capabilities, only to discover that their most significant competition was coming from Japan. In telecommunication equipment, AT&T worried most about Northern Telecom until deregulation in 1984 opened the door to Siemens, Ericsson, NEC, and Fujitsu. Yet to be successful in the 1990s, all firms in global oligopolistic settings must benchmark themselves against the best of their international competitors, regardless of national origin.

Second, while simply copying one's competition is rarely the road to success, in globally oligopolistic industries it is dangerous not to engage in matching moves to reduce the risk of competitive disadvantage. International trade offers many sources of competitive advantage that earlier movers can realize: we have seen in our studies how first movers can gain advantages by locking in customers (e.g., Northern Telecom in central-office switches and IBM with its 360 mainframe technology), locking up sources of supply (e.g., Inco in nickel), and building global distribution (e.g., Caterpillar in construction equipment). While late movers sometimes had an "attacker's advantage"[6] in global competition, the benefits of waiting rarely exceeded the benefits of quickly matching a global competitor's moves on technology, location, distribution, and so forth.[7]

A closely related implication is that in global oligopolies firms cannot allow their rivals to have sanctuaries at home. In virtually all the studies, competitors that were not challenged on their home turf built significant competitive advantages in the contested markets. A home market that is not contested by global competitors can provide a myriad of advantages, some of which are country based, others specific to the firm. At the country level, there may be special comparative advantages that firms can access, like unique features of domestic demand or advanced suppliers of particular components. At the firm level, the most important advantage of sanctuaries from global competitors at home is that firms can build and maintain the cash flows needed to support a global network and a global strategy. A secure monopoly or oligopoly at home, where firms can sustain a profitable mix of collaboration and competition, should be the most feared combinations for foreign competitors. If a firm does not require high levels of cash flow or profits from overseas activities to support its ongoing global battles, then that firm can set the rules for price and other forms of competition.

Many of the strongest competitors in our studies had markets that were relatively uncontested by foreign competitors at home for long periods of time: IBM in computers in the United States; Caterpillar, also in the United States, in construction equipment; Ericsson in Sweden, Alcatel in France, Northern Telecom in Canada, and Siemens in Germany in telecommunication equipment; and Japanese firms in autos, insurance, and semiconductors. Our studies also showed that the weakest performers were usually those firms which stayed at home or refused to challenge their direct competitors head-on: e.g., Zenith in television in America; many of the American bearings firms that were bought by conglomerates, such as Fafnir under Textron; several European auto, computer, and semiconductor manufacturers, like British Leyland, Bull, and Plessey. Virtually all the American manufacturing companies we studied suffered serious setbacks against their Japanese competitors in the past 20 years, but those which suffered most were usually inactive in Japan. Caterpillar and IBM had the advantage of a long-standing history in Japan's market, dating back prior to the 1970s. Although both firms were suffering in 1992, they were still number one worldwide by a large margin, and they generally outperformed, within their industries as well as in televisions, semiconductors, bearings, and autos, their American brethren, most of whom could not or would not prevent their Japanese competitors from keeping the home market to themselves.[8]

A fourth implication from our analyses relates to the role of alliances in global oligopolies. Alliances were prevalent in many of our studies, the two most obvious being in construction equipment and computers. Especially in computers, alliances were ubiquitous, serving as vehicles for the transfer of technology between firms (and countries) as well as achieving adequate scale economies, building technical standards, creating mechanisms for gaining access to markets, complementary skills, and resources (e.g., distribution or manufacturing capabilities). The consequences of alliances for the firms involved suggest a cautious approach toward these international linkages. On the one hand, Benjamin Gomes-Casseres illustrated in Chapter 3 that the most successful Japanese firms were those which acquired much of their core technology through alliances with second-tier American firms in the 1960s and 1970s. On the other hand, those second-tier firms all subsequently exited the business, and Japanese success has put the leaders, like IBM and DEC, on the defensive. Alliances have become even more pervasive in the 1990s as the oligopolistic structure dissolved in computers, especially in low-end desktop computers, and groups of allied firms are now forming the basis of competition. This research suggests that alliances can be a powerful vehicle for firms to acquire technology from rivals; but while the recipients can become major beneficiaries, the firm giving up technology can also become a casualty.

REGULATED COMPETITION

In telecommunications, semiconductors, mainframe computers, and to some extent automobiles, we found that government's heavy and visible hand often sculpted, manipulated, or even directly determined the direction and volume of international trade flows. The all-important role of country factors in explaining international trade frequently disappeared in these heavily regulated oligopolistic industries. Under these circumstances, international trade and competition became a game of strategic business-government relations in which neither government alone nor firms and industry alone can explain the pattern of exports and investments. It was the interaction of business strategy, government policy, and industry structure that were the key drivers of global winners and losers.

In several of the industries we studied, government policy had only marginal effects, such as tipping the balance between two countries as a location site for investment or accelerating decisions that were already under way. In bearings, for instance, Collis found that Japanese and European firms increased their investment in the United States after the U.S. government decided to impose dumping duties. Since a number of firms had already started investing prior to protection and there were already follow-the-leader activities, it is reasonable to assume that government action simply accelerated those decisions. A similar effect occurred in minerals, when environmental regulations among all the industrial countries accelerated the decisions of multinationals in copper and aluminum to move smelters offshore to lower-cost locations, which probably would in any case have occurred at a later time.

However, governments' impact on the patterns of trade and investment were far more profound in semiconductors, mainframes, and telecommunication equipment because of the intrusive nature of intervention. In telecommunications, for example, government policies around the world mandated those which could and could not serve a particular market for almost a century. Even as official protectionist policies receded during the mid- and late-1980s, implicit or explicit subsidies, domestic content regulations, and nationalist buying preferences often dictated which firms and countries were allowed to sell or invest. While government intervention in semiconductors and mainframe computers was generally less onerous, it was no less pervasive. IBM had to set up local facilities, which often included manufacturing and R&D, in virtually every country in the world to satisfy political demands, regardless of economic rationality. Similarly in semiconductors, government procurement and antitrust policies in the United States were crucial in lifting the domestic industry to a position of global prominence in the 1960s, just as explicit protectionist policies and subsidized cooperative ventures in Japan were essential to that country's subsequent rise. Government's management (and most often, mismanagement) of the economies and industrial policies in Mexico and Brazil had equally strong influences on the automobile industries in those countries.

Lessons from Government Intervention

Sequencing.   Recognizing that international trade in these industries is as much a product of regulation as oligopolistic competition has significant implications for both government policies and firm strategies. The first lessons are related to the sequencing of regulation and deregulation. We learned from Chapter 4 that in a globally interconnected world, regulatory policy cannot be made in isolation. Policies that appear theoretically sound, such as fostering competition through unilateral deregulation, can be destructive in a world of strategic players. In globally oligopolistic competition, deregulation in one country can be undermined by foreign governments. If foreign governments accommodate higher prices at home, effectively subsidizing the national champions abroad, they can provide real strategic advantages. The decision by the United States to deregulate telecommunications, without considering its impact on the international competitiveness of its domestic firms, had precisely this effect: although competition forced AT&T to become more efficient, the transition costs in terms of lost market share and frustrated investments abroad have been very high. AT&T's margins have suffered while decisions by the Japanese, French, and German governments to delay intense competition at home have implicitly or explicitly subsidized AT&T's competitors. This suggests that government policies in an interdependent world should seek to coordinate major regulatory and trade moves. If regulatory policies are taken unilaterally, then trade policy should be used to ensure equal national treatment in foreign markets.

Infant-industry policies can work. The semiconductor and computer experiences offered more positive lessons on how government can shape country and competitive advantage. Perhaps the most important was that infant-industry protection could work. We found concrete evidence that in mainframes and semiconductors, two industries in which barriers to entry were extremely high and American firms had significant first-mover advantages, trade restrictions combined with limitations on direct investment provided powerful incentives for Japanese firms to invest aggressively in emerging technologies. However, there were two keys to successful infant-industry protection: limiting the role of the dominant foreign firms in the domestic market and providing incentives for exports. European governments tried protectionist policies similar to those of Japan, but their firms largely failed in both semiconductors and computers. Part of the explanation was that American firms invested around trade barriers and were able to operate autonomously within the European market. As a result, the American companies often pre-empted local competition. Japanese firms, by contrast, had the domestic market largely to themselves. Even when firms like IBM and Texas Instruments entered the Japanese market, their early activities were heavily regulated. In addition, European national champions were usually focused on their small national markets, not the world market. While Japanese firms gained the needed scale by aggressive export expansion, European firms often lacked scale in manufacturing and R&D. We also saw that Korea's explosive growth in semiconductors would have been possible only with Japanese-style infant-industry policies that limited foreign competitors at home and aggressively promoted exports.

Managed trade can reverse patterns.   A third lesson was that governments can successfully manage trade, even reversing trends that appeared irreversible. Despite the common perception that managed trade is an unnatural act, doomed to failure, we found that in settings like semiconductors, trade policy can fundamentally alter trading patterns with potentially positive results for a nation. In other words, a good case can be made for strategic trade policy in oligopolistic industries, especially high-technology ones in which the spillovers from research and development and the dynamic learning economies may be lost to a country forever in the absence of government intervention. The United States reversed its decline in semiconductors with the negotiation of the Semiconductor Trade Agreement in 1986. The agreement had significant defects, which carried short-term costs, but it did stabilize the overall position of American firms and helped to strengthen U.S. leadership in product lines such as microprocessors and EPROMs.

Comparative government advantage.   A fourth lesson is that different governments demonstrated varying capabilities to execute infant-industry or strategic trade policies. Governments excelled (at least relatively) at different activities, a phenomenon one might describe as *comparative government advantage.* Some governments are consistently better than others at encouraging the success of domestically based firms. Political institutions, like countries and firms, are not all created equal. The configuration of interests groups, the voting and bureaucratic structure of different nations, the role of the courts and public opinion play dramatically different roles in different societies. Ex ante and ex post, there is no reason to believe that two governments with different political institutions, trying to do exactly the same thing, should be equally successful. In fact, our studies showed that different institutional settings produced markedly different results. Japan was clearly more successful than Europe at infant-industry protection in many industries, including semiconductors, bearings, computers, automobiles, and construction equipment, and the United States was generally the best at promoting nascent technologies, like semiconductors and computers in the 1950s, and parallel supercomputing (through DARPA) in the 1990s. The implications of comparative government advantage are that politics and political institutions should be viewed as a constraint or limit on intervention for any given nation: like comparative advantage in the economic realm, success generally comes from building on natural strengths rather than swimming against the tide. However, one should recognize that just as comparative advantage can evolve, government institutions can also learn and improve. American efforts at regulating trade in semiconductors were far more sophisticated than earlier efforts to manage trade in steel or textiles. As political institutions evolve, so does their appropriate role.

Strategic Implications

The lessons for firms and firm strategies are equally important. A prerequisite for international and even domestic success in such politically salient industries as semiconductors, mainframe computers, and telecommunications is dealing effectively with government relations. American semiconductor firms stemmed the tide of Japanese dominance by effectively collaborating on a series of collective goods, including SEMATECH (a $500 million joint government-industry effort at regaining leadership in manufacturing technology) and the Semiconductor Trade Agreement with Japan. Similarly, IBM's ability to transform itself into a "local" company wherever it operated gave it better entrée into the major markets of the world compared with all its major competitors. Close collaboration between Siemens and state-owned Deutsche Bundespost, Northern Telecom and state-supported Bell Canada, Alcatel and the French government, NEC and Fujitsu with (largely) state-owned and (heavily) state-supported Nippon Telephone and Telegraph, were essential in telecommunication equipment. Even AT&T found that, without high-level American government support, it could not act effectively in diverse locations such as Italy, Spain, Japan, and Indonesia. In essence, political strategy in globally regulated industries has to be elevated to be on a par with financial, marketing, and other functional strategies.

POLITICAL COMPETITION

In insurance and numerous other highly fragmented industries[9] that were subject to significant government intervention, we found that *political competition* supplemented competition among countries. While *com-*

parative advantage was still the best predictor of trade patterns in industries with low global concentration, the way different governments regulated their industries at home or used trade barriers at their borders influenced the timing and pace of shifts in country advantage as well as the level of trade. The differences between political competition and regulated competition are important to note. In industries dominated by regulated competition, government policy has a direct strategic impact on individual firms: a government's commitments to AT&T or NEC can fundamentally alter the strategic calculations of domestic and foreign competitors. In industries characterized by political competition, by contrast, governments often tip the balances between countries at the margin. For example, John Goodman found in his study of insurance that governments did not alter the fundamental structure of national competitive or comparative advantage, but the degree and structure of regulation could pre-empt most foreign entry (in the case of Japan), build highly profitable domestic businesses that could create enormous leverage for foreign expansion (as occurred in both Japan and Germany), reinforce opportunities for first-mover advantages (an American firm, AIG, had a highly profitable business in Japan because it entered prior to restrictions and Japanese government policy kept new competitors out), or even reduce the incentives to expand overseas (as regulation did in the United States).

In other industries characterized by political competition, like textiles and apparel, steel, machine tools, and color TVs, how various governments intervened determined the longevity and exporting success of local industries. For example, the structure of American protectionism in textiles and apparel has been a critical determinant in explaining the continued leadership of Taiwan, Korea, and Hong Kong in world textile trade: American trade barriers locked in East Asian producers and limited the new low-cost manufacturers in South Asia and elsewhere.[10] In addition, protectionism has kept American producers in the textile business long after most models of comparative advantage would have predicted their exit. Similarly in steel, American and European producers have propped up domestic manufacturers for decades, skewing the direction and volume of its international trade.[11]

The implications of political competition supplementing the economics of comparative advantage are relatively straightforward. While country characteristics will still drive patterns of international trade and production, even local government policies will have international ramifications. In our increasingly interdependent world, heavy government regulations can have second-order effects that may be completely unanticipated. In industries with traded goods, like textiles, or in which globalization is unfolding, like insurance, policymakers must look beyond their borders to appreciate the consequences of their actions for domestic as well as international welfare. In addition, as Goodman found in insurance, when there are patchworks of national policies without any international coherence, governments can undermine the prospects for any rational division of labor between nations. If government intervention is extensive across nations, then global rules, like the GATT, remain the best mechanism for firms and countries alike.

CONCLUSIONS

This book has offered a different view of the world. We have suggested that comparative advantages and national competitive advantages continue to be important features of the global landscape. However, to understand fully the nature of global competition and the origins or direction of international trade and production, one must also explore the structure of the global industry, the level and style of government intervention, the characteristics of leading firms, and the inertia of history. Even more important, to make the right strategic choices in the future, successful firms and governments must identify whether they are playing a game of comparative advantage, political competition, oligopolistic competition or regulated competition, *and* how that game is changing. The most successful firms and governments will ultimately be those which adapt quickly to their shifting industry and political environments as well as those which seek to change the rules by overcoming historical inertia and even altering the global structures of the industries in which they compete.

NOTES

1. This argument is analogous to Monty Graham's "exchange-of-threat" model. Edward M. Graham, "Transatlantic Investment by Multinational Firms: A Rivalistic Phenomenon?" *Journal of Post Keynesian Economics*: 1, no. 1 (1978): 82–99. Jean Tirole also discusses pre-emption as a strategy for filling product space and locational space in *The Theory of Industrial Organization* (Cambridge, Mass.: MIT Press, 1989), 285.

2. Occasionally, second-tier firms would also lead the parade of foreign in-

vestment, only to be followed by the leader. For instance, Freeport, in copper, was often the pioneer.

3. This is a variation of Frederick T. Knickerbocker's argument in *Oligopolistic Reaction and Multinational Enterprise* (Boston: Division of Research, Harvard Business School, 1973). Whereas Knickerbocker limited his discussion to domestic oligopolies, it would seem that the same principles apply to global oligopolies.

4. Gene Grossman and Elhanan Helpman, National Bureau of Economic Research, "Hysteresis in the Trade Pattern," National Bueau of Economic Research Working Paper No. 3526.

5. For similar examples, see Yair Aharoni, *The Foreign Investment Decision Process* (Boston: Harvard Business School, 1966).

6. Richard Foster, *The Attacker's Advantage* (New York: Summit Books, 1986).

7. The flip side of this point is that when oligopolies break down, firms should *stop* copying their competitors. As barriers fall and new firms enter a market, the sources of competitive advantage usually change.

8. There were exceptions among firms in these industries; Texas Instruments, for instance, understood these issues explicitly and made every effort to penetrate Japan in the 1960s. While Texas Instruments was successful to some extent, as Laura Tyson and David Yoffie describe in Chapter 2, TI alone was unable to mount a sufficient challenge to Japanese firms at home, because of government intervention, which is discussed in the next section.

9. Another good example of political competition is the textile and apparel industry, in which the high degree of protectionism for more than thirty-five years had dramatic effects on the pattern of exports. While the textile industry is not covered in this volume, the influence of political bargaining and government intervention in it has been extensively covered elsewhere. See, for example, David B. Yoffie, *Power and Protectionism: Strategies of the Newly Industrializing Countries* (New York: Columbia University Press, 1983). See also William R. Cline, *The Future of World Trade in Textiles and Apparel* (Washington, D.C.: Institute for International Economics, 1987).

10. Ibid.

11. For a review of protectionism in these sectors, see Gary Hufbauer et al., *Trade Protection in the United States: 31 Case Studies* (Washington, D.C.: Institute for International Economics, 1986).

ABOUT THE CONTRIBUTORS

David J. Collis is an associate professor in the Business, Government, and Competition area at the Harvard Business School. He is an expert on global competition and corporate strategy. His current research is an international comparison of the role of the corporate office in large multibusiness corporations. His work has recently been published in the *Strategic Management Journal, European Management Journal*, and in addition to this volume in the book *International Competitiveness*.

He received an MA (1976) with a Double First from Cambridge University where he was the Wrenbury Scholar of the University. He graduated as a Baker Scholar from the Harvard Business School (MBA, 1978), and received a Ph.D. (1986) in Business Economics from Harvard University, where he was a Dean's Doctoral Fellow. He taught for one year at Columbia University before joining the Harvard faculty in 1986. From 1978 to 1982 he worked for the Boston Consulting Group in London, advising European companies on corporate strategy and global competition. He is currently a consultant to several large U.S. and European corporations.

Benjamin Gomes-Casseres is associate professor at the Harvard Business School. He holds a BA from Brandeis University (summa cum laude, Phi Beta Kappa, 1976), an MPA from Princeton University (1978), and a DBA degree from Harvard University (1985). His dissertation on ownership strategies of multinational enterprises won the Academy of Management's award for best dissertation in international management. Dr. Gomes-Casseres's work on this topic has appeared in the *Sloan Management Review*, the *Columbia Journal of World Business*, the *Journal of Economic Behavior and Organization*, the *Journal of International Business Studies, Strategic Planning, The President*, and *Spectrum*, and as chapters in edited books. He is also co-editor of the forthcoming book *International Political Economy of Foreign Direct Investment*. He has developed numerous case studies at Harvard on joint venture management, alliance strategies, intellectual property, and technology transfer. His current research and consulting are on the management of international alliances in high-technology industries.

John B. Goodman is an associate professor at the Harvard Business

School. He received his bachelor's degree from Middlebury College, summa cum laude, and his master's and Ph.D. degrees from Harvard University. He is the author of *Monetary Sovereignty: The Politics of Central Banking in Western Europe* (Cornell University Press, 1992), as well as a number of articles on European integration, financial deregulation, and privatization. His current research focuses on the changing pattern of business-government relations in Europe.

Michael G. Rukstad is a visiting associate professor at the Stanford Business School. He received his Ph.D. in economics from the University of California at Berkeley in 1981, and has since taught courses in economics and business strategy at the Harvard Business School and Stanford. His research has focused on the interactions of business strategies and the international macro-economic environment. He has also been a consultant and lecturer for numerous companies.

Helen Shapiro has been an assistant professor at the Harvard Business School in the area of Business, Government and Competition since 1988. She received her Ph.D. in economics from Yale University, where she also taught as a lecturer. Her research focuses on industrial policy and state intervention in less-developed countries. Her extensive research on the history of the Brazilian auto industry formed the basis of several articles and a book, *Engines of Growth: The State and Transnational Auto Companies in Brazil* (Cambridge University Press, forthcoming). She has consulted with the World Bank, the United Nations Development Program, and Brazil's Institute of Economic Policy and Analysis on industrial policy. She has just completed research on the determinants of recent trade and investment patterns in the Brazilian and Mexican auto industries as part of the Harvard Business School World Trade and Global Competition Project, and is currently looking at more general issues of business-government relations during periods of economic transition.

Laura D'Andrea Tyson is a professor of Economics and Business Administration and director of the Institute of International Studies at the University of California (Berkeley). She received her BA from Smith College and her Ph.D. in economics from the Massachusetts Institute of Technology.

Professor Tyson is the chair of the Council of Economic Advisers in the Clinton administration. She is also a member of the Cuomo Commission on Trade and Competitiveness, the Advisory Board of the Economic Strategy Institute, the Conference Board Economics Colloquium, and the Economic Policy Institute Research Council on Foreign Relations, as well as the *Los Angeles Times* Board of Economists.

She has written and edited extensively on the economics of competitiveness, beginning with *American Industry in International Competition* (co-edited with John Zysman) in 1983 and most recently with *Who's Bashing Whom: Trade Conflict in High Technology Industries*, 1993. She also publishes on the economics of Eastern Europe, her most recent publication in this area being *Power, Purpose and Collective Choice: Economic Strategy in Socialist States*, 1986.

Richard H. K. Vietor is a professor at the Harvard Business School, where he teaches courses on the regulation of business, environmental management, and the international political economy. He received an economics degree from Union College and graduate degrees in history from Hofstra University and the University of Pittsburgh. Before coming to the Harvard Business School in 1978, he held faculty appointments at Virginia Polytechnic Institute and the University of Missouri.

Professor Vietor's research, which focuses on business-government relations, has been published in numerous journals and cases and several books, including *Energy Policy in America Since 1945* (1984), *Telecommunications in Transition* (1986), *Strategic Management in the Regulatory Environment* (1989), and most recently, *Contrived Competition: Regulation and Deregulation in America* (Harvard University Press, forthcoming). He serves on the editorial board of the *Business History Review* and is president of the Business History Conference.

Louis T. Wells, Jr., is the Herbert F. Johnson Professor of International Management at the Harvard Business School. He holds a BS in physics from Georgia Tech and an MBA and a DBA from the Harvard Business School. He is chairman of the Faculty Council of the Harvard Institute for International Development.

Professor Wells co-authored, with David N. Smith, *Negotiating Third World Mineral Agreements* (Ballinger, 1975). He has published articles or books on third-world multinationals, promotion of foreign investment by host countries, the screening of foreign investment by host governments, and other topics concerning international business. With Raymond Vernon, he wrote *Manager in the International Economy* (Prentice-Hall, 1991).

David B. Yoffie is a professor at the Harvard Business School. Prior to coming to Harvard, he received his bachelor's degree summa cum laude and Phi Beta Kappa from Brandeis University and his masters and Ph.D.

degrees from Stanford University, where he was a lecturer for two years. Professor Yoffie is currently head of the required MBA course on Competition and Strategy, and faculty chairman for the HBS executive program on Managing Global Opportunities.

Professor Yoffie's research and consulting have focused on international trade and competitive strategy. He is a director of Intel Corporation and consults for several *Fortune* 500 industrial firms as well as large service companies. He has written more than twenty articles on international trade and firm strategy for such journals as the *Harvard Business Review, California Management Review, Journal of Forecasting, International Management,* and the *American Political Science Review*. He is the author of *Power and Protectionism: Strategies of the Newly Industrializing Countries* (Columbia University Press, 1983) and *International Trade and Competition: Cases and Notes in Strategy and Management* (McGraw-Hill, 1990); and co-editor for *The International Political Economy of Direct Foreign Investment* (Elgar Press, 1993). Professor Yoffie has also written more than forty-five case studies on competitive strategy and international management issues.

INDEX

Acquisitions. *See also* International alliances
  in bearings industry, 280, 281, 285–286
  in insurance industry, 415–417
Advanced Computer Environment (ACE) consortium, 120–121
African minerals industry
  aluminum trade in, 338, 346–350
  copper, 335, 352, 353, 354–357, 359, 360,
    362–363, 440
AIG, 401, 402, 403, 448
Alcan, 341, 346, 350, 377
Alcatel, 429, 447
  globalization and trade by, 153, 155, 156,
    159, 181, 182, 183, 184
  markets and competition, 161, 162–167,
    168, 170, 171, 176
  strategy and organization of, 177–178, 438,
    442
  technological developments of, 130, 136,
    137, 138, 139
Alcoa (Aluminum Company of America),
    339, 346, 347, 349, 352
Allianz, 391, 402, 409, 413, 415–416, 417
Allis-Chalmers, 313, 317, 318, 323
Aluminum industry, xv
  alumina smelting in, 339–341, 381
  bauxite mining and production in,
    337–339, 372–373, 381, 430
  characteristics and nature of, 335–336,
    435–436
  restructuring of, 341–346
  trade in, 346–352, 437
Alusuisse, 339, 342, 343, 347
Amax, 342, 365, 367
AMD, 62, 63, 70
Amdahl, 107, 114, 115, 116, 117
Anaconda, 354, 357, 429
Aneka Tambang
  aluminum production and trade by,
    345–346
  nickel production and trade by, 367,
    369–371
Antidumping laws
  in bearings industry, 290, 300
  of Semiconductor Trade Agreement, 49–50
Antitrust laws, 32, 145, 376, 405
Apple, 100, 107, 121
Asian automobile industry, 194, 198, 199,
    202, 240–243, 432
Asian bearings industry, 257–259, 431, 432
Asian computer industry, 80, 81, 431
  competitive advantage of, 90–91
  trade patterns in, 83–89, 91–93, 94, 95

Asian semiconductor industry
  establishment of, 33, 35, 61
  evolution of, 63–64, 68, 69, 70, 71, 73
Asian telecommunication industry, 156, 158,
    159, 170, 176, 431
AT&T, 32, 40, 105, 107, 429, 448
  globalization and trade by, 152, 153,
    154–155, 156, 159, 181, 182, 183,
    184
  markets and competition, 160, 161,
    162–167, 173, 174, 175, 435
  monopoly system of, 144–145, 444
  strategies and organization of, 168–172,
    176, 177, 439–440, 441
  technological developments of, 129, 130,
    135, 136, 137, 138, 139, 141, 143
Australian minerals industry
  aluminum, 338, 343, 346–347, 348, 349,
    350
  copper, 353, 355, 356, 358, 360, 362–363
  nickel, 367, 369–370
Autolatina, 220, 221, 238, 239
Automobile industry, xiii
  Brazilian exports and markets in, 212–216,
    217–219
  firm strategies in Brazil, 216, 220–223, 438
  firm strategies in Mexico, 230–235
  global competition and trade in, xv, xvi,
    199–202, 434, 440
  Korean, 240–243
  Mexican exports and markets in, 223–230
  national environment and evolution of,
    193–199, 237–240, 436
  production in Brazil, 202, 203–206
  production in Mexico, 202, 206–212
  results of import-substitution policies in,
    235–237
Axa-Midi, 402, 417

Barden, 262, 263, 264, 265, 276, 280
Bauxite industry, xvii, 337–339, 340, 372,
    430, 435, 437. *See also* Aluminum
    industry
Bearings industry, 430, 432
  company performance and markets in, 259,
    261–265, 438, 440–441
  country performance in, xii, xiii, 257–259,
    260
  economics and production in, xv, 252–257
  government regulation of, 296–297
  location of firms and customer service in,
    290–296
  nationality and growth of firms in, 273–284

455